"In this wise, passionate, and persuasive book, Alan Wolfe draws on decades of reflection and scholarship to elucidate and champion one of the most important concepts of the human enterprise. While fully living up to its title by providing hope and guidance for the century just begun, *The Future of Liberalism* is also a tour de force of intellectual history—and an astute commentary on the great political issues of our time." —Strobe Talbott, author of *The Great Experiment: The Story of Ancient Empires, Modern States, and the Quest for a Global Nation*

"As befits the kind of intellectualism he sees as a defining virtue of liberalism, Wolfe's arguments are nuanced and twisty. . . . This book is the best guide I know to sussing out what Obama's liberalism means." —Bob Moser, *The Texas Observer*

"A terrific analysis of the last three hundred plus years of political thought. . . . Published on the cusp of a new political era in Washington, Wolfe's tome is likely to grow more relevant with time. Highly recommended for anyone with even a passing interest in politics or history." —*Kirkus*

"If you're into history and philosophy, *The Future of Liberalism* will be a delight. . . . Engrossing. . . . An important book." —David M. Kinchen, *Huntington News*

"Engrossing [and] comprehensive." —Michael Skube, *The News & Observer* (Raleigh)

ALAN WOLFE

The Future of Liberalism

Alan Wolfe is Professor of Political Science and Director of the Boisi Center for Religion and American Public Life at Boston College. A contributing editor of *The New Republic*, *The Wilson Quarterly*, *Common-Wealth*, and *In Character*, Professor Wolfe also frequently writes for *Commonweal*, *The New York Times*, *Harper's*, *The Atlantic Monthly*, and *The Washington Post*. He lives in Brookline, Massachusetts.

ALSO BY ALAN WOLFE

THE FUTURE OF LIBERALISM

THE FUTURE OF LIBERALISM

ALAN WOLFE

VINTAGE BOOKS

A DIVISION OF RANDOM HOUSE, INC.

NEW YORK

FIRST VINTAGE BOOKS EDITION, FEBRUARY 2010

The Library of Congress has cataloged the Knopf edition as follows:
Wolfe, Alan, [date]
The future of liberalism / Alan Wolfe.
p. cm.
Includes bibliographical references and index.
1. Liberalism—United States.   2. Liberalism.   3. United States—Politics and
government—21st century.   I. Title.
JC574.2.U6W65 2009
320.51'3—dc22
2008039673

Vintage ISBN: 978-0-307-38625-0

Author photograph © Lee Pelligrini
Book design by Soonyoung Kwon

www.vintagebooks.com

Printed in the United States of America
10 9 8 7 6 5 4 3 2 1

To

RSK, JNW, and AWW

In the first place, such liberalism knows that an individual is nothing fixed, given ready-made. It is something achieved, and achieved not in isolation but with the aid and support of conditions, cultural and physical—including in "cultural," economic, legal and political institutions as well as science and art. Liberalism knows that social conditions may restrict, distort and almost prevent the development of individuality. It therefore takes an active interest in the working of social institutions that have a bearing, positive or negative, upon the growth of individuals who shall be rugged in fact and not merely in abstract theory. It is as much interested in the positive construction of favorable institutions, legal, political and economic as it is in removing abuses and overt oppressions.

—*John Dewey, "The Future of Liberalism," an address presented at the twenty-fourth annual meeting of the American Philosophical Association, Eastern Division, New York University, December 28, 1934*

CONTENTS

INTRODUCTION TO THE VINTAGE EDITION

One of the oddest aspects of U.S. politics to have emerged since the election of Barack Obama has been the effort to portray his views as borrowed from either the extreme right or the extreme left. Some on the right, such as the popular television and radio commentator Rush Limbaugh, have insisted that Obama's policies represent a return to the Nazi years, as if such horrendous evils like euthanasia or the crushing of political opposition are central to the administration's way of carrying out the public's business. (An equally preposterous idea is that Obama, far from being a symbol of post-racial America, is actually a racist at heart.) Others have simply flipped the ideological switch and claimed that Obama's policies are in fact socialistic, that they borrow more from Karl Marx than from James Madison or Abraham Lincoln, and that they are bound to transform Americans into captives of an all-powerful state. No matter how contradictory or removed from reality such claims may be, they have won followers among more extremist elements in the Republican Party and have even received serious attention from mainstream political commentators. It is as if the United States lacks political traditions of its own and has to turn to those associated with European extremism to characterize its new president.

In fact, American political ideas work quite well in defining Obama, especially those liberal ideals shaped by thinkers from Thomas Jefferson in the eighteenth century to John Dewey in the twentieth. Liberalism, I argue in this book, is the political philosophy best suited to manage the complex realities of the modern society in which North Americans and Western Europeans live. Americans seem to have understood this in

2008 and voted accordingly. Frustrated by senseless war in Iraq, watching the first major signs of an emerging economic meltdown, and clearly disenchanted with religious extremism and attack-dog styles of politics, they chose a man who not only urged the adoption of liberal policies but whose pragmatic style and calm reassurance possessed decided appeal, especially in contrast to his more erratic opponents. In 2008 the left defeated the right. But in that election as well reason and rationality defeated emotion and polarization. A majority of Americans decided to reject the culture war and were looking instead for someone actually capable of governing.

Politically speaking, American liberalism in the age of Obama finds itself in the best position it has occupied in decades. The U.S. House of Representatives has not only a Democratic majority, it has a liberal one as well. With the delayed election of Al Franken, Democrats, for at least the moment, hold a filibuster-proof majority in the Senate. Only in the U.S. Supreme Court do liberals lack a majority, and while the prospect is unlikely, there is always the chance that Democrats could hold power long enough to shift that balance as well. For a way of thinking about the world that just ten years ago could read its obituary in just about any influential magazine of ideas, left or right, this constitutes quite a comeback.

Liberalism's success, moreover, has been accompanied by a decided failure on the right. It is not merely that the 2008 Republican candidate John McCain lost. In the aftermath of his defeat, the Republican Party has turned its back on its heritage of enlightened leadership in favor of a demagogic populism that looks with hostility on immigrants, disdains science, hates government, and wraps itself in one particular, and exceedingly cramped, vision of God. Conservative Republicans approach the battle of ideas these days by waiting until liberals make proposals— and then opposing them. Politically speaking, such a strategy can work if liberals overreach. But even if Republicans and conservatives make a political comeback in the future, it will be many years before their ideas can help them solidify national majorities.

Liberals, in a word, have achieved an unusual amount of political power. But will they use their power to advance liberal ideas? The answer to this question, as it happens, is anything but self-evident.

At one level, the administration of Barack Obama is strongly committed to advancing a liberal agenda. Liberalism's key substantive principle, I argue in this book, can be summarized this way: "As many people as possible should have as much say as is feasible over the direction their lives will take." Once we accept this definition we can understand why Adam Smith, who admired the market and distrusted the state, and John Maynard Keynes, who reversed the formula, can both be called liberals: in eighteenth-century Scotland, laissez-faire was compatible with liberalism's twin beliefs in autonomy and equality while in the twentieth century state intervention is required to meet both goals. In this regard, it is worth noting that the Obama administration's two major domestic policy initiatives—the $787 billion economic stimulus package passed in 2009 and the plans for health care reform working their way through Congress in the fall of that year—fit squarely within the liberal tradition. If people are thrown out of work because of a severe recession, or if they cannot afford to protect themselves against illness, they lack control over the direction of their lives. No liberal can look upon the human costs of recession or disease and say, as many did in earlier times, that nothing can be done when misfortune strikes. Government exists to minimize these effects of misfortune and liberals use government for precisely that purpose.

Along similar lines, the Obama administration has also been pursuing liberal objectives in its foreign policy. The most obvious example is its determination to remove U.S. troops from Iraq, hoping thereby to restore support for the United States among its allies in line with liberal ideas about international cooperation that rose to prominence in the late 1940s. In addition, Obama has also made clear his determination to close the Guantánamo Bay facility in which torture clearly took place, as well as to extend more legal rights to those charged as enemy combatants. Compared to his predecessor, Obama's popularity outside the United States has soared, and one of the reasons has to do with a clear understanding that under his leadership the United States is less likely to preach the virtues of liberal democracy while violating liberal democratic ideals in practice.

Still the affinity between Barack Obama and the liberal tradition is anything but complete. For all the administration's repudiation of the Bush approach to foreign policy, for example, it has also accepted at least a few of the ideas of former Vice President Dick Cheney that in times of war the executive branch possesses unusual powers, including that some detainees can be held indefinitely without trial, that the president can withhold information from the public in the name of national security, and that it is constitutional to use the controversial tactic known as signing statements in which the president reserves the right not to follow what congressional action mandates. (Such signing statements can be used in domestic matters as well as foreign affairs). How one evaluates the liberalism of the Obama administration's approach to foreign policy depends upon how liberal one is: compared to what went on before he became president he is definitely moving in a liberal direction, but compared to some of liberalism's historical ideals, he is not moving fast enough. The administration's overall record with respect to the wars in Afghanistan and Iraq has won surprising support among conservatives and has disappointed legions of liberal bloggers.

One can find the same ambivalence with respect to domestic policy. For many on the left, Barack Obama is not so much a liberal as a "neoliberal," a post–New Deal Democrat not enthusiastic enough about government intervention, moderate in his political instincts, and all too willing to strike deals with Republicans. From their perspective, the Obama administration rejected a single-payer approach to health care such as the one that works so well in Canada and has allowed Congress, with its close ties to lobbyists, to further water down its proposals for reform. Along similar lines, they point out that Obama's environmental policy is based on ideas about "cap and trade" that rely on market-like incentives rather than strong regulations to promote clear air and water. Neither Franklin Delano Roosevelt nor Lyndon Johnson serves as a model for the administration, these critics charge, but Bill Clinton. That president became famous—or for those to his left infamous—for what was called "triangulation," positioning himself in the middle between the left and the right in Congress. Obama's victory is therefore for some not so much a triumph for liberalism as a sign of how far liberalism has strayed from the days when it reigned supreme.

There is no doubt some truth in what these critics charge. To take only one example, Obama has appointed to key positions in his administration policymakers and thinkers fascinated by "behavioral economics," a way of conceiving of economic matters based on the proposition that real-world people often act against their own best interest. The most prominent such appointment, the distinguished legal scholar Cass Sunstein, who heads the White House Office of Information and Regulatory Policy, is coauthor of a book called *Nudge*, which argues on behalf of what its authors call "libertarian paternalism." According to this way of thinking, laissez-faire economics is problematic because it is based on the notion that people make rational decisions when in fact they rarely do. But it is equally problematic to rely on government and its heavy-handness through regulation, since this substitutes for individual choice the coercive power of the state. Public policy should seek a middle ground—what its advocates call a "choice architecture"—that guides people to make decisions that will benefit them without forcing them to do what the government decides is best for them. Whatever one thinks of such approaches—I, for one, am not persuaded by the many experiments presuming to prove how irrational we really are— they clearly represent a movement away from the regulatory state once advocated by liberals such as Keynes and John Kenneth Galbraith.

If the direction taken so far by the Obama administration is any indication, then, liberalism is both essential to modern Western societies and at the same time too ambitious for even American presidents with an electoral mandate to undertake in full. Even in the Obama years liberalism remains on the political defense. Nothing else can explain why a small number of "blue dog" or conservative Democrats have so much influence compared to the far larger number of liberal ones in the U.S. House of Representatives. A similar reluctance to lean too far left prompted Obama to appoint prominent Republicans to key posts and to seek to gain bipartisan support for his proposals even as his own party has sufficient votes to ensure passage of much of his agenda. The ideas of neoconservatives, whose advocacy of the war in Iraq so conspicuously resulted in failure, continue to gain respectful hearings in newspapers and on television and even to influence the new administration's approach to Afghanistan, suggesting that liberals are as on the defensive in foreign policy as they are in domestic. Much of American public life remains conservative even in an era of liberal success.

Some liberals would find the reason for this ambivalence to lie in the disproportionate influence of entrenched interests and their inherently conservative ways of doing business. They would argue, for example, that the very structure of politics designed by the U.S. Constitution enables a conservative minority to block a liberal majority: senators from small and nearly all white states, for example, played a key role in the health care debate, in part because the two senators from Montana have the same power as the two from New York. Since sixty votes are now required to pass ordinary legislation in the Senate rather than fifty—the higher number is required to stop a filibuster—the odds that liberal measures will have to be tailored to win conservative support have hugely increased. Lobbyists spend fantastic sums to get what they want and their spending is frequently unregulated. The media feature "human interest" stories, neglect policy details, and in some cases, such as Fox News, are little more than propaganda vehicles for the right. There is the elected government that is liberal and the more permanent establishment that is conservative and the latter, if it is patient enough, can either defeat or modify the ambitions of the former.

No one can doubt that structural factors such as these benefit conservatism at the expense of liberalism. Conservatives may be out of power and bereft of ideas, but they are very good at opposition tactics and know how to find liberal weaknesses. Ambitious new programs will have to be financed, and deficits present major obstacles in finding ways to fund them, especially including raising revenue through taxes. For all of Barack Obama's electoral success in 2008, Democrats still have problems attracting the votes of less well-off whites, especially white men, and while their gains among Latinos bode well for the future, they remain vulnerable politically among other key electoral groups. When all these conditions combine, no Democratic president can afford to swing too far to the left, Obama included. We do not live in the 1960s, let alone the 1930s.

Still, *The Future of Liberalism* contains an alternative account of Obama's political affinities with liberalism that deserves a hearing. This book points out that liberalism in its substantive sense is committed to autonomy and equality. But there are two other kinds of liberalism as well. Procedurally speaking, liberalism is committed to the moral idea of fairness; everyone, whether liberal or not, should be committed to the same rules of the game. In addition, there is a temperamental liberalism, a psychological propensity to be generous and inclusive rather than sectarian and dogmatic, again, irrespective of one's own substantive views. The Obama administration, it is possible to argue, has been going slow on the substantive front because it also wants to be liberal in the two other senses of the term.

From this broader liberal perspective, it makes sense that the Obama administration would try to reach out to Republicans, even if they resist such overtures, because it understands that policies need broad support if they are to be accepted as legitimate by the citizens whose behavior will be affected by them. Such an approach, in addition, grows out of a recognition—again, liberal in the most generous meaning of the term—that ideas on the left, no matter how strongly held, may not contain the whole truth and that it makes a certain amount of sense to incorporate ideas from the other side if they contain something of value. Obama's lack of dogmatism—his willingness to show a pragmatic and experimental approach to policy—can in this sense be viewed as more liberal than strict adherence to a substantive liberal script.

To appreciate more fully this more capacious sense of the Obama administration's liberalism one has only to realize how it differs in procedure and temperament from the Bush administration that preceded it. On many of the key issues he faced, President Bush used his own Republican majority to pass legislation over Democratic opposition and shaped his programs to win the support of lobbyists whether or not the policy details made sense. The Obama administration, by contrast, cares about governing well, or as well as it can; from this point of view, the compromises with liberal ideals that Obama is making in policy may be offset by gains in public sympathy and understanding for a way of conducting politics that works to the benefit of those who respect their opponents and agree to fair rules. If the Republican Party continues to be perceived by many voters as too extremist and shrill for their taste, this trend toward a more open conception of politics could do more to ensure a more positive future for liberalism than gains in health care or environmental regulation.

However successful Obama proves to be in his domestic and foreign policy agenda, the mere fact of his election, especially the willingness of so many Americans to put their long history of racial discrimination behind them and vote for an African-American, suggests how much the United States has changed in the past few decades. Never again, it seems safe to say, will America be a country in which race, gender, and age trump ideas and competence in the election of political figures. The United States remains polarized and in particular the white South retains a preference for very conservative politicians and policies, but overall, and especially as today's younger voters move on with their lives and new immigrants settle here and raise their children, America seems to have taken a giant step toward a more diverse, cosmopolitan, and skill- and knowledge-based direction. If liberalism has an affinity with modernity, more modernity suggests more liberalism.

All of which is a way of saying that, as my book concludes, liberalism very much has a future. In the book's last chapter, I identify three major challenges to liberalism in the coming decades. One of them, the challenge presented by the radically illiberal rise of terrorism, is difficult to predict, for if another major terrorist strike against the United States takes place, the demands for immediate retaliation, even at the cost of violating democratic liberties, will be difficult to resist. Still, there can also be little doubt that any future administration is unlikely to respond to a terrorist attack as the Bush administration did, by going to war against a country that had little or nothing to do with the attack. Multilateral responses to terror, rather than assertions of American power, will be the dominant ones in the future, and that is good news for liberalism.

Liberalism will also continue to face a challenge from globalization; the economic integration of the world economy shows no sign of abatement. Here again what seemed not long ago to be an illiberal backlash has not materialized. Although some television commentators continue to harp on the theme of immigration, xenophobia never became an issue in the 2008 presidential election, reflecting the fact that closing off this country to global movements of people is not only impossible but not worth doing. Some protectionist sentiment continues to exist among Democrats and the labor movement, and a number of liberals remain wary of globalization because they associate it with a weakening of economic regulation, union-busting, and high corporate profits. Yet even the major recession that preoccupied the United States in the first year of the Obama administration did not produce fervent economic nationalism. Globalization in one form or another appears here to stay. There are reasons for liberals to cast a skeptical eye when profits are unregulated and wages reduced to subsistence, but there is also much to appreciate when goods, people, and ideas are free to move around the world. Liberalism remains the most appropriate political philosophy under globalizing conditions.

Lastly, *The Future of Liberalism* challenges liberals to confront conservative populism even if doing so opens them to the charge of elitism. Here too the future of liberalism seems bright. Sonia Sotomayor, a judge who had handed down decisions defending affirmative action, is now on the U.S. Supreme Court despite conservative efforts to paint her as hostile to working-class white men. *Roe* v. *Wade* remains alive and well and it is difficult to imagine a future U.S. Supreme Court overturning it. The Republican 2008 vice-presidential candidate Sarah Palin portrayed herself as an ordinary American and accused her opponents of being elitist, but to little effect (and to downright ridicule). As the Palin nomination strongly suggests, Americans, while sometimes receptive to appeals to them as ordinary people, also value leaders who possess knowledge of the world and are familiar with the actual details of public policies, an attitude that will help liberals resist the notion that, in order to lead, all you need are the right instincts and the common touch.

All in all the years after 2008 will not be a bad time to be a liberal. To appreciate the ideas likely to have the greatest impact on the lives of North Americans and Western Europeans over the next few decades, understanding (and hopefully appreciating) what the liberal tradition has always been about is crucial. This is what I have set out to do in *The Future of Liberalism*. Many reviewers of the hardcover edition of the book pointed out how much its analysis helped explain the rise of Barack Obama. I hope the paperback edition will help explain what will continue to happen in the wake of his election—and long after.

—Alan Wolfe,
September 2009

THE FUTURE OF LIBERALISM

CHAPTER 1

THE MOST APPROPRIATE POLITICAL PHILOSOPHY FOR OUR TIMES

AT THE ENDING

"In the beginning," wrote John Locke in his *Second Treatise on Government,* "all the world was America."

Locke, the late-seventeenth-century English philosopher as well known for his explanation of how our ideas are formed as for his insistence that government be based on the consent of the governed, viewed America, at least before the white man arrived, as a land in which, because "no such thing as money was any where known," conflicts over that particular root of all evil would not be necessary. From that seemingly simple idea sprung a political philosophy thoroughly alien to the absolutist monarchies of Europe. Because everyone possesses the capacity to work, all have a right to the property created when their labor is mixed with the blessings offered by the land. It follows that societies are best organized by freedom (no one can legitimately take away what naturally belongs to you), as well as equality (nor can they take it away from anyone else). To say that in the beginning all the world was America is to claim that freedom and equality would become forces too powerful to resist. That, in turn, became the single most influential component of liberalism: the dominant, if not always appreciated, political philosophy of modern times. Three centuries after Locke wrote his masterpiece, liberalism offers the best guide not only to our own times, but to the future as well. It will be my task in this book to show why.

Liberalism is a way of thinking and acting so easily taken for granted that one can easily forget how it struggled to come into existence; solved many of the problems it was asked to address; spread its influence around the world, not through coercion, but because of its universal appeal; and remains to this day far more attractive than its leading alternatives. As important as liberalism has been to the development of modern citizens and the societies they inhabit, it suffers today from a crisis of confidence. To flourish, liberalism needs to be recovered, and the stakes in its recovery are much greater than which party wins a forthcoming election, proposes the latest social reform, or even launches the next war. Modern citizens all too often forget that the liberal way of life is a good way of life, indeed, under the political conditions in which they live, the best way of life. It is liberalism's underlying philosophy—its understanding of human nature, its respect for both individualism and equality, its discovery of the social, its passion for justice, its preference for experience over theory, its intellectual openness, its commitment to fairness—that offers us the surest path toward both individual freedom and a collective sense of purpose. We need liberalism if we are to respect the integrity of human beings, design institutions that serve their needs, and enable them to shape their destinies. John Locke pointed the way, and we remain indebted to him every time we insist that we be recognized for our own accomplishments or demand that nobody be treated as inherently more superior (or inferior) than anyone else.

There was a time when Americans appreciated the importance of the political philosophy that John Locke did so much to bring into being. "Locke's little book on government is perfect as far as it goes," Thomas Jefferson wrote to Thomas Mann Randolph, his brand-new son-in-law, exactly one hundred years after the publication of *The Second Treatise*. Jefferson was hardly revealing state secrets; the whole literate world knew the extent to which he had relied on Locke when he wrote the Declaration of Independence. So closely connected were Lockean ideas with the development of the United States that one of the classics of modern political thought, the Harvard political scientist Louis Hartz's *Liberal Tradition in America* (1955), was devoted to exploring every aspect of them. Like any transformative book, Hartz's generated fierce controversy, and some of the criticisms, especially those pointing out his insufficient treatment of race, have stuck. But no one has effectively undermined Hartz's overall thesis. Lockean truths, as

Jefferson put it in the Declaration, were "self-evident," which meant, in contrast to Europe of the *ancien régime,* that no one could easily mount an attack against them.

In the beginning all the world may have been America, but, if current political arguments and election results in the United States are any indication, one must wonder about the present. The country that once embraced John Locke so warmly has been turning its back on the liberal political philosophy he did so much to inspire. Far from self-evident, liberalism in the United States remains conspicuously unpopular; twice as many Americans say that they are very or somewhat conservative compared to those who say they are very or somewhat liberal. After eight years of right-wing government under George W. Bush, these sentiments changed. Although the ultimate historical judgment on these years is yet to be delivered, the Bush administration's combination of ideological rigidity and persistent incompetence— demonstrated from its response to Hurricane Katrina to its conduct of the Iraqi war—produced widespread dismay, not only among liberals, but among significant numbers of conservatives, causing, along the way, serious dents in the alliance between small-government advocates, religious-oriented values voters, and unilateralist national security policymakers that had characterized the era of Ronald Reagan. Still, conservatism's increasing problems in no way guarantee liberalism's political success. With the election of Barack Obama in 2008, liberals in the United States have the opportunity to advance some of their most deeply held conceptions of the proper role of government. Only time will tell how successful they will be, but the early signs are mixed at best. Liberals may well succeed in moderating some of the more entrenched forms of inequality in American public life, but it is highly unlikely that any new programs will have the breadth of either the New Deal or the Great Society.

The problems facing liberalism, moreover, are not just confined to the United States. Throughout the nineteenth and early twentieth centuries, Great Britain produced the most impressive collection of liberal thinkers ever associated with one country, nearly all of whom will make their appearance in the pages that follow; yet the Liberal Democrats, the inheritors of their ideas, have been a third party for quite some time in British politics, and the other political party on the left, the Labour Party, has been in deep trouble because of the support its former leader, Tony Blair, gave to an American conservative president. On the Continent, liberal parties are either out of power or unsure what to do with whatever, generally minimal, power they have. With the exception of Margaret Thatcher, Europeans rarely elect conservative politicians recognizable to Americans. But nor do they select liberal ones with a well-articulated sense of the direction in which their societies ought to be headed. Stalemate is more likely to characterize European politics than right-wing reaction, which means that Europeans, no doubt to their relief, are spared anything resembling America's Christian right. But no one can make a credible argument that European liberalism is a vibrant political force. Europeans are unsure whether liberalism instructs them to ban Muslim head scarves or welcome them, support globalization or oppose it, or choose jobs over environmental protection rather than the other way around.

None of this means that the world has suddenly been stripped of liberal thinkers. On the contrary, liberal political theory is flourishing in the English-speaking world, especially in the work of the late American philosopher John Rawls, who asks us to evaluate the fairness of any policy or program based on the assumption that we do not know whether we personally will benefit from it or not. Although French and German philosophy throughout much of the twentieth century was inspired by one or another form of Marxism, the collapse of socialism has given rise to serious liberal thinking there as well; some French intellectuals, rather than shifting from their left-wing enthusiasm of 1968 to the neoconservative right three decades later, stopped instead with the liberal tradition in between, and many of Germany's most important thinkers, in the aftermath of Marxism's collapse, turned to American pragmatists for inspiration. But although liberalism remains something of a growth industry in the contemporary academy—endless books pour out from university presses addressing how liberals should treat multiculturalism, religion, equality, free speech, affirmative action, and a number of similar topics—many if not most of these books, technical in approach and densely written, are intended not for general readers but for other liberal political theorists. In them, moreover, liberalism frequently comes off as unappealing, as if it were a set of formulaic abstractions written from on high to guide less principled ordinary people down below. In the United States over the past few decades, any one conservative theorist in a Washington, D.C., think tank has had the public influence of at least ten liberal philosophers in America's most prestigious universities.

There also exist compelling accounts of liberalism outside the academy; some prominent journalists have written in defense of liberal ideas, and they have been joined by academics who write for the broader public. These books aim for a general readership, yet they tend, in their focus on policy debates and current events, to lack historical and comparative depth. The aim of these writers is to persuade contemporary citizens that liberalism, far from problematic, is not so bad after all. They do this in different ways; some of them argue that liberals need to remind themselves of the great leaders and policies they once produced and to reclaim their connections to ordinary voters; others spend most of their time attacking conservatives; still others insist that liberals will recover their popularity when they better learn to "frame" their beliefs in more publicly appealing ways or learn to speak not just to matters of fact but to the power of emotions. Liberals are not rolling over and playing dead. They have much to say and are saying it energetically.

Still, there is an apologetic tone to these books, which leaves the impression that those writing them are not quite convinced of their own case. When liberals address issues of foreign policy, they frequently do so as if conservatives are peering over their shoulders ready to pounce on any false move or thought. When they propose new domestic programs, their ideas tend to be pale carbon copies of the ambitious liberal programs of the past. Feminists defending a woman's right to choose are more likely to base their argument not on liberal beliefs about equality but on libertarian, and even conservative, ideas about freedom from government interference. The response of many liberals to the growth of the religious right is not to make a defense of separation of church and state, and to show how that might be good for both reason and revelation, but to urge the creation of a religious left. Liberalism, in both theory and practice, all too often represents an effort to stop further losses rather than a strategy to make additional gains. Its best offense has become a cautious and conservative defense.

This, then, is the proper time to try to close the gap between what liberalism used to mean and what the citizens of contemporary political systems all too often take it to mean. "The 'L word' implies unelectability and marginality," the historians Neil Jumonville and Kevin Mattson, liberals themselves, have written in their introduction to *Liberalism for a New Century*. "The situation has become so bad that some in America are seeking a new name for liberalism: 'progressivism.' But this move is mistaken. The term *liberalism* should be championed today and reinvigorated as a source of pride and a reminder of Americans' connection to basic values that stretch back centuries. To avoid the moniker is to run from the past, and liberals have no reason to do so." They are right. "Progressive" is the wrong term and the wrong turn;

by returning us to the days of Woodrow Wilson and others who once adopted the label, it would take liberals back to a political agenda too convinced of its own moral superiority and too hostile to civil liberties to serve the needs of an open and dynamic society. If liberals run away from their own tradition by hiding behind other labels, they will hardly be in a position to make the case for liberalism's relevance both to their own times and to the future.

Despite the ambivalence that so often seems to surround the term, liberalism does not lack for important, indeed vital, things to say. Its problem, at least in more recent times, has been its inability or unwillingness to say them clearly, positively, and convincingly. Reminding ourselves about what liberalism has stood for ought to encourage liberals to overcome some of their insecurities. It should also enable liberal societies to better find their way. And—who knows?—it might just help liberals not only to win elections but to know what to do once that happens.

AMATEURS IN INVECTIVE

No better illustration of the difference between what liberalism once meant and what it means today can be found than in the way liberalism is treated by the more inflammatory political activists and pundits prominent on the American right. Consider some typical examples. The most influential presidential adviser in a century, Karl Rove, who made the containment of liberalism a major part of his life's work, told the New York State Conservative Party in June 2006 that liberals "saw the savagery of the 9/11 attacks and wanted to prepare indictments and offer therapy and understanding for our attackers." Sean Hannity, the host of a popular American television news show, insisted that liberals "have rendered our society more vulnerable to evil's influence," are "far less suspicious than they should be of totalitarian regimes," and "have shown a constant reluctance to confront the enemies of freedom around the world." Ann Coulter, a particularly publicity-hungry polemicist who admires Senator Joseph McCarthy, began one of her books by saying, without dint of a qualification, that "when the nation is under attack, from within or without, liberals side with the enemy." And then, in 2007, the conservative firebrand Dinesh D'Souza put it all together: liberals, he wrote, not only failed to respond to September 11, they actually caused it; so horrendous are the things liberals believe,

D'Souza argued, that American conservatives should join forces with religious traditionalists in the Muslim world to defeat them.

These are, to say the least, strong words. It is not just that liberals stand accused of being misguided, impractical, hypocritical, or wrong; charges such as these are the stuff of democratic debate, there to be proven or refuted by example and evidence. Liberals, rather, are treated as carriers of infectious political diseases, people who hold views so toxic that, should those views become the basis for public policy, the United States—and by implication all modern societies—would be destroyed from within. Start with liberalism, these writers proclaim, and before you know it your country will be taken over by its enemies; your fellow citizens will be consumed with sin; your leaders will become weak-willed and duplicitous; and your democracy will turn into tyranny, most likely of the Communist variety, but even, as one right-wing critic has recently alleged, the Fascist variety as well.

Today's critics of liberalism, although they may not be aware of the fact, are repeating charges that have been around since liberalism first began to make its impact on the modern world. Over the past two hundred years, liberals have been denounced for their egoism and taste for luxury, their absurd belief in progress, their overweening rationalism, their rootless cosmopolitanism, their affinity with madness, and their naïve failure to recognize the central role played by decisive leadership in the modern world. Compared to the liberal critics of the past, those of today are amateurs in invective; none of them has matched the rhetorical flourishes of the nineteenth-century Spanish priest Félix Sardá y Salvany, for whom liberalism was "this monster of our times . . . an insidious enemy . . . the root of heresy, the tree of evil in whose branches all the harpies of infidelity find ample shelter . . . the evil of all evils." American conservatives who routinely denounce Europe for its welfare state and distaste of militarism rarely recognize how much they owe to Europe for the liberal bashing they find so attractive.

Politics ought to be a rough-and-tumble business. When life itself is at stake, or when disagreements about the meaning of life are pervasive, there is nothing wrong with passion in defense of position. Still, one has to wonder exactly *why* liberalism brings about such shrill attacks. If liberalism had been responsible for a return to the Dark Ages, one could understand the furious nineteenth-century opposition to it; but life was far better for most people in the year 1900, when liberal ideas had been put into practice, than in 1800, when they had not.

And in the twentieth century, when totalitarian systems of both the left and the right threatened global stability and the most basic of human rights, liberalism's record, despite the denunciations voiced by a few angry American conservatives, was a distinguished one. Liberals were firm in their opposition to fascism, and although some were apologists for Stalinism, others became its stern antagonists, in the process separating themselves not only from fellow travelers on the left but also from isolationists on the right. Because ideas can kill, ideology implies apology. By that criterion, liberalism has relatively little to regret; charge, if you must, liberals with naïveté, but it strains the imagination to charge them with mass murder, cruelty, or thirst for war.

The critics of liberalism so prominent on the American scene today nonetheless serve an important purpose. The very fury of their attacks, while reminding us of liberalism's vulnerabilities, also testifies to its strengths: you do not write books accusing your ideological opponents of treason unless you suspect that those opponents have ideas capable of attracting widespread support. By denouncing liberalism in the tones they do, these critics challenge liberals, not to respond with invective of their own, although I confess to having done so from time to time, but to rethink why they became liberals in the first place. The best place to begin is with definitions.

LIBERALISM IN FULL

Three ways of defining liberalism have come down to us. One emphasizes substance, the second procedure, and the third temperament.

The core substantive principle of liberalism is this: *As many people as possible should have as much say as is feasible over the direction their lives will take.* Expressed in this form, liberalism, as in the days of John Locke, is committed both to liberty and to equality. The question is what those terms mean under the conditions of modern political life.

With respect to liberty, liberals want for the person what Thomas Jefferson wanted for his country: independence. Dependency, for liberals, cripples. Human beings have minds and bodies, and both, liberals believe, should be free to exercise their full capacities: minds, through open societies that allow everyone to develop their intellect, and bodies, through societies that guarantee sufficient economic security to individuals so that they are not dependent upon the arbitrary will of others for the basic necessities of life. When we have no choice but to accept someone else's power over us, we fail to think for ourselves, are confined to conditions of existence resembling an endless struggle for survival, are unable to plan for the future, and cannot possess elementary human dignity. The autonomous life is therefore the best life. We have the potential, and are therefore responsible for realizing it, to be masters of our own destiny. This is why liberals insist on the importance of rights, including the right of people to practice their religion as they see fit, to speak for and assemble around causes in which they believe, and to possess a significant degree of control over their personal livelihood. Take away such individual rights—imagine a world in which religion (or irreligion) is coerced, freedom of speech curtailed, economic activity directed and controlled by the state, and no one allowed to organize and bargain collectively to improve their economic condition—and you have a political system that can only be called illiberal, whether it leans backward toward absolute monarchy or forward to some alleged socialist utopia.

Liberalism's core commitment to individual autonomy does not mean that it refuses to accept the existence of authority, including authority that derives from supernatural forces or governmental power. On the contrary, John Locke was a religious believer and an exponent of natural law; key American founders such as Thomas Jefferson were theorists of republican virtue who worried about the corrosiveness of individual self-interest; and the pathbreaking eighteenth-century German philosopher Immanuel Kant struggled his whole life to derive a philosophy based on obedience to universal moral commands. Liberals do not envision a world of heroic Ayn Rand stalwarts refusing to bend their implacable wills to the opinions, or even the existence, of others. Much like conservatives, liberals believe that individuals live within an ordered world that necessarily constrains the ability of people to do whatever they want whenever they want to do it. For liberals, however, such constraints are not imposed by authorities over which people have no control or shaped by traditions they cannot influence; they are established instead by people themselves through some form of consent or social contract. Independence cannot exist without interdependence. Once we have left the state of nature, we require the existence of society.

This insistence on the importance of the social is frequently overlooked, but it cannot and should not be. "Men are not born free; they become free by means of Society and the State, which, while limiting the claims of individuals, in reality bestow upon these claims an effectual recognition and sanction, and elevate them from precarious facts to rights whose fulfillment can be confidently demanded," wrote

Guido De Ruggiero, an Italian historian of European liberalism, in 1927. "That is the real gain which the individual makes when he exchanges the uncertainty of natural liberty for civil liberty." Or, as James Oakes, a historian at the City University of New York, put the point in more of an American context:

> *Society* was the great discovery of enlightened liberals. They felt liberated by their conviction that most of the things that previous generations had taken to be "natural" or "divinely ordained" were, in fact, the products of human history. Families, political systems, even economies were, as liberals realized (and as we would put it), "socially constructed." For liberals, humans were above all social beings. They were born *tabula rasa* and were thus the products of their upbringing, their environment. To function freely as a flourishing human being, everyone had to be, well, socialized. And if humans are the products of society, then the social institutions that shape them must be constructed so as to produce the kind of individuals each society wants.

Equality is liberalism's second substantive goal. Liberals are not satisfied when only some people—members of an aristocratic class here, representatives of a business elite there—have the chance to determine how they will live. Liberals believe in equality, but not as an end in itself; radical egalitarianism is more associated with the socialist tradition than with the liberal one. Liberals, rather, believe that the freedom to live your life on terms you establish does not mean very much if society is organized in such a way as to deny large numbers of people the possibility of ever realizing that objective; if independence is good for the few, it ought to be good for the many. How much actual equality there is in a society will vary from one to another, and one can imagine different kinds of liberal societies with different degrees of it. But any society that closes off opportunities for people to achieve their full human capacities, or that allows persistent inequalities to stifle the desire on the part of its least fortunate members to develop them, would not be a liberal one.

One frequently hears that liberalism's commitments to liberty and equality contradict each other. I certainly do whenever I address conservative audiences: Which liberalism are you talking about, they immediately want to know, the "classical" form or the "modern" one? Classical liberalism, in this rendition, is all about respecting private property and allowing individuals to pursue what they determine to be in their own self-interest without the coercive hand of government interfering in their decisions. Adam Smith, the Scottish moralist who published *The Wealth of Nations* in the same year that Jefferson wrote the Declaration of Independence, is the philosopher par excellence of classical liberalism; were he alive today, many of his followers insist, he would be a champion of Thatcher or Reagan, leaders who are called conservatives but are better described as libertarians, or advocates of the free market. Libertarians, to rely upon a distinction associated with the twentieth-century British philosopher Sir Isaiah Berlin, are advocates of "negative" liberty, the key principles of which are not difficult to grasp: one is that freedom consists in the fact that no one can tell me what to do; and the other holds that when I am free to make my own decisions, my success is due to my own efforts and my failures are my own responsibility.

For those who think this way, classical liberalism, because it puts freedom first, is worlds apart from the form liberalism has taken in the twentieth century, which asserts the primacy of equality. Modern liberalism promises equality through what Berlin calls a "positive" conception of liberty: it is not sufficient for me merely to be left alone, I must also have the capacity to realize the goals that I choose for myself. If this requires an active role for government, then modern liberals are prepared to accept state intervention into the economy in order to give large numbers of people the sense of mastery that free market capitalism gives only to the few. Positive conceptions of liberty hold that human beings ought not to be reduced to their passions or even their interests. They live for some higher sense of purpose than getting and spending and ought to be able to realize those ideals in the here-and-now through their own collective efforts. If Adam Smith is the quintessential classical liberal, the twentieth-century British economist John Maynard Keynes, whose ideas paved the way for massive public works projects and countercyclical economic policies meant to soften the ups and downs of the business cycle, best represents the modern version. Although an economist by training, Keynes, heretically for his profession, believed that economic problems were not all that interesting; if we can find a way to produce more abundance, something he believed we could do with the assistance of government, people could direct their attention to more worthwhile pursuits.

Frightened by the specter of twentieth-century totalitarianism, which he interpreted as an attempt by coercive governments to impose some higher purpose on human beings against their will, Isaiah Berlin argued that between negative and positive liberty one must choose: "Everything is what it is: liberty is liberty, not equality or fairness or justice or culture, or human happiness or a quiet conscience." If Berlin and those who have been inspired by him are correct, then liberalism's effort to stand substantively in favor of both liberty and equality is not only internally contradictory, it is politically unstable, always threatening to decompose into its constituent parts.

Yet classical and modern liberalism are not nearly as distinct as those who insist on dividing them maintain. One, in fact, follows, if not logically, then certainly sociologically, from the other. Liberalism's substantive commitments have to be understood in their historical context. In the eighteenth century, dependency was fostered by legacies of feudalism that made individuals subservient to their presumed superiors and, given the fixed status categories of the old regime, simultaneously created conditions that made it all but impossible for those in the lower orders to overcome their dependency. Under such conditions, autonomy and equality could both be furthered through the operations of a free market, for markets would provide opportunities for individuals to escape from the ties to which they were bound as well as give them a chance to improve their condition.

In more recent times, by way of contrast, dependency happens when people are too poor or too much the objects of invidious discrimination to develop sufficient autonomy. The eighteenth-century idea that people's fates were intertwined because of the existence of society was transformed, during the twentieth century, into the conviction that government had to be called upon when necessary to make concrete the idea of the social; no more effective means existed by which those who already led independent lives could fulfill an obligation to offer assistance to those who did not. This was a solution not without its problems, for reliance on government, as I will argue later in this book, put a crimp into the consistency of all modern political worldviews. But the liberal proposition, tested by long experience, is that whatever dependencies result from using public policy to address modern inequalities, the resulting gains in individual mobility, development of physical and mental capacity, and racial and gender equality far outweigh them. This is why Smith, writing in the eighteenth century in opposition to the regulation of business by government, and Keynes, writing in the twentieth century in support of it, were, substantively speaking, both liberals. Their disagreements were over the means by which large numbers of individuals could achieve control over their lives, not over whether they should.

The same is not true of twenty-first-century Smithians. To advocate today what Smith advocated yesterday—a free market unregulated by government—is to foster greater, rather than lesser, dependency and less, rather than more, equality. This is not always the case; in the aftermath of communism in the Soviet Union and Eastern Europe, a reliance on the market could and did unleash pent-up human potential in ways that contributed, at least for a time, to both greater liberty and equality. But in the highly organized and concentrated forms taken by capitalism in the contemporary world, removing government from the marketplace does not allow large numbers of people to become entrepreneurs in ways that enable them to set the terms by which their lives will be led; it instead allows firms to reduce their obligations to their employees and thereby make them more dependent on the vagaries of the market. At the same time, it increases the gap between rich and poor such that, even if the poor improve their condition, which they do not always do, they do so in ways dramatically unfair compared to the other improvements taking place around them. And by ignoring the tendency of employers or other people in authority to prefer people like themselves to those who are different, it sanctions forms of irrational prejudice that keep members of stigmatized groups from reaching their full potential. You do not give people more control over their lives by reducing their real income, increasing their fears of unemployment, exposing them to greater risk of accident, threatening to take away their health care, lowering how much income they receive relative to society's most well off, allowing their talents to be overlooked for purely arbitrary reasons of race and gender, and making them more dependent in their last years.

Liberalism's substantive commitments to freedom and equality represent a political position; they are meant to defend particular goals against other political positions that either oppose such goals or assign a low priority to them. In the eighteenth century, liberalism's opponents were those who protected a caste system in which favorable birth gave a small minority advantages available to no one else. In the twenty-first century, liberalism stands in opposition to forms of conservatism that justify hierarchies of unequal opportunity; versions of libertarianism that, by giving big business too much power, give ordinary people too little; and lingering legacies of socialism that run roughshod over individual rights in their determination to achieve greater equality. Liberalism in the substantive sense of the term is partial as well as partisan; to realize their substantive goals, liberals must organize on behalf of them and influence public opinion to obtain them.

In addition to its substantive content, liberalism can also be defined according to procedural means. Liberalism emerged in the late eighteenth and early nineteenth centuries when constitution writing was all the rage, and the constitutional imperative reflected a desire to create rules that would enable competing interests within society to peacefully negotiate their differences. For liberals, proceduralism is the only realistic alternative we have to violence. In the absence of agreed-upon rules in the international arena, war is inevitable. Without adherence to procedures in domestic life, civil war threatens. Liberal thinkers have come up with a variety of terms to express this commitment to proceduralism, ranging from Locke's social contract to such American constitutional practices as the separation of powers and checks and balances to the movements of the twentieth century to create international bodies designed to prevent war such as the League of Nations and the United Nations. What links all of them are the shadows cast by two political philosophers who called attention to the ubiquity of, and need for, force in the world of public affairs: Niccolò Machiavelli, the Florentine Renaissance man who gave the rulers of his day strikingly cold-blooded advice about how to retain their power; and Thomas Hobbes, the seventeenth-century Englishman, and rival of John Locke, who insisted that only a powerful sovereign could prevent a return to a barbaric state of nature in which life is, in one of the most chilling phrases ever written by a political philosopher, "solitary, poor, nasty, brutish, and short." To avoid such a fate, liberal proceduralists held, government must achieve sufficient neutrality between contending parties to win their trust, and that can be accomplished only through agreements to which all parties commit themselves.

Procedural liberalism, in contrast to substantive liberalism, refers to a moral ideal rather than a political goal; its goal is fairness or impartiality, the idea that anything that applies to any one person must apply to every person. Liberalism in this meaning of the term is not necessarily opposed to political conservatism, certainly not the anti-ideological conservatism of the twentieth-century British philosopher Michael Oakeshott or those followers of Leo Strauss, the German émigré to the United States and inspiration for contemporary neoconservatism, who have done so much to help us appreciate the importance of the American founding. Nor does it stand in opposition to libertarianism. If anything, libertarians have been even more vigilant than liberals in the protection of civil liberties against arbitrary power. And even those forms of socialism that left behind the idea of government ownership of the means of production in favor of a less intrusive commitment to the welfare state adopted a sympathy toward liberal proceduralism. Procedural liberalism's real opposition is to absolutism: the notion that a ruler need not be bound by rules.

Understood in a procedural sense, a liberal is anyone who supports a constitutional form of government; believes in a government of laws rather than of men; holds that exceptions to general rules should be rarely if ever granted; and accepts the principle that the party in power cannot change the rules of achieving power to benefit itself. It is for this reason that one can properly call an entire country such as the United States liberal, even though it obviously contains many people whose substantive views are conservative. What unites nearly all Americans is loyalty to a set of rules put in place by the framers of the Constitution that borrowed extensively from a liberal proceduralist way of thinking.

Although formulated in opposition to the monarchies of the *ancien régime,* liberal proceduralism is surprisingly relevant to the twenty-first century, not only because illiberal societies threaten liberal ones with the prospect of terrorism but because liberal societies are tempted to take procedurally illiberal actions to counter the threat. So long as some use arbitrary means to impose their will on others, proceduralism will be a crucial element of liberalism. Suspend the Constitution (or interpret it in ways impossible to justify), break the law when you are in charge of enforcing it, grant pardons to some while increasing the severity of the punishments handed out to others, treat the political opposition as if it were an enemy—and you are no longer a liberal in the procedural sense. If a conservative is a liberal who has been mugged by reality, a liberal proceduralist is anyone who has been treated arbitrarily and does not want to be treated that way again.

Despite its importance, liberal proceduralism is subject to widespread criticism among contemporary thinkers. To the American political philosopher Michael Sandel, a "procedural republic," by valuing fair rules over substantive ends, is incapable of offering guidance to its citizens about the right way to live; against procedural liberalism, Sandel would prefer forms of civic republicanism that, in paying greater attention to the qualities of a virtuous citizen, encourage discussions about the nature of the good. For the literary and legal theorist Stanley Fish, perhaps the most prominent and prolific critic of liberalism in the contemporary world, liberal proceduralism is an impossibility; it speaks in terms of neutrality between different ways of life, but its real aim is to force one way of life, the one that values neutrality, on others. In theory, liberal proceduralism, because it is inclusive of different political worldviews, ought to be less controversial than substantive liberalism, which defends one set of political goals against others. But in reality, liberal proceduralism finds itself under attack from left, right, and center, as if the one thing that people who disagree over substantive ends can all agree upon is that no set of rules can rise above the fray and look down disinterestedly upon those rules.

Liberal proceduralism has its vulnerabilities. There *is* something amiss about thinkers who insist that government should always be neutral among competing conceptions of the good life and yet who always manage to conclude that government should be on their side on such controversial matters as abortion or affirmative action. Others are more consistent; they genuinely do try to remain neutral when questions of morality are at stake, but their effort to do so only exposes them to the charge that government *ought* to defend one version of the good life against others. Liberal proceduralism, like all other forms of liberalism, should not be taken to the extreme of caricature.

Still, the critique of liberal proceduralism, no matter how vigorously advanced, fails to offer any credible alternative. If we conclude that no neutrality between competing outlooks on the world is possible, as Stanley Fish does, we are back in a Hobbesian state of nature, obeying a sovereign for fear of societal conflict—not the most enviable place, even more so in our weapons-filled times than in the days of Hobbes, to find oneself. If we instead try to find substantive points on which everyone can agree, an approach favored by those who call themselves communitarians, we end up either with fairly vacuous platitudes that lose the capacity to bind us to anything important or with more deeply etched conceptions of the good life that unfortunately define those who do not conform to such conceptions as leading bad lives. For all the talk of civic republicanism or communitarianism as an alternative to liberalism, no one has shown how they might work in complex, pluralistic, political conditions. Compare liberalism to its alternatives, and it tends to win by default. How, after all, would we even make such a comparison unless we all agreed on the procedures for doing so?

In addition to sharing core substantive convictions and a preference for procedural means, liberals are characterized by a distinct temperament. The first use of "liberal" in a political sense took place in 1810, when Spanish delegates to the Cortés, or parliament, meeting in Cádiz, adopted the term to characterize a program seeking to end feudal privileges and to establish a more modern government. But the word "liberal" existed etymologically long before it existed politically. "Liberal" stems from the Latin *liber*, or "free." Because it originated as an adjective whose meaning was dependent on whatever noun it was modifying, "liberal" has always had a rather capacious—dare one say liberal?—meaning; the *Shorter Oxford English Dictionary* points out that "liberal," besides meaning free, can also mean generous, abundant, large, gentlemanly, unstinting, lax, candid, and unprejudiced. Legacies of that broad meaning abound today: students do not study something called the conservative arts and many societies claim to be liberal democratic while none call themselves conservative democratic. In ordinary usage, "liberalism" refers not only to a substantive political program and a morality emphasizing fairness; it also possesses a connotation emphasizing an openness to the world.

The liberal temperament has more to do with psychology than with politics or morality. "Liberalism" in this meaning of the term seeks to include rather than to exclude, to accept rather than to censor, to respect rather than to stigmatize, to welcome rather than reject, to be generous and appreciative rather than stingy and mean. Temperamentally, liberals are impatient with arguments rooted in fear and self-protection. They tend to see the past's improvements in the human condition as reason for anticipating continued improvement in the future. To be sure, liberals recognize that evil can lurk in the hearts of men and women and that some political systems—by definition, illiberal ones—have been evil in the extreme. But they hold that the existence of the bad does not make impossible the realization of the good. On the contrary, the fact that some societies lack liberalism's generosity of spirit is all the more reason for liberals to insist on reform, not only in the public and political sense but in the private and human one.

As was true of liberal proceduralism, temperamental liberalism is trans-ideological. A conservative who opposes liberalism's commitment to the welfare state but who gives generously to charity is acting liberally in this temperamental sense—more liberally, in many ways, than the leftist who supports the welfare state but gives less to the poor and needy. A libertarian who votes Republican and welcomes new technologies is more liberal than a party-line Democrat who insists that nothing of which he disapproves shall be built in his backyard. A Christian who argues that religious liberty applies to Muslims and Buddhists is more temperamentally liberal than a secularist who dismisses all religion as superstitious nonsense. An academic department composed of liberals that refuses to hire conservatives does not live up to the liberalism it preaches. Temperamentally speaking, liberalism is not defined by the positions one takes, but by the spirit in which they are taken.

The danger posed by the kinds of conservative attacks on liberalism that characterize the present political environment is of throwing out the procedural and temperamental baby with the substantive bathwater. Conservatives can and do object to liberalism's insistence on freedom and equality, even if they find it difficult, at least in the contemporary world, to make the case for unfreedom and hierarchy. But the more extreme of them, through the shrill distemper of their rhetoric, undermine the conditions under which all political arguments, liberal as well as conservative, can make their best case. These are voices that in many ways are not even conservative, lacking a skeptical sensibility to the same degree they possess a radical confidence in their ability to change the world around them. Such critics fail to understand that temperamental and procedural liberalism are as valuable to everyone, whatever their views, as substantive liberalism is and ought to be contentious. Understood in its broadest sense, liberalism is open to conservatism in ways that conservatism, understood in its narrowest sense, is not open to liberalism.

Conservatives are not the only ones who oppose liberalism these days; criticism aplenty comes from the left as well. Leftist thinkers do not reject all of liberalism's component parts; that is difficult for any modern political worldview to do. But many of them select one while downplaying the others. Civil libertarians, for example, defend a proceduralist commitment to free speech irrespective of the substantive content of the speech being defended. Others, including those protective of the rights of stigmatized minorities, would assign more weight to achieving the substantive goal of equality, even if that means curtailing the free speech rights of people who say hateful things about them. Both are convinced that choices have to be made between liberalism's commitments, and they are prepared to make such choices. In so doing, however, they fail to appreciate the extent to which choices can work at cross-purposes: a strict civil libertarian defense of free speech, for example, by assigning the same right to speak to well-funded corporations as to underfunded corporate protesters, undermines commitments to equality by allowing the views of the corporations to effectively drive out of existence the views of the protesters. Defending unpopular minorities against hateful speech, done in the name of equality, can easily lead to forms of political correctness that deny people the liberty to express their deeply held convictions, no matter how unpleasant those convictions may be to others. Criticize liberalism in one area of life and you are likely to pay the price in others.

In contrast to those who appreciate none, or only some, of the features that made liberalism what it is, Western societies need a reminder that all three of its components—substantive, procedural, and temperamental—are essential to the way we live now.

Modern democratic societies may give widespread credence to liberalism's substantive goals of liberty and equality, but this does not mean those objectives are secured. Liberty these days would seem to be safe because it is the official philosophy of both the right, in the form of economic freedom, and the left, in the form of personal freedom. Yet governments remain ever on the lookout for new ways to keep tabs on their citizens, now emboldened by new technologies unimaginable to those who first insisted on rights to privacy and freedom of conscience. It is difficult to lead an autonomous life if someone in power knows precisely what kind of life you are leading. So long as there are threats to autonomy, there will be a case to be made for liberty.

Nor can we conclude that the liberal commitment to equality has been safely secured in modern times. It is not just that the gap between rich and poor in recent years has been growing, although in the United States it has. It is that we lack basic agreement about what equality means. Are conditions of equality met when everyone has the same chance to improve their condition or when improvements in condition are actually achieved? Does a rising tide lift all boats or submerge the less well-crafted ones? Do subsidies for the most well off benefit the least well off by trickling down to them? Is racial equality best achieved by ignoring race or taking it into account? To what extent are citizens of wealthier societies under an obligation to help those who, through no fault of their own, happen to live in poorer societies? If liberalism has a future, it ought to be because the idea of as many people as possible leading autonomous lives has one as well; yet, uncertain how to achieve such an objective, Western societies are uncertain how strong their commitments to equality really are.

Although substantive liberalism is a necessary condition for the realization of the good life, it is not, by itself, a sufficient one. Procedural liberalism is required whenever a society is tempted to take short-cuts around its constitutional rules. The fact that the West is no longer engaged in fighting world wars has not stilled cries to suspend liberal proceduralism; on the contrary, in response to the events of September 11, 2001, some argue that the West is fighting an enemy so determined and fearsome it has little choice but to modify its historical commitments to fair procedures and constitutional norms to meet it. Their cries have not fallen on deaf ears. In the United States in particular, liberalism's commitment to fair procedures was severely put to the test when America's leaders during the administration of George W. Bush permitted torture, suspended such rights as habeas corpus, increased surveillance without following established rules, and concentrated unprecedented powers in the White House. In such ways are liberal societies constantly reminded to take seriously the liberalism that defines them; pleas for the rules to be suspended ought to be taken as opportunities for remembering why rules are important.

Nor should we neglect liberalism of the temperamental sorts, one that is open to a sense of discovery, anticipates the future with excitement and approaches the world with generous spirit. It is one thing for conservatives to defend such time-honored practices and institutions as the classical tradition, Western culture, and the rural way of life, as the mid-twentieth-century essayist and cultural commentator Russell Kirk did, or even to add fox-hunting to them, in the case of the contemporary British philosopher Roger Scruton; this is what conservatives are supposed to do. But it is another thing when leftists turn into temperamental conservatives, unwilling to see their ways of life change, their ideas challenged, or their prejudices exposed. No one is more temperamentally conservative than a Manhattan leftist living in a rent-controlled apartment and holding tenure at a university; his or her way of life is inevitably bound to breed a sense of complacency that is incompatible with liberalism's historical commitment to be open to the new. Liberalism is unlikely to make major gains in politics if it continues to suffer such losses in spirit.

Treating liberalism in the broadest meaning of the term will not take place without problems. Given its tripartite usage, some linguistic confusion will inevitably follow. The term has been used in a different way in Europe, for example, where a liberal might find himself comfortable with the American Republican Party, than it has been in the United States. Liberalism's multiple understandings, moreover, do not always work in tandem; although substantive ends commit liberals to choosing one way of life over another, procedural means aim for impartiality among competing ways of life. Because liberals have supported a variety of ends to reach the goal of improving and equalizing human capacities, finally, they have not made unalterable commitments to the idea that the market (or the state) always rules, that freedom of speech must be an absolute, that human nature is either inherently good or inherently bad, or that peace is always preferable to war. Seeking to find some common thread in the liberal tradition, one writer sympathetic to it, the twentieth-century Brazilian diplomat and philosopher J. G. Merquior, all but gave up and argued that instead of speaking of liberalism, we should speak of many different liberalisms.

This is a suggestion that ought to be resisted. By focusing on only one of liberalism's meanings, inconsistencies can be avoided. But there is also a significant cost to be paid: liberalism loses the appeal that did so much to make it the dominant political philosophy of modern times. We need liberalism because without its politics, we are less free and less equal. But we also need liberalism because without its morality, we are less fair, and because without its psychology, we are less generous. Our goal should be the recovery of liberalism in full.

LIBERAL DISPOSITIONS

To appreciate liberalism's future, it is necessary to return, not just to the New Deal or the Progressive Era, for those were the periods in which substantive liberalism achieved its goals, but to the period between 1787 and 1815 when liberalism in its most capacious sense made its political debut. The last years of the eighteenth century, as the historian Jay Winik has argued in *The Great Upheaval*, gave birth to the modern world as we know it, and when we add to that the decade or so that followed, the case for major historical transformation is strengthened even more. People alive during this relatively brief interval of Western history found themselves witnessing the writing and ratification of a Constitution for the recently formed United States of America; the French toppling their monarchy through violent modern revolution; significant movements to contain the power of established churches; the first stirrings of the feminist movement; the beginnings of the international campaign against slavery; Luddite rebellions and working-class protest in Great Britain; the effort by Napoleon to conquer Europe; increasing repression and authoritarianism in Russia; the planting of the first seeds of national self-consciousness in the countries Napoleon tried to subdue; and the Congress of Vienna that brought about a century's worth of relative peace to Europe. If these were times that tried men's souls, they were also ones that liberated them from political authoritarianism and freed them from religious orthodoxy.

The years that gave birth to modernity also inspired the ways we think about it. Out of such events emerged the major political philoso-

phies of our era: besides liberalism, they include conservatism, nationalism, romanticism, and socialism. Never in the history of the world, it
seems fair to say, did so many significant and competing visions of
organizing and understanding politics come into being simultaneously.

The late eighteenth and early nineteenth centuries, it follows, were
a time of intellectual as well as political intensity, producing one of
the greatest collections of thinkers and artists ever assembled in one
twenty-five-year period: Thomas Jefferson, James Madison, Tom Paine,
Mary Wollstonecraft, Edmund Burke, Samuel Taylor Coleridge, William Wordsworth, Jeremy Bentham, Benjamin Constant, Carl von
Clausewitz, Ludwig van Beethoven, Johann Wolfgang von Goethe,
Immanuel Kant, and G. W. F. Hegel—and those in just four countries.
It is as if a century's worth of political, social, and intellectual transformation was compressed into the experience of one generation. We
are more likely to recognize ourselves—our ideals, our dilemmas, our
solutions—at the end of this brief period of political and intellectual
ferment than at the beginning.

Today, we lack the genius of those who dominated those years, and
our era, while exciting in its own right, also lacks the other's drama. But
like defenders of the Enlightenment influenced by Voltaire and Denis
Diderot, we continue to debate whether reason and revelation are in
conflict. Much as Tom Paine and his intellectual sparring partner
Edmund Burke did during the French Revolution, we disagree over the
importance to be attached to human rights. In the spirit of Napoleon
Bonaparte's defenders and critics, we ponder whether leaders should or
should not claim for themselves the power to go to war. Our concern
with protecting nature comes right out of the pages of the followers of
Jean-Jacques Rousseau, as does our preoccupation with leading lives of
authenticity. Like the Romantic poets, we worry about losing touch
with the spiritual and emotional sides of life. Our concerns with gender
equality leap out of the pages of Wollstonecraft's *Vindication of the
Rights of Woman*. Even though socialism—a term invented during this
period by the British writer and activist Robert Owen—failed in our
time, its original concerns with equality continue to be at the heart of
contemporary political debate. The events and thinkers of the modern
age could not be more relevant in an era all too many are willing to call
postmodern. For all the talk about how the Enlightenment project failed,
we live with the consequences of the Enlightenment all around us.

Liberalism emerged as a response to events that were as destabilizing to established ways of thinking as they were exciting anticipations
of new ways of living. Born in an era of flux, liberalism tells us not so

much what to think but more about how to think. It is not a software program that can spit out the answers to whatever questions we may have, nor is it a set of abstract principles or an inchoate bundle of well-meaning platitudes. Liberalism, rather, is best treated in its prepolitical form. It is characterized by a set of dispositions toward the world that defines what kinds of creatures we are, establishes goals for us to reach, and lays down guidelines for the fairest ways to reach them. Seven such dispositions—each of which will get its own analysis in chapters 2–8 to follow—strike me as especially important if we are to understand the contributions liberalism can make to the world in which we live.

A disposition to grow. Contemporary libertarians are right to insist that human beings must have the freedom to choose. But human beings must also have the freedom to develop who they are. You cannot choose what you do not know. Liberals therefore insist that people be encouraged to grow beyond whatever state they find themselves in. We are not, liberals hold, destined by forces beyond our control to lead lives whose outcome we cannot influence. Human nature is neither so perfect that we can live like angels nor so horrendous that we are consumed by sin. We are products of culture more than we are creatures of nature; we make the world around us, and in so doing, we make ourselves.

A sympathy for equality. It is widely believed that people are by nature unequal and that any attempt to use government to make them more equal is therefore doomed to fail. For some, the case is even stronger: artificial attempts to create equality lead inevitably to totalitarianism. Liberals hold that, if anything, the reverse of this way of thinking is true. Modernity creates inevitable pressures toward equality; once the industrial and democratic revolutions took off, unjustified inequalities could no longer be sustained. It is therefore efforts to prevent equality—or in especially ugly times to bring about greater inequality—that are unrealistic. Debate in modern politics should focus not on whether equality ought to be a goal of public policy, but on what kinds of equality society wants and how they can best be achieved. Liberals recognize that inequality, even if it benefits some people economically, imposes huge costs socially. Inequality serves the interests of some; equality is in the interest of all.

A preference for realism. Liberals distrust reliance on the emotions in favor of a less dramatic, but more secure, reliance on fact. Indeed, liberalism developed throughout the nineteenth century as a reaction against Romanticism, an exuberantly creative force in literature, music, and poetry, but one that when applied to such issues as war and nationalism became extremely dangerous. Liberals treat the world with a certain kind of ironic detachment that resists ideological thinking. Wary of heroes, Romantic or any other kind, they believe that leaders should be guided, above all else, by a sober sense of responsibility. Let the imagination soar, but keep politics and policy close to the ground. Sometimes the prosaic offers a better guide to the way we ought to live than the poetic.

An inclination to deliberate. Deliberation and debate are not, to liberals, obstacles in the path of making strong decisions but necessary ingredients for making wise ones. Liberal proceduralism is therefore not just a formulaic insistence on rule-following; in democratic times, the more individuals who share in the responsibility for a decision, the more legitimate and binding that decision will be. Liberalism cautions against those who insist that we face an enemy so grave, a crisis so portentous, or a situation so unprecedented that the rules promising discussion and negotiation must be suspended. A political system that encourages leaders to make decisions in the absence of widespread deliberation is an illiberal one.

A commitment to tolerance, even for those who do not tolerate you. Liberals are committed to the idea of an open society. But what should liberals do about those who are not open to them? The earliest liberal answer to this question was shaped by its reaction to organized religion. Some liberal thinkers, both during the Enlightenment and at the present time, insist that since religion is hostile to reason, liberalism should be hostile to religion. But if liberalism, in the interest of promoting openness, closes itself off to faith, will it still be liberal? The answer is no. To pronounce religion wrongheaded and dangerous is not to be enlightened but is to mimic the sectarian sensibilities one is presumably denouncing. Liberalism ought to be in favor of freedom for religion and not just freedom from religion.

An appreciation of openness. Liberalism developed in reaction to societies that closed the minds of their subjects against new ideas, their borders against foreigners, and their governments from the eyes of the public. All three spheres will continue to pose challenges to liberals for the foreseeable future. Liberalism is at its most robust when it views freedom of speech not merely as the absence of restraint but as an opportunity to learn. It can be most proud of itself when it develops viable ways to protect open borders against xenophobia, as it insists in return that newcomers, even if they are inclined to resist doing so, learn liberal rules of the political game. And despite arguments to the effect that times of terror and war require an unusual level of secrecy, the liberal commitment to open government is too valuable a resource to be casually thrown away.

A taste for governance. If individuals are to gain control over their emotions, should society gain control over its destiny? The liberal answer is yes. Liberals believe in government because they believe in governance; just as people can establish directions for themselves, they can use their intelligence to plan for their collective future. Modern people are not likely to return to a time when one illness could deplete their life savings, one natural disaster could wipe out their city, or one ill-planned war could undermine their security. Government is a fact of life in modern society, and the reaction against it has more to do with romantic longings than practical needs. Better to welcome an approach that accepts government and wants to see it improve than one which, in rejecting its importance, all too often presides over its ineffectiveness.

BRIGHT IDEAS IN DARK TIMES

Robust, optimistic, forward-looking, liberalism made the case for modernity against forces of tradition and superstition. It helped usher in social reforms that brought both personal dignity and material gain to ordinary people. Under the influence of liberal ideas, people stopped believing that the conditions of their lives were determined by forces beyond their control, rendering all efforts toward human improvement futile. Liberalism gave people a language for asserting their individual rights in situations in which governments were prepared to take them away. It prepared the ground for people to live at peace with recent arrivals to their society. It took some time, but, again due to liberalism, people also learned that however necessary war may be to protect a nation's security, it ought always to be treated as a last resort; talk between nations, however frustrating, is better than armed conflict between nations, however tempting.

This does not mean that everything liberals have thought and done has been correct: Immanuel Kant's commandment that we act out of a sense of duty to strangers we do not know rather than loyalty to those we love and cherish could easily become too burdensome to follow; John Stuart Mill, the Victorian reformer and advocate of woman's suffrage, will appear many times in this book as a courageous defender of liberty, but also as someone who expressed churlish contempt for the views of ordinary people; the twentieth-century educational reformer and philosopher John Dewey, America's Mill, possessed an admirably generous faith in human capacity, but did not fully appreciate the human capacity for depravity; and contemporary academic liberal philosophers, who insist that we be guided in our deliberations by a common commitment to principles, have been unable to find a place for those for whom revelation counts for more than reason. Liberalism is by no means perfect. No political philosophy can be, and perfection, in any case, is appropriate for religious visions, but not for the give-and-take of politics in societies containing different visions of what perfection means.

Still, liberalism presents a challenge, indeed, one of the most important challenges of our time: it asks people to reach higher in order to live better. It is a way of thinking and doing that refuses to accept that we can do nothing while remaining suspicious of the idea that we can do everything. It accepts human beings for what they are while recognizing that what they are is inextricably connected to what they can become. It tells us that we can be free, but it also reminds us that freedom in the world in which we live is dependent upon finding ways to work together with others. Understood in the fullest sense of the term, liberalism is modernity's guide for the perplexed: its advice is designed to help us make sense out of a world far more confusing, but also filled with far more potential, than the one inhabited by our pre-liberal ancestors. If liberalism sometimes appears overly nuanced and complicated, that is because the conditions of modern lives are as well.

Not that long ago, an American writer, Francis Fukuyama, proclaimed the end of history—with liberalism, or more precisely Western liberal democracy, as its victor. Fukuyama's book had its flaws, especially its triumphalist tone and its failure to anticipate that Western societies would soon be under attack from decidedly nonliberal and nondemocratic forces. Still, his thesis at least gave credit where credit is due. For all the talk throughout the twentieth century of how nonliberal, sometimes totalitarian regimes would prove themselves infinitely superior to liberal ones, the latter survived not only intact but in significant ways improved. Liberal ideals may be under attack, but they retain a powerful appeal. Most societies with a choice—there are, alas, many societies without a choice—would, if they could, be liberal ones. Liberal democracies won out over fascism and communism for a reason: equality and freedom are too compelling to resist for long. They are likely to survive any current threats from any of today's deeply illiberal forces for the same reason.

Yet despite liberalism's appeal, the tone of some of the West's leading thinkers is far gloomier than anything found in Fukuyama's *The End of History*. The ever-engaging but often over-the-top British philosopher John Gray informs his fellow human beings that any thoughts they might entertain about their inherent goodness are presumptuous, any conceptions that they might have of being subject to moral laws are vain, and any beliefs they might have in progress are absurd. It is not the end of history we witness, writes the distinguished European-born but American-based historian Walter Laqueur, but merely the last days of Europe, as its affinity with Judeo-Christian values becomes lost in a wave of Islamization, its welfare states crumble under impossible demands, and its new political entity, the European Union, has no means of defending itself.

The future of the United States does not offer much of an alternative either, at least according to the political scientist Samuel P. Huntington in his book *Who Are We?*, because its historical association with Protestant ideas of freedom and responsibility is being overwhelmed by immigrants from Mexico who do not share Anglo-Saxon culture. It would be bad enough if the challenge to the West represented by militant Islam amounted to World War III; but, according to the neoconservative writer Norman Podhoretz, it actually has launched World War IV—and there is reason to believe that the West might not be up to the task of winning it. Such accounts of Western gloom and doom stand in sharp contrast to the optimism of a Locke, a Smith, or a Mill. Far from liberalism having much of a future, we will be lucky, if we pay attention to books such as these, to have any future at all.

Let's not give up just yet. It is true that modern societies face significant challenges, both on the environmental front in the form of global warming and on the foreign policy front in the form of international terrorism. It is also true that in at least some liberal societies, the United States being one of them, political polarization, demagoguery, and electioneering as expensive as it is unenlightened are at work. But political life has never been without its challenges; if anything, in comparison with the years in which liberalism was born, our era seems rather staid. There is no reason to look around us and to conclude that liberalism's optimism, openness, and confidence doom it to irrelevance. Apocalyptic scenarios, in either the religious or secular form, offer more self-pity than self-understanding. The world in which we live is a world we still have the capacity to shape. That, more than any other reason, is why liberalism's future is our future.

CHAPTER 2

IN PRAISE OF ARTIFICE

ROUSSEAU V. KANT

In 1749, the thirty-seven-year-old Jean-Jacques Rousseau walked the twelve miles from Paris to Vincennes to visit the polymath Denis Diderot, who had been imprisoned for the irreligiosity of his writings. Along the way, Rousseau, who had yet to accomplish much of anything in life, read in the newspaper *Mercure de France* that the Dijon Academy was sponsoring an essay contest on whether the development of the arts and sciences had been beneficial to humanity. In a flash, he decided to answer in the negative. His argument—or more precisely, the ideas of those who challenged his argument—would go a long way toward establishing key features of what liberals believe.

Liberalism begins with the conviction that the question of human nature is up to human beings to decide; even if their nature makes them bad, their works can make them good. Liberalism's greatest contribution to thinking about society is a different way of thinking about ourselves: we are not merely what God ordains us to be or what nature determines we must be, but what we create through our own deliberate acts. Economists tell us that there is no such thing as a free lunch. The same wisdom applies to politics. The liberal premise is this: if you put little or nothing in, you get little or nothing out; liberal citizens use the powers given to them by society to improve their lives by working together with others for purposes chosen by themselves. Design a world in which people have little or no role to play, and you do not need liberalism. Liberalism matters only because people do.

Rousseau started the discussion that eventually produced this generous understanding of human capacity. Upon his return from the prison at Vincennes, Rousseau wrote two discourses, both attacking civilization and defending nature in ways so thought-provokingly audacious that other leading thinkers, especially the late-eighteenth-century German philosopher Immanuel Kant, felt compelled to make the contrary case for artifice and culture. The arguments in which these two thinkers engaged continue to rage until our own time. Rousseau's skepticism toward human accomplishments finds its echoes in surprising places: the sermons of conservative preachers, the assumptions of ecological activists, the findings of behavioral economists, and the speculations of sociobiologists and evolutionary theorists. Kant's appreciation of society, by contrast, has influenced every subsequent liberal thinker who followed in his footsteps, down to those who insist that we have obligations toward all human beings in the world and not just to those with whom we happen to share a nation. Every era, it would seem, develops its own ways to question human accomplishment, which means, from the standpoint of liberalism, that every era also needs thinkers prepared to make the case for human inventiveness and social cooperation. Rousseau's walk turned out to be a fateful one indeed.

At first, Rousseau's ideas were greeted with remarkable enthusiasm by those committed to the principles of the Enlightenment, the great eighteenth-century intellectual movement defending reason and progress against superstition and reaction. Diderot, the man Rousseau so much wanted to see, in the years after leaving the prison in Vincennes had launched the *Encyclopédie*, his multivolume effort to summarize everything known to man in ways designed to help individuals understand the world around them. Enchanted by Rousseau's critique—this was before hostilities broke out between the two of them, not only over their contrasting views of science and industry but over their personalities and achievements—Diderot helped arrange for the publication of the *Discourse on the Sciences and the Arts*. Yet Rousseau, as Diderot quickly learned, shared little of the *encyclopédiste*'s desire to bring reason to bear on all things human. Not one for throat-clearing, Rousseau began his essay by blaming "the stupid Moslem" for the terrible decision to translate, and thus to keep alive for posterity, the writings of the ancient Greek philosophers. Although he sometimes compared himself to Socrates, Rousseau distrusted those who spoke on behalf of the intellect. "The needs of the body constitute the foundation of society," he wrote, "those of the mind its ornamentation." The problem with the arts and sciences is that they distract us from the real virtues associated with simple ways of life. Influenced by them, "we no longer dare appear as we really are."

Artificiality has a name, according to Rousseau, and its name is "civilization." Thinking they are free to benefit from progress, civilized people are in fact subject to "a loathsome and deceptive conformity." In their atrophied condition, they drive away real friendships, trust, and deep personal regard, and replace them with "suspicions, resentments, fears, coldness, reserve, hatred, and betrayal. . . ." Anticipating Alexis de Tocqueville's *Democracy in America,* as well as the best-selling criticisms of the United States associated with such 1950s classics as William Whyte's *The Organization Man* and Sloane Wilson's *The Man in the Gray Flannel Suit,* Rousseau condemned "the herd known as society" for being filled with people who "behave in exactly the same ways, unless more powerful motives prevent them from doing so." Trying to impress others, we lose touch with ourselves. What does it matter, Rousseau wondered, paraphrasing Jesus, if the arts and sciences advance progress but, in the course of so doing, corrupt man's soul?

Three years later, Rousseau sent his second essay to the academicians at Dijon. He posited in his *Discourse on the Origin and Foundations of Inequality Among Mankind* a state in nature in which people lived in equal harmony, only to be undone by the development of a human society in which "we have nothing but a deceitful and frivolous exterior, honor without virtue, reason without wisdom, and pleasure without happiness." Perhaps the best way to convey the power of his critique is to focus on a subject as interesting to him as it is to us: food. Eating was a pretty straightforward matter for the savage man, Rousseau argued: he took what he wanted from nature, and even if he sometimes had to fight with others over who got what, "it ends in a few cuffs; the victor eats, the vanquished retires to seek his fortune; and all is quiet again." When it comes to "man in society," however, the food is dreadful—and so, by extension, is everything else:

If you reflect a moment on the monstrous mixture, and pernicious manner of seasoning so many dishes; on the putrefied food; on the adulterated medicines, the tricks of those who sell them, the mistakes of those who administer them, the poisonous qualities of the vessels in which they are prepared; if you but think of epidemics bred by bad air among great numbers of men crowded together, or those occasioned by our delicate way of living, by our passing back and forth from the inside of our homes into the open air, the putting on and taking off of our clothes with too little precaution, and by all those conveniences which our boundless sensuality has changed into necessary habits, and the neglect or loss of which afterwards costs us our life or our health; if you set down the conflagrations and earthquakes, which devouring or overturning whole cities destroy the miserable inhabitants by thousands; in a word, if you sum up the dangers with which all these causes are constantly menacing us, you will see how dearly nature makes us pay for the contempt we have showed for her lessons.

Rousseau, as the cascading rhetoric of this passage ought to make clear, is an incredibly seductive thinker. He certainly was to the late Harvard political theorist Judith Shklar. Shklar, a refugee from totalitarian-torn Europe, remembered how she was "mesmerized" by Rousseau during her undergraduate years in Canada: "It is not just that debates about him always seemed to touch upon the most vital and enduring questions of politics, but that when I read him, I knew that I was in the presence of an unequaled intelligence, so penetrating that nothing seemed to escape it." Shklar dedicated her life to identifying what made the liberal tradition valuable, and for that task Rousseau was "addictive" because "his writings are so perfect and lucid, and yet so totally alien to a liberal mentality."

To appreciate what liberalism is, it is important to know what it is not. Rousseau is exemplary in this regard for, while no liberal, he was also no conservative; Edmund Burke, who was one, called him, in his "Letter to a Member of the National Assembly," "the insane Socrates of the National Assembly," as if Rousseau's *Social Contract*, and its antimonarchical conception of the general will, contained a plot outline for the French Revolution. Yet so powerful were Rousseau's ideas to other right-wing thinkers that those who wanted to restore the authority of the Catholic Church in the aftermath of the Revolution were attracted to his denunciation of modern man and his preference for sentiment over reason. To revisit Rousseau is not to begin a discussion of liberalism's meaning with a substantive focus on politics. It is instead to transcend all contemporary political categories in order to appreciate liberalism's commitment to improving who we are. Rousseau had strong views on the matter: he did not think much of us. All the efforts we make to improve ourselves through social cooperation are doomed to fail, he believed; we would have been far better off if we had never left the state of nature behind.

If Rousseau is alien to a liberal way of thinking, Kant, as much an eighteenth-century republican as a modern liberal, expresses ideas that every liberal thinker ought to welcome. Kant's politics, like Rousseau's, are agonizingly difficult to categorize: his writings on perpetual peace would inspire global humanitarians, while latter-day German politicians cited his arguments on behalf of a duty to obey as one of the foundations for a quasi-authoritarian state. To add to the confusion, Kant was full of praise for Rousseau, even if his ideas were decidedly anti-Rousseauian. (Like so many people wrestling with thoughts they dislike from a thinker they do, Kant simply argued that Rousseau did not understand his own writings: "The hypochondriac [ill-humored] account that Rousseau gives of a human species daring to emerge from the state of nature as extolling a return to the state of nature and into the forests," he wrote, "should not be understood as his real position.") Still, Kant understood that Rousseau had asked the right question. Indeed, he informed his readers precisely what that question was: "whether the character of species is, according to its natural predisposition, better found in the brutishness of his nature or in the artifices of culture."

Kant's answer would prove to be quite different from Rousseau's. Just as much an admirer of reason as Rousseau was a detractor, Kant defended the forms of modern society that Rousseau found so oppressive. "The human being," he insisted, "is destined by virtue of his reason to exist in society with other humans, and to cultivate himself through arts and sciences, to civilize himself, and to become moral in this society . . . and . . . to actively make himself worthy of humanity by struggling against the impediments that come with his brutish nature." The language here is instructive. As cultivating a field yields a better product, the arts and sciences cultivate us by improving the quality of who we are. No wonder, then, that when we look for a term that expresses the way we improve upon nature, we use "culture," which has the same root as "cultivate." And civilization—expressed in German not only as *Zivilisation* but also as *Kultur*—far from corrupting our soul, makes it possible for us to bring good out of evil. Kant, in other words, turned Rousseau's distinction between nature and culture upside down. It is not that we are inherently good and made bad by society. On the contrary, as Kant famously put it in his essay "Toward Perpetual Peace," even a nation of devils can establish a state—that is to say, can find ways to cooperate with each other—so long as they possess understanding.

The gains given to human beings through culture are secured, in Kant's view, by forming a civil constitution, "which embodies the highest degree of the artificial elevation of humankind's predisposition to the good. . . ." As is true of "cultivation," the term "artificial" had an exact meaning for Kant. For all those who would come under the influence of Rousseau, artificiality is a bad thing because it is false or insincere. But for Kant, "artificiality" (*künstlich*) had much in common with "art" (*Kunst*), one reason why Kant could put "artificiality" and "elevation" in the same sentence—indeed, right next to each other. By disciplining his talent and working as hard as he can, an artist creates an object of beauty that appeals to our highest aesthetic sensibilities. For similar reasons, a civil constitution, because it tames our natural inclination to act as pure egoists struggling to break free of any constraints, enables us to act morally by treating other people as ends in themselves rather than as means to our own end. We do not need a state merely to protect ourselves against each other, as Thomas Hobbes had argued. We need one instead to live together in freedom, for the only freedom that enables us to act as moral beings is freedom within civil society rather than freedom against it.

Kant was a believer in progress, but he never argued that progress would come easily. Our bestial nature is always there, holding out the possibility that we can lapse back into a state of amorality. But so long as we are rational, we can take the necessary steps from "brutishness to culture" that will enable us to appreciate "the social worth of human beings." Once again there is a key word here, and this time it is "social." Society, as one of Rousseau's biographers summarizes his argument, "far from being the solution to our problems, *was* the problem." This was hardly true of Kant; nature does have intentions for us, Kant believed, but they can "be realized only in society" where the "freedom of each is consistent with that of others." So powerful is human reason, moreover, that eventually the advantages of human cooperation will extend beyond any particular society to the world as a whole; cosmopolitanism, from Kant's perspective, is our destiny. Sustaining these forms of social cooperation will not be easy; but although the task of building a society is difficult, it is not impossible, and so long as human beings act prudently, it is one that they can accomplish.

The contemporary American economist Thomas Sowell has argued that nearly all social theorists can be placed into one of two camps: those who hold that human nature is fundamentally bad and therefore in need of the constraints of firm laws and strong institutions, which Sowell identifies with conservatives such as himself; and those who believe it is fundamentally good and therefore compatible with utopian longings, a property of liberals and radicals. Such a distinction, however, is of little help in appreciating what Rousseau and Kant were arguing about. Rousseau was an optimist on human nature before the creation of civilization and a pessimist after it came into being, while Immanuel Kant, like the American political theorist and Constitution builder James Madison, saw matters the other way around. The important question is not whether human nature is good or bad; it is whether human beings can do anything about it, whatever it happens to be. For Rousseau, they could not. For Kant, as indeed for Madison, they could. Liberals hold that human beings are neither naturally free nor naturally equal; in fact, they are not naturally much of anything. Freedom and equality and, even more, the ability to realize them, depend upon the determination of human beings to govern nature so that they will not be governed by it.

A TALE OF TWO CITIZENS

Perhaps because so few at the time would have been familiar with Rousseau's name, he did not identify himself as the author of the *Discourse on the Sciences and the Arts*. Instead, the title page proclaimed that the essay was written by a "citizen of Geneva," now part of Switzerland but then an independent city-state. Being a citizen of Geneva was no easy task at the time Rousseau was born there in 1712. Geneva's most famous resident before him had been John Calvin, the titanic Protestant reformer who lived from 1509 until 1564, and Calvin left behind a city distinctively marked by his ideas about the proper way to worship God. No one could be a citizen, for one thing, unless he was a Calvinist. (The same thing is true today of Calvin College in Grand Rapids, Michigan. No one can teach there unless he or she endorses a statement of faith compatible with Calvinist theology and agrees to attend a church in the Reformed tradition.)

Anything but an adherent to separation of church and state, Calvin fully integrated the government of Geneva with his church, creating the first true theocracy within Protestantism. And although the Calvinist doctrine of predestination held that human beings could not determine their ultimate fate through their own deeds—only God chose who was to be saved and who was not—Calvinist Geneva, through its ominous-sounding Consistory, or quasi-religious governmental body, rigorously monitored the behavior of its residents, ever on the watch for sinful conduct that could be taken as an offense to God. Teaching false ideas, uttering profanity, engaging in infidelity, all were subject to strong punishment, from public shaming to excommunication (no small matter if leaving the church meant living in hell), and, in extreme cases, to a recommendation to a criminal court for treatment that might rival something from the Spanish Inquisition.

Rousseau was never comfortable with what today we would call organized religion. Something of a seeker, he converted to Catholicism early in his life, only to have that act annulled before he could return home. But he was nonetheless a deeply religious thinker, especially when compared to such Enlightenment giants as Diderot and Voltaire. (If Rousseau's relationship with Diderot turned frosty, the one with Voltaire, who possessed a decided fondness for the civilized good life in which France has so long specialized, was hostile from the start.) At first glance, Rousseau's religious sensibility seems the opposite of Calvin's; instead of man being inherently evil only to be redeemed by God's grace, man is inherently good until corrupted by society. But as the Berkeley sociologist Robert Bellah has pointed out, "Rousseau's view of human nature is perhaps closer to that of orthodox Protestantism than is usually recognized." In Christian terms, Adam and Eve led blissful lives in the Garden of Eden before their thirst for knowledge led them to commit mankind's original sin. In Rousseau's more seemingly secular terms, human beings were innocent in the state of nature until corrupted by the invention of society. Rousseau was a Calvinist minus God, a thinker able to transpose one of the most enduring ideas associated with strict religion—the utter depravity of human nature—into terms compatible with modern psychology and anthropology.

Because of its history, Geneva would have a special relationship to Calvinism not fully reproducible elsewhere. Still, the Calvinist emphasis upon the sinful nature of human beings would become a feature of religious life wherever Calvinism spread. One place to which it spread was Northampton, Massachusetts, home of America's most famous preacher (and most famous Calvinist) Jonathan Edwards. A scientifically inclined intellectual familiar with the writings of Locke and Sir Isaac Newton, Edwards was at the same time a fiery and unforgiving preacher. His sermon "Sinners in the Hands of an Angry God," with its image of human beings being held over the fires of hell by something as fragile as a spider's web, was read in fear and trembling by generations of Americans ever afterward. Whatever the tone he took, enlightened and curious or hortatory and emotional, Edwards had no doubt that in the absence of God's capricious grace, human beings would be doomed by their deformed nature to lead lives as wasteful as they were wicked.

If we were to look today for thinkers who insist on the inherent depravity of human nature, the best place to find them would be in those religious precincts that hold to a pessimistic account of man's fall. In some of them—such as Calvin College—conservative Protestantism takes a form that is intellectually rigorous and, in its own countercultural way, attractive: however intolerant Calvin may have been, he was a major theologian and inspired serious moral and religious reflections among his disciples. Nor is a focus on sin just the province of conservative believers. Reinhold Niebuhr, America's greatest twentieth-century liberal Protestant theologian, was constantly on guard against the sin of pride, man's tendency to think of himself as godlike. Sin will be of interest so long as human beings are imperfect, and all the evidence suggests that such a state is likely to continue indefinitely into the future.

But then there are those fundamentalists such as the late Jerry Falwell and Pat Robertson who offer all the limitations of Calvinism without any of its strengths. "Sin is a transgression of God's law and God's law is unalterable," Falwell writes in *Listen, America!* "To sin is to voluntarily disobey God and His divine laws." Nothing in these words is all that different from what would have been uttered by Calvin or Jonathan Edwards: like all conservative religious thinkers, Falwell argues that what dooms us more than anything else is the poor material out of which we human beings are made. "I here propose that man by nature is not good," he intones, proposing something that had been advanced many times in the past. For Falwell, our depraved condition makes essential a rebirth in Christ, and a particularly gruesome one at that. "Man must be born again; he must be regenerated and believe in the death, the burial, and the resurrection of Jesus Christ and accept the shed blood of the Savior as the atonement for his sin in order to be complete." Short of that—and most of us, imperfect creatures that we are, will always fall short of that—we have no remedy at hand to improve on our corrupted nature. The problem, in other words, is not just that we are bad. It is also that we are by our own efforts unable to be good.

The more Falwell explains his views on the human condition, the more his differences with earlier Calvinist thinkers become apparent. Something interesting happened to the concept of sin as it made its way from sixteenth-century Geneva to twenty-first-century Lynchburg, Virginia. John Calvin had no objection to blending religion and politics, but the sins with which his Consistory were concerned were mostly matters of individual conduct: a blasphemous comment here, an act of sexual license there. (Calvin could hardly point the finger of blame at the city of Geneva as a whole since he effectively ran it.) For Falwell and his like-minded fundamentalist preachers, by contrast, America's sins are public as well as private. It is not just that a woman has had an abortion or that a man has had sex with another man— although, to Falwell, those things are bad enough. The truly egregious matter is that the United States condones such conduct. Sinning, in short, is not just something that people do but also something that a people does. "Sin brings reproach upon a people. This is the reason we are in a nosedive as a nation." What is at stake for Falwell is not the saving of a soul but the redemption of a country. America was once a nation blessed in the eyes of God, Falwell believed, but it lost that special dispensation when it opted no longer to believe in Him. No wonder, then, that "we have become one of the most blatantly sinful nations of all time." In the absence of the Savior, not only are we as individuals helpless, so is the country to which we belong.

Once Falwell shifts from viewing sin as an individual act to a social characteristic, his views come closer to the spiritually eclectic Rousseau than to the theologically more orthodox Calvin. Falwell's evidence for our fall, like Rousseau's, rests on secular things: the Equal Rights Amendment, food stamp programs, opposition to missile defense, deficit spending, and, as befits a contemporary Rousseauian, public education and the false beliefs it inculcates in children. (Rousseau's *Emile*, his treatise on education devoted to finding ways to ensure that children will be true to their nature in a society determined to corrupt it, may have inspired countercultural parents under the spell of the 1960s to educate their offspring at home, but homeschooling would ultimately prove far more popular among Christian conservatives.) Falwell, in addition, blames our fall from grace on exactly the same forces that Rousseau does, even if the terms they use differ: Rousseau calls these forces the sciences and the arts, while Falwell characterizes them as naturalism and humanism. For both men, a fatal preference for the life of the mind over the life of the spirit causes society to oppress its members. "We are living in a society that is quite sophisticated and very educated," Falwell writes at one point. The problem with America is not that its people have become so dumb that they have lost the sense of majesty offered by belief in the Creator. It is because they have become so smart that they convince themselves it is all right to follow their own laws rather than those ordained by God.

Rousseau did not challenge liberalism directly; liberal ideas were relatively undeveloped at the time he wrote, and no political party or society had yet been established calling itself by that name. The same cannot be said of Falwell. He is preaching after some two centuries of experience with liberalism, and it is not surprising that when he looks for a culprit responsible for America's fall from grace, liberalism springs automatically to mind. "The hope of reversing the trends of decay in our republic now lies with the Christian public in America," he posits. "We cannot expect help from the liberals. They are certainly not going to call our nation back to righteousness and neither are the pornographers, the smut peddlers, and those who are corrupting our youth." Liberalism is to politics as X-rated movies are to popular entertainment: wanton, hedonistic, unbridled. The great mistake of the liberals is to believe that human beings are "good and can pick themselves up with their own bootstraps." The whole idea is absurd because, stained by sin, human beings can never be masters of their own fate. "God is the Author of our liberty, and we will remain free only as long as we remember this and seek to live by God's laws," said Falwell.

For all the attention Jerry Falwell received when he was alive, Falwellism, the movement he started and the ideas he advocated, has proven to be a decided flop. Some contemporary societies, such as those in Western Europe, are not especially religious, let alone preoccupied with sin. And even in the one that has experienced a religious revival, the United States, fundamentalists who have inherited Falwell's mantle remain deeply unpopular and speak for relatively few. For all the talk of America's Puritan heritage, most of its religions and religious thinkers do not share John Calvin's dour outlook on the world. The Reformation theologian who most influenced the United States was Calvin's critic, the sixteenth-century Dutchman Jacobus Arminius, who argued that because human beings have free will, salvation is available to anyone who earns it. Yes, human beings are inclined to sin, America's unofficial national religion holds, but that is all the more reason to insist on forgiving them so that they can get on with their lives.

To find a richer and more influential account of our poorly constituted nature as well as our inability to overcome it, one has to travel about as far from religion as one can go. Of all the accomplishments brought about by the human capacity to transform nature, none is more impressive in its intellectual brilliance, and at the same time more transformative of the world in which it found itself, than modern science. Yet one important scientific discipline, biology—especially the use of methods and reasoning associated with biology to understand human behavior—has witnessed nothing short of a determined campaign to reduce human beings and their accomplishments to insignificance. If Jean-Jacques Rousseau were alive today, he might well have become an adherent of evolutionary psychology, that branch of Darwinian theory that is prone to argue that what we call culture is really just a side effect of a process of natural selection over which we human beings have little or no control. Rousseau receives his triumph over Kant in our day not through the kind of philosophy Rousseau practiced, but from the sciences whose presence in the society around him he found so corrupting.

SELF-INCAPACITATION

For fundamentalist Christians, the mere fact that we teach Charles Darwin in the schools is evidence of how sinful we have become. Ever since the Scopes Trial of 1925, where the theory of evolution was put on trial, fundamentalists have not relented in their war against it. With every defeat they seem to arise again, determined to win control of a school board here or a town meeting there. Large numbers of conservative religious believers in America live in post-modern suburbs, work in demanding professional jobs, send their children to respectable colleges and universities—*and* believe that God created the world in seven days not all that many years ago.

Darwinists, in turn, have taken up the challenge and launched a full-scale countercampaign against religion in general and conservative religion in particular. For Richard Dawkins, the Oxford professor who is today's leading popularizer of Darwinian ideas, "intelligent design," the latest wrinkle in the anti-Darwinist crusade, aims "to make propaganda among gullible laypeople and politicians, rather than to discover important truths about the real world." Fortunately, Dawkins informs his readers, we have a better explanation of reality: "Any creative intelligence, of sufficient complexity to design anything, comes into existence only as the end product of an extended process of gradual evolution." It is understandable that people might conclude that something beautifully designed required a designer, Dawkins argues, but it is nonetheless wrong. "The central insight of Darwinian theory," writes another evolutionary theorist, the psychologist Paul Bloom, "is that a purely physical process—the gradual accretion of whatever random variants lead to increased survival and reproduction—can mimic, and often surpass, the efforts of the most thoughtful designer." So much for God. Based upon their insights into how natural creatures have evolved over time, scientists and philosophers trained in or familiar with the insights of neurobiology and evolutionary psychology—not only Dawkins, but the Tufts University philosopher Daniel Dennett and the best-selling author Sam Harris—have become among the most publicly prominent skeptics of religion in the world today.

Thinkers associated with sociobiology will have nothing to do with the language of sin and redemption so central to the outlook of conservative religious activists. Yet despite their attack on conservative religion, contemporary Darwinian theorists share its pessimistic views about human nature. "It's not that people have a well of goodness that moral exhortations can tap," writes Harvard's prominent linguist Steven Pinker, in trying to explain why good things sometimes happen in the world. "It's that information can be framed in a way that makes exploiters look like hypocrites or fools." Dawkins perfectly captured the gloomy perspective of sociobiology with the title of his best-seller *The Selfish Gene* (1989). He would later take pains to argue that just because genes are selfish, it does not follow that human beings are, but this was more a change of rhetoric than one of outlook. For one thing, Dawkins still believes that the conditions of social life resemble those of natural life to a sufficient extent that unselfish behavior is relatively rare. And even when altruism does take place, regard for others is never reflective of deeply held convictions, a product of learned behavior shaped by history and tradition, or an outgrowth of a decision made by an autonomous agent to do the right thing.

Nor does the comparison between Darwinian theorists and their religious antagonists stop there. Both are persuaded not only that we are inherently flawed but that we can do very little about our fallen state. Kant, as we have seen, believed that our most bestial instincts could be tamed and turned to our advantage through artificial means such as culture. That insight became a staple of modern humanistic social science, itself closely allied with liberal political theory. "Believing, with Max Weber, that man is an animal suspended in webs of significance he himself has spun," wrote the anthropologist Clifford Geertz, "I take culture to be those webs." Although Geertz would never have used the term, implied in his famous definition is the idea that culture— man-made, artificial, capable of multiple interpretations—is an intelligent designer; human beings create culture, and culture in turn gives them the resources—language, ritual, meaning, morality—to advance civilization. There is an enormous power—a wonder-working power, as evangelical Christians would put it—in culture. Without it, social solidarity would be impossible, and without social solidarity, there would be no sense of collective purpose or capacity for moral obligation. "It is civilization that has made man what he is," wrote the Kant-inspired Emile Durkheim, the late-nineteenth- and early-twentieth-century social theorist who was one of the key founders of the discipline of sociology. Because he both creates and depends on civilization, man, Durkheim continued, possesses a dual nature. On the one hand, he is driven by his hard-wired instincts—writing long before the invention of the computer, Durkheim called them "sensory appetites"—to regard only himself. On the other hand, he is restrained by the cultural institutions and practices he creates to regard the interests of others.

In contrast to Durkheim, Richard Dawkins describes himself as a "dyed-in-the-wool monist," who explicitly rejects the major form that dualism has taken in Western philosophy, the distinction between mind and matter: minds, for him, are merely clumps of matter organized in particular ways. Equally as vehemently, Dawkins rejects any duality between nature and culture. He does not deny the existence of cultural products—Shakespeare's plays, moral taboos, reputations, rumors, customs, rituals. But cultural practices have their own means of evolutionary survival—Dawkins calls them "memes"—and these follow the same reproductive strategies as genes; if cultural forms survive, it is because they prove efficient in replicating themselves. Dawkins acknowledges that meme theory, as he calls it, is too premature "to supply a comprehensive theory of culture, on a par with Watson-Crick genetics," but this does not stop him from suggesting that the more similar memes are to genes, the more likely it will be that meme theory is true.

Committed to the proposition that culture offers us human beings no escape from our evolutionary destiny, sociobiologists go out of their way to show that the cultural practices and customs that appear to elevate what is human about us—romantic love, responsibility for future generations, artistic creation, and, of course, religion itself—are really little more than survival strategies. Moral conduct, for an evolutionary psychologist, is, as Pinker puts it, "an innate part of human nature": it is a by-product rather than a product, an accident of natural forces rather than a humanly created cultural practice. Evolutionary theorists just cannot come out and say that human nature is purposive because that might imply that people make deliberate choices, and if people make deliberate choices, their behavior cannot be so easily predicted by forces more powerful than themselves. We have, it would seem, freed ourselves from a supernatural power only to find ourselves enslaved to a natural one.

The state of nature in this Darwinian account is neither the paradise pictured by Rousseau nor the jungle warfare imagined by Hobbes; it is coterminous with the families in which we raise our children, the organizations within which we work, and the cities in which we live. At least conservative Christians believe that through a personal relationship with Jesus Christ we can redeem ourselves; sociobiologists do not hold out any such hope. Culture, rather than serving as a protection against nature, is just one more way in which nature imposes its designs upon us.

The overlap between conservative Christians and evolutionary theorists is not complete: of the two forces identified by Jerry Falwell as responsible for our decadent condition—humanism and naturalism—evolutionary psychologists are determined advocates of just one, since their account of how we came to be what we are is as naturalistic as any can be. But it is just as true that evolutionary theorists are in agreement with Falwell about the limitations of a humanistic point of view. Neither he nor they view human beings as autonomous agents capable of building the world around themselves, the one because such an act infringes on God's turf, the other because it infringes on nature's.

These thinkers may not believe in sin, but they do insist on the vital role played by genes, which, for them, play the same role in human conduct that sin does for religious believers: inscribed so deeply inside us that there is nothing we can do to control them, our genes, and not our intentional thoughts and actions, determine the kind of people we will be. Both Calvinism and evolutionary theory thus end up in the camp of predestination: in the one case, grace is granted by an arbitrary supernatural force, while in the other, the random and meaningless struggle for survival will be won by those preprogrammed in the right way. Politically, intelligent design and evolutionary psychology could not be further apart. Temperamentally, they are cut from exactly the same cloth.

No wonder, then, that evolutionary psychology has become the single most influential illiberal current of our time. This does not mean that we are witnessing a period such as the Gilded Age in which the leading defenders of inequality, such as the Victorian advocate of laissez-faire Herbert Spencer or the American sociologist William Graham Sumner, used Darwinian theory to explain why social classes owed each other nothing. There are some on the right who maintain that "conservatives need Charles Darwin," and some scholars have relied on sociobiological arguments to develop theories of international relations supportive of neoconservative understandings of how the world works. But conservative administrations in the United States are too afraid of alienating religious voters to become the explicit enthusiasts for the same evolutionary theory that characterized late-nineteenth-century defenders of the capitalist free market. Right-wing politicians in America seem to prefer natural selection selectively, appropriate for the economy, where only the fittest ought to survive, but not for the moral sphere, where embryonic stem cells and fetuses deserve the right to be protected against the allegedly neo-eugenic designs of liberals and feminists.

It is, rather, contemporary sociobiologists who best illustrate how liberal political positions can be combined with illiberal temperamental ones. The great bulk of today's evolutionary psychologists do not believe that market forces should be unleashed in ways akin to natural selection. Nor are they adherents of thoroughly discredited versions of Darwinism which argued that only superior races or peoples have the capacity to win nature's struggles, thereby damning inferior ones to conditions of second-class citizenship. (Historically speaking, it was not just conservatives who made such arguments but progressive thinkers such as the U.S. Supreme Court justice Oliver Wendell Holmes, Jr., and Margaret Sanger, the prominent advocate of birth control.) It is wrong, argues Steven Pinker, to confuse a scientific theory such as evolutionary psychology with a moral and political agenda. These days, he continues, one is likely to find arguments from genetics coming from the left rather than the right; those in favor of gay rights insist that homosexuality is not a choice, for example, while those opposed to them believe it is. If we focus on political positions, Pinker is right. But my focus here is on the pre-political—on ideas about what human beings really are and what they are capable of achieving. And on those issues, Pinker, I believe, is wrong. Whatever the specific political views of one evolutionary theorist or another, all of them agree that human beings rarely accomplish very much independent of what nature has bequeathed to them, and that even when they do accomplish something, it is frequently the opposite of what they intended.

The usually perceptive pundit David Brooks, who presents a conservative point of view in newspapers and on television, is therefore correct to view evolutionary biology as supporting the political positions of people on the right end of the political spectrum. Brooks does not quite get the political philosophy right: he emphasizes the differences between a Rousseauian view of human nature and those of the evolutionary biologists without seeing some of their similarities. But he does appreciate the extent to which the idea that we are a species incapable of improving upon what nature bequeaths to us undermines the case for progressive reform, or, indeed, for any attempt to use that artificial method called "society" to improve the human condition. "From the content of our genes, the nature of our neurons and the lessons of evolutionary biology, it has become clear that nature is filled with competition and conflicts of interest," Brooks wrote in one of his *New York Times* columns. "Humanity did not come before status contests. Status contests came before humanity, and are embedded deep in human relations." For Brooks, biology really is destiny: "Human beings operate according to preset epigenetic rules, which dispose people to act in certain ways. We strive for dominance and undermine radical egalitarian dreams. We're tribal and divide the world into in-groups and out-groups."

As Brooks's use of sociobiological themes makes clear, evolutionary psychology is anything but an arcane academic literature read only by specialists. Not only do such arguments appear in the op-ed columns of leading newspapers, but books purporting to explain the science of human nature frequently become best sellers. This should not be surprising. Science these days has considerable cultural authority. When a religious figure writes a book about daily life—such ventures, usually called self-help books, are a publishing phenomenon in their own right—it contains advice about how we ought to live. Books written by scientists or by those popularizing science intend, by contrast, to characterize how we actually *do* live—indeed, once we understand the science involved, how we *must* live. Reading the former, we aspire to do better. Reading the latter, we learn why we cannot. It makes little sense, therefore, to view popular works explaining the principles of evolutionary psychology as falling into the self-help category. A better term is "self-incapacitating." Their aim is to show that leading any kind of life we think we are choosing is impossible.

Most people do not believe themselves capable of running a country or even a corporation; the skills involved are multifaceted, the time demands onerous, and the risks of failure spectacular. But most people do think of themselves capable of running a family: despite declining birth rates, children continue to come into the world and parents take upon themselves the task of raising them. How should parents plan for the responsibilities that parenthood places upon them? Perhaps they should not plan at all, argue the authors of *Freakonomics*, the best-selling of all the self-incapacitating books to have reached the market of late. Parents may love their children, but their decisions about how to raise them are guided by fear. And the fears they have turn out to be terribly misguided. Many parents, for example, would hesitate to send their children to a home where guns were on display but would be happy to send them to one with a swimming pool. But this is decidedly myopic: swimming pools, the data show, are far more dangerous than guns. In fact parents, say the University of Chicago economist Steven Levitt and his co-author Stephen Dubner, citing the psychologist Judith Rich Harris, may not matter much at all. In this highly secularized version of Calvinism, it is not what parents do, but who they are, that counts: "Most of the things that matter were decided long ago—who you are, whom you married, what kind of life you lead." All those advice books written by experts telling parents how to give their child a head start in life can be safely ignored.

The inability of parents to influence their children's future stems from the fact none of us is well equipped to understand what the future means. In *Stumbling on Happiness*, the psychologist Daniel Gilbert, summarizing in just a few words the main theme of all the literature of self-incapacitation, writes that "each of us is trapped in a place, a time, and a circumstance, and our attempts to use our minds to transcend those boundaries are, more often than not, ineffective." Gilbert offers an explanation of why our efforts to ensure future happiness for ourselves are likely to fail: human beings have evolved in such a way that "the eye looks for what our brain wants." We routinely filter out information we do not want to hear, Gilbert believes, and give undue weight to information that supports our instincts. We regret not doing things more than we lament doing them, even when the consequences of both action and inaction are the same. We imagine the future will be much like the present even if the future, in a world of constant change, cannot be like the present. We *are* decision-making creatures. The problem is that nearly all the decisions we make are wrong.

Evolution helps explain why we are so often wrong. False beliefs about how the world works, Gilbert argues, act like "super-replicators," memes, in the language of Richard Dawkins, that reproduce themselves efficiently precisely because they are inaccurate. Wealth, except in rare cases, does not produce happiness. But people insist that it does. Why do they maintain something so obviously untrue? "The production of wealth does not necessarily make individuals happy, but it does serve the needs of an economy, which serves the needs of a stable society, which serves as a network for the propagation of delusional beliefs about happiness and wealth." Modern life, in short, is characterized by millions of people running around utterly clueless about their goals in life, yet the unintended consequence of such mass cluelessness is social stability. (Gilbert's unacknowledged guide here is the eighteenth-century thinker Bernard de Mandeville, whose *Fable of the Bees* was meant to demonstrate how good results can come from bad motives.) The whole thing is a game, and a rigged game at that. "We are," Gilbert writes, "nodes in a social network that arises and falls by a logic of its own, which is why we continue to toil, continue to mate, and continue to be surprised when we do not experience all the joy we so gullibly anticipated."

As dystopias go, Gilbert's strikes me as even more depressing than Rousseau's diatribes against conformity. Rousseau, after all, hated modern man's tendency to look to other people for the proper clues about how to lead a virtuous life. "Incessantly we obey rituals, never our own intuition," he wrote in his *First Discourse,* perfectly anticipating the conclusion of yet another best seller informed by evolutionary psychology, Malcolm Gladwell's *Blink* (2005). Evolutionary psychologists address with cheery anticipation what drove Rousseau to desperate distraction. "What makes us think we're so darned special?" Gilbert asks. If we just realized what sociobiologists teach us—which is that we are remarkably like everyone else—we would get over our individualistic delusions and realize that the way millions of people act is a pretty good guide to how we act as well.

For all the appeals to science in these works of self-incapacity, there is very little scientific proof. Evolutionary psychology is highly speculative, at least when it comes to the role culture plays in social reproduction, because modern cultures are recent things and evolution occurs over extremely long periods of time. Economists, by comparison, do offer concrete data, but the data usually illustrate rather than resolve the claims they make; the hypothesis that the efforts of parents do not matter much, for example, is tested with data involving test scores, handy enough when you want to measure things, but only one of the many things that parents do to influence the fate of their children. Rather than viewing these books as proving much of anything, it makes far more sense to understand them as part of the centuries-old conversation that engaged so much of the attention of Rousseau and Kant. To be sure, evolutionary theorists are entering this conversation a bit late, for they pick up the story about a generation after Rousseau and Kant argued out their differences. Daniel Gilbert is particularly helpful in this regard, for he identifies exactly when, in his view, the debate over human nature should be entered: sometime between 1789, the year in which Jeremy Bentham laid down the principles of Utilitarianism, and 1861, when his most famous disciple, John Stuart Mill, began to question them.

Utilitarianism holds that people seek to maximize pleasure and minimize pain. In this, they are not that different from other animals. Bentham, an early exponent of animal rights, argued that pleasure and pain are sensations and that any sensate creature is sufficiently like us to be treated with respect. As he worked his way out of strong versions of Utilitarianism, Mill, by contrast, came to believe that human beings "have faculties more elevated than the animal appetites." Borrowing from the German philosopher Wilhelm von Humboldt, Mill argued in *On Liberty* that we strive toward excellence in what we do. "Human nature is not a machine to be built after a model and set to do exactly the work prescribed for it," he claimed, as if anticipating the evolutionary psychologists who would come long after him, "but a tree, which requires to grow and develop on all sides, according to the tendency of the inward forces which make it a living thing." It is because we live for something more than mere sensation, Mill held, in one of the most famous sentences he ever wrote, that "it is better to be a human being dissatisfied than a pig satisfied; better to be a Socrates dissatisfied than a fool satisfied."

Daniel Gilbert disagrees. One of the main arguments of *Stumbling on Happiness* is that none of us is in a position to judge the claims about happiness made by others. "For two thousand years philosophers have felt compelled to identify happiness with virtue because that is the sort of happiness they think we *ought* to want." We ought, he believes, to throw out that "ought." If a person says that killing his parents makes him happy, "the sentence is grammatical, well formed, and easily understood," and Gilbert therefore sees no reason to question such a statement in principle. Twins joined at birth, a condemned man standing at the gallows, a famous actor paralyzed from the neck down—all, according to Gilbert, say that they are happy. Happiness only has meaning to the degree it can be measured, and when it comes to an emotion as subjective as happiness, the answers of the people involved are the only ones that count. People's emotions are important to them, and we should not confuse their emotions with lofty ideals such as virtue, which instruct people that their happiness is somehow misplaced or wrong.

In such a way does the modern debate about human nature return us to the era in which it began. Gilbert is far more comfortable in the sensate world of Jeremy Bentham than the striving-after-excellence world of John Stuart Mill. If we allow ourselves to be guided by Gilbert, or by the insights of evolutionary psychology more generally, we will lead lives without meaning, make plans without purpose, and blink more than we think. There is not much specifically human about all that, but then again, that would seem to be the point. For a conservative Christian like Jerry Falwell, man's great sin is to imagine that he can substitute himself for God. For popularizers of evolutionary psychology, man's great mistake is to believe that he can escape the destiny evolution has in store for him. Perhaps fundamentalist Christians and atheistic Darwinists should stop taking each other to court and instead join forces, united by their mutual contempt for the quintessential liberal idea that human beings have the capacity to create that monument of artifice called "culture," which, in turn, enables them to bring meaning and direction to their lives.

PURPOSE-DRIVEN PEOPLE

No matter how many copies it might sell, few books written by evolutionary psychologists or economists will ever approach the popularity of Rick Warren's *The Purpose Driven Life* (2002), which, by some accounts, has found some 25 million buyers. One has to wonder why. Warren is neither an original thinker nor a scintillating writer; most of his book simply repeats, in one form or another, the idea that God has a plan for you, which, if you know what is good for you, you will follow. Nor can Warren's success be attributed to a warm and fuzzy version of therapeutic religion that has no harsh edges. On the contrary, Warren insists that salvation is to be found only through a born-again relationship with Jesus, which cannot be good news for non-Christians (or even those Christians who stubbornly refuse to be born again).

One possible reason for Warren's success is that he has identified, and made central to his book, the idea that human beings hunger for purpose. Of course Warren believes that we do not determine our purposes for ourselves; God does that for us. Warren, for that reason, is hardly a liberal. But if John Stuart Mill's question were rewritten to ask whether it is better to be a Christian dissatisfied or a pig satisfied, Warren would surely opt for the former. At least in Warren's formulation we can choose Jesus, which is more choice than most of sociobiology offers us.

The idea that human beings live for purpose can be traced to that great theorist of liberalism, John Locke. "God gave the world to men in common," Locke wrote in his *Second Treatise on Government*, "but since he gave it to them for their benefit, and the greatest conveniences of life they were capable of drawing from it, it cannot be supposed he meant it should always remain common and uncultivated. He gave it to the use of the industrious and rational (and labour was to be his title to it), not to the fancy or covetousness of the quarrelsome and contentious." Had Locke lived long enough to read Rousseau's idyllic descriptions of man in the state of nature, he would have been appalled. Casting about for a way to distinguish human beings from other animals, Rousseau had settled on the idea of improvement (*perfectibilité*), which may to us sound like a good thing but to him was "the source of all man's misfortunes." For Locke, by contrast, people who do not improve upon what God or nature has given them are wasting their powers. None

of what today we consider the bourgeois virtues—industriousness, fru-
gality, prudence—are available to us in the state of nature. We leave
that state behind, not because we fear the war of all against all but
because we need what civil society can offer—law, restraint, impartiality, morality—if we are to appropriate it for human use. Locke is widely
considered a theorist of individualism, even, as one well-known commentator writes with some disparagement, of "possessive individualism." But for Locke even something as individualistic as private
property requires general adherence to rules that are made with the
consent of all and apply to all, a condition never found in nature but
only in society.

This insistence that human beings bring purpose to their lives
through acts of intentional cooperation with others is common to all
thinkers who followed Locke's lead. Thomas Jefferson, for example,
who paraphrased Locke in the Declaration of Independence, also borrowed liberally from Locke's conception of human purpose when he
wrote that "the earth is given as a common stock for man to labour &
live on" and that "man was created for social intercourse." As much as
Locke's emphasis on liberty and equality helped shape the United
States, so did his understanding of human purpose. The American
Revolution was all about a people taking control over their lives by
ending their dependence on forces outside themselves.

Another thinker writing in Locke's wake who held to a strong conception of human purpose was Adam Smith. Some may be surprised to
find him so identified. Smith, these days, is claimed as a hero by libertarian theorists who argue that people ought to be left to follow the
selfish instincts that grow out of their less than perfect human nature.
But this is an incorrect reading of Smith's anthropology. For Smith, as
well as for David Hume, the other major eighteenth-century Scottish
Enlightenment philosopher, self-interest was not an adaptation to
what is found in nature but a repudiation of it. (Hume, as luck would
have it, tried to befriend Jean-Jacques Rousseau and even brought
him, somewhat surreptitiously, to England. But like Diderot before
him, Hume would tire of Rousseau's unceasing self-absorption, just as
Rousseau would find himself ungrateful for, if not hostile to, Hume's
hospitality.) As the New York University political philosopher Stephen
Holmes points out, Hume "conceived of commercial self-interest as a
peaceful alternative to hot-gospeling and sectarian zealotry"; if you
have an eighteenth-century equivalent of Jerry Falwell reminding
you of the inherent depravity of your sins, insisting on your own self-
interest can be a way of improving upon the corrupt human nature

assigned to you by God. For similar reasons, self-interest for both Hume and Smith allowed individuals to possess a modicum of dignity in a courtly world characterized by fawning subservience and random cruelty. Self-interest was neither an emotion nor a passion but a rational corrective to both. In that sense, it is a step we have to take if we are to lead a life under our own direction. Once we do that, we can enter the social world described in Adam Smith's *Theory of Moral Sentiments,* in which the actions of particular individuals are judged for their moral worth from the point of view of an impartial spectator.

If one were in any doubt that Smith belongs among the great liberal thinkers of the past, the popularity of behavioral economics should put them to rest. Those contemporary thinkers who read *The Wealth of Nations* literally are wont to apply self-interest to every sphere of activity, down to raising children and policing communities. In its more extreme forms, libertarianism of this sort is not especially attractive to liberals, especially to those who believe that without government intervention to counter self-interest, life would resemble jungle warfare. Yet even purely selfish people still act rationally, choosing both their objectives and the most efficient means to achieve them. This is not how behavioral economists view human beings. Influenced by utilitarianism, a considerable number of psychologically informed economists, many of whose books have also reached the best-seller lists, have taken to arguing that in contrast to what Adam Smith says about us, we are irrational to our core, constantly making confident decisions that work against what is in our own best interest. In developing so bleak a version of human purpose, behavioral economics has performed the amazing trick of making free market economics seem appealing. If Rick Warren's Christians can at least choose Jesus, pure libertarians can at least maximize their utility.

No thinker in the liberal tradition better illustrates how living for purpose depends on the efforts of others as much as ourselves than John Stuart Mill. *On Liberty* can be read as one of the great individualistic manifestos of all time. "He who lets the world, or his own portion of it, choose his plan of life for him, has no need of any other faculty than the ape-like one of imitation," Mill wrote. "He who chooses his plan for himself, employs all his faculties. He must use observation to see, reasoning and judgment to foresee, activity to gather materials for decision, discrimination to decide, and when he has decided, firmness and self-control to hold to his deliberate decision. And these qualities he requires and exercises exactly in proportion as the part of his conduct which he determines according to his own judgment and feelings is a large one." A more powerful statement of the need for human beings to hold fast to their autonomy as choosing creatures has never been written.

But if room must be made for individual judgment, that judgment only has meaning if challenged through interaction with others. After rejecting Calvinism for its "narrow theory of life" and "pinched and hidebound type of human character," Mill went on to write,

> It is not by wearing down into uniformity all that is individual in themselves, but by cultivating it and calling it forth, within the limits imposed by the rights and interests of others, that human beings become a noble and beautiful object of contemplation; and as the works partake the character of those who do them, by the same process human life also becomes rich, diversified, and animating, furnishing more abundant ailment to high thoughts and elevating feelings, and strengthening the tie which binds every individual to the race, by making the race infinitely better worth belonging to.

Mill is widely regarded for his insistence that freedom can be curtailed only when it causes harm to others. But he is also arguing that freedom in the absence of individual growth causes harm to ourselves. "It really is of importance, not only what men do, but also what manner of men they are that do it." For Mill, individualism without society is impossible: "In proportion to the development of individuality, each person becomes more valuable to himself, and is therefore capable of being more valuable to others."

Each of these great liberal thinkers would, if somehow transported to the early twenty-first century, recognize a figure such as Rick Warren. For some two hundred years, liberals have argued the importance of individuals freely choosing for themselves by contrasting freedom with the compulsions of religious orthodoxy. (Even religion is improved, John Locke maintained, when faith is voluntary.) By the same token, they would have a difficult time understanding the appeal of sociobiology. To claim that epigenetic rules determine who we are and what we become is to argue that we do not; far from being a scientific advance, the liberal thinkers of the past would view such an idea as a reactionary concession to human hopelessness. Liberals today should therefore be as concerned by the implications of sociobiology as the liberals of yesterday were by strict forms of theology. We are what we make of ourselves, and if we are prevented by our dependence on nature from making much use of the tools offered to us by culture, we are not very much indeed.

NATURE AND CULTURE, LEFT AND RIGHT

Ever since Rousseau and Kant began to argue with each other, two different visions of human capacity have competed for the attention of modern citizens. Should we try our best to live according to the limits placed upon us, whether those limits grow out of respect for God the Creator or nature the designer? Or do we have an obligation to take what nature offers to us and to transform it for our purposes, using all those powers we have at our disposal, especially including our ability to work together with others to realize ends defined by ourselves? Throughout most of the nineteenth and twentieth centuries, conservatives typically found themselves at home with the former view while liberals adopted the latter. If you were God-fearing and traditional, you worried about the prideful arrogance of upending the natural in favor of the human. If you considered yourself a believer in progress, you marveled at human capacity to transform the inherited world.

The political right today shares much of the suspicion of progress held by conservatives of yesterday. There are, to be sure, some who locate themselves on the conservative end of the political spectrum who are enthusiasts for extending human longevity, using drugs to improve the mental and physical capacities of human beings, and meddling with nature to improve the life prospects of their children. "Even if there were such a thing as a 'real' personality," asks the science journalist and libertarian advocate Ronald Bailey, "why should you stick with it if you don't like it? If you're socially withdrawn and a pill can give you a more vivacious and outgoing manner, why not go with it? After all, you're choosing to take responsibility for being the 'new' person the drug helps you to be." Bailey's objection is to efforts by governments either to compel or forbid new technologies, but he sees nothing wrong with individuals making such decisions for themselves. If conservatives are genuinely committed to the free market, he believes, they ought to allow industries to invent new, even revolutionary, technologies and refrain from regulating their consumption.

Such forms of what has been called "liberation biology" are decidedly unpopular among conservative neo-Rousseauians more likely to worry about what they see as progress spun radically out of control. One of them, the University of Tennessee historian Wilfred McClay, criticizes "a shortsighted and impoverished vision of life: the dream of complete and unconstrained personal mastery, of the indomitable human will exercised on the inert and malleable stuff of nature by the heroically autonomous and unconditioned individual who is ever the master of his fate and captain of his soul, and whose own existence is, or deserves to be, infinitely extensible." Others, including the ethicist Leon Kass and the political philosopher Francis Fukuyama, share McClay's concerns, especially when they involve the prospects of biotechnology. All these writers bring up to date one of the more powerful ideas in the conservative tradition, the notion that in abandoning the city of God for the city of Man, we have cut ourselves off from our very essence to pursue the false dream of human liberation.

It is not just the reactions against biotechnology that illustrate the Rousseauian inclinations of contemporary conservatism. Like Mario Savio, the leader of the Berkeley free speech movement calling for his fellow students to put their bodies on the machine and bring it to a stop, all too many conservative politicians look out on the modern world and cry out for protection against it. In the face of a more cosmopolitan world characterized by increased personal freedoms and unprecedented mobility, this form of conservative Rousseauism seeks to defend children against sexuality, the presumed wholesomeness of Kansas against the equally presumed degeneracy of New York, the people already here against the people who want to come here, the nation against the world, the market against the majority, religion against secular humanism, and, in some of its less attractive precincts, the neighborhood against the stranger. And just in case any comparison between the Berkeley New Left and the contemporary New Right seems farfetched, we have witnessed the emergence of "crunchy cons," conservatives who live, dress, and act like hippies of old while voting for politicians who believe in God and question the benefits of progress. Rousseau the antiliberal was never really a conservative as we understand the term today, but conservatives today, with few exceptions, share the instincts of the man from Geneva.

Conservatives may be discovering what they have in common with Rousseau, but not all that many on the left recognize what they ought to share with Kant. If anything, Kantian sympathies with society, culture, and civilization remain decidedly out of fashion on the left, many of whose leading thinkers and activists oddly share the Rousseauian sentiments so prominent on the right.

One place where Kantianism has all but disappeared from the left is among the more radical thinkers concerned with protecting the natural environment. There are good reasons to worry about what is happening to nature: global warming is real enough that even conservatives have come to accept the science behind it, and only those with no sense of beauty can accept with equanimity the rapacious depletion of resources characteristic of capitalism unleashed. Still, it is one thing to argue for environmental protection and another to jump from Rousseau's disdain for humanity to the conclusion that, if human beings ever were to disappear from the face of the earth, "eventually," as the best-selling science writer Alan Weisman puts it, "the Earth would do fine without us." It might or it might not, but if human beings were not around to make the judgment, it would be hard to know one way or another.

"The human race ought to and can be the master of its own good fortune," Kant once wrote; but mastery, many ecological activists argue, is precisely what the human race should avoid. "It is an intensely disturbing idea that man should not be the master of all," insists Bill McKibben—the ecological activist and author of *The End of Nature* and other books—"that other suffering might be just as important. And that individual suffering—animal or human—might be less important than the suffering of species, the ecosystems, the planet." For McKibben, along with the more extremist wing of the ecology movement, the idea that nature's value has something to do with human needs is an arrogant attempt to conquer blameless nature on behalf of a prideful species no longer able to regulate its appetites. More so than Christian conservatives, radical ecologists achieve something of a synthesis between Calvin and Rousseau: on the one hand, they issue puritanical jeremiads against the sins of gluttony and greed, and on the other hand, they see themselves as romantic rebels against modern civilization. To save nature, they are perfectly willing to condemn humanity, an odd choice given that our best hope for nature is to use our human capacities to protect it.

Another area of contemporary left-wing politics that flirts with the natural at the expense of the social involves claims of inherent differences between groups based upon biological characteristics such as sex and race. Essentialism of this sort had been seemingly discredited in the wake of Nazism's defeat. Stunned by the consequences of a rabidly evil effort to divide people along presumably racial lines, and then to take such divisions as an opportunity for genocide, liberal thinkers in the years after World War II were committed with striking unanimity to the proposition that all human beings are biologically the same. When the Harvard psychologist Richard Herrnstein and the conservative political scientist Charles Murray published *The Bell Curve* in 1994, arguing on behalf of racial differences in intelligence, the "science" supporting their findings was widely discredited. With the exception of a few diehards who believe that the authors of *The Bell Curve* were speaking truth to power (alas including the DNA co-discoverer James Watson), we no longer take seriously arguments to the effect that inequalities in natural capacity justify inequalities in social achievement.

All of which makes it surprising that political liberals do tolerate, and sometimes even welcome, arguments in favor of nature if they are viewed as promoting equality instead of attacking it. Feminists such as the psychologist Carol Gilligan have tried to demonstrate that men and women have inherently different styles of moral reasoning. Claims to the effect that homosexuality is genetic in origin, which for all I know (I am not a scientist) may very well be true, enable activists on behalf of gay rights to argue against the fundamentalist claim that their acts represent a sinful choice, but they open up a Pandora's box of appeals to other arguments based on genetics that may not have such egalitarian ramifications. While arguments from *The Bell Curve* are unlikely to gain adherents from the left, some writing in support of racial equality, such as that of the political scientist Andrew Hacker, can assert that "black children are . . . more attuned to their bodies and physical needs" than white children and endorse claims that black and white children have different learning styles. Identity politics easily descends into essentialist politics, and essentialist politics, by ascribing importance to features of our bodies that are beyond our capacity to change (or, in these days of medical miracles, to change very much), remind us of the extent to which our destiny was determined before we were born. People imprisoned by the biology of their bodies are not people who can direct their minds toward ends established by themselves.

Sympathy toward nature is inevitably accompanied by suspicion toward "cosmopolitanism," yet another Kantian term that, like mastery, testifies to our ability to shape how and why we live. A cosmopolitan is a person who, not content with the truths and traditions of the particular place in which he or she is born, strives to become a citizen of the world. "Cosmopolitanism . . . starts with what is human in humanity," the philosopher Anthony Appiah points out in good Kantian fashion. "My people—human beings—made the Great Wall of China, the Chrysler Building, the Sistine Chapel: these things were made by creatures like me, through the exercise of skill and imagination." Cosmopolitanism is nonetheless distrusted in a time of cultural relativism, an era dominated by the idea that local cultures have their own, time-honored ways of engaging in the arts and sciences. Like nature, local cultures, relativists believe, need protection against the universalizing and therefore homogenizing force of cosmopolitanism, which, for some, is just another synonym for imperialism. Unlike radical ecologists, cultural preservationists, as their name suggests, protect culture. But it is those forms of culture closest to nature that exercise their protective instincts most: indigenous practices, not universal truths; tools that till the earth, not machines that uproot it; artifacts that mimic nature, not those, such as the Chrysler Building, that dominate it. Lost in this appreciation of everything close to us is the stretching of the imagination to appreciate things far away. Take away cosmopolitan longings, and one removes the whole point of growing into something better.

One final example of liberalism's unease with progress involves the same biotechnological revolution welcomed by libertarians. Michael Sandel certainly has reservations about it, which he cogently expresses in his book *The Case Against Perfection*. Unlike religiously oriented conservatives, Sandel strongly defends the morality of stem cell research using human embryos. But he worries that, seduced by advances in genetics, we can manipulate not only nature but human nature. If athletes can enhance their performance and parents the height and intelligence of their children, we run the risk of diminishing the moral agency of the very people whose physical or mental capacities are being expanded. "There is something appealing, even intoxicating, about a vision of the human life unfettered by the given," Sandel writes, yet it is crucial, if we are to lead lives worth living, that we accept that there is a role for chance in life as well as for choice. Genetic engineering represents a form of liberal eugenics. To the degree that it includes a "resolve to see ourselves astride the world, the masters of our nature," it is flawed and best resisted. The best political arrangements, including liberal ones, should be designed in ways "more hospitable to the gifts and limitations of imperfect human beings."

Sandel is dealing with profound questions for which there are no easy answers. It is not difficult to imagine technologies capable of tampering with human nature to such a degree that we are left with little or nothing recognizably human about ourselves; if that is where artifice takes us, no liberal should want to go there. But there clearly are dangers in the other direction as well. The opposite of mastery, after all, is slavery. Becoming so fearful of new advances in technology that we refuse to take steps that would alleviate human suffering represents a form of cruelty alien to liberalism's promises of freedom and equality. We should never become so afraid of choice that we leave too much to chance. It is, moreover, all but impossible to stop new technologies from developing. Even if one fears the consequences associated with some of them, one is still best off relying on human capacities for discernment and reason to decide upon their proper use. The fact that we are now exploring technologies that raise fundamental questions about what it means to be human offers even more support for a political philosophy based on the fact that human beings matter.

Nature, identity, locality, the gift of life—all appear as places of refuge to which people on the political left turn when they are no longer persuaded that human beings can or should direct their actions in purposive ways. The most cited philosophers on the contemporary left, especially but not exclusively in the academy, are not those who speak of human purposiveness, but the worshippers of the irrational, such as the twentieth-century German philosopher and Nazi sympathizer Martin Heidegger, who wrote in the shadow of the man who has been called the inventor of modern pessimism, Jean-Jacques Rousseau. Indeed, when compared to more academic metaphysicians, Rousseau's disdain for contemporary civilization seems stunningly familiar because it anticipates with unerring precision an era in which liberals have become fearful of the world around them.

Like Rousseau, leftists today worry about the food we eat and go on from there to the air we breathe, the dangers to our neighborhoods posed by gentrification, the loss of jobs threatened by globalization, the impact of computer games on children, the gains in personal autonomy under attack from the religious right, the electromagnetic currents that bring electricity into our homes, the side effects of the medications we swallow and the diseases in store for us if we do not swallow them, the debilities that accompany the miracle of our longer lives, the consequences of military actions abroad, and any number of other possibilities that upset their ways of life as much as they challenge some of their convictions. All too often, people on the left, just like people on the right, seek a philosophy of protection, a place calling for a halt to everything destabilizing and unsettling. For them, life in modern society consists not of opportunities to be welcomed but of dangers to be avoided.

One reason why liberals lack a sense of purpose politically is that they have abandoned the sense that human beings live for purpose philosophically. The missing ingredient in much of contemporary liberalism is not a failure to develop policies for sustained economic growth or national security; if anything, contemporary liberalism suffers from a surfeit of policy proposals that show every indication of working better than conservative bromides. The problem, rather, is a failure to link liberalism's politics to the kind of generous and creative conception of human purpose associated with the great liberal thinkers of the past. Question the capacity of human beings to build societies capable of realizing their objectives and one has little choice but to conclude that progress is an illusion, self-direction impossible, pessimism appropriate, and the future unknowable. If liberalism is to have a future, these forms of leftist caution will have to be overcome. Before it can once again be a powerful political force, liberalism must recover its more hopeful understanding of who we are and what we can achieve.

That understanding will come about when liberals once again take the side of culture over nature. The miracle of human cooperation—the ability of larger numbers of people to find ways to direct their actions toward purposes decided by themselves—is fully as remarkable as faith in the unseen or the complexities of design without a designer. Obtaining the first glimpses of what modern people could do once they learned to depend on each other, Rousseau saw nightmares while Kant anticipated possibilities. Living at the other end of the era they began, Rousseau may inspire our imagination but Kant describes our reality. Once we accept that reality, we will be less likely to put our faith in either God or our genes and more likely to realize that it best belongs in ourselves.

CHAPTER 3

EQUALITY'S INEVITABILITY

APRÈS LA RÉVOLUTION

Liberté, égalité, fraternité—the rallying cry of the French Revolution is to this day capable of evoking powerful images: the storming of the Bastille, the decadence of Marie Antoinette, the relentless guillotine. Yet for all the fervor such images convey, the words themselves long ago lost their incendiary connotations. Now inscribed on the French Republic's logo and stamped on its version of the one-euro coin, the slogan—actually, two thirds of it—refers to quite conventional political ideals. Liberty, in the past capable of toppling monarchs, developed such a capacious meaning in the nineteenth and twentieth centuries that business corporations routinely evoked it to protect their privileges. And fraternity dropped its political connotations entirely: to the degree that the term still resonates, it is with drinking parties and crude, sexist behavior.

Equality, by contrast, was a bitterly contested concept before the French Revolution happened, while it was taking place, and long after it ended. From Plato and Aristotle through Machiavelli and Hobbes, the West's most important political philosophers had justified philosopher kings, slavery, war, and monarchy, but had not been willing to endorse the notion that all people are of equal worth. Even some of the leading thinkers of the Enlightenment, whom we generally view as anticipating the French Revolution, were inegalitarian in their outlook. Equality, wrote Voltaire, "is at once the most natural and at the same time the most chimeral of things," appropriate to human beings when they are most like animals but not realistic for people in society, where there will inevitably be differences between the rich and the poor. And then there was Edmund Burke, the founder of modern conservatism, who, while watching the Revolution from across the English Channel, concluded in his *Reflections on the Revolution in France* that equality was that "monstrous fiction which, by inspiring false ideas and vain expectations into men destined to travel in the obscure walk of laborious life, serves only to aggravate and embitter that real inequality which it never can remove, and which the order of civil life establishes as much for the benefit of those whom it must leave in a humble state as those whom it is able to exalt to a condition more splendid, but not more happy."

Nor did equality fare well as an ideal in the aftermath of the French Revolution. One twentieth-century writer, the Israeli historian Jacob Talmon, blamed the egalitarian thrust of the Revolution, and especially the ideas of Rousseau, for the totalitarian dictatorships of his time, while other thinkers who experienced those dictatorships at first hand, including Leo Strauss and the right-wing German philosopher Carl Schmitt, found it easier to defend secrecy, elitism, and dictatorship than to endorse anything resembling egalitarian principles. As late as the 1950s, an American conservative man of letters could still look back to the French Revolution as the ultimate cause of an egalitarian condition in which "the people subsist only as an inchoate mass of loosely cohering units, a tapioca-pudding state, which condition many utilitarian and social planners contemplate with equanimity," but which he, Russell Kirk, viewed with a sense of dread.

Despite the reluctance of political philosophers to endorse egalitarian ideals, those ideals nonetheless became part and parcel of the way politics would be conducted in the modern world. It is not that modern societies attempt to make everyone equal; that notion, associated with the socialist movements that developed in the aftermath of the French Revolution, rather than fulfilling liberalism's promise, became, until their demise in the late twentieth century, one of liberalism's closest rivals. Socialism, moreover, never managed to achieve the equality it advocated. The Communist governments that claimed to be putting scientific socialism into practice proved to be anything but egalitarian in the way they did so; party status, national and ethnic identification, and contributions to economic growth or military prowess divided the haves from the have-nots. Some governments calling themselves Socialist, especially the Scandinavian ones, developed forms of equality compatible with liberal principles, but in most places at most times socialism failed liberalism's tests on nearly all fronts: even if it achieved equality, which it rarely did, it suppressed liberty; its preference for authoritarian governments resulted in assaults on liberal proceduralism; and it lacked liberalism's temperamental preference for openness in favor of extreme bureaucratic caution.

Liberal equality, rather, is to be found in the ideals expressed in the Declaration of Independence and the Declaration of the Rights of Man and Citizen, with their assertions that, in the French case, "men are born free and remain free and equal in rights," or, in the American, that "all men are created equal." At first glance, this seems hardly credible. Thomas Jefferson, the author of the Declaration of Independence, was a slave owner, and whatever equality he may have had in mind would therefore seem to bear little relationship to the kind to which we aspire today. The same could be said of the Declaration of the Rights of Man and Citizen; it abolished the privileges once given to the nobles and the clergy, but it did not treat women as equal to men and it did not call for the legal abolition of slavery. Equality in the eighteenth century was a lofty goal, so lofty that it never came down to earth. In their earliest manifestations, calls for equality were, at best, a form of procedural liberalism; they lacked substance, and not all that many thinkers of the era were intent on providing some.

Yet as the historian Lynn Hunt has argued in *Inventing Human Rights*, "the rights of man provided the principles for an alternative view of government. As the Americans had before them, the French declared rights as part of a growing rupture with established authority." By breaking so radically with the past, the eighteenth-century revolutionaries set in motion a process in which, since people themselves were the only source of legitimacy, all of them, irrespective of their social status, race, or gender, would come to be viewed as possessing fundamental human rights. "Does Mr. Burke mean to deny that man has any rights?" Tom Paine demanded to know of the man who had written the most famous critique of the French Revolution. "If he does, then he must mean that there are no such things as rights anywhere, and that he has none himself, for who is there in the world but man?"

Rights, as the Enlightenment philosopher and mathematician the marquis de Condorcet put it during the Revolution, were an all-or-nothing proposition: "Either no individual in mankind has true rights, or all have the same ones."

•Paine and Condorcet proved, in their own way, to be prophets. While political philosophers were picking the ideal of equality apart, ordinary people took the ideals of the two declarations as gospel. In the more than two hundred years since the French and American revolutions, modern citizens have come to look upon equality as a right, fully as important as the right to free speech or freedom of religion. Not only do people have a right to equality, they also insist, it is a right that ought to be realized; there is a direct line from the ideals of those revolutions to the welfare states of the contemporary world. Equality proved to be something other than an illusory or even dangerous ideal. Its rise to the top of policy and politics was inevitable, and none of its philosophical opponents, no matter how eloquent their voices, has been powerful enough to stop it.

The inevitability of equality changes the way we think about what is possible and what is only a dream. Premodern societies were so divided by class and status, so intent on insisting that advantages of birth were to be honored while merit and individual achievement were to be ignored, and so willing to view the inequalities that resulted as the work of divine planning, that all those who insisted on equal worth or treatment could be dismissed as hopelessly naïve. Realism demanded that we accept the world as it was, and the world that then existed was inegalitarian to the core. In modern society, by contrast, equality has become such an entrenched fact of life that those who oppose it become the true romantics and those who accept it the clear-sighted realists—that is, if it is possible to find people who oppose it. These days, as we shall see later in this book, even political reactionaries claim to be friends of equality; it is the left, they insist, that represents the truly elitist forces in contemporary society.

For liberals, this is a transformation of enormous significance. To achieve equality, modern societies are not required, as critics of egalitarian ideals insist, to bend human nature out of shape. On the contrary, it is equality's opponents who ask the impossible, demanding as they do that modern people ignore all the improvements that the realization of greater equality has brought about in favor of a presumed state of nature that not only never existed, but that even if it could somehow be achieved would reduce human beings to their most prim-

itive instincts. Just as liberals need to recover the sense of human purpose that enables individuals to shape their destinies, they need also to
remember that liberty without equality would be as empty as equality
without liberty would be authoritarian.

THREE EMINENT VICTORIANS

Edmund Burke was not the only British observer to look in horror
upon what the desire for equality had unleashed in France. John Stuart
Mill had planned to write a book on the French Revolution, but unable
to find the time, he encouraged his friend Thomas Carlyle, who had
already published his first major work, *Sartor Resartus,* to undertake the
task instead. Carlyle responded with alacrity and, anxious to win the
approval of his country's most prominent Victorian political philosopher, sent his copy of the first volume—the only copy of the first
volume—to Mill, whose maid inadvertently threw into the fire. Eventually, Carlyle rewrote the lost portions, and *The French Revolution,*
published in 1837 in three volumes, became, thanks to a well-placed
review by the no doubt guilt-ridden Mill, an immediate best seller.
Less sympathetic to the monarchy than Burke, and in that sense not
nearly as partisan, Carlyle turned his book into an argument for the
importance of heroic action in society. Still, like Burke, he realized that
once the aristocracy was overturned to make way for the middle class,
all kinds of disaster would follow. Significant chunks of Carlyle's book
portray the French Revolution as endless seas of blood let loose by the
passion of those below to tear away the privileges of those above.

We will never know what kind of book Mill might have written
about the French Revolution. But we do know from his other writings
that, however much Mill may have respected Romantics such as Carlyle and the poet Samuel Taylor Coleridge, he would not have become
the alarmed defender of inequality that they were. This is not because
of much that can be found in *On Liberty,* Mill's most famous work; in
that essay, Mill wrote about the masses in unflattering terms. Mill's
truly egalitarian thoughts were the ones inspired in part by his wife,
Harriet Taylor, and published in 1869: *The Subjection of Women.*

The Subjection of Women is a fascinating text because it anticipated
so acutely the forces that would coalesce around the campaigns for
women's rights in the twentieth century. Mill was appalled that women
could not own property in their own name. He attacked the idea that it

is somehow in the nature of femininity to become a wife and mother rather than a writer or a scientist. He made the case for women's suffrage long before any country came close to adopting such a policy. Most remarkably of all, he recognized that underneath the Victorian glorification of marriage lay the possibility of real, and deadly serious, violence against women, including marital rape. "However brutal a tyrant she may be unfortunately chained to—though she may know that he hates her, though it may be his daily pleasure to torture her, and though she may feel it impossible not to loathe him—he can claim from her and enforce the lowest degradation of a human being, that of being made the instrument of an animal function contrary to her inclinations." Although Mill was not the first in his country to express these thoughts—much of what he had to say had been anticipated by Wollstonecraft in her *Vindication of the Rights of Woman* in 1792—his book, as one of his biographers writes, "was a founding document of radical feminism and remains one of the finest polemics in the English language." More powerful words about what were, for his time, some of the most conventional of everyday cruelties have rarely been written.

Mill argued for women's equality specifically because he understood something about equality more generally. Victorian England was a highly moralistic society, yet at least as far as equality is concerned, not a very moral one: we owe to the era's most famous novelist, Charles Dickens, some of the most gripping accounts we have of the ways in which inequality can stunt human character. Despite the pervasive inequality of his time, Mill somehow recognized that inequality had no real future. It used to be the case, he pointed out, that physical strength determined who ruled and who did not. So long as this was so, society became little more than the codification of a brute nature in which masters could own slaves or men could control women. Social customs and institutions grew up around such relationships, but they "convert what was a mere physical fact into a legal right." If you look beneath the tales that such societies tell about themselves, you will discover that they are governed by the law of force; the taint of their brutal origins can never fully be removed because, when, so to speak, push comes to shove, brutal methods were always used to keep inequalities in place.

We no longer live in such a way. "The truth is," Mill continued, "that people of the present and the last two or three generations have lost all practical sense of the primitive condition of humanity." Trying to govern by sheer physical force can no longer work, because the modern world is dominated by one overwhelming sociological reality:

"Human beings are no longer born in their place of life, and chained down by an inexorable bond to the place they are born to, but are free to employ their faculties, and such favorable chances as [they] offer, to achieve the lot which may appear to them most desirable." It took a thousand years or so to bring this result about, but now that it is here, the ability of men to control women by relying on their superior strength will eventually go the way of such brutalities as impressment, the whisking off of men to sea against their will. As Mill put it, "We are entering into an order of things in which justice will again be the primary virtue; grounded as before on equal, but now also on sympathetic association; having its root no longer in the instinct of equals for self-protection, but in a cultivated sympathy between them; and no one being left out, but an equal measure being extended to all."

Like Kant, and very much unlike Rousseau, Mill did not believe that human beings had much to learn from nature. "All praise of civilization, or art, or contrivance," he wrote in his essay "Nature," "is so much dispraise of nature, an admission of imperfection which it is man's business and merit to be always endeavoring to correct or mitigate." Such a way of thinking extended to his ideas about equality. In nature, some have power over others because of their superior strength, and for that very reason the natural world is an inherently inegalitarian one. But because modern people do not live in nature but are shaped by culture, sympathy in modern times is as important as strength was at a time of brutes. Modernity results in large numbers of people living together, the accomplishment of one dependent on the potential of everyone else. Under these conditions, "conduct, and conduct alone, entitles to respect," as Mill argued in *The Subjection of Women.*

One might think that the dependence modern people have on each other would reduce the freedom each person has to do whatever he or she wants. But Mill held the opposite to be the case. Modern society gives individuals unprecedented freedom, but, like all societies before it, it also insists that people have duties that require them to restrain their actions. How can a society committed to freedom ensure that its citizens fulfill those duties? Only by relying on people themselves to recognize "the liberty of each to govern his conduct by his own feelings of duty, and by such laws and social restraints as his own conscience can subscribe to." For this reason, the existence of freedom, far from standing in opposition to equality, as it often seems to do in *On Liberty,* makes equality that much more necessary, for it is only when as many people as possible possess the ability to make the choice for restraint that choice can be exercised at all. "Any society which is not improving, is deteriorating," Mill wrote. Modern society can either flourish by encouraging equality among all its citizens or restrict such equalities and stagnate.

Not all the eminent Victorians agreed with Mill. One who took up the cudgels against him was James Fitzjames Stephen. Mill's father may have been a famous philosopher in his own right, but Stephen came from an even more illustrious background. Grandson of a member of the evangelically oriented reformist society known as the Clapham Sect who married the sister of the abolitionist William Wilberforce; brother of Leslie Stephen, a prominent editor, writer, and mountain climber; and uncle to Leslie's daughter Virginia Woolf, Stephen took upon himself the task of refuting Mill's arguments. His magnum opus, written in 1873–74, was titled *Liberty, Equality, Fraternity*, a thoughtful if cantankerous summing up of everything that a certain kind of aristocratic conservative viewed as having gone wrong since the Revolution in France. Liberty, equality, and fraternity, Stephen believed, had become a religion, and John Stuart Mill was its prophet. Mill's ideas would have to be thoroughly discredited if respect for the moral order was once again to be valued.

Although Stephen subjected all three components of the French Revolution's slogan to critical analysis, his comments on equality are particularly relevant because they anticipate just about every subsequent attempt to prove how futile the quest for equality would have to be. Should society be fashioned around people as they are, or should people be educated and encouraged to live up to an ideal of what they can be? Stephen answered resolutely in favor of the former. "Government," he wrote, "ought to fit society as a man's clothes fit him." (Stephen shared with Carlyle a special fascination with clothing.) Since a man's size in shirts is not something he chooses but is determined by the body given to him by nature, Stephen argued, government must respect the fact that people come in all sorts of shapes: "To establish by law rights and duties which assume that people are equal when they are not is like trying to make clumsy feet look handsome by the help of tight boots." We might be tempted to believe that when it comes to rights and duties, everyone ought to be treated equally. But this would be a serious mistake: "Rights and duties should be so moulded as to clothe, protect, and sustain society in the position which it naturally assumes."

As Mill believed that the case for equality in general could best be made by demonstrating the value of equality between the sexes,

Stephen argued that the natural inequalities between men and women proved the necessity of inequality overall. Because "the physical differences between the two sexes affect every part of the human body, from the hair of the head to the sole of the feet, from the size and density of the bones to the texture of the brain and the character of the nervous system," it follows that "all the talk in the world will never shake the proposition that men are stronger than women in every shape." Try as we might, therefore, we can never do away with the role of force in the world:

> Political power has changed its shape but not its nature. The result of cutting it up into little bits is simply that the man who can sweep the greatest number of them into one heap will govern the rest. The strongest man in some form or other will always rule. If the government is a military one, the qualities which make a man a great soldier will make him a ruler. If the government is a monarchy, the qualities which kings value in counsellors, in generals, in administrators, will give power. In a pure democracy the ruling men will be the wirepullers and their friends; but they will no more be on an equality with the voters than soldiers or Ministers of State are on an equality with the subjects of a monarchy. Changes in the form of a government alter the conditions of superiority much more than its nature.

Once Mill and Stephen set the stage, arguments about equality versus inequality reproduced the earlier debates between Rousseau and Kant on nature and culture. As the nineteenth century turned into the twentieth, the most powerful case for inequality borrowed its arguments not from those inegalitarians from Plato to Hobbes who wrote long before the French and American revolutions, but from Charles Darwin. Biology seemed to offer far more secure grounding for inequality than did metaphysics. And the most compelling case on behalf of equality came not from Marx and Engels, for they, and especially Engels, were Darwinians, but from versions of moral philosophy based on humanistic ideals, including those with a distinctly religious bent. Once we had a better understanding of who we human beings really were, both sides seemed to agree, we would also know more about the conditions under which we would live.

"HALF-WAY" PESSIMISM

Herbert Spencer, who, as visitors to London's Highgate Cemetery usually learn, is buried facing Karl Marx, was another thinker who emerged out of Victorian England to make his mark on the way we think about equality. James Fitzjames Stephen is remembered mostly for his illustrious niece; Spencer, not Charles Darwin, is known for coining the term "survival of the fittest." A recent biography argues that Spencer was not quite the caricature of an unfeeling Social Darwinist usually associated with him; he was a serious philosopher of altruism and a supporter of women's suffrage; John Stuart Mill was in his circle; and the great if unconsummated love affair of Spencer's life was with the novelist George Eliot (Mary Ann Evans). All of which may be true. Yet it remains the case that whatever Spencer's private doubts, his most popular works, the ones that gave him influence in his and subsequent times, not only defended the free market with dogmatic enthusiasm but viewed it as the natural outcome of a progressive evolutionary process. Few British thinkers find themselves cited in a major U.S. Supreme Court decision, but Spencer did when Oliver Wendell Holmes, Jr., argued in dissent that the justices of that Court had no business reading his economic theories into the text of the American Constitution.

Social Statics (1851), the book to which Holmes referred, was not Spencer's strongest work, at least in his own eyes. But it was his first book and it laid out some basic ideas from which he never retreated. Spencer was a radical individualist, indeed something of an anarchist, as his assertion of what he called his "first principle" makes clear: "Every man has freedom to do all that he wills, provided he infringes not the equal freedom of any other man." In Social Statics, Spencer asked whether we have a duty to obey the state, and his answer was that we do not: freedom, for him, includes the capacity "to drop connection with the state—to relinquish its protection, and to refuse paying towards its support." Although Spencer may have thought of himself as a liberal, it is not difficult to understand why twentieth-century liberals such as Holmes would object to such an assertion. If we can legitimately remove ourselves from the authority of the state whenever we choose, government can play no role in helping us realize, in any purposive sense, our commonly chosen ends. The result is a morality that can be only indirect at best; morality, as Spencer put it, "can give us no direct information as to what a government ought to do [but] can merely say what it ought not to do."

Spencer was fully aware that the capitalism evolving everywhere around him was generating significant inequality: he could not help but notice, as he stepped in and out of London cabs, the "idlers" and "loungers about tavern doors" who "swarm" in the "tens of thousands" through the city. What should we do about them? Our instinct may be to help them, even by passing laws designed to relieve their plight, but so long as people are of bad character—and Spencer was in no doubt that these people were of very bad character indeed—such efforts will prove delusional. "The defective natures of citizens will show themselves in the bad acting of whatever social structure they are arranged into," he wrote. "There is no political alchemy by which you can get golden conduct out of leaden instincts." We are therefore best off letting nature take its course: "There is a notion, always more or less prevalent and just now vociferously expressed, that all social suffering is removable, and that it is the duty of somebody or other to remove it. Both these beliefs are false. To separate pain from ill-doing is to fight against the constitution of things, and will be followed by far more pain. Saving men from the natural penalties of dissolute living, eventually necessitates the infliction of artificial penalties in solitary cells, on tread-wheels, and by the lash." For thinkers such as Kant and Mill, artifice saves human beings from nature's brutality; for Spencer, artifice interferes with nature's seemingly harsh but ultimately fair justice.

Herbert Spencer came to the United States in 1882, where he was fêted at Delmonico's in New York City by, in Richard Hofstadter's phrase, "a Who's Who for letters, science, politics, theology, and business." (Spencer did not like the United States—he thought Americans worked too hard—and left right after the Delmonico's banquet.) Of all those who volunteered to carry forward his work on American shores, the most notable was the late-nineteenth-century Yale sociologist William Graham Sumner. More than any other writer in the Social Darwinist tradition, Sumner gazed upon the ideal of equality and found it vile. "It is a great delusion," he wrote in *What Social Classes Owe to Each Other*, "to look about us and select those men who occupy the most advanced position in respect to worldly circumstances as the standard to which we think that all might be and ought to be brought. All the complaints and criticisms about the inequality of men apply to inequalities in property, luxury, and creature comforts, not to knowledge, virtue, or even physical beauty and strength. But it is plainly impossible that we should all attain to equality on the level of the best of us." It was not enough for Sumner to attack any attempt to use government to promote equality. His aim was deeper: to criticize the very notion that anyone is under any obligation to come to the assistance of anyone else. The idea that social classes owe each other something is "radically erroneous and fallacious." Demands for equality must be resisted with all the force that superior classes can muster. "The yearning after equality is the offspring of envy and covetousness, and there is no possible plan for satisfying that yearning which can do aught else than rob A to give to B; consequently all such plans nourish some of the meanest vices of human nature, waste capital, and overthrow civilization."

Like Spencer before him, Sumner concluded that given the nature with which we are endowed, inequality will be our destiny. Yet with Sumner we begin to see the realization, which would come to dominate conservative thinking in the twentieth century, that the case for inequality, no matter how seemingly grounded in science, would eventually become a losing one. In Sumner's writing, any acceptance of inequality's inevitability contained a rejection of modernity's promise. Modern people like to believe they are in control of things. They may not always want more equality, but if they decide that they do, they expect that positive steps will be taken to realize their objective. By instructing his readers that any such efforts were impossible to achieve, Sumner put himself in opposition to the can-do spirit with which his fellow Americans approach even the most intractable of difficulties. To an optimistic people, Sumner offered the gloomy pessimism of David Ricardo, whose "iron law of wages" held that the pay workers received would rarely exceed the costs of their subsistence, and Thomas Malthus, who believed that the world's population would always grow faster than its food supply. Sumner, for all his apologies for capitalism, was an antimodern thinker. While his country looked forward, he could only look backward. As Hofstadter put it: "In an age of helter-skelter reforms, he tried to convince men that confidence in their ability to will and plan their destinies was unwarranted by history or biology or any of the facts of experience; that the best they could do was bow to natural forces."

However unappealing the ideas of Spencer and Sumner may sound to contemporary readers, who expect at least rhetorical commitments to doing right by the unfortunate, their ideas about inequality's inevitability have not been consigned to the dustbin of history. These days our inegalitarian fate is more likely to be associated with the science of economics than with the science of biology. Belonging to the most rigor-

ous of the social science disciplines, economists, specifically the resolute defenders of the free market among them, typically hold that we
are hard-wired to be selfish; so relentlessly will we try to maximize our
self-interest that any effort to interfere with the workings of the market, including those designed to equalize wages or income, will prove
to be counterproductive at best and dangerous at worst. Our destiny
lies not in the stars, and not necessarily even in our genes, but in our
calculations; design a system intended to produce more equality, and
human nature will find ways to achieve less. And yet with economics,
as happened with Social Darwinism, doubts have begun to creep into
the analysis. It is because modern people want equality that so many
free market economists are so determined to show that they cannot
have it.

This ambivalence can be seen in the writings of one of the most
influential twentieth-century economists, F. A. Hayek. An Austrian
emigrant first to Britain and then to the United States, Hayek, in *The
Road to Serfdom*, first published in 1944, offered an argument in favor of
laissez-faire capitalism. His book, however, could also be read as a
warning that the road to serfdom was so broad and easily traveled that
considerable efforts had to be made to discourage people from taking
it. "As soon as the state takes upon itself the task of planning the whole
economic life," Hayek wrote, "the problem of the due station of the different individuals and groups must indeed become the central political
problem." Still, there is one way to avoid such a fate, and that is by
relying on the free market.

Hayek might have at this point argued for the superiority of markets on the grounds that reliance on them would produce more equality than would state planning, but his economic understanding was too
filled with Ricardian gloom to take such an easy way out. Instead, he
argued that the market's advantage lay in its capacity to diffuse responsibility for the inequalities that capitalism generates. The trouble with a
planned economy, he noted, is that once government becomes active,
"it cannot refuse responsibility for anybody's fate or position." Fortunately, however, "inequality is undoubtedly more readily borne, and
affects the dignity of the person much less, if it is determined by impersonal forces than when it is due to design." By disguising the amount of
inequality that capitalism produces now, free markets can help reduce
the inevitable pressures pushing for greater equality in the future.
However perverse it may sound, this must be considered an argument
in favor of equality's close association with modern ways of life.

Capitalism's other major twentieth-century defender and popular-izer, Milton Friedman, longtime professor of economics at the Univer-sity of Chicago and author of such best sellers as *Capitalism and Freedom* and (with his wife Rose) *Free to Choose*, also argued for inequality's inevitability while implicitly conceding how powerful the attraction of equality can be. He did this by making a distinction between equality of opportunity, which he held to be natural and desirable, and equality of outcomes, which he believed to be unattainable as well as wrong. For Friedman, the trouble with liberals is that they take equality of oppor-tunity and transform it into equality of outcomes through the coercive mechanism of the state. This was not as telling a criticism of liberalism as Friedman might have imagined. Liberalism has always been about giving people the ability to control their lives, not about telling them how to lead them. Far from holding to some ideal of what the con-temporary political philosopher Michael Walzer has called "primitive equality," or a society in which everyone's outcome is basically the same, liberals have long insisted, as the British economist and Fabian Socialist R. H. Tawney put the matter in *Equality* (1931), that people need equality of opportunity in order to ensure inequality of outcomes; it is only when we have roughly equal chances to choose what we want that we can choose to be different from each other. (The Fabians, named after the Roman general Quintus Fabius Maximus, a master of the strategy of delay and misdirection, were committed to the realiza-tion of equality through the most cautious and deliberate means.)

Friedman's effort to defend equality of opportunity while denounc-ing equality of outcomes nevertheless tells us something important about the fate of equality in the modern world. Worried that the descendants of the original Pilgrims could not live up to the strict Calvinism once expected of them, seventeenth-century New England divines created the "half-way covenant," which allowed people into the church even if they lacked a full conversion experience. Compared to the Social Darwinists of the nineteenth century, Milton Friedman belongs to the "half-way" school of pessimism: unlike them, he ack-nowledges that equality is a powerful ideal, even if he insists it can never be realized. Lurking behind his warnings lies a recognition that even if actual equality is economically impossible, people will strive to realize it nonetheless.

Defenders of inequality rest their case on the seemingly hard sci-ences of biology or economics because it has become so much more difficult in the modern world to make a case for inequality on moral grounds alone; if one cannot just come out and say that inequality is good, one can at least claim that there is nothing much we can do about it. Inequality's advocates view themselves as realists: the bad news they deliver is the only news that can be delivered. It does no good, in their view, to tell a terminal cancer patient that he is disease-free, and it does no good to respond to the deep sense of fairness modern people possess by telling them that the world can and should become more fair. We must follow our instincts because we cannot follow our consciences. Yet for all their appeals to realism, and indeed for all their occasional worship of cynicism, economists such as Hayek and Friedman want to prevent us from doing what they know full well we are going to do anyway. John Stuart Mill was right: once we understand that the few can no longer dominate the many through force, the many will use their faculties to extend sympathy and justice to all. It is an illusion to think the process can be stopped; those who argue that it can base their conclusions on fantasies about how the world ought to work, not on the realities of the ways it actually does.

LEGISLATING MORALITY

"You can't legislate morality"—or so we are often told. The basis for the claim goes back to the failed efforts to regulate the consumption of alcohol in the United States after World War I. Here was a classic case in which artifice confronted nature—and nature won. People like to drink. Moralistic do-gooders tried to impose on them strictures alien to what they really wanted to do. The result was as counterproductive as could be: not only the creation of a black market in bathtub gin, but the growth of organized crime capable of supplying it. Sanity was restored only when a subsequent constitutional amendment repealed the meddling one.

So firmly ingrained are the lessons of Prohibition that we often fail to recognize just how often, and how successfully, we *do* regulate morality. No better example, with the exception of the abolition of slavery, can be provided than the emergence of the welfare state. The welfare state proved to be everything that Prohibition was not. The inequalities created by capitalism were increasingly denounced as immoral, frequently by the very same ministers who viewed alcohol consumption as sinful. Although Social Darwinists and economists had held that inequality was our natural condition and that intervention by government would only make matters worse, people demanded that government do something to bring about greater equality—and such intervention by government made things better. Without in any way downplaying the evils of drink, the evils of economic inequality are far worse than those of alcoholism; indeed, the former may be a contributing cause of the latter. It is therefore odd that we so often point to our failure to legislate morality in an arena of lesser importance while neglecting our ability to legislate morality in one of the most important of all human endeavors.

The welfare state has many parents: socialist as well as liberal political philosophies contributed both to its emergence and to its development. But it would never have achieved its ubiquity without the presence of religious voices. The idea that social classes owe each other something after all was not based on an economist's calculation of how things must work but on moral and religious ideals about how they ought to. Three British and American thinkers deeply inspired by their faith are worth singling out for the contribution they made to the idea that greater equality could be had in the here-and-now—and that government would be the appropriate instrument to bring it about.

The first, the Victorian philosopher Thomas Hill Green, was quite familiar to Herbert Spencer. The two engaged in a spirited debate over evolution, which Green found too materialistic and reductionist to account for human creativity. Green was not an evangelical Christian; Calvinistic conceptions of human nature were too dark and unforgiving for his generous temperament. (Readers interested in his religious views are best guided not to his philosophical writings, which are especially turgid, but to *Robert Elsmere,* a novel by Matthew Arnold's niece, Mrs. Humphry Ward, much praised by Henry James and the bestselling British work of fiction of the 1880s, one of whose characters, Mr. Gray, is based on Green.) For Green, God wanted human beings—created, after all, in His image—to live up to their full potential, and that goal could be realized only by mobilizing the capacity of the state to engage in social reform. One way was through temperance. Green was a passionate opponent of the traffic in liquor, perhaps because his brother was an alcoholic. The other was through education, where Green's egalitarian commitments were on full display; he identified in particular with "the men whose heart is with their books, or in the Lord's house, while they are behind the counter or at the clerk's desk." Green helped give birth to a school of thought known as the "new liberalism"; his major contribution to it, as two later writers put it, was that "the state was ultimately a moral institution which aimed at the common good. It, thus, had certain basic responsibilities and obligations to its citizens, to provide the conditions for the self-realization of individuals." Because Green's theory advocated a role for government in the economy, Herbert Spencer in turn denounced the new liberalism as a "new Toryism," determined to bring back the coercive power of the feudal state.

Walter Rauschenbusch was the Rochester, New York, Baptist preacher responsible for creating the Social Gospel, a religiously inspired movement closely linked to Progressivism that urged social reform in the name of Christian teachings. Like T. H. Green, Rauschenbusch was a moralizing reformer. "Gambling is the vice of the savage," he wrote in his own best seller, *Christianity and the Social Crisis* (1907), and he urged "a new temperance crusade with all the resources of advanced physiological and sociological sense." In part a historical reconstruction of who Jesus was and what he taught, Rauschenbusch's book was also a passionate denunciation of the Gilded Age for the inequalities it produced. The brutal realities of unregulated industrial capitalism and the harsh conditions of urban life, he argued, were destroying the family and degrading the person. Commerce "exalts selfishness to the dignity of a moral principle." Democracy is being corrupted by money. Because "nations do not die by wealth, but by injustice," the United States needed "statesmen, prophets, and apostles who set truth and justice above social advancement" so that "the stifled energy of the people will lead forward . . . and a regenerate nation will look with the eyes of youth across the fields of the future."

Like Green, Rauschenbusch was not an evangelical; he did not believe that an individual's soul could be saved simply by developing a personal relationship with Jesus. But he did believe that a society could be saved if it took upon itself the task of responding to vast inequities it generated: "Equality," as he put it, "is the only basis for Christian morality." Along with Upton Sinclair's novel *The Jungle*, an attack on the conditions of America's meat-packing plants, which was published the year before *Christianity and the Social Crisis*, Rauschenbusch's book was instrumental in leading the United States to abandon laissez-faire in favor of active government.

The most eloquent of the trinity of religious thinkers who did so much to shape how modern people think about the welfare state was R. H. Tawney. Noting that John Stuart Mill's concern was not with the inequality of "personal gifts" but only with the effects of unfair social and economic arrangements, Tawney wrote that Mill and thinkers like him "are concerned, not with a biological phenomenon, but with a spiritual relation and the conduct to be based on it. Their view, in short, is that, because men are men, social institutions—property rights, and the organization of industry, and the system of public health and education—should be planned, as far as possible, to emphasize and strengthen, not the class differences which divide, but the common humanity which unites, them."

That word "spiritual" seems a stretch, since Mill himself had little use for religion. But Tawney was talking more about himself than about the thinker in whose steps he was following. For Tawney, as for T. H. Green, God commands that we live up to the best ideals we have. This conviction led him to take all the words deployed by earlier liberal thinkers to make the case for humanity's triumph over nature and to deploy them to make a Christian-inspired argument for equality over inequality. Modern people like to think of themselves as civilized, Tawney wrote, but civilization, that quintessentially Kantian ideal, does not mean "violent contrasts of wealth and power, and an indiscriminating devotion to institutions by which such contrasts are maintained and heightened" so much as it refers to conduct "guided by a just appreciation of spiritual ends, in so far as it uses its material resources to promote the dignity and refinement of the individual human beings who compose it." Or take the word "humanism," which for Tawney is not opposite to, but complementary with, Christianity: the aim of the humanist spirit "is to liberate and cultivate the powers which make for energy and refinement" and to oppose efforts "to reduce the variety of individual character and genius to a drab and monotonous uniformity." And then there is culture itself. "Culture," wrote Tawney, "is not an assortment of aesthetic sugar-plums for fastidious palates, but an energy of the soul. It can win no victories if it risks no defeats. When it feeds on itself, instead of drawing nourishment from the common life of mankind, it ceases to grow, and when it ceases to grow, it ceases to live." We should stop thinking of culture as a dead thing found in museums, but appreciate that for human beings its task is "to broaden and enrich them by contact with an ever-widening range of emotional experiences and intellectual interests."

Tawney's writings should alert us to two ironies concerning the liberal defense of equality. One is that in today's political discourse, critics of religion sympathize with the political left, while believers are often pictured as conservatives in both theology and politics. But for a considerable period of time, the roles were reversed. Spencer and Sumner were both nonbelievers, the former a dedicated materialist who refused to credit the existence of an unobservable force, the latter a lapsed clergyman who ran afoul of Noah Porter, a Congregational minister who had become Yale's president, by insisting on teaching from Darwinian texts. Meanwhile, Green, Rauschenbusch, and Tawney were by no means the only religious figures who insisted upon greater equality. They were joined by such figures as Richard T. Ely, one of the founders of the American Economics Association; Norman Thomas, who would run for president of the United States on a Socialist ticket numerous times; Monsignor John A. Ryan, a strong advocate for the New Deal; Dorothy Day, the Catholic advocate of social justice; Martin Luther King, Jr.; and Stephen Wise, the Reform rabbi and early Zionist who helped formulate a Jewish version of the Social Gospel. If people engaged in political debate today went back to their roots, we would likely have a secular right in the United States being confronted by a religious left.

A second irony involves the inevitable question of inevitability. We usually think of writers inspired by their faith as idealists; indeed, Green used just that term to characterize his own writings. Yet Green's defense of the necessity for government to represent the common good proved to be quite realistic; it was more in accord with the actual political dynamics of twentieth-century capitalism than Spencer's advocacy of laissez-faire. Religiously oriented philosophers understood better than more practical men of affairs something that seems obvious to us now but was not so clear then: modern people, once they become aware of the fact that inequality need not be inevitable, will do whatever is in their power to ensure that equality will be.

Through the prophetic voices of religiously inspired thinkers, then, the modern idea of equality, which had first been articulated by the declarations associated with the French and American revolutions, led directly to the efforts by twentieth-century reformers to rely on government to improve the conditions of life for society's worst-off inhabitants. The thinker who did the most to draw a straight line from the rights of man to the right to welfare was yet another in a long tradition of British writers, although this time the man in question, T. H. Marshall—a sociologist and longtime member of the faculty of the London School of Economics—while clearly a moralist, was not motivated by religious convictions. Marshall's 1950 lecture "Citizenship and Social Class" has become a classic document in the analysis of the welfare state. In it, Marshall distinguishes between civil, political, and social rights, the first associated with the eighteenth century, the second with the nineteenth, and the third with the twentieth. By "civil" rights, Marshall meant essentially procedural ones, those "necessary for individual freedom—liberty of the person, freedom of speech, thought and faith, the right to own property and to conclude valid contracts, and the right to justice." "Political" rights included the Reform Acts of 1832 and after, which expanded the right to vote, including, a century later, the extension of the suffrage to women. "Social" rights, finally, were those associated with such welfare state policies as unemployment insurance, legal aid, and the provision of health care. "What matters," Marshall wrote of social rights, "is that there is a general enrichment of the concrete substance of civilized life, a generalized reduction of risk and insecurity, an equalization between the more and less fortunate at all levels—between the healthy and the sick, the employed and the unemployed, the old and the active, the bachelor and the father of a large family."

In Marshall's schema, one kind of right leads to the next. Civil rights include procedural guarantees of due process of law, but since law is enforced by the courts, and because the courts are political institutions, once people possess basic civil rights they will demand equality in political rights as well. To exercise a political right such as the right to vote, in turn, imposes on the individual the duties of democratic citizenship. But fulfilling the duties of citizenship then implies something beyond merely possessing the right to vote: "It was increasingly recognized, as the nineteenth century wore on, that political democracy needed an educated electorate, and that scientific manufacture needed educated workers and technicians. The duty to improve and civilize oneself is therefore a social duty, and not merely a personal one, because the social health of the society depends upon the civilization of its members." Rights are contagious. Once people get the idea into their heads that they deserve dignity and respect, they will see no reason to stop with procedure and go all the way to substance.

Like so many writers in the liberal tradition, Marshall did not equate the arrival of social rights with the nightmare of equality of outcomes imagined by Milton Friedman. It is true that the welfare state was intended to moderate the effects of extreme inequalities associated with capitalism. And it is also true that the idea of citizenship implies a basic commitment to political equality. But "the extension of social services," Marshall insisted, "is not primarily a means of equalizing incomes." The aim of the welfare state "is not a classless society, but a society in which class differences are legitimate in terms of social justice, and in which, therefore, the classes co-operate more closely than at present to the common benefit of all." The rights promised by the welfare state lie somewhere between equality of opportunity and equality of outcomes; their aim is to realize opportunities without guaranteeing outcomes. Liberals believe that we should all have a chance, not only in the abstract but also concretely; equality has no meaning unless there exists the capacity to make it happen. At the same time, unlike socialists to their left, they do not call for the abolition of class differences across the board. It is not the elimination of inequality that the welfare state seeks but, to use the framework developed by Michael Walzer, the building of a series of dams that prevent inequalities in some spheres of life from spilling over into others where they do not belong.

Theorists of the welfare state such as Tawney and Marshall understood something about markets that economists tend to downplay. In theory, markets allow everyone to exercise freedom of choice and in that sense they advance human autonomy. But markets in turn create dependencies, and dependencies injure self-respect. The most important of these dependencies is that without work, one cannot live, making people dependent not only on work itself but on the employers who furnish it. This, however, is only the tip of the dependency iceberg that market societies leave in place. Left to operate on their own accord, markets will also keep wages below the level necessary for most people to escape from the vicious spiral of earning just enough to get along but not enough to plan for the future, let alone meet a sudden emergency. It is true that many Western societies, realizing that no one ought to be forced to live in conditions of desperation, created charities designed to offer some level of help to people whose conditions of life spun out of control. Charities, though, create new dependencies, and even if the generally meager economic assistance they offer can help in the very short term, reliance upon the generosity of others encourages those who receive their largesse to beg for more. In seeking to bypass the dependencies associated with both markets and private charity, the welfare state aims to give individuals the autonomy they need to make their own choices about the kind of life they wish to lead. The welfare state in this sense is an exercise in self-governance; just as liberals in the eighteenth century held that people need not be ruled by the arbitrary powers of a monarch, twentieth-century liberals insisted that people's lives need not be determined by the arbitrary gyrations of economic performance.

But doesn't the welfare state create an even greater form of dependency by linking people's fate to the actions of public bureaucrats? It does if those bureaucrats possess discretion in the distribution of the funds they control. Besides reducing dependency, then, the welfare state aims to reduce discretion. It does so not only by providing assistance, but by considering such provision as a right. Because rights are nonnegotiable, the welfare state, by guaranteeing them, removes the groveling homage those lower in the pecking order once had to pay to those higher up. Critics of the welfare state tend to call such rights "entitlements" and find them problematic because once people think they are entitled to something, they no longer need expend much initiative to obtain it. If people feel entitled to things they do not deserve, such critics would have a point. But the rights historically associated with the welfare state are something that everyone deserves. No one deserves to die because medical assistance is priced too high for them to use it. No one deserves to live a life whose last years will be dominated by fears of economic insecurity. No one should be completely excluded from competing for a better job that requires an education because the job they have does not allow them to obtain an education. When such things happen—people, after all, do die because they cannot afford health care—the response among the welfare state's critics is that such things are unfortunate or tragic. But that is precisely why we have welfare states. The welfare state is premised upon the assumption that while nature's effects can be tragic, society's need not be.

It is for this reason that the welfare state, although it obviously has a huge economic impact, is primarily a moral institution. As the contemporary British political philosopher Brian Barry argues, the welfare state transforms the idea of justice into the concept of social justice. Justice seeks a sense of proportion between an act and its reward or punishment: we say a wage is just when it corresponds with the work expended to earn it, just as we say a sentence is unjust if it exceeds the severity of the crime that brought it on. Similar considerations apply to society more generally: it is unjust if one person gets to keep his job and an equally deserving person loses her job just because the latter's firm was bought out by a cost-cutting multinational corporation and the former's was not, and the same can be said if a child who deserves an education is denied one by the poverty of his or her parents. The social justice sought by the welfare state seeks to curtail the role that purely arbitrary phenomena play in the distribution of sought-after goods. Its moral premise, as Christian as it is liberal, is: there, but for the grace of God, go I. The welfare state is an institutionalization of the moral idea of empathy. It asks that we put ourselves in the place of others less fortunate than we are—and then that we tax ourselves to help them. The welfare state thus fulfills a moral obligation. Because we can be just, we must.

Not only does the welfare state help people to realize their rights, achieve autonomy, reduce discretion, and express their collective sense of moral obligation; it is also purposive. Hayek's objections to it are not confined to the idea that planned economies will be more inefficient than unplanned ones because the state will take over the making of economic decisions best left to the market. His criticism is far more radical. He argues that because individuals make decisions under conditions of imperfect knowledge, any form of social order, because it arises spontaneously from the uncoordinated actions of so many, cannot be designed to reach a predetermined outcome. It is in that sense not just socialism to which Hayek objects but the fundamental premise of modernity. Planning is unachievable because purposiveness is impossible. If we try to direct the whole machinery of modern society in ways we predetermine for ourselves, we will merely cause the whole thing to collapse. Our fate is to recognize that we cannot control our fate. "We have never designed our economic system," as Hayek once put it. "We were not intelligent enough for that."

In opposition to that way of thinking, liberals have always insisted that it is because human beings live for purpose that they can establish and realize goals they themselves set. It does not automatically follow that society can also have a sense of purpose; individual purposes can cancel each other out, making efforts at social planning incoherent. But twentieth-century liberals nonetheless believed in what John Maynard Keynes called "directive intelligence" or "intelligent judgment" in matters of public policy. We are not, Tawney, Marshall, and Keynes all concluded, prisoners of economic calculations and therefore unable to influence the moral character of the societies we inhabit. Instead, we are quite capable of deciding what moral purposes we want our societies to serve and then designing our economic arrangements accordingly. It is not a planned economy liberals seek—that is a goal more properly identified with socialism—but a society that can decide what it stands for and do its best to realize it. There is a common good. We can know what it is. And we can achieve it.

For all these reasons, the welfare state corresponds with the way modern people live. Without it, most people would be at the mercy of forces beyond their ability to control and in that sense little better off than creatures struggling with the brutal realities of nature. To say this, however, does not mean that equality is inevitable in quite the same way that thinkers from James Fitzjames Stephen to Herbert Spencer held that inequality was inevitable. The welfare state, Marshall once pointed out, "is a mutual benefit arrangement of a special kind . . . and the rights it confers are not rights rooted in the nature of man as a human being, but rights created by the community itself and attached to the status of citizenship." It might seem to lessen the significance of rights to remove them from the realm of nature; if rights are rooted in human nature, they cannot be taken away without taking away our humanity. Compared to nature, culture, as we have seen, is artificial, and because it is artificial, it is always contingent; if a right has been established by the community, the community can abrogate it. Rights that are contingent upon political arrangements would appear to be a contradiction in terms.

Yet it makes a significant amount of sense to view the right to equality as social and cultural rather than natural. Natural rights tend to be broad in scope but narrow in application. Assigned to nature, there is no need for people to work for their realization; the same permanence that presumably makes them sacrosanct also means that, in taking them for granted, we need do nothing to bring them about. Social rights, by contrast, are premised on the assumption that if people view the extension of rights as a product of their own efforts, they will be more likely to be more protective of them. Such rights may be thinner—the right to unemployment insurance lacks the grandeur of the rights proclaimed in the eighteenth-century declarations—but they are also more concrete. The American-born political philosopher Robert E. Goodin, who now lives in Australia, published his *Reasons for Welfare* in 1988. The book begins by noting that "the welfare state is, first and foremost, a political artifact." Goodin is correct, but artificiality does not lessen the welfare state's significance. Instead, it serves as a reminder of the fact that equality is always a product of culture, even if inequality remains a product of nature. Modern people have learned, sometimes through bitter experience, that they can take some of their fate into their own hands. But there is no guarantee that just because they have the means, they will use them. The logic of modernity renders equality inevitable, but the politics of modernity do not.

THE COUNTERREVOLUTION THAT NEVER HAPPENED

Everything that Green, Tawney, and Marshall stood for seemed to come to a crashing end with the election of Margaret Thatcher as British prime minister in 1979. Strongly influenced by Friedrich Hayek and Milton Friedman—though more by the former than the latter—Thatcher viewed her election as an opportunity to rein in the welfare state that had become so much a part of British life. And if the welfare state went, so would the modern conception of equality underlying it. "Equality, properly understood," Mrs. Thatcher said in her James Bryce Lecture of September 1996, "does not mean that men are equal in every respect. It only means that they are equal in their right to be free, and to enjoy all the rights bestowed on them by 'the laws of nature and of Nature's God.' This notion of equality acknowledges and accepts that there will be differences—often glaring differences—among men when it comes to abilities; true equality can produce inequalities in wealth and station." There was no doubt in her mind that the welfare state had produced so much equality that it threatened liberty. Cutting back the welfare state might return us to the state of nature, but since, as Thatcher also once famously said, there is no such thing as society, she believed that that would not in itself be a bad thing.

Mrs. Thatcher, of course, was not alone in the conclusions she reached. The year after she became prime minister, Ronald Reagan was elected president of the United States, and Reagan as well pointed to Hayek and Friedman—more often, in his case, to the American than to the European—as thinkers who shaped his views on the evils of socialism and the benefits of capitalism. Reagan had come to the attention of the Republican Party through a speech—usually called "the speech"—which he had been delivering around the country starting in the 1960s. The speech attacked liberals for wanting to replace the profit motive with the welfare state. Given his reputation as a friend of industry, an advocate of tax cutting, and an opponent of welfare, Reagan's election to the presidency in 1980 led both his supporters and his opponents to conclude that extensive rollbacks of the welfare state would be forthcoming.

The Thatcher and Reagan counterrevolutions were counterrevolutions that never happened. To be sure, as the Berkeley political scientist Paul Pierson has shown, there was a significant retrenchment of the welfare state in both countries. Yet in neither case did events produce a return to the conditions of political life before the idea of the welfare state came to its fruition in the first decades of the twentieth century. In Great Britain, Thatcherism's success, the British essayist and historian Geoffrey Wheatcroft argues, spelled Mrs. Thatcher's political demise; once she cleared away the brush that accumulated after many years of earlier Labour and Conservative misrule, there was little left to put in its place. And even though Mrs. Thatcher led her country in a direction that was accepted in large measure by Labour under Tony Blair, Blair's neoliberalism, despite the hostility it provoked from the left, remained a far cry from Social Darwinism. Nor did the Reagan revolution result in a rollback of the welfare state. Reagan's legacy was entrusted to George W. Bush, and while Bush proved to be in many respects more conservative than Reagan, he was also something of a big-government conservative. Perfectly willing to cut taxes, Bush was not at all willing—indeed, as Reagan was not before him—to cut the programs that the taxes paid for. Both societies, moreover, were part of a worldwide pattern. One study of public attitudes toward the welfare state in eighteen different countries conducted by the sociologists Clem Brooks and Jeff Manza determined that in only two of them was the welfare state significantly cut back during the past few decades; in thirteen of them, expenditures on welfare state activities actually increased. No one can doubt either the determination or the political skills of Mrs. Thatcher and Ronald Reagan. Why, then, did they fail to obtain so much of what they wanted?

The most compelling answer is that, for all its faults, the welfare state remains popular. "Whatever the level of support for social provision," Brooks and Manza conclude, "those attitudes are deeply rooted and tend to move slowly over time." This means that people tend not to be passionately in favor of the welfare state, but neither are they its determined opponents. On the one hand, they are attracted to politicians who promise tax cuts and evince little sympathy for the fate of the most downtrodden; in that sense, they do not subscribe to the universality of the welfare state as outlined by T. H. Marshall. On the other hand, they have come to accept the idea that society must provide certain basic benefits, usually including health care, old age provision, and unemployment insurance; it is literally unthinkable to them that people should be forced to rely entirely on their own efforts without help from their fellow citizens.

Milton Friedman believed that even if equality could be justified in theory, it could not be realized in practice. The actual experience in Western liberal democracy is almost exactly the opposite. People are not especially responsive to theoretical justifications in favor of equality, but they are quite practical in making sure that at least some of it is made available to them. Although the form of the welfare state in the future is open to debate, the argument over culture versus nature to which such thinkers as Mill, Spencer, Green, and Tawney contributed is no longer open to discussion. We accept as a matter of obvious fact that people can, through their collective efforts, put limits on selfishness. The only question left is the extent to which they will.

HAS THE DRIVE FOR EQUALITY RUN OUT OF FUEL?

Despite the continued political viability of the welfare state, a clear sense exists in Western liberal democratic societies that the political energy behind equality is running low; it frequently has proven as difficult to expand the welfare state in new directions as it has been to roll it back. As much as equality remains a fact of life in modern society, the morally crusading and religiously inspired language in which it once expressed itself has all but disappeared. In part because Socialist parties took ideas of equality much further than most liberals were prepared to accept; in part because conservative parties were fairly successful in conflating socialism with liberalism; and in part because at least some liberals overestimated the appeal that equality would have, it is no easy task for contemporary politicians and policymakers to pursue an egalitarian agenda. With what the American sociologist Herbert Gans has called "more equality" harder to come by, Western liberals typically engage in a politics of indirection, urging, for example, strategies of economic growth that will produce greater equality without ever suggesting that this is their intent. This is an approach pursued just about everywhere in the contemporary political world, but most especially in the United States. The leaders of the Democratic Party, the party more committed to egalitarian objectives, rarely let the word "equality" escape from their mouths.

So long as the goal of equality is pursued in such hesitant ways, however, liberals, besides being disingenuous, are unlikely to live up to the ideals established by such thinkers as Mill, Green, Tawney, and Marshall. It therefore makes sense to ask whether liberals have any prospect, under future political conditions, of putting more substance into the words associated with the Declaration of Independence and the Declaration of the Rights of Man and Citizen. Two pieces of advice might help them get started.

Ever since the Elizabethan Poor Law of 1601, there has existed a tendency to divide recipients of public assistance into those who deserve it and those who do not. In modern times, the criterion most frequently used to reinforce the distinction involves taking responsibility for one's actions: people who obey the law and refuse to engage in self-destructive behavior deserve our support, while those who drink, take drugs, or have children out of wedlock do not. This way of thinking has special appeal for conservative politicians who encourage those near the bottom of the ladder to channel their resentments not against those at the top, but at those in even more desperate straits.

Liberals frequently react to this way of thinking by downplaying the distinction between those who deserve and those who do not. This, I believe, is a mistake. Conservatives touch very real sentiments when they use the language of deservedness because questions of what we deserve are intimately connected to questions about the kind of creatures we are. A better strategy is to reflect on what it means to be deserving—or, for that matter, undeserving—as well as what it means to be responsible. This means stepping back for a moment from questions of public policy to ponder, as the early theorists of liberalism did, questions about the difference between nature and culture. Are all human beings deserving of equal respect? If so, what is it about us that deserves respect? If we are products of nature, do we have free will? If we are instead products of culture, are we or the culture that shapes us responsible for what we do? Before we can know who is deserving, we need to know more about what it means to deserve.

By taking the side of culture rather than nature, earlier liberal political theorists also took the side of free will. Culture is not a given but is something people make. Because we possess free will, we are responsible for our actions; liberals cannot, and should not, adopt the idea that people are inevitably helpless victims of forces larger than themselves. If liberals respond to conservative insistence on personal responsibility by claiming that the very poor cannot be held responsible for their actions, they transform culture back to nature: human beings are viewed as impersonal pawns thrown hither and yon by huge cataclysms over which they can exercise no control. If the price paid to keep welfare state programs funded is the denial of human agency, that is too great a price to pay.

But it does not follow that because people must be held responsible for their acts, some people are more deserving than others. From a liberal point of view, all human beings are capable of leading lives of purpose. What they deserve, more than anything else, is the opportunity to do so. We are all deserving because we are all human beings who share a common culture. If I am successful and another person is not, that person deserves my support because if he has the chance to lead a life of purpose, my ability to do so improves as well; if, with public assistance, he gets a job, the economy we share is enriched, and if, with public assistance, he becomes more law-abiding, my personal security is enhanced. Once culture replaces nature, in short, everyone becomes dependent on each other, and because of that, everyone deserves the support of everyone else. We can no longer be guided by ideas about social policy inherited from the Elizabethans. Or, more properly, we are best off being guided by the famous Elizabethan poet John Donne, who wrote that no man is an island.

To further reflection on these kinds of questions, a second step would be in order. A stronger and more substantive liberal case for equality could benefit in the twenty-first century, as it did in the nineteenth, from a broader inclusion of religious voices. This is more than an abstract possibility. Historically speaking, those adherents to the Social Gospel movement who once spoke most movingly on behalf of equality were not evangelical in their outlook but—at least the Protestants among them—leaned more toward what we now call "mainline" versions of the faith. Yet although in recent years white evangelicals have strongly identified with the Republican Party, there exists an increasing sense among them that considerations of social justice cannot be dismissed by those who call themselves born-again Christians. Because African-Americans, who are disproportionately evangelical in their religious practices, have long belonged to the party of equality, this movement among whites raises the prospect of a biracial commitment to a language of equality among one of the most theologically conservative forms of American religion. Liberals would be foolish not to seek to join with evangelicals around common concerns in this area. Moral and religious arguments in favor of equality are likely to have far greater resonance, at least in the United States, than economic and practical ones.

This, in turn, requires that liberals not only become more comfortable with the language of religion but that they also begin to familiarize themselves once more with the language of morality. Here the legacy of the 1960s has not served liberals well. In the face of the efforts by leaders of the religious right to portray themselves as a moral majority, too many people on the left concluded that the state ought not to be in the business of morality at all. Decisions about who (and how many) to sleep with, whether or not to obtain an abortion, or how to properly raise children ought, they believe, to be left to individuals themselves to determine without the heavy hand of government. This proved to be a rather ironic course to follow: in their determination to carve out space for individuals to avoid the condemnatory moral judgments of the religious right in their personal and sexual lives, liberals adopted arguments similar to the laissez-faire positions once used to justify rampant economic inequalities. Whatever you do, don't regulate. People have to find their own best ways to lead their lives. We can and must resist the meddling of others. Keep the government out. Negative liberty is not necessarily a bad thing.

Morality, alas, is not so easily divisible. If the state studiously avoids telling a teenager that promiscuous sexuality is a bad thing, how can it make the case that obligations to the poor and needy are a good thing? For Western societies to achieve greater equality, let alone to hold on to the equality they have already achieved, they need to insist that the fate of every person is tied to the fate of every other person, and that cannot be done if we claim that, when it comes to matters of sexuality and the family, every person is an island after all. This does not mean making abortions illegal or demanding that gays step back into the closet. On the contrary, it suggests that homosexuals be allowed to marry, in that way promising to love and care for another person with the same legal rights that heterosexuals possess, just as the decision to terminate a pregnancy, which on grounds of individual liberty ought to be permitted, nonetheless cannot be isolated from the interest society has in all reproductive decisions, without which it would be impossible to offer public assistance to mothers and children. There are ways to be moral without meddling. It is more important that liberal societies remind their members of the common moral goals they share, especially the equal dignity of all who inhabit them, than that they try to impose particular conceptions of morality by force upon those who do not share them.

A conservative reaction against the liberatory politics associated with the 1960s has taken place in recent years (although, as with welfare state retrenchment, it is remarkable how much of the sexual and cultural transformations of the 1960s remains with us). This is something that many liberals can properly bemoan. The conventional morality that preceded the 1960s was a cruel one, and real gains for equality for large numbers of people were made when it went into abeyance. Yet once again ironies abound. It was surely never the intent of the leaders of the religious right, so fervent in their political conservatism, to make a case for the modern welfare state, but this is indirectly what they have done. Evangelical Christians who are making questions of poverty and social justice central to their concerns—the efforts of Rick Warren, who has turned his attention to AIDS in Africa, spring immediately to mind—are following out the logic of the morality-based considerations they have introduced into contemporary politics. If we start out by asking why we all have an interest in each other's sexual behavior, it is not long before we ask ourselves whether we can ignore the sufferings of others living with poverty or afflicted by disease. And if we seek to do something about those conditions in Africa, it will not be long before we try to do something about them at home. As evangelical Christianity turns back to the days of the Social Gospel for inspiration, it would be a tragedy if the secular left found itself on the side of Social Darwinism.

Inegalitarians have long insisted that because we are unequal by nature, any attempt to make us more equal, because it violates who we really are, is bound to fail. We now know that this gets the matter backward. The case for equality in the modern world is frequently made awkwardly, and equality itself is politically contingent. Yet the movement toward equality that began as early as the days of the French and American revolutions has become so much part of the established universe of contemporary politics that interference with it is frighteningly difficult to pull off. In the face of all this, the reluctance of liberals to talk about equality is difficult to understand. Modernity gives us a stake in how each other lives. The question is not whether we should link our fates with others, for that has already happened, but whether we can use our collective efforts to strengthen those links in the future.

CHAPTER 4

WHY GOOD POETRY MAKES BAD POLITICS

THE POETIC AND THE PROSAIC

John Stuart Mill was the Mozart of political philosophy. Trained to be a prodigy, he not only surpassed his father's own quite considerable accomplishments, he left his mark on all who came after him. *On Liberty* and *The Subjection of Women,* his best known works, may not have achieved the greatness of *Don Giovanni* or *Così fan tutte*—nothing written by anyone in the last two hundred years has—but they remain core texts in the history of liberalism. The former is relevant any time people in the contemporary world argue over the limits of liberty, the latter is unsurpassed in its willingness to take the case for equality further than anyone of his period was prepared to go.

Mozart aficionados love to point to lesser known pieces of the master that truly exemplify his genius—the viola quintets, for example, or the Adagio and Fugue in C Minor, K. 546. One can be similarly carried away by the more obscure writings of Mill. In particular, two rather journalistic essays, originally published in 1839 and 1840 but difficult to find until they were brought to light by F. R. Leavis at Cambridge in 1950, shed special insight into the liberal temperament. One dealt with the Utilitarian philosopher Jeremy Bentham; the other with the Romantic poet Samuel Taylor Coleridge.

In these two essays, Mill contrasted the passionless calculations of Bentham with the profound, quasi-spiritual sensibility of Coleridge. In so doing, he posed a question that subsequent liberal thinkers would have to address as well: whether to opt for an emotional commitment to feelings, however destabilizing, or for a scientific emphasis on fact, however uninspiring. Mill himself leaned in the former direction. Most of the liberals who followed him chose the latter. Romance has its appropriate settings, these later thinkers believed, but politics is not one of them. European and American history since Mill wrote his essays contains all too many examples of bloodshed in the cause of passion: war, including civil war; nationalism and its appeals to the heart; and ideological conflict posing utopian visions of a new world against one another. In the face of such movements, the grounded empiricism of Bentham came to be trusted over the organic holism of Coleridge. Of all of liberalism's dispositions, a wariness toward what William Wordsworth in his preface to the second edition of *Lyrical Ballads* called "the spontaneous overflow of powerful feelings" is one of the most important.

Jeremy Bentham, as it happens, was decidedly easy to mock. Dickens could not resist the temptation when he created Mr. Gradgrind, the no-nonsense educator in *Hard Times* who proclaims, "In this life, we want nothing but Facts, Sir, nothing but Facts." Against such caricatures, Mill's treatment of Bentham was sympathetic. Bentham, he wrote, was "the great questioner of things established," who "for the first time introduced precision of thought into moral and political philosophy." But despite Mill's appreciation, he found in Bentham's writings insufficient respect for the complexities of human behavior: "Man is never recognized by him as a being capable of pursuing spiritual perfection as an end; of desiring, for its own sake, the conformity of his own character to his standard of excellence, without hope for good or fear of evil from other source than his own inward consciousness." Lacking a tragic sensibility, Bentham could not come to terms with such "powerful constituents of human nature" as a sense of honor, a love of beauty, or a thirst for action. No worthwhile conception of society can be built on such a simplistic conception of human character, Mill argued. If living together with others is to bring out the best in us, we require something more than Bentham's famous observation that "Prejudice apart, the game of push-pin is of equal value with the arts and sciences of music and poetry."

Who, then, better to offer a contrast to Benthamite emotional sterility than a poet, indeed one of England's greatest poets, who also dabbled in moral and political philosophy? Mill was no great lover of hypocrisy; the fact that churches reached for the spiritual by emphasizing the selfish, or that politicians spoke of the public good while lining the pockets of private interests, brought on his scorn. There are two ways to reform such imbalances, he pointed out, "the one demanding the extinction of the institutions and creeds which had hitherto existed; the other, that they may be made a reality." Coleridge embodied the latter in much the way Bentham did the former. Since Tories were not likely to disappear, Mill asked, what kind of Tories should we have? For him, it was far better to have an idealist such as Coleridge than a practical politician such as Sir Robert Peel, the Conservative prime minister of the 1830s and 1840s. Mill is famous, especially on the right, for having called the Conservatives "the stupidest party." ("I never meant to say," he later wrote, "that the Conservatives are generally stupid. I meant to say that stupid people are generally Conservative.") One sees no such contempt in Mill's essay on Coleridge, a thinker who, according to Mill, offers "the natural means of rescuing from oblivion truths which Tories have forgotten, and which the prevailing schools of Liberalism never knew."

Mill's essays on Bentham and Coleridge need to be read against the backdrop of those powerful political and artistic forces unleashed during the first half of the nineteenth century that helped usher in the modern world. One way of responding to changes of this magnitude was to identify oneself as a liberal; this is, after all, the period in which that term first made its appearance on the scene as a political ideal. But liberalism was not unchallenged during these years. By the time Mill published his essays, no one could make a credible case for going back to the politics of the old regime, although some, especially in France, tried. But there was an alternative to both reactionary conservatism and newly emergent liberalism. As classical forms gave way to Romanticism in art and music, an emphasis on emotions, purity, spontaneity, and adventure appealed to many swept up in the political fervors of their time.

Romanticism, however much valued as an artistic movement, is an underappreciated political force; its impact on the political and social views of early-nineteenth-century thinkers and artists was considerable. Coleridge himself, along with Wordsworth, both once supporters of the French Revolution, discovered in the Lake District a love of nature that substituted for the ecstasy politics was no longer able to provide. Military leaders such as Napoleon or Andrew Jackson were worshipped as liberators or, sometimes by the same individuals, condemned as devils. (The most famous case of Napoleonic obsession is Beethoven's removal of the Bonapartist dedication of his Third Symphony, renaming it, still in the Romantic mode, as the "Eroica"). An all-star list of the British Romantic poets was enchanted by the battlefield as a theater for sacrifice and glory, and even though some of them later turned their backs on militarism and its horrors, the images they fashioned of war as the appropriate ground for displays of manly virtue lived on after them. For a philosopher such as G. W. F. Hegel, the radical changes of the time seemed to offer a new, and higher, synthesis, in the form of a state embodying a true conception of freedom. Religious revivals broke with sterile dogma to emphasize the importance of personal conversion and enthusiastic worship. Nationalism emerged as a profound political movement, recovering lost languages and literatures and rediscovering folk traditions. Western societies were in the process of exploring new worlds, and as they did, contacts with indigenous people furnished the themes of exotic novels, poems, and paintings. Slavery, far from disappearing in the United States in the aftermath of the compromises that characterized the Constitution, developed its passionate defenders, who turned to the novels of Sir Walter Scott and traditions of chivalry and honor to champion their way of life. In comparison to John Locke's legalistic emphasis on contractual obligations or Adam Smith's rather colorless invisible hand, Romanticism offered something fresh, vibrant, and resonant, even—or especially—when it defended the old.

Romanticism appealed to the left as well as the right. Karl Marx, Hegel's student, wrote a doctoral dissertation on Prometheus, the proto-Romantic Greek god, and penned, in *The Communist Manifesto,* an epic poem that, in the words of Marshall Berman, owed a considerable debt to "the thought of Goethe and Schiller and their romantic successors." Southern defenders of slavery were Romantics at heart, but so were the New England Transcendentalists Henry David Thoreau and Ralph Waldo Emerson, among slavery's most eloquent opponents. The bohemianism that filled the garrets of mid-nineteenth-century Paris had no particular political disposition, but it was clearly part of the same hothouse atmosphere brought to Europe by the revolutions of 1848. Anarchist movements that attracted rabid adherents throughout the latter half of the nineteenth century made Marx, who opposed them vigorously, seem insufficiently Promethean and, in the extreme case, led to what we now call terrorism. Romanticism could stand in protest against the present by looking back to an idyllic past, but it could just as easily look forward to a utopian future.

Because of Romanticism's broad appeal, it had its attractions to some liberal thinkers, Mill most definitely included. In his essays on Bentham and Coleridge, Mill, although occasionally critical of the poet, especially the Germanically inspired pontifications of his metaphysics, never applied to him the barbs he reserved for the philosopher. One reason is because, liberal to a fault, Mill bent over backward to find more of value in the political philosophy he disagreed with than the one that guided so much of his upbringing. But of more consequence is the fact that Mill was himself something of a romantic; his evocation of the self-sufficient dissident willing to brave the scorn of conventional opinion echoes Thomas Carlyle and foreshadows Friedrich Nietzsche. "Whoever could master the premises and combine the methods of both," Mill writes of Bentham and Coleridge, "would possess the entire English philosophy of the age." Mill never pulled that off. (He never really tried.) But the fact that he could even think it suggests that, to him, liberalism needed something more than a set of procedures designed to maximize happiness or to promote efficiency.

Yet for all that, Mill is too soft on Coleridge and, difficult as it may be to acknowledge, too hard on Bentham. The Utilitarian portrayal of human nature may be too thin, reducing human beings to what is most animalistic about them, but the Romantic portrayal is likely to be too rich, holding them up to standards appropriate for *Übermenschen* but ill-fitting for everyone else. Human beings are moved by beauty and possessed with a love of action, but Bentham's—or even Gradgrind's—preference for facts constitutes a better standard for public action than a desire for vengeance or the defense of honor. The most impressive eighteenth-century arguments for capitalism, suggests the American economist and intellectual historian Albert Hirschman, were those ideas associated with the Scottish Enlightenment to the effect that people's interests should be allowed to constrain the power of their passions.

The same could be said for the liberalism that grew up alongside capitalism's triumph. The best way to create a stable society, in the absence of the state-enforced order no longer available through the *ancien régime*, was to tame the emotions of collective enthusiasm through the dispassion of law, the impersonality of morality, and the reasonableness of what thinkers of the period were prone to call *doux commerce*. Liberalism must stand for something larger than the morally indifferent pursuit of self-interest. Yet it also must resist the irrational fervor associated with the rejection of this world in favor of the glories of heaven or in fear of the horrors of hell, whether in religious or secular form. Liberalism seeks a sense of balance as well as a sense of purpose. It insists that we stand for something without believing that we should stand for everything.

Mill's essays on Bentham and Coleridge speak to us today because the Romanticism toward which Mill had such ambivalent feelings continues to color our politics, even if one finds it in somewhat unusual places. One of them is among neoconservative intellectuals. Rejecting the placid politics of peace, they recall the Romantic poets by finding in military valor a compelling alternative to mundane commercial civilization, and, in the wake of 9/11, they sought out heroes, even finding that the awkward and inarticulate George W. Bush counted for one. Another is among ethnic nationalists who, at a time when civilizations are presumed to be clashing, rediscover the appeal of indigenous cultural roots; even in the United States, with its long-lasting liberal tradition, such forms of romantic ethnic nationalism can be witnessed. Yet a third outbreak of romantic fever is the ideological hardening on both the left and the right, based on the inherently romantic notion that the grandeur of the passions takes precedence over the mere fulfillment of the interests. Romanticism, in short, is neither a historical anachronism nor is it solely confined to matters of creative expression; it is part of the way we think and act now. The poetic or the prosaic? In politics, as in literature and philosophy, there is always a choice.

MERE SAFETY

"Riddance, mere riddance, safety, mere safety, are objects too far defined, too inert and passive in their own nature, to have ability either to arouse or sustain." William Wordsworth was protesting the Convention of Cintra, which allowed the defeated French to withdraw from Portugal during the Napoleonic Wars. (It was the French occupation of the Iberian peninsula that had led to the meeting at Cádiz where the term "liberalism" was first used in its modern political sense.) Wordsworth was aghast that caution had triumphed over courage. Nor was he alone. "And ever since that martial synod met," despaired Lord Byron in *Childe Harold's Pilgrimage*:

> *Britannia sickens, Cintra! at thy name;*
> *And folks in office at the mention fret,*
> *And fain would blush, if blush they could, for shame.*
> *How will posterity the deed proclaim!*

Will not our own and fellow-nations sneer,
To view these champions cheated of their fame,
By foes in fight o'erthrown, yet victors here,
Where Scorn her finger points, through many a coming year?

Byron wrote his poem between 1812 and 1818. During those same years, an officer named Carl von Clausewitz briefly left the Prussian army in protest against its alliance with Napoleon, returned to fight in the battle of Waterloo, and was eventually named director of the War College in Berlin. Clausewitz's writings on war were unavailable to Wordsworth, Byron, and the other Romantic poets because *On War* would not be published until 1832, a year after Clausewitz's death. Although he shared many of the Romantic sensibilities of his time, Clausewitz understood, as the Romantic poets did not, that the proper approach to war is a realistic one. In *On War,* heroism and glory recede into the background while organization and tactics occupy the foreground. War is not an art but a science. Fighting war successfully requires dispassion and clinical precision, not risky adventurism. It is true that war is above all else a theater of uncertainty and unpredictability. But that is why strength of character in war "is not vehement expressions of feeling, nor easily excited passions . . . but the power of listening to reason in the midst of the most excitement, in the storm of the most violent passions."

Clausewitz was no liberal, but his reflections on war offer words that liberals need to ponder. Liberalism is not pacifism; even in his essay on perpetual peace, Kant wrote that "one cannot demand of a state that it abandon its constitution . . . so long as the danger exists that it could be swallowed up by other states." If war is necessary, one can ask in the spirit of Mill's question about the Tories, then what kind of wars should we have? Recognizing that success in war requires controlling one's emotions, the liberal answer must be that war is necessary when the dispassion required to keep the peace breaks down. The way peace is pursued, moreover, inevitably influences the way war is fought. If the conditions of civilian life are dominated by images of guts and glory, preoccupied with quests for national honor, and filled with either joyous anticipation of victory or apocalyptic anticipation of defeat, the conditions of war are likely to be more violent and more lengthy than necessary. If, on the other hand, domestic politics is characterized by compromise and negotiation, political parties treat each other as competitors rather than as enemies, and public discussion focuses on questions of national interest rather than wars to end all wars, then conflict in the international arena is more likely to be handled as a problem to be solved than treated as a crusade to be won. Clausewitz is best known for saying that war is politics by other means. This does not mean that domestic politics should be understood as a struggle to the death. On the contrary, it means that politics must be carried out with the same sense of realism required to win battles.

The Romantic militarism of Wordsworth, Coleridge, and Byron burned itself out in Europe after the defeat of Napoleon, that "poet in action," as the writer and royalist sympathizer François-Auguste-René de Chateaubriand, who was also Alexis de Tocqueville's uncle, called him. But, in a case of an export lasting longer in the place to which it was sent than the place from which it originated, the adulation of military virtues continued unabated in the American South, an area Chateaubriand had visited in the aftermath of the French Revolution. Americans like to view their revolution as a break from European customs, which, with respect to such issues as an established church, it was. But rather than bypassing the European discussion over the proper role of the military in an expanding commercial society, the United States imported the two sides of the argument into the two main regions of the country. The North, as the historian William Taylor has suggested, modeled itself after the Yankee: frugal, businesslike, impersonal, High Church Protestant, rational; the South fashioned its self-image after the Cavalier: impetuous, chivalric, glory-seeking, evangelical, or even at times aristocratically Catholic, and, above all else, romantic. Consider the famous 1830 debate between Daniel Webster of Massachusetts and South Carolina's Robert Y. Hayne concerning the nature of the Union. Ostensibly about whether political power was lodged in the federal government or reserved by the states, the two orators, according to Taylor, evoked radically different conceptions of life: "Hayne cast himself as a passionate Cavalier and slipped frequently into a military terminology of defense and attack. Webster was the transcendent Yankee, peaceable, cool, and deliberate." The passions and the interests were here being contrasted not by defenders of the free market writing in eighteenth-century Scotland, but by politicians arguing the pros and cons of slavery in nineteenth-century Washington, D.C.

As they are wont to do, historians dispute the extent to which the South was possessed by a martial spirit. Some have written about the region's peculiar bellicosity, its eagerness to take offense, its insistence on righting wrongs to its honor, its sympathy toward violence, while others downplay the South's distinctiveness from the rest of the country. Still there is little doubt that, in the words of Samuel P. Huntington, "sectional self-interest, an atavistic allegiance to feudal romanticism, and an agrarian economy—all fueled Southern militarism." Southerners dominated the U.S. military before the Civil War, and some of them, especially Andrew Jackson, distrusted West Point and any tinge of military professionalism in favor of the highly Romantic notion, inspired by the French Revolution, that natural military genius would emerge, more or less spontaneously, from the ranks of ordinary fighters.

Yet the military romanticism so long identified with the South could not last forever. Modern military professionalism, whatever its geographic origin, simply cannot ignore a Clausewitzian understanding of war. "The military man," writes Huntington in *The Soldier and the State*, "normally opposes reckless, aggressive, belligerent action. . . . He always favors preparedness, but he never feels prepared. Accordingly, the professional military man contributes a cautious, conservative, restraining voice to the formulation of state policy." It can be no surprise, then, that during and after the Civil War, the South, while retaining its affinity with militarism, dropped its inclination toward romanticism. Military academies flourished in the South, and in distinct contrast to Andrew Jackson, Southerners flocked to West Point and assumed positions of leadership in the armed forces throughout the nineteenth and twentieth centuries. Romanticism survived in the form of nostalgia for the tactical brilliance of "Stonewall" Jackson and the aristocratic courtliness of Robert E. Lee. But just as the North moved into the modern era through industrialization and urbanization, the South became modern through militarization, bureaucratization, and the growth of government. Nostalgia remained where nostalgia properly belonged, in literature and memory, not in battle.

Romanticism would nonetheless continue to flourish in odd nooks and crannies of American life, not only in Southern nostalgia but in the romance of the Wild West, artistic revolts against bourgeois convention in early-twentieth-century Greenwich Village, and, extending into our times, that Emersonian revival known as the counterculture of the 1960s. When romanticism appeared in its twentieth-century form, moreover, it manifested itself, as it had in earlier times, on both ends of the political spectrum. This is why, as we search around us today for examples of the Romantic imagination at work, we are just as likely to find it, not only among those who identified with the counterculture but among those who condemned it. A good deal of what passes for conservatism in American politics is better understood as romanticism, and no figure embodies those nostalgic longings more than that child of small-town America who grew to maturity in the dream factories of Hollywood: Ronald Reagan.

In *Ronald Reagan: Fate, Freedom, and the Making of History,* the historian John Patrick Diggins has made the best case for viewing Reagan as an embodiment of the romantic imagination. Reagan's favorite among the founders, Diggins notes, was not a sober realist such as James Madison, known for writing the Constitution, but a firebrand such as Tom Paine, who, having helped bring about one revolution in North America, went to France to participate in another. Although Reagan appealed to Christian conservatives, his personal religious views owed more to Ralph Waldo Emerson than to John Calvin; cheery transcendence, not sin-laden despair, characterized whatever spiritualism he possessed. His economic views seemed to borrow from Adam Smith, but they replaced Smith's cynicism toward unearned wealth with wide-eyed wonder at all the good things money can buy. He may have called the Soviet Union the "Evil Empire," but he also opted for a utopian view of foreign policy that insisted, against all military expertise, that a foolproof military weapons shield could protect the United States against incoming missiles and at the same time maintained, against all professional diplomatic advice, that the president could sit down with the Russians and negotiate nuclear weapons out of existence. To the cynical world of inside-the-Beltway politics as usual, Reagan brought an innocence more associated with the popularity of the western than the decline of the West.

It was during Reagan's presidency that neoconservatism began to emerge as a significant intellectual and political force in American life, and, like the man to whom they owed so much, neoconservatives were attracted to the kind of Romantic vision that led the early-nineteenth-century British poets to glorify the battlefield. One of the more interesting neoconservatives is Victor Davis Hanson, a former farmer and scholar of ancient Greece. Historians once examined famous battles in order to draw lessons about the human condition and the nature of societies, Hanson argues, but we have lost this tradition and need to bring it back. "Battles bring out the coward or hero in all of us," he writes in *Carnage and Culture.* "The nineteenth-century logic was that there is no better way to form our character than through reading of the heroism and cowardice inherent in the fighting of the past." For Hanson, "the power and mystery of culture" helps explain why some countries are good at fighting battles and others are not. He is especially enamored of the Western way of war: "The idea of annihilation, of head-to-head battle that destroys the enemy, seems a particularly Western concept largely unfamiliar to the ritualistic fighting and emphasis on deception and attrition found outside Europe." Hanson wants to bring his readers directly into the experience of battle so that they can witness human behavior in its extreme form. If Westerners are free to live lives of order and accomplishment, it is because they are guarded by soldiers willing to bleed and die on their behalf. We should never be ashamed of the presence of the warriors in our midst, Hanson concludes, but instead should feel a sense of obligation to them for having the courage we too often lack.

Hanson wrote *Carnage and Culture* before the attacks of September 11, 2001. When President George W. Bush responded to the events of that day by declaring a war against terror, Hanson watched as his countrymen, at least in his view, failed to respond adequately to the military challenges with which they were faced. In one of his more interesting essays written after the attacks, Hanson returns to late-eighteenth- and early-nineteenth-century speculation over the passions and the interests. "The suburban soccer fields of Seattle," he writes, "are not quite the same places as the wilds of Yemen, the palaces of Riyadh, or the barracks of the Republican Guard." He makes the comparison, not to praise latte culture but to bury it. Representing Seattle—literally—is its senator Patty Murray, and Murray, to Hanson's disdain, believes that if we just offer the militant Arabs money in the form of foreign assistance, they will be less likely to hate us. It is a nice, therapeutic gesture, Hanson charges, but it utterly fails to acknowledge our enemy's love of violence. "The United States cannot lose the struggle on the battlefield," he concludes. "But we most surely can fail in this war if our citizens and leaders reach for their checkbooks as the fundamentalists reach for their gun." Our task is not to get them to love us, but to reach for more guns, and to reach for them quicker, than they are capable of doing against us.

Commentators have found it difficult to choose the right term to characterize the strategic views of those neoconservatives, including such thinkers and pundits as William Kristol and Charles Krauthammer, who, during the younger Bush's administration, became such enthusiastic advocates of war. Traditionally, foreign policies are classified as either realist or idealist. Neoconservatives strongly reject the term "realist," a designation that, in their view, refers to someone who assigns priority to global stability without regard for the ideologies of the states that offer such stability. Brent Scowcroft, James Baker III, and other foreign policy officials of the elder Bush's administration, they believe, were too willing to accept a corrupt and undemocratic government in Saudi Arabia and too unwilling to finish the job against Saddam Hussein in Iraq when they had him on the run. If that is realism, neoconservatism will have nothing to do with it.

If the term "realism" does not apply to neoconservatism, however, neither does the term "idealism." For a brief moment, neoconservatives seemed willing to accept the label, for they justified the invasion of Iraq, after threats due to weapons of mass destruction proved false, as an effort to bring democracy to countries that had been governed by brutal dictatorships. But the paradigmatic idealist in American history was Woodrow Wilson, and the neoconservatives were as far removed from Wilson as they were from George H. W. Bush. Wilson's singular contribution to diplomacy was the League of Nations; neoconservatives, by contrast, have been forthrightly contemptuous of the body that replaced the League, the United Nations. It is not some Wilsonian ideal of cooperating with other nations that neoconservatives prefer, but unchecked American power. Whatever else it is, this is not idealism but a form of American-centered unilateralism.

Neoconservatives such as Hanson, Kristol, and Krauthammer are better understood as romantic. Not all neoconservative intellectuals became romantics. Some, such as Francis Fukuyama, retained a temperamentally cautious suspicion of zealotry. Fukuyama, indeed, provides the best analysis of how some members of the club to which he once belonged lost their hearts to romanticism. The first-generation neoconservatives, he astutely notes in *America at the Crossroads*, were skeptical of the ability of human beings to draw up plans capable of guiding the world toward ends chosen by policymakers. In domestic policy, this led neoconservatives to raise the possibility that political reforms designed to alleviate poverty or to promote social justice could wind up doing the exact opposite. The foreign policy views of the early neoconservatives were similarly marked by an absence of zeal, most illustratively in "Dictatorships and Double Standards," an article written by the political scientist (and later U.S. ambassador to the United Nations) Jeane Kirkpatrick. That article, published in *Commentary* in 1979, drew a distinction between totalitarian and authoritarian governments and warned against efforts to topple the latter while urging strong opposition to the former. Formerly on the political left, neoconservatives typically adopted a sober outlook on the world suspicious of perfectionist utopianism.

The same was not true of a younger generation of neoconservatives, some of whom were literally the children of the previous ones. First-generation neoconservatives were social scientists made humble by the world's unpredictability. Those who followed in their footsteps were political philosophers, novelists, historians, polemicists, and humanists made arrogant for the certainty of their understanding of the human heart. William Kristol, editor of *The Weekly Standard* and one of the most prominent of the second-generation neoconservatives, shares the general views of his parents: Irving Kristol, who had all but single-handedly invented the neoconservative movement, and the historian of Victorian Britain Gertrude Himmelfarb. But when it comes to foreign policy, he sheds all caution and skepticism to argue that the United States can implant democracy in previously hostile climes and help create a new world order in which American supremacy would render the notion of a balance of power obsolete. He has been joined by others who inherited the romanticism of the Reagan years but, in doing so, dispensed with Emersonian optimism in favor of romanticism's Gothic side: the world as they understood it was filled with dark forces, against which only resolute action offered any prospect for a happy ending.

Iraq proved to be the neoconservatives' great test case, and no better term describes the strategy and tactics followed by its planners than "romantic." Iraq's history was ignored. Its rivalries with other states in the Middle East were downplayed. The consequences of removing Saddam Hussein from power, spelled out with realistic foresight by George W. Bush's father in his memoirs, were downplayed. A Jacksonian distrust of the sober caution of professional military officers and diplomats guided the strategic thinking of the neoconservatives, as well as a determination to bend other countries to America's will. Planning for postwar reconstruction was guided by the fantasy that a reliance on free markets could restore the Iraqi economy in miraculous ways. This is not the world according to Machiavelli or Clausewitz. It is the world according to such dreamy enthusiasts for Empire as Rudyard Kipling, the British writer of children's tales, and T. E. Lawrence of "Lawrence of Arabia" fame. There would be, as Thomas Carlyle had hoped, a hero in history, only it would be a great nation rather than a great person. And the epic task undertaken by that heroic land would be to bring the benefits of Western civilization to a backward people who would be forever in its debt.

Neoconservatism's conspicuous foreign policy failures in Iraq raised the important question of what would follow it. Fukuyama argues in favor of what he calls "realistic Wilsonianism," a combination of multilateral, democracy-yielding strategies on the one hand and a cold-eyed appreciation for balance of power necessities on the other. But there is no reason for Fukuyama to invent a new term, and an awkward one at that. "Realistic Wilsonianism" is just another phrase for "liberalism." Guided by interests rather than passions, a liberal foreign policy is realistic in the empirical sense; its first order of business, before a decision is made on whether troops should be used, is to gather as much information as possible about how they should be used. But neither is a liberal foreign policy amorally cynical; liberals believe that the peace is best kept when as many possible partners to war are themselves liberal. It does not seek to impose liberal democracy upon countries unable to make it work. It does try to create a liberal global order in which as many governments as possible avoid romantic dreams, shun unrealistic expectations, and dampen religious and ideological enthusiasms.

The relevant contrast before the West is not between Mars and Venus, as the neoconservative Robert Kagan puts it in *Of Paradise and Power*. It is between Apollo and Dionysus. When it comes to human affairs in general, but especially when it comes to that form of human affairs whose consequences are destruction and death, the best advice is to keep the inebriating stuff at home just in case it proves necessary, but to bring sobriety to the negotiating table and to maintain it instead. Safety, more safety, is not always a bad thing to seek.

BIRTH OF THE NATION

Nationalism, for the Romantics of the early nineteenth century, was militarism's first cousin. As Napoleon's forces swept across Europe in the aftermath of the French Revolution, intellectuals in countries threatened by France, especially in the German lands that were not yet organized into a nation-state, reacted by insisting on their own distinct history, folkways, ideas, language, and manners. Everything French— Cartesian rationalism, intellectual snobbery, frivolous fashion, Voltairian skepticism—struck them as hollow and inauthentic. Their names—the philosophers Johann Gottfried von Herder (1744–1803) and Johann Gottlieb Fichte (1762–1814) and the poet and essayist Ernst Moritz Arndt (1769–1860)—are not especially well known today. But the intellectual movement to which they gave birth, nationalism, became an unstoppable force throughout the nineteenth and twentieth centuries. Out of the chaos created by war and revolution, nationalism offered a balm. "The idea, sometimes invested with a mystical or messianic fervor, of the nation as a supreme authority, replacing the Church or the prince or the rule of law or other sources of ultimate values," Isaiah Berlin writes in his essay "Nationalism," "relieved the pain of the wound to group consciousness, whoever may have inflicted it—a foreign enemy or native capitalists or imperial exploiters or an artificially imposed, heartless bureaucracy."

Berlin identifies four features that illustrate why romantic nationalism and liberalism represent two contrasting outlooks on the modern world. First, nationalists believe that "men belong to a particular human group, and that the way of life of the group differs from that of others; that the characteristics of the individuals who compose the group are shaped by, and cannot be understood apart from, those of the group, defined in terms of common territory, customs, laws, memories, beliefs, language, artistic and religious expression, social institutions, ways of life . . . and that it is these factors which shape human beings, their purposes and their values." Nationalism, in other words, implies particularism; human beings everywhere and anywhere are not the same. You are where you were born. Forces that existed long before you appeared in this world shape what you will become. Just as your first language is never your own choice, your entire way of life is a product of the decisions made by your parents, and before them, their parents, all the way back, in some cases, to ancestors lost to history. It is therefore foolish on your part to insist, as liberals such as Mill do, that you can—indeed must—choose your way of life. Your way of life has already been chosen.

The second characteristic of nationalism is a preference for the natural over the artificial. As Fichte put it in his "Address to the German Nation" of 1806, "Those who speak the same language are joined to each other by a multitude of invisible bonds by nature herself, long before any human art begins." Nationalists, like romantics, stand with Rousseau rather than Kant. The nations to which people belong are wholesome in two senses of the term: they are pure and they cannot be reduced to their component parts. Nations, like species, evolve, and any attempt to interfere with their process of evolution—say, by opening the borders to newcomers or by adding a second language as an alternate to the dominant one—will set them off on a false course. Unlike the evolution of a species, however, the evolution of a society is not governed by scientific rules. Artifice is inappropriate to the work of nations, not only because they are natural but also because they are mystical. You are tied to your nation by forces you can never fully understand.

Isn't this natural evolution?

Why should you be subject to a state's authority? The nationalist's answer, according to Berlin, is because its authority is designed for you and those like you. "This is tantamount to saying that these rules or doctrines or principles should be followed, not because they lead to virtue or happiness or justice or liberty, or are ordained by God or Church or prince or parliament or some other universally acknowledged authority, or are good or right in themselves, and therefore valid in their own right, universally, for all men in a given situation; rather they are to be followed because these values are those of *my* group." Nations make a virtue of the "we." The worst thing a nationalist can do is to judge his own society's values by comparing them to some abstract standard—what any rational entity would choose behind a veil of ignorance, for example—because, to the nationalist, there is no neutral standard that exists above the competing standards associated with particular nations. Just as free trade benefits those who dominate a global market, universal standards of right and wrong benefit those countries that identify their principles with universal principles. When asked how we can justify our actions, the nationalist has only one answer: This is how we do things here. The more curious may be inclined to find out how other people do things there, but this is not essential. Our world, as far as we are concerned, is the only world that counts.

Finally, nationalism must have room to breathe. "If my group—let us call it a nation—is freely to realize its true nature, this entails the need to remove obstacles in its path," as Berlin puts it. "Nothing that obstructs that which I recognize as my—that is, my nation's—supreme goal can be allowed to have equal value with it." The nation's integrity, in theory, could be preserved by retreating behind its borders and sealing itself off from the rest of the world. But because nationalists cling to a negative understanding of human nature, they typically believe that other nations will become so jealous of their own nation's goodness that they will threaten to take it over. Protecting one's own nation becomes intertwined with anticipating threats from others and being prepared, by preemptive actions if necessary, to ensure that those threats never materialize. In such a way does romantic nationalism link with romantic militarism. Those who guard the nation best embody its soul. For Berlin, there is a direct line from the Romantic nationalism of the early nineteenth century to the irrational racism, let alone the foreign policy messianism, characteristic of twentieth-century fascism. Worship of Il Duce or Der Führer follows in the extreme cases once all standards of reason and Enlightenment are swept away in the emotional flames that nationalists stoke.

The United States experienced neither the French Revolution nor the turmoil surrounding the Napoleonic conquests; if anything, Napoleon strengthened the United States by granting it Louisiana on ridiculously favorable terms. As odd as it may therefore sound to contemporary readers accustomed to belligerent displays of American power on the part of American leaders, the United States throughout much of its history experienced very little of the Romantic nationalism so characteristic of nineteenth-century Germany. In calling attention to the ubiquity of Lockean liberalism in the United States, Louis Hartz pointed out that America's greatest early-nineteenth-century nationalists were Alexander Hamilton and John Marshall, and that their nationalism "was legal rather than social, defending a federal government but not embracing in any Rousseauian sense—as, ironically, Jefferson's 'anti-nationalism' did—the American popular community." Nationalism in the United States was too preoccupied with expanding its territory to pay much attention to worshipping the land. Its attention was more directed to making an *unum* out of the *pluribus* than to glorifying the folk traditions of any one of its constituent parts. American nationalists were bankers and jurists, not poets and linguists.

American nationalism, to rely on a distinction made by numerous historians and political scientists, has historically been civic rather than ethnic. Civic nationalism, as the Canadian writer and politician Michael Ignatieff defines it, is achieved rather than ascribed; it comes into existence as an act of political will—it is, so to speak, artificial—by people determined to forge allegiance, not to a specific racial or religious group but to a set of ideas founded on Enlightenment principles. Ethnic nationalism, by contrast, is the form that romanticism takes under modern political conditions. Holding the integrity of the blood-based group to be of greater significance than the shallow wants of individuals, ethnic nationalists believe that the nation exists first and the state comes afterward; you are a Serb or a Kurd irrespective of whether you have a country, and you remain one even after a legal entity is formed around you. Where civic nationalism reigns, different nations generally resolve their differences through negotiation and compromise. Where ethnic nationalism dominates, military campaigns—sometimes, as in the Balkans, carrying forward slights that are a thousand years old—tend to predominate.

Nothing did more to bring more extreme forms of ethnic nationalism to a halt in most of Europe than the twentieth century's two world wars. "Too many people were killed, maimed, raped, or starved to death in wars," writes the British political scientist Anatol Lieven of King's College London, "for the language of militant, outwardly directed nationalism to be acceptable, not merely in political or intellectual circles but in the vast majority of the populations." Romantic nationalism is no longer a significant force in most of the world's liberal democracies. Europe has its xenophobes, to be sure. But in Western Europe, it is not just an aversion to war that tempers old-fashioned nationalist fervor but also the presence of large numbers of immigrants and their children, born in other nations or still in one way or another attached to them, that makes it so difficult to speak about the nation in nineteenth-century terms. Influenced by the German liberal philosopher Jürgen Habermas, whose ideas about the public sphere we will encounter in a later chapter, European liberals have been exploring at length the concept of "constitutional patriotism," the notion, as the German-born Princeton political scientist Jan-Werner Müller defines it, "that political attachment ought to center on the norms, the values, and, more indirectly, the procedures of a liberal democratic constitution." When it comes to the Romanticism that inspired Europeans, and especially Germans, in the past, the feeling seems to be that enough, finally, is enough.

As Europe's nationalism becomes more civic, Lieven argues that America's is becoming more ethnic; increasingly in the United States, he believes, populistically inclined, racially motivated, and religious-inspired forms of reactionary nationalism are gaining ground, specifically among those who constitute the electoral base of the Republican Party. Lieven acknowledges that American nationalist movements, including the more romantic ones, historically found their authoritarian inclinations checked by the institutions of constitutional democracy. But he worries that such checks may no longer be very operative. For one thing, Americans are increasingly involved in the Middle East, where intense and bloody conflict is the rule. For another, the United States has its share of populistic politicians blaming foreigners for any of the country's economic woes. If middle-class jobs begin to disappear, Lieven concludes, the United States may discover that "as in the European countries of the past, such a development would create the perfect breeding ground for radical nationalist groups and for even wilder dreams of 'taking back' America at home and restoring the old moral, cultural, and possibly racial order."

For now, it is impossible to know whether Lieven's forebodings will prove correct. My own view is that civic nationalism is more robust than he suggests, even if some of the more vehement anti-immigration sentiment in the United States seems to confirm his analysis. But in the meantime, various versions of ethnic nationalism have been advocated among leading thinkers and political commentators in the United States. On the right, Samuel P. Huntington, who is clear-sighted toward romantic militarism, has been far more receptive to romantic nationalism. Worried about immigration from countries such as Mexico, Huntington asks who Americans are—and he answers that they are defined by their culture. That culture, moreover, far from being something artificially created, is for Huntington a by-product of a particular place (Great Britain) and a particular religion (Protestantism). Huntington's *Who Are We?* is a lament for a culture that was once whole but has been fractured by the relentless cosmopolitanism of a globalized world. It speaks to a widespread longing in the United States for a nation with secure borders that can protect its own kind from alien influence. The fact that the United States has always been an immigrant nation, and that its defining features have been creedal rather than cultural, is ignored by romantic thinkers of this disposition. They speak about early-twenty-first-century America in terms that would be familiar to the way Fichte, Herder, and Arndt spoke of early-nineteenth-century Germany.

On the left, the analysis is in some ways radically different but in other ways much the same. One example is offered by strong multiculturalists, who have an ambivalent relationship to liberalism at best. It is no longer possible or desirable to create a nation based on a common understanding of civic ideals, multiculturalists argue. This does not mean that they want to replace the civic nation with an ethnic nation; most multiculturalists are opposed to an insistence on any form of national identity in a world characterized by diversity. Multiculturalists prefer the ethnic group to the nation; they urge the teaching of a frequently romanticized history of each of the nation's major ethnic blocs and a desire to ensure the integrity of each of its components against forms of assimilation that would blend all together into one. For them, as for Huntington, culture—in the ascribed rather than the achieved sense—counts for more than creed. It is, as it nearly always is with romantic nationalism, the conditions under which you are born, and not those to which you aspire, that determine who you are. Identity is still destiny; it is just the identity of the particular community and not the national community that determines it.

Of all the philosophers in the liberal tradition, Kant was the most hostile to Romantic versions of nationalism: to assert that each nation has its own particular sensibility is to challenge, directly or indirectly, Kant's insistence on examining particular circumstances from a cosmopolitan point of view. Today, as in the early nineteenth century, the Kantian tradition offers to contemporary liberals an alternative to romantic nationalism; once we agree to treat everyone as morally equal, we no longer have a rational basis for preferring someone of our own ethnic or racial group just because he happens to belong to that group and not another. There is a principled universalism built into Kant's way of thinking that contemporary liberals ought to admire. Perhaps the most eloquent voice speaking in those universalistic cadences is that of the philosopher Martha Nussbaum. "Becoming a citizen of the world," she writes in "Patriotism and Cosmopolitanism," which first appeared in the *Boston Review*, "is often a lonely business. It is, in effect, as Diogenes said, a kind of exile—from the comfort of local truths, from the warm nestling feeling of patriotism, from the absorbing drama of pride in oneself and one's own." Yet becoming a citizen of the world is something, Nussbaum believes, that we still must do. "The air does not obey national boundaries," she writes. Neither do the demands of justice. Against nationalism, liberalism offers internationalism.

As admirable as such principled universalism may be, however, it cannot be the sole basis upon which liberal citizens act. We are not rootless individuals unattached to any particular community, liberals believe, but instead live in societies that continue to define themselves as nation-states with particular histories, policies, traditions, and rights. Liberals believe in justice, but they also recognize that the way to achieve a more just society is by taking seriously one's obligations to the society of which one is a member. Without a nation, neither liberty nor equality can be realized, for the former presupposes the existence of society and the latter requires policies provided by the state. A citizen of the world must also be a citizen of a particular country. The difficult problem facing liberals is not whether to choose between national and global responsibilities but how to find ways to balance them.

Fortunately, as the example of constitutional patriotism in Europe suggests, there are ways they can be balanced. So long as nationalism is understood in creedal rather than cultural terms, liberalism includes a love of one's own country. The question is always what about one's country one ought to love. "What holds a society together," as Ignatieff writes in *Blood and Belonging*, "is not common roots but law. By subscribing to a set of democratic procedures and values, individuals can reconcile their right to shape their own lives with their need to belong to a community. This in turn assumes that national belonging can be a form of rational attachment." Constitutional patriotism is, as another writer has put it, post-nationalist rather than post-national. It does not object to the idea of collective obligation, the necessity to sacrifice from time to time for the common good, or even the need for military action to protect national security—so long as all of them can be justified by appeals to the head as well as the heart. Unlike Nussbaum's citizen of the world, the constitutional patriot loves her own country first. But unlike the romantic nationalist, the constitutional patriot loves her country in a cosmopolitan manner; she recognizes that it is one country among many, hopes to see it live up to the principles enshrined in its founding documents, and wishes it to adhere to international norms of justice and human rights.

In the early nineteenth century, nationalism and Romanticism joined forces, especially in Europe. It remains an open question whether the United States, which historically has resisted blending them together, will continue to do so. But there seems little doubt that outside the United States, there exists widespread recognition that in the potentially combustible world in which we live, love of one's country is best expressed by respect for the principles for which it stands rather than emotional attachment to people who are just like us.

THE ENDS OF IDEOLOGY

Militarism and nationalism were not the only Romantic currents to emerge in reaction to the intensity of the French Revolution and the struggles over the Napoleonic restoration. Ideology joined them. Its path, however, would prove to be more circuitous than those taken on behalf of armed battle or national aspirations.

Comte Antoine Destutt de Tracy, imprisoned during the Terror only to be elected later to the French Academy, spent the first two decades of the nineteenth century writing and then publishing *Eléments d'idéologie*. A *philosophe* who was close to the other French proto-liberals of his day, Destutt de Tracy used the term he had just coined in a favorable sense: "ideology" meant to him, as it would have meant to the Greeks from which the word was derived, the science of ideas. His purpose was to argue for the essential unity between such notions as "free thought, free press, individual liberties, the integrity of representative assemblies, and secularization," as the historian Emmet Kennedy puts it. Still, it was a new word and its use engendered considerable confusion. "Three vols. of *Ideology*," wrote John Adams to Thomas Jefferson near the end of the lives of both men:

> Please explain to me this Neological title! What does it mean? When Bonaparte used it, I was delighted with it, upon the Common Principle of delight in everything we cannot understand. Does it mean Idiotism? The science of Non compos Menticism? The Science of Lunacy? The Theory of Delirium? Or does it mean the Science of Love? Of Amour Propre? Or the Elements of Vanity?

Jefferson, who was fascinated by Destutt de Tracy and supervised the translation of his work into English, responded: "Tracy comprehends, under the word 'Ideology'[,] all the subjects which the French term *Morale* as the correlative to *Physique*. His work on Logic, government, political economy, and morality, he considers as making up the circle of ideological subjects."

In retrospect, there was good reason for Adams's confusion, as well as his sarcasm. So bourgeois were the political ideas of Destutt de Tracy that his notion of ideology would be attacked both by Napoleon, for whom it lacked grandeur, and by Karl Marx, for whom it was missing revolutionary fervor. If we consider Napoleon and Marx two of the great Romantics of the nineteenth century, ideology, when it first emerged as a new political term, sided with the very opposite of the Romantic imagination; its realm was that of science and system, not passion and promise. Had that trend continued, liberalism today would proudly call itself ideological.

Yet the trend did not continue. Our ways of thinking about ideology went through a considerable role reversal throughout the nineteenth century. As liberals became the party of reform, their politics sacrificed vision for purpose. Liberals would campaign on behalf of expanding the suffrage or reforming the most blatant ills of laissez-faire by arguing for moderate change in piecemeal fashion; politics, for them, was about gaining ground in a long-term campaign to make the world a fairer place, not about radical transformation that would bring about a more just world in the here-and-now. If liberals suffered from any ailment during the latter part of the nineteenth century, it was an excess of caution. In *The Prime Minister*, Anthony Trollope allows his protagonist, Plantagenet Palliser, to inform fellow parliamentarian Phineas Finn that liberalism stands for "lessening differences," only to then suggest that such an ideal—which he refuses to designate by the term "equality"—should be put off until a millennium "so distant that we need not even think of it as possible."

If nineteenth-century liberals lacked passion, they also lacked anything resembling an apocalyptic sense of expectation. Toward the latter half of the nineteenth century, Great Britain experienced a flowering of liberal political philosophy. The thinkers associated with "the new liberalism"—among them T. H. Green, L. T. Hobhouse, Bernard Bosanquet, and J. A. Hobson—resolved the tension in John Stuart Mill's work between individual liberty and social purpose by shifting their focus away from laissez-faire in favor of a positive state that could provide for the welfare of all. In so doing, they also resolved Mill's ambivalence about Romanticism and realism. Green, in particular, the religiously motivated reformer who did so much to advance the idea that all people should be treated with equal dignity, lacked the appeals to heroic individualism one can find in *On Liberty*. Green's respect for social institutions and his insistence on the slow but steady course of human improvement were the exact opposite of a Romantic outlook on the world.

Marxism, by contrast, not only came to be viewed as an ideology but became the nineteenth-century ideology par excellence. Despite Marx's efforts to identify ideology with the bourgeoisie's attempts to mask the oppressiveness of its rule, ideology increasingly was defined not as the science of ideas but as a comprehensive theory about how the world ought to be organized. By that revised definition, Marxism more than qualified: to identify with it was to stand in radical protest against the world as it was in favor of a dream about what the world could be, all based on a comprehensive account of the human condition and the specification of a historical agent that could make our fallen world whole once again. And in the fervor unleashed by war, revolution, and ultimately the rise of totalitarianism, Marxism would not become the only ideology. Today, the term is used to characterize socialism, fascism, populism, anarchism, or religiously inspired movements such as Islamism or Christianity, all of which express a longing for a world more perfect than the one in which we currently live.

It is common to view both liberalism and conservatism as ideologies. But both come in forms that do not correspond to that characterization. There can certainly be found ideological conservatives in the modern world; neoconservative romantics easily qualify. Yet conservatism has other varieties, especially including those who insist on resisting passion in favor of reason or raise flags of caution toward any overly ambitious schemes whether they emerge from the right or the left. Along similar lines, liberals have at times been known for their susceptibility to ideological thinking, especially when they reveal soft spots toward more militant comrades to their left. Yet temperamentally speaking, liberalism is truest to its heritage when it rejects ideological thinking in favor of the idea that the first step necessary in changing the world is to understand it as it actually exists.

Liberals of this realistic bent have been uncomfortable with ideology for the same reason they have distrusted militarism and nationalism: ideological thinking can slide too easily into romantic thinking. It surely did for Marxism, which aimed, above all else, to shatter the chains that kept human beings from realizing their full potentiality. Much the same was true of all the ideological currents of the nineteenth and twentieth centuries, which were distrustful of the compromises necessary for political stability, looked with sympathy upon black-and-white struggles between good and evil, condemned moderation for its prudence, were persuaded that the ends justified the means, and expressed suspicion toward those near them on the political spectrum while being willing to ally with those furthest apart. In ideological times—perceptively characterized by the New School for Social Research political scientist Aristide Zolberg as "moments of madness"—liberalism's belief in individualism can transform itself into a defense of heroism and its preference for pragmatism can seem synonymous with opportunism. But for liberalism in general, "cold rules," as another political scientist, Harvard's Nancy Rosenblum, puts it, "offer relief to overheated sensibilities." Liberalism's preference is always to side with the interests over the passions. Isaiah Berlin captures this liberal sensibility when he quotes, as he does with some frequency, Kant's observation that "out of the crooked timber of humanity, no straight thing was ever made."

The term "ideology" originated in Europe. European politics, moreover, have historically been more tempted by extremism than have politics in North America. Yet in the years after World War II, a group of American thinkers produced one of the great milestones in the history of liberal thought: as persuasive a case on behalf of liberalism's anti-ideological stance as has ever been made. Interestingly enough, none of them was a political philosopher, although one of them, Louis Hartz, was well versed in American political thought (which, before he wrote *The Liberal Tradition in America*, was a widely neglected subject). Their intellectual backgrounds were eclectic: literary criticism (the Columbia University English professor Lionel Trilling); religion (Reinhold Niebuhr, the liberal Protestant theologian); history (Richard Hofstadter, also of Columbia, as well as the presidential adviser Arthur Schlesinger, Jr.); sociology (Harvard's Daniel Bell and Berkeley's Seymour Martin Lipset); and even a longshoreman (Eric Hoffer). Only a few of them preferred writing books; most were more comfortable with essays. Their work was not especially well regarded in the academy; Hofstadter, for example, would be criticized for spending insufficient time in the archives. They did not always agree with each other, and not all of what they had to say stands the test of time. But read together, their work continues to resonate, especially at a time when ideological thinking—more these days on the right than on the left— dominates public discussion.

Writing in 1949, the year before Mill's essays on Bentham and Coleridge became widely available, Trilling turned to those essays to sharpen his reflections on the liberal imagination. Coleridge's writing in particular, Trilling believed, helps us realize that "the conscious and the unconscious life of liberalism are not always in accord." In other essays published after that one, Trilling argued that literature—broadly defined to include not only novelists such as Nathaniel Hawthorne and Henry James but thinkers such as Sigmund Freud and David Riesman, author of the best-selling *The Lonely Crowd*—can fill the resulting gap by adding "an awareness of complexity and difficulty" to liberalism's tendency "to organize the elements of life in a rational way." Absent a serious conservative tradition in America—whether Trilling was right or wrong on that point is certainly open to debate—any checks on liberalism's ambitions would have to come from liberalism itself. For Trilling, the liberal imagination was an ironic imagination; nothing, including liberalism itself, ought to be taken literally.

Irony—the need to distance oneself from what seems most apparent because life tends to be complicated rather than simple—became the signal contribution postwar American liberals made to the way we think about politics. Just as Trilling found a world in turmoil under the seemingly placid surface of a Jane Austen novel, Hofstadter discovered that the historical figures liberals love to love—Andrew Jackson, the populists, even the revered Franklin Delano Roosevelt—may have had dark motives of their own. Hofstadter applied to American history the lesson taught by his Columbia University colleague Robert Merton in 1936: that while we intend by our acts to do one thing, the consequences of those acts may result in something else entirely. Based upon that insight, it was a short step to conclude, as many a neoconservative did, that government intervention into the economy to right a wrong could wind up creating a new form of injustice, or that the necessary work of defending liberal democracy against communism could bring to power anti-Communist demagogues with little appreciation of the virtues of liberal democracy.

Postwar liberals remained liberals; indeed some of them, such as Bell and Hofstadter, were among the first to perceive the dangers associated with the radical right. But theirs was a post-totalitarian form of liberalism, bound, after the experiences of communism and fascism, to be different from the liberalism of a more innocent age. Tempered by the experience of ideological extremism, liberalism would have to occupy what Schlesinger called "the vital center," a place obviously distinct from the totalitarian right, but at the same time marked off from what Schlesinger called "doughfaced progressivism," which believes in "the more subtle sensations of the perfect syllogism, the lost cause, the permanent minority, where life can be safe from the exacting job of trying to work out wise policies in an imperfect world."

Irony, in the mind of these thinkers, came to be associated with maturity. In our youth, whether as an individual or as a nation, we are given to romantic longings. But as we age we grow wiser, as Niebuhr put it, "because so many of our dreams of our nation have been so cruelly refuted by history." Niebuhr was instrumental in informing his fellow intellectuals that, with the arrival of the Cold War, the United States could never return to its more innocent ways. "Our American nation," he wrote in 1952 in *The Irony of American History*, "involved in its vast responsibilities, must slough off many illusions which were derived from the experience and the ideologies of its childhood. Otherwise either we will seek escape from responsibilities which involve unavoidable guilt, or we will be plunged into unavoidable guilt by too great confidence in our virtue." Niebuhr's warning anticipates with remarkable accuracy what happens when ideology and innocence combine, as they did so tragically in Iraq, to produce a foreign policy that, based on the premise that the United States can do no wrong, was incapable of getting anything right.

Daniel Bell brought all the threads of this way of thinking together in his seminal essay "The End of Ideology." Read as a prediction about the future, which in some ways it was, Bell's essay failed to anticipate the rise of both the New Left and the New Right; it is especially problematic to read, after leaders such as Margaret Thatcher and Ronald Reagan vociferously pledged themselves to the laissez-faire economics of Adam Smith, that "few 'classic' liberals insist that the State should play no role in the economy." But Bell's essay is dead-on correct in understanding that ideology is what happens when thinkers are deaf to irony. "What gives ideology its force is its passion. . . . For the ideologue, truth arises in action, and meaning is given to experience by the 'transforming moment.' He comes alive, not in the contemplation, but in 'the deed.' One might say, in fact, that the most important, latent function of ideology is to tap emotion." With this portrayal, Bell evokes the Romantic poets longing for battle so that human beings can experience at the margins what they lack in their conventional lives. His ideologue is as well the nineteenth-century nationalist identifying the existence of his country with the improvement of mankind. "The young intellectual," Bell wrote, "is unhappy because the 'middle way' is for the middle-aged, not for him; it is without passion and it is deadening." Consider this, then, the tragedy of the intellectual: in his youth he lacks for caution, while in his maturity he lacks for zeal.

Yet a lack of zeal is not necessarily a bad thing, because, lacking it, we are more likely to act responsibly. For the liberal ironists who wrote explicitly about politics, and especially for Daniel Bell, no text was more important in developing their distaste for ideology than "Politics as a Vocation," a lecture delivered by Max Weber in 1918. In his lecture, Weber drew a distinction between "an ethic of responsibility," which seeks to contain the violence always implicit in politics, and an "ethic of ultimate ends," which views political power as an opportunity to bring into being a particular goal, irrespective of the means used to achieve it. Weber's preference was for the former. Echoing Clausewitz, who stressed calm in the face of the turbulence of battle, Weber insisted that the responsible politician lets "realities work upon him with inner concentration and calmness." He ought to be a man of passion, Weber believed, but passion "in the sense of matter-of-factness," not passion in the form of what another German sociologist of Weber's era, Georg Simmel, called a "sterile excitation," which leads to the "romanticism of the intellectually interesting." Distance, including distance toward oneself, Weber argued, is an essential requirement of responsible political conduct. Let the ethic of ultimate ends remain where it belongs, for example in the Sermon on the Mount. Only a leader who understands the nature of responsibility can be trusted with the realities of power because he will be sure "that he shall not crumble when the world from his point of view is too stupid or base for what he wants to offer."

Weber's understanding of moral responsibility, which owes much to the dispassion of Kant, was, as Bell pointed out, foreign to a romantic sensibility. In relying on him, postwar liberals brought to the United States a way of thinking about politics that stood in sharp contrast to well-meaning but frequently naïve forms of populism and progressivism. Progressivism in particular differs from liberalism because the former lacks an ironic imagination while the latter does not; from the days of Woodrow Wilson to the fellow traveling of Henry Wallace's Progressive Party of 1948 so strongly criticized by Arthur Schlesinger, Jr., to those on the left who would rather be called by that term today, Progressivism, as its identification with progress implies, views the world in straight-and-narrow terms with little allowance made for the byways and indirection that life in a liberal society frequently requires.

There was, of course, a danger to leaving left-wing idealism behind; the journey of the ironic liberals might have ended in conservatism. (Walk down the path explored by Dostoyevsky and Freud, and the ultimate destination will be a fatalism undermining any possibility that human beings can direct their efforts toward purposive ends chosen by themselves.) But nearly all of the liberal ironists never went that far. To be sure, some neoconservatives, such as the longtime *Commentary* editor Norman Podhoretz, trace their roots back to Trilling, and in particular his heavily ironic notion of an "adversary culture," in which the rebels against the established order end up as a new class defending their own self-interest. But even Podhoretz concludes that Trilling, who died in 1975, was a bit soft on the student movements of the 1960s and may never have emerged as a full-blown neoconservative.

Whatever Trilling's political views, others from his era, including Schlesinger and Bell, lived into the twenty-first century, and they clearly never succumbed to the neoconservative temptation. (Bell eventually resigned his editorship of *The Public Interest*, the magazine he had edited with Irving Kristol that had published so many of the most influential neoconservative essays of the 1980s and 1990s, while Schlesinger became a determined critic of George W. Bush.) It is not difficult to understand why. Postwar American liberalism developed its ironic stance to distance itself from the ideological left. Over time, it faced an even greater challenge with the development of the ideological right; if you were repulsed by the failure of Progressive presidential candidate Henry Wallace to appreciate the complexities of politics in 1948, you were likely to be appalled at the romantic simplicities of Ronald Reagan in 1980. Once an ironist, always an ironist. If we learn to appreciate that things may not be as we convince ourselves they are, we cannot fall victim to the ideologue preaching the black-and-white message that the world around us is corrupt while the world of the future, whatever form its prophets insist it will take, is filled with unambiguous promise.

Although the ideas of Trilling, Hofstadter, and Bell fell out of favor during the heyday of the New Left, when romantic dreams about violent revolution and complete personal transformation became all too prominent, a taste for irony remains prominent in contemporary thought, especially in the work of the late philosopher Richard Rorty, an iconoclastic thinker and engaging essayist whose ideas drew opposition from all corners of the political spectrum. (Rorty's maternal grandfather was Walter Rauschenbusch, the founder of the Social Gospel.) Rorty's take on the problem is not the same as the one that attracted the early postwar thinkers. For them, irony offered protection against ideology whereas for Rorty it is a defense against metaphysics. The ironist, as Rorty understands him, gives up on the notion that any set of truths, including the truths that inspire liberals, can be grounded in such a way as to make them uncontestable. "An ideal liberal society," Rorty wrote, "is one which has no purpose except freedom, no goal except a willingness to see how much such encounters go and to abide by their outcome." Such a passage evokes John Stuart Mill at his most heroic. Indeed, just like Mill, Rorty searched for the contingent truths a liberal society needs in creative works of literature. "A liberal utopia would be a *poeticized* culture," as he put it in *Contingency, Irony, and Solidarity*, implying that the best of all possible worlds would be one inspired by the dreams of the imagination. In Rorty's thought, irony becomes more of an expression of a romantic temperament than a corrective against it.

It is not clear, however, that Rorty really takes irony to a point where it exists outside the liberal tradition. Rorty's ironic stance is directed primarily against philosophical claims to truth; it is not directed against liberal society per se. As he expresses the point: "The social glue holding together the ideal liberal society . . . consists in little more than a consensus that the point of social organization is to let everybody have a chance at self-creation to the best of his or her abilities, and that that goal requires, besides peace and wealth, the standard 'bourgeois freedoms.'" If the poetic shows the way, the prosaic, in Rorty, still guides how most of us live. This is how Rorty ends up in the same camp as one of American liberalism's most important, and certainly most prosaic, thinkers: the American pragmatist John Dewey. To function well, liberal society, Rorty believes, does not require its citizens to engage in "Socratic requests for definitions and principles." It can get along instead through what he calls "Deweyite requests for concrete

alternatives and programs." Rorty's liberalism may be of the most minimal sort, but it is liberalism nonetheless. "Solidarity has to be constructed out of little pieces, rather than found already waiting, in the
form of an ur-language which all of us recognize when we hear it," he
contended. Expressed that way, Rorty does not seem that far away from
the early postwar liberal ironists after all.

Irony will be needed whenever ideology runs rampant. In the early
days of the Cold War, the threat posed by ideology came from the left
in the form of communism abroad and a certain progressive sympathy
toward communism at home. With communism now dead and socialism on the defensive, ideology is more likely to make an appearance
from the right, whether in the form of free market utopianism or unrealistic hopes in what military power can achieve. Against such
ideological thinking, Jeremy Bentham's empiricism—what Mill calls his
commitment to "never reasoning about wholes till they have been resolved into their parts, never about abstractions till they have been
translated into realities"—seems fairly good advice. No one, to be sure,
can turn to Bentham without at least some qualms about the flatness of
his intellectual surface. Yet for all his faults, Bentham's major contribution to liberalism was to insist on the importance of facts: "He introduced into morals and politics," Mill wrote, "those habits of thought
and modes of investigation, which are essential to the idea of science."
In ideological times, a little testing of theory by the collecting of empirical evidence is surely in order.

ROMANTICISM'S COSTS

"The attack on everything that hems and cramps, that persuades us
that we are part of some great machine from which it is impossible to
break out, since it is a mere illusion that we can leave the prison—that
is the common note of the romantic revolt." This is Isaiah Berlin defining the romantic imagination in a way that, however critical, also man-
ages to capture its appeal. In part a reaction against the modern world,
romanticism also embodies some of modernity's key features. It is a
way of asserting one's identity, either as a person or as a nation, against
convention and complacency, a protest against everything that prevents
us from being what we aspire to be. Without at least some attachment
to romanticism, our lives as individuals would be barely worth living
and our collective identities barely worth defending. No wonder that

Mill, Trilling, and Rorty all ask us to read poetry. There is, or at least there ought to be, a romantic in all of us.

Nonetheless, political romanticism, as we have seen, has been with us since the early nineteenth century and we are thus in a position to assess its consequences. And those consequences have been by and large baleful. Militarism, nationalism, and ideology, all of them romantic in temperament, however appealing in private life, offer temptations to public life that a liberal society must resist.

One might be inclined to overlook the attraction of the Romantic poets toward militarism, for they wrote before America's Civil War and the twentieth century's two world wars showed how truly brutal military engagement can be. But their views cannot be so easily explained away, not when other thinkers of the time, such as Clausewitz, recognized the realities of armed combat. And even if one were to pass over Lord Byron's more fervid rhapsodies on the grounds that, as a poet, he was entitled to a certain license, the same cannot be said of those who have adopted the mantle of romantic militarism in our own time. Max Weber's warning that the state's monopoly of violence ought to produce disinterested and careful leaders stands as a sober rebuke to those spectacularly amateurish neoconservative intellectuals who helped launch America's fantasy-laden war in Iraq. Five years after the invasion of that country, George W. Bush had this to say to Americans stationed there: "It must be exciting for you . . . in some ways romantic, you know, confronting danger. You're really making history, and thanks." That an American president could still speak of the romance of war after so many years of violence producing so little success says much about why Byronic enthusiasm is wildly inappropriate to the actual world in which we live.

Between romantically conservative and pragmatically liberal ways of fighting wars, moreover, there exist considerable grounds for concluding that the latter is preferable. Aristocratic societies do not call upon the full energy of their citizens when they go to war and are frequently marked by a leadership that, based on birth rather than merit, lacks expertise and the legitimacy to command those of ordinary status. Liberal democracies, by contrast, although frequently charged with being insufficiently hard-nosed for the tough business of war fighting, have proven remarkably successful at winning international conflicts. Thanks to the careful empirical research of two political scientists, Dan Reiter and Allan C. Stam, it is now generally accepted that Clausewitz was right: "Armies are microcosms of the societies they come from and, to a large extent, the military mirrors the qualities of the society from which it is drawn. The emphasis on individual initiative in liberal political culture, therefore, spills over into superior initiative on the battlefield." Liberal democracies, Reiter and Stam show in their *Democracies at War*, are slower to go to war than other kinds of societies; but once they do, their soldiers are likely to fight better, their citizens are more likely to give those soldiers their support, and for these reasons and others, they are more likely to win. Wars always produce a demand for heroes. But it remains true today, as it was in the time of Clausewitz, that matter-of-factness wins wars, and liberalism offers a firmer appreciation of matter-of-factness than romantic enthusiasm.

Equally problematic have been the consequences of romantic nationalism. John Patrick Diggins, whose views about Ronald Reagan were discussed earlier, does not think so; he finds Reagan's romanticism inspiring, a much needed corrective to the despair that had taken over the United States before Reagan came to office. Yet it is by no means clear that the United States in the late 1980s required more romantic nationalism than it already had. With the possible collapse of the Soviet Union on the horizon, Americans needed a Niebuhr—someone to remind them that although they were becoming the world's most powerful country, they would need to use their power responsibly and with an appropriate sense of its limits. Instead, their president appealed to their childish innocence, their sense that they are immune from the corruptions that inevitably come along with power, one reason why, despite efforts to include him in the pantheon of great presidents, Reagan in the long run is unlikely ever to belong there. Reagan's true legacy is not the end of the Cold War but a refusal to recognize reality that led directly to America's ill-fated venture in Iraq, a war Americans initially supported because they thought military power could accomplish anything and then turned against when they discovered that military power, by itself, cannot remake the world. Hello, Vietnam?

Ideology, finally, is not serving the world well. Ideology does not win wars, provide hurricane relief, fight hunger, and improve transportation. "What is at stake in our economic decisions today," John F. Kennedy said in his Yale University commencement speech of 1962, "is not some grand warfare of rival ideologies which will sweep the country with passion, but the practical management of a modern economy. What we need is not labels and clichés but more basic discussion of the sophisticated and technical questions involved in keeping a great economic machinery moving forward." It is relatively easy to mock such "end of ideology" pronouncements today, for they seemingly have so little to say to a world caught up in a clash between different religious and ideological worldviews. Even if what we are witnessing is not a clash of civilizations but a competition between cultures, a defense of the liberal way of life—and not just a defense of the policies liberals favor—is in order.

Yet Kennedy's words make considerable sense in the wake of George W. Bush, who brought an ideological approach to every problem he tackled—and left just about every one of those problems worse off. Ideologues are persuaded that there is no such thing as global warming, only to discover, hopefully not too late, that it really exists. They pledge themselves not to talk to countries they find hostile, only eventually to talk to them anyway. They bring the market to bear on problems they believed are caused by too much government, only then to bring government to bear on problems caused by excessive reliance on markets. It takes ideological politicians to bring out the true virtues of realistic ones. Postwar liberal ironists were premature in declaring that ideology will end. But they were not wrong in thinking that ideology must be contained—at least if we are to have a politics capable of recognizing the existence of realities that policies are designed to improve.

On matters of the heart, romanticism touches on the deepest emotions, expands the human imagination, and produces world-class music and art. But however much romanticism can serve as a corrective to liberalism, it ought never to be a substitute for it. "Politics," Max Weber wrote, "is a strong and slow boring of hard boards." That does not sound very dramatic, but its undramatic quality is what makes politics a blessing in disguise. When liberal politics works—either at home or abroad—fewer people are killed in the name of a cause, fewer lives are disrupted to serve as characters in someone else's drama, and leaders who make decisions, including decisions that bring pain and death to the innocent, assume responsibility for their acts. Liberals cannot allow romantic longings to interfere with the awesome responsibilities politics brings in its wake. They ought to be aware of the powerful attractions of militarism, nationalism, and ideology, and they also ought to be strong enough to resist them. Let the passions reign in the museums and concert halls. In the halls of government, reason, however cold, is better than emotions, however heartfelt.

CHAPTER 5

MR. SCHMITT GOES TO WASHINGTON

TIMES OF TURMOIL

Suppose that, during the course of your lifetime, you had been living in France and had witnessed, in your country alone, a violent revolution resulting in the Jacobin Reign of Terror; the rise and fall of the world's first modern dictator; the restoration of the Bourbons, and, with it, the return to prominence of a deeply conservative Catholic Church; and, five months before you died, yet another revolution that brought an end to the Bourbon dynasty and replaced it with the house of Orléans. How would you have responded? If your name had been Benjamin Constant, you would have become one of the most important of modern political philosophers.

Constant, like Rousseau, was a Swiss Protestant by birth. Like Kant, he had praised Rousseau, even calling him a "sublime genius," but his ideas, again like Kant's, had little in common with Rousseau's. Constant is best known for comparing the liberty of the ancients with that of the moderns—and finding the former problematic. In the context of late-eighteenth-century political thought, such a position was decidedly out of the mainstream. In both Europe and the United States at that time, one heard nothing but praise for the ancient Greeks and Romans. Readers were told that the ancients understood the need for virtue, a willingness to turn one's back on self-interest and promote altruistic dedication to the common good, much as Pericles had proclaimed his fellow citizens did in his Funeral Oration for the Athenians who had died in the Peloponnesian War. Great leaders were those who, like the Roman orator Cicero, relied on the brilliance of their rhetoric to call upon men to lead lives of character rather than convenience. Self-government was primarily about governing the self. Politics should be a noble calling, a way of perfecting the imperfections of human nature. It was not about asserting individual rights against the common good; it was about realizing the common good through individual actions.

Constant had seen too much of Maximilien Robespierre, the most bloodthirsty of the French revolutionaries, to be seduced by appeals to republican virtue. An avid reader of Rousseau, Robespierre had learned from the master the necessity to make men good, a well-intentioned enough disposition, but one that led Robespierre himself to the guillotine. All this, Constant believed, had been foreshadowed by the political philosophy of the ancients; as he summarized the way that philosophy had been interpreted by the abbé de Mably, one of Rousseau's disciples, it "demands that the citizen should be entirely subjected in order for the nation to be sovereign, and that the individual should be enslaved for the people to be free." Look behind the classical commitment to virtue, Constant advised, and you will discover a liberty hardly worthy of the name: "All private actions were submitted to a severe surveillance. No importance was given to individual independence, neither in relation to opinions, nor to labour, nor, above all, to religion." As in Greece, so in Rome: "the individual was in some ways lost in the nation, the citizen in the city."

Against this, the liberty of the moderns, distrusted by both the Jacobins on the left and royalists on the right, was far superior. Constant told his listeners—his essay was originally a speech given in 1819 to the Athénée Royal in Paris—to think about what a British citizen, a Frenchman, or an American would say about modern liberty:

For each of them it is the right to be subject only to laws, and to be neither arrested, detained, put to death or maltreated in any way by the arbitrary will of one or more individuals. It is the right of everyone to express their opinion, choose a profession and practice it, to dispose of property, and even to abuse it; to come and go without permission, and without having to account for their motives or undertakings. It is everyone's right to associate with other individuals, either to discuss their interests, or to profess the religion which they and their associates prefer, or even simply to occupy their days or hours with their inclinations and whims. Finally, it is everyone's right to exercise some influence on the administration of government, either by electing all or particular officials, or through representations, petitions, demands to which the authorities are more or less paid to pay heed.

Constant's words—one of the most eloquent statements of the liberal commitment to proceduralism on record—anticipate debates over the concentration and use of political power that would become vitally important in the twenty-first century. Should political leaders be constrained by constitutional rules, including those protecting individual rights and limiting the power of the executive, even in conditions of emergency? Or should those leaders have the flexibility to make decisions as they think best, even if doing so means setting aside constitutional agreements appropriate for normal times but a presumed hindrance when the security of the society is at stake? Constant's answers to those questions were clear: people have rights, constitutions lay down procedures, and leaders must respect both. But not all subsequent political philosophers and statesmen agreed. As a result, we are still arguing on the terrain established by Constant two centuries ago.

Although many philosophers of Constant's time thought that society should return to the liberty of the ancients, he did not believe it would—or could. Ancient Rome and to a slightly lesser degree ancient Greece were small states constantly threatened by, and thus continually preparing for, war. For some writers, especially the British Romantic poets who found in war such virtues as courage and honor, the martial spirit improved the character of a people. Constant, whose writings on this topic were published in 1814 just as Lord Byron was bringing out *Childe Harold's Pilgrimage,* strongly disagreed. In the contemporary world, war, in Constant's view, had become "a disastrous anachronism." Modern societies were commercial ones, and commerce offers so many more advantages to modern citizens than war that it would be the wave of the future. "Commerce rests upon the good understanding of nations with each other; it can be sustained only by justice; it is founded upon equality; it thrives in peace," he wrote. Once exposed to enlightened commerce, society would be reluctant to return to states of unenlightened conflict. So thoroughly would the beneficiaries of modern liberty find war distasteful, Constant believed, that the only way leaders could engage in it would be through lies and hypocrisy. Never would such leaders acknowledge that their aim was to conquer other countries; instead, they "would talk of national independence, as if the independence of a nation were in jeopardy because other nations are independent," and they would "talk of national honour, as if a nation's honour were injured because other nations retained their own."

Throughout his writings, Constant, reflecting on the tumultuous events of his era, developed a series of ideas meant to protect citizens against the zeal of their leaders. Individuals, as we have seen, are entitled to rights—explicit protections against the designs on their private life held by public officials. Those rights, moreover, ought to be embedded in constitutions that establish firm rules about how political power should be organized. The best constitutions, Constant held, were those that separated powers, enabling one branch of government to check the others. While Constant understood the need for a strong executive, he also insisted on the special significance of the legislative branch; bicameralism was a method through which one house of the legislature could oversee the other, and all legislative activity would be committed, as the French term *parlement* implied, to discussion and talk. The political theorist Stephen Holmes defines Constant's purposes this way: "Within the political realm, rules became more fundamental than values. Procedures were fixed and held in common, while ideologies were open to question and subject to peaceful contestation." Constant's accomplishment was to bring an aura of calm to the realm of politics. With all these checks in place, no one, but especially no dictator, would be able to appeal to people's passions in pursuit of objectives defined by himself. Men ought to be governed by constitutions to avoid being governed by emotions.

The American Constitution was drafted and ratified before the outbreak of the French Revolution. There were, nonetheless, important assumptions shared between its authors and Benjamin Constant. Both, for one thing, were influenced by the baron de Montesquieu, the eighteenth-century philosopher and literary figure who had developed the idea of the separation of powers. The Bill of Rights and the French Declaration of the Rights of Man and Citizen were complementary documents, each contributing in important ways to furthering respect for basic human rights. But most important of all, the main author of the Constitution, James Madison, was not especially swayed by the taste for classical virtue held by his fellow Virginian Thomas Jefferson. The liberty of the ancients may have helped frame Jefferson's Declaration of Independence, but Madison's Constitution was a product of the liberty of the moderns. "If all men were angels,"

Madison famously wrote in *The Federalist,* "no government would be necessary."

The United States did not adopt its Constitution to make men more virtuous; if anything, the three-fifths clause, which increased the political power of slaveowners by allowing them to count their slaves as 60 percent of a citizen for purposes of the census, was immoral to a fault. The Constitution was designed to take the passions out of politics by formulating procedures through which political compromises could be reached without taking sides on the ethical views of the parties to those compromises. The trick, as Madison understood it, was not to give any one leader free rein to fulfill his ambition but to make the ambition of leaders in one branch of government counter the ambitions of those in the others.

The period from the Congress of Vienna in 1815 to the eve of World War I in 1914 was, save for the American Civil War and the Crimean War immortalized by Alfred Lord Tennyson, the longest period of peace in modern Western history. Not coincidentally, these were also the years of liberalism's greatest political ascendancy. It is not as if, politically speaking, these were easy years to manage: revolutions and nationalist fervor frequently disturbed the peace. Yet liberal proceduralism's insistence that leaders be guided by rules derived from common agreements among their citizens helped Western societies steer their way through conflicts that, in a pre-liberal age, might have resulted in wars lasting thirty years, or even a hundred. It is true that liberals, in order to accomplish this, held to relatively thin conceptions of the common good; making sweeping ideological claims was not part of the liberal agenda for most of the nineteenth century. But it is just as true that liberalism's inclination to sublimate the quest for virtue into formal rules embodied in constitutional texts permitted one conflict after another to be resolved by means short of violent conflagration.

Still, all good things come to an end, and eventually the liberal world of the nineteenth century collapsed. So, to construct another thought experiment, suppose you were a prominent jurist and political theorist who entered the world sixteen years after your country, Germany, had become a nation-state and who, in the course of *your* life, experienced its defeat in World War I; an attempt to create a revolution based on the Soviet system in the years immediately after that defeat; the creation of Germany's first republic, however shaky; a putsch and ultimately a right-wing revolution displacing that republic in favor of Nazism; the Holocaust that followed; the military defeat of the Nazi regime during World War II; an international trial determined to establish guilt for those who had participated actively in the regime; the eventual division of your country into a democracy in the West and a Communist state in the East; and the building of a wall to prevent those in the latter from mixing with those in the former. (Had you lived just five years longer, you would also have witnessed the crumbling of that wall.) Would you, like Benjamin Constant, have concluded that events as tumultuous as these ought to lead to the reestablishment of a liberal and constitutional order? If your name were Carl Schmitt, you would have done the exact opposite: you would have interpreted the tumult of your times as the best reason for getting rid of liberalism altogether.

Although he did have a brief flirtation with apolitical forms of bohemianism in his early adult years, Schmitt was not one of those thinkers who shifted from one side to the other in the course of his life. Born to conservative Catholic parents in Plettenberg, Westphalia, in 1888, the same town in which he would die ninety-six years later, he was a consistent political reactionary who devoted himself to attacking every aspect of liberal political philosophy. Schmitt, who had worked as a censor in Bavaria during World War I, witnessed at first hand the revolution that exploded in Munich after the Versailles Peace Treaty: an officer working next to him was shot by Communist revolutionaries during the insurrection. By 1921, when he accepted his first position as a law professor, he had already begun to publish the works that would establish his reputation as one of the most darkly seductive political philosophers of modern times.

Schmitt's first book, *Political Romanticism*, came out in 1919. Schmitt correctly understood romanticism as a search for an organic wholeness associated with a simpler way of life, marked above all else by an unwillingness to take responsibility for political action. The romantic, he wrote, "ironically avoids the constraints of objectivity and guards himself against becoming committed to anything. . . . In this way, he preserves his own inner, genial freedom, which consists in not giving up any possibility." Many liberals, seeking inoculation from the Romantic spirit, would have agreed with this critique, but for Schmitt, rather idiosyncratically, liberalism was not an alternative to romanticism but a philosophy sharing its escapism: "tolerance, human rights, individual freedoms—that was all revolution, Rousseauianism, unbridled subjectivism, and thus romanticism." (Even Constant, who so strongly criticized the romantic militarism of his era, could nonetheless be classified by Schmitt as a romantic because he placed such importance on parliamentary discussion, which presumably is engaged in only by dilettantes.) Although *Political Romanticism* never mentioned the recently concluded Great War, it is easily read as an attack on a certain kind of bourgeois sensibility that, in treating politics as an opportunity for self-expression rather than as a struggle for power, left Europe unprepared for the catastrophe about to descend upon it.

Schmitt's most productive years as a political philosopher overlapped with the brief history of the Weimar Republic, and a government that was at one and the same time Germany's first real attempt to put into practice the principles of liberal constitutionalism and the product of a series of unstable compromises capable of falling apart at any time. For Schmitt, Weimar was a hopeless experiment in political naïveté. In *The Crisis of Parliamentary Democracy*, first published in 1923, he argued that the liberal principles behind parliamentary government—openness, competition, discussion, balance—were all becoming obsolete in the face of modern, mass democracy. Rousseau may have been a Romantic but, according to Schmitt, he rightly understood that democracy depends upon the existence of a general will; it is therefore absurd to conclude, as so many liberal thinkers did, that a democratic state achieves its legitimacy through a contract between the people and their representatives. The general will is either present or absent. "Where it exists a contract is meaningless. Where it does not exist, a contract cannot help." If there is no unanimity in society, democracy will degenerate into anarchy. If there is, democracy will transform itself into dictatorship. Indeed, Schmitt believed, democracy and dictatorship are not opposed to one another; what unites them is that neither needs liberal proceduralism.

"The situation of parliamentarism is critical today," Schmitt wrote in a 1926 preface to the second edition of his book, "because the development of modern mass democracy has made argumentative discussion an empty formality." Having a parliament in which great matters of state would be subject to Constant's desired argument and counterargument was little more than "a superfluous decoration, useless and even embarrassing."

If parliamentary government was in crisis, executive government was not. "Legislation is *deliberare,* executive *agere,*" Schmitt wrote: one branch of government talks, while the other one acts. (Here Schmitt relied on Hamilton's call, in *The Federalist Papers,* for "energy" in the executive.) This was not merely some academic point relevant to professors of law. "In case public safety is seriously threatened or disturbed," proclaimed Article 48 of the Weimar Constitution, "the Reich

President may take the measures necessary to reestablish law and order, if necessary using armed force." As with any constitutional text, this one could be interpreted narrowly or broadly. Throughout the 1920s, Schmitt argued that it should be interpreted as broadly as possible. Although the text of Article 48 gave the executive the authority to suspend seven specific articles of the Weimar Constitution, especially those involving basic civil liberties such as freedom of speech and assembly, Schmitt argued that to save the constitution it might be necessary to abrogate nearly all of it, including provisions establishing the separation of powers. In a crisis situation, only the executive is capable of responding in ways that reflect Rousseau's general will. The one branch of government chosen directly by the people ought to be the one whose powers trumped all the others.

Article 48 was eventually invoked. After the Nazis began to show their strength in German elections, a grand coalition of right-wing forces joined together to transfer power from the legislative branch to the executive, instituting a series of complicated political maneuvers that resulted in the ascendancy of Adolf Hitler to the chancellorship with dictatorial powers. Schmitt provided them the intellectual rationale for doing so. Germany faced a state of emergency, he argued, and because it did, extraordinary actions were not only justified but necessary. In *Political Theology*, first published in 1922 and reissued in 1934, he laid out the reasons. "The exception," Schmitt wrote, "is always more interesting than the rule." Real power consists not in following rules but in deciding when rules ought to be followed. Laws can be suspended; the state never can. Power, in other words, is best understood not in times of normality but in times of exception, for it is when laws are suspended or constitutions ignored that we can really appreciate where sovereignty lies. This was Constant turned upside down: instead of procedures restraining power, power determines whether procedures will be permitted.

Besides the idea of the exception, Schmitt is also well known for his "decisionism." If people obey a law, it is because they assume that the law is authoritative. The law's authority, however, stems from political leaders whose own authority enables them to pass legislation. Where, then, lies the authority behind those leaders? If you go far enough in this infinite regress, you will discover, Schmitt argued, that just as theology is dependent upon an ultimate authority vested in God, politics must be invested in a sovereign who "has the monopoly over this last decision." Schmitt himself offered the most succinct definition of his approach: "Making a decision is more important than how a decision is made." It was this no-nonsense insistence on the priority of decisions that led Schmitt to support Hitler. Using decisionist arguments to justify the Nazi seizure of power, Schmitt no longer insisted that the executive embodied the will of the people but argued instead that executive power ought to be supreme because it was the power of last resort; if democracy and dictatorship are really the same thing, the fact that Schmitt changed his ground for justifying supreme authority hardly mattered.

Schmitt was in many ways more Nazi than a number of prominent Nazis. In the summer of 1934, noting in characteristic fashion that "the Führer protected the law," he justified the bloody purge Hitler launched against the leaders of the S.A., or *Sturmabteilung*, the "brown-shirt" thugs upon whom Hitler once relied, in the so-called Night of the Long Knives. To win the Nazis' favor, Schmitt had been willing to engage in ugly Jew-baiting. The most notorious example was the 1936 conference he organized on "Judaism in Legal Studies," which aimed to purge the law of Jewish influences. Schmitt opened and closed the conference by citing Hitler's dictum that "in defending myself against the Jew, I am fighting for the work of the Lord," while adding his own observation that "the Jew does not concern us for his own sake. What we seek and what we are struggling for is our unfalsified own kind, the intact purity of our German *Volk*." His opportunism, however, did not prove to be particularly helpful to his careerism. Schmitt, to his discredit with the Nazi leadership, had once been close to Jewish thinkers, including Leo Strauss. He also joined the Nazi Party relatively late, which was why his party number was 2,098,860, and in the internecine conflicts characteristic of the movement, his tardiness—dare one call it indecision?—would be held against him. The Nazis, who controlled the state, had no need for a theorist of the state.

Still, Schmitt's contribution to political authoritarianism did not end with his emphasis on decisionism. *The Concept of the Political*, published in 1932, offered yet another idea, the friend-enemy distinction, that, although anticipated before him by thinkers from Plato to Machiavelli, would become his most widely cited contribution to political philosophy. In this book, Schmitt wrote that every realm of human endeavor is structured by an irreducible duality. Morality, for example, is concerned with good and evil, aesthetics with the beautiful and ugly, and economics with the profitable and unprofitable. In politics, the core distinction is between friend and foe. That is what makes politics different from everything else. Jesus' call to love your enemy is perfectly appropriate for religion, but it is incompatible with the life-or-death stakes politics always involves. Moral philosophers are preoccupied with justice, but politics has nothing to do with making the world fairer. Economic exchange requires only competition; it does not demand annihilation.

Not so politics. "The political is the most intense and extreme antagonism," Schmitt wrote. War, he believed, is the most violent form that politics takes, but even short of war, politics still requires that you treat your opposition as antagonistic to everything in which you believe. It's not personal; you don't have to hate your enemy. But you do have to be prepared to vanquish him if necessary. *The Concept of the Political* ought to be read not only as a justification for fascism, but as the intellectual foundation for any kind of extremist politics; what liberals have always found distasteful—bitter conflict that inevitably results in violence—Schmitt found essential, if not downright attractive.

The Concept of the Political brought Schmitt's crusade against liberalism to its logical conclusion. Liberalism, Schmitt argued, was not a mistaken form of politics; it was not a form of politics at all. "All genuine political theories presuppose man to be evil," he argued, and in so doing, they recognize the need for a strong government capable of restraining man's base instincts. But liberalism, lacking any political equivalent of original sin, sees no need for a strong state. Instead of identifying the enemy and then strengthening the state to fight him, liberals, in Schmitt's view, put their faith in "a doctrine of the separation and balance of powers, i.e., a system of checks and balances and controls of state and government," and such a form of government, divided against itself as it is, "cannot be characterized as either a theory of the state or a basic political principle." Searching for a liberal whose ideas most embodied such a desiccated vision of politics, Schmitt settled on Benjamin Constant, a man who, he wrote, "maintains that we are in an age which must necessarily replace the age of wars."

Liberalism, in a word, is dangerous; by seeking to disarm the state in the face of its enemies, "it joins their side and aids them." At the same time, and in something of a contradictory fashion, it is also self-defeating. For Schmitt, politics is everywhere; to deny a role for politics as Schmitt defined it, which he claimed that liberals do, is to engage in politics without acknowledging that this is what one is doing. A classic case presents itself in foreign policy, where liberals frequently insist that they represent the best interests of humanity. But war cannot be fought on behalf of humanity because humanity as such has no enemy. "When a state fights its political enemy in the name of humanity,"

Schmitt therefore concluded, "it is not a war for the sake of humanity, but a war wherein a particular state seeks to usurp a universal concept against its military opponent." The same holds true in domestic politics. Although liberals try to make a distinction between society, where politics does not rule, and the state, where it does, "it remains self-evident that liberalism's negation of state and the political, its neutralizations, depoliticizations, and declarations of freedom . . . have a certain political meaning, and in a concrete situation these are polemically directed against a specific state and its political power." Claiming to be above the fray is just a way of being in the fray, and a particularly deceptive one at that.

Had Schmitt's theories been applied to himself, his life might well have come to an end after Germany's defeat in World War II; from the perspective of the Allies, after all, Schmitt had worked assiduously on behalf of the enemy and seemed to deserve the fate of others who had aided and abetted the regime. He was, however, lucky enough to be treated if not exactly as a friend then better than most of his fellow enemies. Captured first by the Russians and then by the Americans, who sent him to an internment camp, Schmitt was brought before the War Crimes Tribunal in Nuremberg in 1947. There he took the position that he had never been much of an anti-Semite, and he denied that his writings provided any intellectual foundation for the Nazi regime. Evidently persuasive, he was not charged at Nuremberg but was released to live in his hometown, where he spent the last forty years of his life writing mostly about international affairs and promoting himself among a younger generation of political theorists. Those writings were as conservative as ever. Schmitt defended the idea of what he called "great spaces" (Großräume) in international politics, or arenas in which imperial powers could hold sway, and he became an avid defender of the Franco regime in Spain. He died without having ever once apologized for the role he played in the destruction of Weimar, the success of the Nazis, his refusal to help Jewish fellow academics threatened by the Nazi authorities, or the death of the Jews.

Because their ideas work at cross-purposes, the writings of Constant and Schmitt frame a debate over liberalism's search for fair procedures that can channel violent emotion and conflicting conceptions of the good in peaceful ways. Liberal democracies have survived two world wars intact with their constitutional principles very much still in place, and so it might appear that the winner in the contest between these two thinkers ought to be Constant. Yet among political theorists, Constant, although undergoing an important revival in contemporary

France and to a lesser degree in the United States, has not been given nearly as much attention as Schmitt, whose ideas seem to be discussed everywhere. If any indication was needed that today's political thinkers might have their priorities wrong, this would be it. Schmitt's approach to politics treats tumult as the justification for more tumult, while Constant's treats it as a warning against losing your head. There will always be those who, convinced that we live in exceptional times which demand firm decisions, will insist on Schmitt's way of thinking. In reality, even in moments of crisis, we are best off resisting such pressures and resolving the problems of politics through agreed-upon procedures.

SCHMITT'S SURPRISING LEGACY

The years immediately after World War II gave every indication of the West returning to the liberalism that had dominated Europe before World War I. Totalitarianism, whether in Communist or Fascist form, suppressed such basic rights as freedom of speech and religion; surely, then, the defeat of the latter, combined with determined Western opposition to the former, would lead to a renewed appreciation of the importance of constitutional government. Although the Soviet Union played a major role in the Allied victory over Nazism, very few turned to it as a model for how to run a modern economy, and as Five-Year Plans gave way to economic inefficiencies and new forms of inequality, even the few who did began to have second thoughts, preparing the way for a general consensus behind both the liberal belief in an open economy and the equally liberal commitment to a welfare state that would temper capitalism's extremes. For roughly two decades, from World War II's end in 1945 until the student-led outbreaks of 1968, liberalism seemed consensual, conservatism nonexistent, ideology dead, and history over.

One group of intellectuals clearly not happy with the liberal consensus of the postwar years were those associated with the ultra right. Nineteen sixty-eight, the year of revolution, was also, as it happened, the year a new European right came into existence. GRECE, the *Groupement de recherche et d'études pour la civilisation européenne*, founded by the philosopher Alain de Benoist and other intellectuals, became a forum for attacks on modernity and the liberal ideologies associated with it, echoing, along the way, many of the key ideas of Carl Schmitt. "The liberal state," de Benoist wrote together with the journalist Charles Champetier, "all too often synonymous with a republic of judges, is committed to the parallel goals of abstaining from proposing a model of the good life while seeking to neutralize conflicts inherent in the diversity of social life by pursuing policies aimed at determining, by purely judicial procedures, what is just rather than what is good." Benoist was not alone in his Schmitt-inspired critique of liberalism; in Germany, *Junge Freiheit,* a weekly newspaper begun in 1986, became another place where Schmitt's ideas were kept alive; and in Italy Gianfranco Miglio, the intellectual inspiration for the Northern League, a right-wing populist secessionist movement, learned from Schmitt and also promoted his ideas among younger generations of right-wing thinkers. For any European philosopher convinced that the path of modernity was the wrong path to take, a trek to Plettenberg, or an exchange of letters with the sage of anti-liberalism, became a *rite de passage.*

There is no exact equivalent of the *nouvelle droite* among British and American thinkers. There do exist so-called paleoconservatives, such as Paul Gottfried, a humanities professor at Elizabethtown College in Pennsylvania, who share with European new rightists an appreciation of Carl Schmitt and especially his willingness to utter, as Gottfried puts it in *Carl Schmitt: Politics and Theory,* "grim truths that democratic idealists chose to ignore." Still, paleoconservatism is less authoritarian in its instincts than Schmitt was. Its leading adherents—Patrick Buchanan, the media commentator and former Republican presidential candidate, is the best known American public figure influenced by its ideas—share at least a smidgen of Schmitt's anti-Semitism. But they are isolationists in foreign policy who worry about any excessive concentration of political power in the executive branch, a position far from Schmitt's point of view.

If paleoconservatives owe only some things to Schmitt, many (although alas not all) neoconservatives owe less. It is not just that Schmitt's virulent anti-Semitism is a rather significant obstacle for neoconservative theorists, a large number of whom are Jewish, to overlook; Schmitt was also a critic of the neo-Wilsonian language that neoconservatives sometimes use to justify American involvement in the politics of the Middle East. Like many European reactionaries, moreover, Schmitt was fiercely anti-American—the United States, after all, is the perfect realization of the modernity that European reactionaries hate—and anti-Americanism sits as uncomfortably with neoconservatism as anti-Semitism. Neoconservatism's great mentor, as I've said, was Leo Strauss, and while Strauss and Schmitt were once close—Schmitt wrote a letter of recommendation for Strauss that helped him leave Germany in 1932, the same year in which Strauss wrote a review of *The Concept of the Political* arguing that Schmitt was not antiliberal *enough*—Strauss's writings in the United States tended to treat modern liberalism as misguided rather than as evil. And Strauss and his students were instrumental in developing an appreciation for the U.S. Constitution that Schmitt frequently held in contempt.

This, however, did not prevent Strauss from adopting Schmittian ways of thinking from time to time; the following passage, from his *Natural Right and History,* published in 1953, could just as easily have been written by Schmitt: "In extreme situations there may be conflicts between what the self-preservation of society requires and the requirements of communicative and distributive justice. In such situations, and only in such situations, it can justly be said that the public safety is the highest law." Strauss and his students could find numerous examples in theory and practice to justify such a point of view, from Machiavelli's writings on leadership to Abraham Lincoln's suspension of habeas corpus during the Civil War; even John Locke wrote of the "prerogative," or the power, inevitably associated with the executive branch of government, "to act according to discretion, for the public good, without the prescription of the law, and sometimes against it." When Strauss noted that "natural right must be mutable in order to be able to cope with the inventiveness of evil," he left considerable room for those inventive in finding ways to justify the suspension of agreed-upon constitutional procedures to combat that evil. Neoconservatives should not be included in the Schmitt camp, but a propensity toward Schmittism can nonetheless be found among them.

Oddly enough, Schmitt fascinates thinkers on the left as well as the right. It is not that left-wing thinkers have any sympathies with Schmitt's Nazism. But Schmitt was, if nothing else, the twentieth century's most powerful critic of liberalism, and for leftist thinkers who view liberalism as too moderate politically and excessively thin philosophically, Schmitt's unapologetic attacks on just about everything in which liberals believe are bound to seem refreshing. To the extent that there is a revival of Schmitt's ideas taking place in Europe and the United States, it is not because of what is happening on the right. It is because Schmitt has become something of a hero to the postmodern left.

The sources of this revival are varied. *Telos,* a journal founded in 1968, the same year in which GRECE came into existence, at first dedicated itself to bringing Marxist critical theory to American audiences before starting a campaign in the 1980s to resurrect Schmitt's legacy. Impressed by Schmitt's critique of liberalism and contempt for Wilsonian idealism, *Telos* published, and showed significant appreciation of, the theorists of the European new right, including de Benoist and Miglio. If *Telos* is relatively obscure, Schmitt also features in the thinking of some of the most influential and representative works of the contemporary left, including *Empire*, a best-selling neo-Marxist manifesto by Duke University English professor Michael Hardt and Antonio Negri, an Italian radical who had served prison time for insurrection against the state; the ideas of Jacques Derrida, perhaps the most influential of contemporary postmodern philosophers; and the books of Slavoj Žižek, the dazzling wordsmith and leftist polymath from Slovenia. Radical thinkers have a special affinity with the Schmittian idea of the "exception": not for them the normal politics of parliamentary give-and-take, not at least when, according to the contemporary Italian philosopher Giorgio Agamben, Schmitt's state of exception, originally formulated during the terrible years of the twenties and thirties, "has today reached its maximum worldwide deployment." The exception will always be more interesting than the rule for those who slide toward the political extremes, whichever extreme it happens to be.

Schmitt's friend-enemy distinction has been as popular on the left as his notion of the exception. *The Concept of the Political*, for example, figures especially prominently in the writings of Chantal Mouffe, the Belgian-born post-Marxist political philosopher teaching at the University of Westminster in London, who describes Schmitt, in the course of just two sentences, as "brilliant," "pertinent," "rigorous," and "perspicacious." "Many people," Mouffe writes of her decision to engage with such a prominent Nazi theorist, "will find it perverse if not outrageous," yet, she continues, "I believe that it is the intellectual force of theorists, not their moral qualities, that should be the decisive criteria in deciding whether we need to establish a dialogue with their work."

For Mouffe, the really important point is that *The Concept of the Political* is, in much the same way Giorgio Agamben views the state of exception, "more relevant than ever." We live in an era of pluralistic conflict in which people belong to groups with radically different identities and conceptions of the good life, she believes. No formula can be found to resolve all these differences, and no procedures exist for domesticating them. Mouffe therefore proposes to think with Schmitt against Schmitt; she agrees with him that efforts to resolve or paper over deep disagreements is "a dangerous liberal illusion which renders us incapable of grasping the phenomenon of politics," even if she is not prepared to go all the way with Schmitt in abandoning liberal democracy. Liberalism, in her view, is blind to politics and Schmitt, for all his

faults, was not. The working class, the stigmatized, the oppressed—
they should not settle for liberal proceduralism but should fight back
against the powerful forces by revitalizing the political, a strategy that
Mouffe advocates but leaves frustratingly vague.

Schmitt's ideas loom so large over the contemporary left that one
need not even refer to him in order to be influenced by him. One of
America's best known academic theorists, Stanley Fish, who writes
about an impressively wide variety of subjects, has never devoted an
essay to Carl Schmitt. Yet significant traces of Schmittism can be
detected in nearly everything he does write. Like Schmitt, Fish is preoccupied, even obsessed, by liberalism, and while he may write something
here or there about conservatives, he has never shown any particular
interest in conservatism. What fascinates Fish about liberalism, moreover, is exactly what drew Schmitt to the subject: the conviction that
liberalism is both dangerous and impossible at the same time; indeed,
Fish believes that liberalism is dangerous because it is impossible,
holding out possibilities to accommodate different points of view that
it can never realize. Examine any liberal principle—free speech, academic freedom, religious tolerance, race blindness—and, according to
Fish, you will immediately discover that its presumed neutrality is at
best a sham and at worst a clever ploy.

Since Fish acknowledges with refreshing honesty that he applies
the same rhetorical strategy to all liberal principles, any one of them can
be used to illustrate his argument. Academic freedom therefore offers a
representative example. Rest assured, Fish tells his readers in *The Trouble with Principle,* that he is all in favor of academic freedom. It is the
arguments used by liberals to defend it that fuel his critical energy. Advocates on behalf of academic freedom claim they are open to all points of
view. "However," Fish continues, "if a form of speech or advocacy will
not offer itself for discussion but simply declares itself to be the truth to
which all must bend, academic freedom will reject it as illiberal." Liberals, in short, just as Schmitt claimed, say that they are neutral between
different points of view when in actuality they are trying to impose one
point of view—their own—on those who disagree with them. "It's a
great move," Fish concludes, "in which liberalism, in the form of academic freedom, gets to display its generosity while at the same time
cutting the heart out of the views to which that generosity is extended."

Not only is the liberal commitment to principle impossible to realize but, again echoing Schmitt, Fish writes that "many bad things are
done in its name." Were liberals to present themselves for what they

are—people with a passionate point of view—they could have arguments with people whose passions lie in other directions. But this is not what liberals do. Instead of defending their politics, they pretend that they have no politics. (Here, then, is one difference between Schmitt and Fish: to the former, liberals are apolitical; to the latter, they are hyperpolitical.) They hide behind words—"fairness," "impartiality," and "justice" are some of them—that are totally devoid of substantive meaning. When liberals, aware, as others are not, of the game they are playing, then rush in and identify their substantive positions with these presumably neutral standards, their true disingenuousness reveals itself: they gain the unusual advantage of capturing not only the low ground of policy but the high ground of procedure. An ideology ostensibly dedicated to fairness thus becomes inherently unfair, forcing its opponents, if they are to make a substantive case for their view of the world, to appear to be against impartiality, mutual respect, due process of law, and all the other good things that everyone, irrespective of their political views, is almost supposed to admire. If liberals were honest—which in Fish's view they never are—they would, to continue with the example of academic freedom, simply say that "the presence of Marxists on campus is beneficial to education and the presence of bigots and racists is not, and that's all there is to it."

Conservatives attack liberals for the positions they take. Fish, whose positions on substantive issues lean toward the left, attacks liberals for the way they take them. "My argument against hewing to liberal platitudes as a matter of principle is also an argument against the dream of procedural justice," he writes. Despite a two-hundred-year period in which liberalism helped sublimate intense political conflicts into legal and constitutional disputes over procedures that helped resolve them, Fish—like Schmitt, or for that matter like Alain de Benoist—is convinced that liberal proceduralism is bankrupt. Substantive liberalism and procedural liberalism do not always go together, but when they do, they do so for a reason. To achieve their political goals of greater freedom and equality, liberals typically believe, one must also be constantly on guard against efforts by dominant groups in the society to rig the rules in favor of unfreedom and inequality. Right-wingers such as Schmitt understand this connection, which is why, to promote a reactionary agenda of racial or religious superiority, they simultaneously come out so strongly against liberal ideas of fairness. But why would someone like Fish, who is anything but a right-winger in his substantive views, find liberal proceduralism so problematic?

This is a question Fish never really answers. Indeed, it is precisely when he reaches this point in his analysis that he runs away from an answer. Like other German theorists of the state, Carl Schmitt held to the idea·that politics is always about violence; if we really and truly disagree with other people, we ought to treat them as enemies. Fish does not follow Schmitt this far. To be sure, he fills his books with examples of people who ought to, and usually do, hate each other: secular liberals dealing with religious fundamentalists; full-stop opponents of affirmative action confronting those who support it; defenders of speech codes and critics of hate-crime laws. But when Fish calls for fundamentalist religious believers and liberal secularists to go at each other rather than to hide behind such abstractions as tolerance or religious freedom, he does not urge them to take up arms and shoot to kill. One wonders why not. If they really do hold completely incommensurable points of view, shouldn't each side in a culture war try to remove the other from the political system they are forced to share?

Perhaps liberals and conservatives, for all their political disagreements, refrain from taking up arms against each other, except on the most far-out extremes, because the world in which we live has come to rely so much on liberal proceduralism and, for this reason, politics nearly always stops short of violence. Through his choice of examples, Fish acknowledges at least indirectly that this is the case; a law professor, he relies on cases adjudicated in the courts, political institutions whose major purpose is to resolve disputes through the application of neutral principles—and then to justify their decisions in writing by appealing to standards applicable to both parties in the case. Had the parties to these disagreements decided instead to treat each other as enemies, their disputes never would have reached those institutions of liberal proceduralism that enable Fish to treat them as examples of how irrelevant liberal proceduralism has become.

Jan-Werner Müller is therefore correct to argue that among many of the leftist thinkers attracted to the ideas of Carl Schmitt can be found the very political tendency against which Schmitt warned in his first book: a form of political romanticism that refuses to accept the consequences of its own line of argument. Writers such as Stanley Fish may think they are standing over liberalism's tombstone delivering its funeral oration. In actuality, they are proving the very viability of the liberal proceduralism they attack. Only if liberalism already exists can one claim that liberalism is impossible—and avoid either the civil war or the dictatorship that would follow if it really were.

DECISIONISM IN D.C.

Carl Schmitt in theory is one thing; confined to a few conservatives on the right and a somewhat greater number of envious postmodernists on the left, Schmitt's ideas have not reached the informed reading public. Schmitt's books are destined to be confined to the political theory seminar room for some time to come.

Schmitt in practice is something else entirely. There will exist a Schmittian temptation whenever the leaders of political movements or parties become convinced that obtaining and holding on to power are the only objectives that matter and that any tactics helpful to realizing those ends, no matter how much they may violate conditions of fairness, understandings of reciprocity, or respect for procedures, are justified. Such proclivities tend to be relatively rare in liberal democracies. In Great Britain, for example, twentieth-century politics was frequently marked by informal agreements between leaders of the major parties *not* to challenge each other too severely, recognizing that each would have its turn in power and that the only effective way to pass legislation would be through some kind of bipartisan agreement. "Butskillism," a term coined by *The Economist* in 1954, is the best example. During the 1950s, the Tory leader "Rab" Butler and Hugh Gaitskell, the leader of the Labour Party, agreed so much on economic policy that it hardly mattered which of them held office. Something similar took place in the United States during the same period when the Republican president Dwight D. Eisenhower worked together with the Democrats who controlled Congress to pass such noncontroversial legislation as the Interstate Highway Act. Under conditions such as these, harsh rhetoric was more likely to be heard within the parties than between them; extreme conservatives detested moderate Republicans, just as the emerging New Left mobilized its anger against liberals in the Democratic Party.

All this has changed in recent years. There are many reasons for the marked increase in ideological politics that took place in both Britain and the United States in the last two decades of the twentieth century. Some of them, such as the rise of new technologies like cable television and the Internet, are not political at all. But the major reason *is* political: on both ends of the political spectrum, but particularly on the right, it became evident that a political movement could win just enough votes to hold office and pass legislation by appealing to the ideological base of its own party rather than by courting independents and moderates. In the United States, the man most responsible for the spread of this kind of politics was Karl Rove. Along with talk radio hosts such as Rush Limbaugh and extreme right pundits like Ann Coulter, Rove engaged in a winner-take-all style of politics quite different from the consensual search for the middle so prevalent a generation ago. Rove's way of doing politics eventually proved to be counterproductive, turning off independently minded voters and contributing to its share of Republican defeats. But when Rovian theories were at the height of their influence, particularly during the first term of the George W. Bush presidency, American politics took on a decidedly Schmittian tone. To say this is not to conclude that because Schmitt was a Nazi it follows that people who practice politics in a Schmittian mode are. My claim, rather, is this: the kind of politics in which people such as Rove and Limbaugh engage have little or nothing in common with the proceduralism of Constant and a great deal in common with the scorched-earth approach to politics emphasized by Schmitt.

Although considerably weakened, right-wing extremism in the Schmittian mode is nonetheless still very much alive among the activists and enthusiasts who constitute the core base of the Republican Party. (The 2008 Republican nominee for vice president, Sarah Palin, excelled in just this kind of political attack.) These are people who have no problem identifying liberals and Democrats as enemies of the state or treating their policy decisions about the war in Iraq as the equivalent of treason. For them, political argument is about talking points rather than talk: one writes or speaks, not to engage in dialogue, but to hammer home an already formulated point of view. Their discipline is impressive, their energy unflagging, their commitment unwavering, and they take politics more seriously than do many liberals. At the same time, they poison the political air by throwing about extreme, biased, and frequently false charges against their opponents, as if "politics" really is another term for "war." You do not call publicly for the assassination of a former vice president of the United States—as Ann Coulter did for Al Gore—unless you really are convinced that liberalism is an evil force let loose in the land.

People of this sort not only advocate conservative goals, they do so through conservative means. Since the days of Constant, Madison, and the framers of the Constitution, liberal proceduralists think of politics as a means to an end. This kind of conservatism treats politics as an end in itself. For liberals of an earlier era, politics stops at the water's edge; for these right-wing activists, politics never stops. Procedural liberals treat conservatives as antagonists today but potential allies on another issue tomorrow; right-wing zealots treat liberals as an enemy at home, never to be trusted, and certainly never to be given the benefit of any doubts. Liberal political philosophers inspired by proceduralism think there are neutral points between liberalism and conservatism; for the hard-core right, anyone who is not a conservative must be a liberal. Liberal proceduralists hold that politics ought to be judged against an independent ideal such as human welfare or the greatest good for the greatest number; conservative cultural warriors evaluate policies by whether they fulfill conservative objectives. Liberals typically treat policy as distinct from politics; Schmittian conservatives view them as identical. Liberals such as Constant hoped that politics could dampen passions; these conservative activists are bent on inflaming them. And, most important of all, procedural liberals want to put boundaries on the political by claiming that individuals have certain rights that no government can take away, while conservative militants of this kind argue that in cases of emergency (they always find cases of emergency) the reach and capacity of the state cannot be challenged.

This last point became more than a matter of academic theoretical speculation when a conservative law professor, John Yoo of Berkeley, became deputy assistant attorney general in the Office of Legal Counsel of the Department of Justice in the administration of George W. Bush. Like Stanley Fish, Yoo never discusses the ideas of Carl Schmitt. But his critique of liberal proceduralism overlaps in remarkable ways with two of Schmitt's concepts: decisionism and the state of exception.

Yoo believes that our times are as tumultuous as any, certainly more so than they were, for example, during the Cold War. But September 11, 2001, changed that equation dramatically, for after that event, he writes, "the costs of inaction can be extremely high—the possibility of a direct attack against the United States and the deaths of thousands of citizens." Three threats are especially worrisome: the ease with which weapons of mass destruction can be created and deployed; the rise to prominence of rogue nations; and terrorism of the kind employed by al-Qaeda. Before September 11, scholars believed "that in the absence of government action peace would generally be the default state." After September 11, Yoo argues, "this assumption is no longer realistic. The United States must have the option to use force earlier and more quickly than in the past." If this means a change in the rules by which the United States fights wars, so be it. "To pretend that rules written at the end of World War II, before terrorist organizations and the proliferation of know-how about weapons of mass destruction, are perfectly suitable for this new environment refuses to confront new realities," Yoo concludes.

Fortunately, or so Yoo would have his readers believe, one set of rules that does not have to be discarded is the one contained in the Constitution. For many if not most legal scholars, one of the most noteworthy features of the Constitution is that, in Constant-like fashion, it separates the different branches of government in order to ensure checks and balances. Yoo disagrees. To be sure, he argues, the Constitution assigns different powers to the executive than it does to the Congress. And at least some of the powers assigned to Congress— to ratify treaties, declare war, and fund the president's foreign policy initiatives—can be viewed as checks on the power of the president in foreign affairs. But none of these provisions in Yoo's view should be taken to mean that Congress and the president have anything like the same level of influence over foreign policy, especially over matters of war and peace. Congress's power to declare war does not mean that Congress initiates a war, only that it "declares" that an already existing war is taking place. Nor does Congress make treaties; the president not only does that, but he and he alone has the authority to interpret how a treaty should be implemented.

The only power Congress really has, especially when it comes to matters of war and peace, is to cut off funding for a war that the president has launched. Yoo acknowledges that in the real world Congress is unlikely to do so, but this is because such a move would be politically unpopular, not because of anything written into America's founding document. The framers of the Constitution did not create—in the spirit of Montesquieu, Constant, or Madison—a system of checks and balances, he believes; instead, they sanctioned "a unitary, energetic executive, but one that took the form of a republican president rather than a hereditary monarch."

Yoo's use of the term "unitary . . . executive" represents the culmination of a way of thinking about presidential power that a determined group of conservative legal scholars have been developing since the Nixon years. During the New Deal and continuing through the years of Lyndon B. Johnson, liberals were generally in favor of expanded presidential authority whereas conservatives, who wanted a smaller government, opposed it. But among this younger generation of conservatives, Congress came to be viewed as an institution very happy to spend money and to raise taxes, policies that only a conservative president could stop. Out of such concerns developed the notion, elaborated in part by John Yoo's brother Christopher, that the president was not only immune from acts of Congress that tried to curtail his power, such as the creation of independent counsels, but he had the authority to curtail the spending proclivities of regulatory agencies within the executive branch itself. The theory of the unitary executive constitutes one of the great intellectual flip-flops in modern constitutional theory. (To be fair here, the same flip-flop occurred on the other end of the political spectrum as liberals such as the late Arthur Schlesinger, Jr., who once believed in a strong and vigorous executive, came to distrust what they called an "imperial presidency" when Republicans rather than Democrats were in office.) Long suspicious of government, and especially the democratically elected president, conservatives had now become enthusiastic advocates on behalf of executive authority.

John Yoo's contribution to this debate has been to argue that September 11 gives the president even more authority than the original theorists of the unitary executive imagined. Yoo took every procedure used by George W. Bush in the war on terror and claimed that all of them could be carried out by the president, and by the president alone, if he determined that they were necessary. The result was not an argument that called for a suspension of the Constitution so much as an interpretation of the Constitution that would have stripped it of its commitments to liberal proceduralism.

Take, for example, the question of warrantless surveillance. In 1978, Congress passed the Foreign Surveillance Intelligence Act, or FISA. Upset with instances of domestic spying within the United States during the Nixon years, Congress created special courts to which the president would have to turn in order to gain approval for wiretapping of foreign agents within the United States. Sensitive to the country's need for intelligence, FISA courts nearly always gave their approval to such requests. To ensure the legality of its intelligence-gathering activities in the aftermath of September 11, the Bush administration could have asked for, and would easily have obtained, not only permission to conduct domestic wiretapping but any revisions of the law it felt necessary.

If one takes seriously Yoo's ideas, as the Bush administration did, no such move was required; the president could simply engage in secret domestic wiretapping without telling anyone, including Congress or any FISA judge, about it. "It is inconceivable," Yoo writes, "that the Constitution would vest in the President the power of commander in chief and chief executive, give him the responsibility to protect the nation from attack, but then disable him from gathering intelligence to use the military most effectively to defeat the enemy." True, there was a law already on the books. But Congress, he believes, has passed unconstitutional laws before and is likely to do so again. "Because the Constitution is the supreme law of the land, neither an act of Congress nor an act of the President can supersede it." President Bush was therefore right to ignore FISA.

Once *The New York Times* revealed the extent to which the Bush administration had been disobeying the law, and once Yoo's arguments for why it could and should engage in such disobedience became public, many constitutional scholars concluded that the Bush administration was engaged in a radical redesign of the U.S. Constitution. But according to Yoo, the exact opposite is the case: it is the critics of the Bush administration who "want to overturn American historical practice in favor of a new and untested theory about the wartime powers of the President and Congress." Only in a Schmittian world is it possible for those who hold the United States to its historical traditions of liberal constitutionalism to be dismissed as radicals, while those who call upon the president to ignore both the text and the spirit of the Constitution are viewed as faithful to it.

Yoo applied the same reasoning to every one of the controversial issues in which he was engaged. Should the United States extend the protections of the Geneva Conventions to the terror suspects it detained? The president, he argued, is not bound by the War Crimes Act of 1996, which made it a crime for any American to violate the Conventions' strictures on how prisoners ought to be treated, nor is the president bound to follow Common Article III of the Conventions themselves, which prohibits torture and cruel treatment. But can the United States engage in torture? In his most infamous memo, Yoo defended the use of interrogation techniques that, while falling short of inflicting permanent damage, are widely viewed as forms of torture. Even if one accepts, improbably to be sure, the Bush administration's claims that it never engaged in torture, could extraordinary interrogation techniques continue after Congress, in 2006, passed the McCain amendment to the Defense Appropriation Act, which mandated that interrogation methods conform to the *U.S. Army Field Manual*?

For Yoo, the McCain amendment was "unwise," a sentiment with which President Bush clearly agreed, for he issued a signing statement indicating that his administration would not be bound by it. (Presidential signing statements, in which the president declares which parts of a law he will enforce and which parts he will not, are another Schmittian innovation; they had been used by presidents before Bush, but the latter relied on them twice as many times as they had been used by all previous presidents combined.) Can the president on his own establish military commissions, thereby bypassing the need to extend basic rights to detainees? The U.S. Supreme Court, in *Hamdan* v. *Rumsfeld*, said it could not, but Yoo believed the Court "displayed a lack of judicial restraint that would have shocked its predecessors." Contrast this with Benjamin Constant, who wrote nearly two centuries ago that "our grandchildren will not believe, unless they are the most abject of people, that legislators, writers and people accused of political crimes were called up before military tribunals, thus setting up, with ferocious irony, blind courage and thoughtless submission as judges of opinion and thought."

For John Yoo, terrorism forces us to confront terrible truths, and one of them is that we ought to end our romance with the law. "Law is critically important to our society generally," Yoo writes, "and to the war on terrorism. But the law is not the end of the matter; indeed, it is often the beginning." Such ways of thinking have led a number of legal scholars to see connections between Schmitt's ideas and those of Yoo and the Bush administration. Even as conservative a legal scholar as Judge Richard Posner, a member of the U.S. Court of Appeals for the Seventh Circuit, who has written his own explanation of why the war on terror requires that the balance between civil liberties and national security be shifted in the direction of the latter, finds Yoo to be offering "an extravagant interpretation of presidential authority" that "confuses commanding the armed forces with exercising dictatorial control over the waging of war, the kind of control exercised by a Napoleon or a Hitler or a Stalin, or by the dictators in the Roman Republic."

Despite the extremism of his views, Yoo was hardly an isolated voice crying out in the wilderness. For two years he worked in the Bush administration and put into legal language the theory of executive authority then held by such influential policymakers as David Addington, Vice President Dick Cheney's key assistant, who, in the words of the former secretary of state Colin Powell, "doesn't care about the Constitution." The administration, in addition, was able to appoint to the Supreme Court two judges, Samuel Alito and John Roberts, whose views on presidential authority were close to those of Yoo and Addington. Not everyone who worked in the Bush administration agreed with Yoo's radical theories of executive power. Jack Goldsmith, a conservative lawyer who had been Yoo's colleague in the Bush Department of Justice, dissented from the more extreme views on executive privilege associated with Bush loyalists. Goldsmith, however, left and Addington stayed. While in office Bush established new precedents that future presidents, Republican or Democratic, can follow if they so choose.

Yoo, moreover, speaks for a movement, a group of conservative scholars who share his faith in unfettered executive action, even if such action violates the law. Harvey Mansfield, Jr., a Harvard political theorist, is interesting in this regard, for Mansfield is a well-known Straussian, as well as a scholar of Machiavelli. For these reasons he illustrates how that strain of Straussian thought sympathetic to declarations of emergency can override other strains respectful of constitutional proceduralism. The framers of the Constitution understood the dangers of any form of tyranny, and so they wrote a document adhering to the rule of law, Mansfield argues. But they also understood the two defects of the rule of law: sometimes adhering to the law will produce a more unsatisfactory result than "the intelligence of a wise man on the spot," and the law, to be effective, needs to be enforced even, if need be, "by one man acting alone." Which view is most appropriate for the times in which we live? "An extreme situation," Leo Strauss once wrote, is one "in which the very existence or independence of a society is at stake." Mansfield has a different view: "In quiet times the rule of law will come to the fore, and the executive can be weak. In stormy times, the rule of law may seem to require the prudence and force that law, or present law, cannot supply, and the executive must be strong." Mansfield leaves no doubt that in his view, our times are so stormy that they require energy in the executive, even if, to achieve that, the rule of law must be suspended. "In other cases," Mansfield writes, "I could see myself defending the rule of law." But not, it would seem, in this one.

Any discussion by serious thinkers and policymakers about abolishing, transcending, or bypassing the rule of law suggests that, to a particular kind of conservative, the United States really is facing a Schmittian moment. The phrase "rule of law," after all, is good shorthand for the major achievement of late-eighteenth- and early-nineteenth-century liberalism. If we are ruled by laws, then adequate procedures are in place to govern us, and hence we have no need of exceptional powers and unitary executives unchecked by the other branches of government. "The rule of law," writes the political philosopher William Scheuerman in *Carl Schmitt: The End of Law*, "renders state action predictable and makes an indisputable contribution to individual freedom." This helps explain why Schmitt devoted so much of his intellectual output to undermining the assumptions that make the rule of law possible. Schmitt believed that no executive can make the decisions he has to make if he is constrained by an authority above him. The same belief is now not only part of the American intellectual debate, it was put into practice by a president of the United States. Somewhere, Schmitt, who viewed the United States as hopelessly addicted to naïve understandings of power, must be smiling.

WARS OF THE IMAGINATION

From the time Thomas Hobbes experienced the English civil war, through the revolutionary conditions that inspired Benjamin Constant, and continuing to Carl Schmitt's participation in the collapse of the Weimar Republic and the rise of Nazism, tumultuous political conditions have had a way of producing profound political philosophy. It is therefore not surprising that September 11 gave rise to reflections on how best to organize liberal democratic governance. It is worth asking two questions about these reflections. One is whether the threat from Islamic-inspired terrorism means that we are living in more tumultuous times than those that confronted the political theorists of earlier eras. The other is whether the political theory produced in the shadow of that threat rises to the level of what the political theorists of earlier periods had written.

Given the fact that even leading liberals such as John Locke had defended executive prerogative in times of emergency, it is not out of the realm of possibility that some shocks to a liberal system may be so great that a suspension of procedures is in order. It is obvious to writers such as John Yoo and Harvey Mansfield that September 11 constituted just such a shock. "We (along with Israel) are the first to face a terrorist enemy intent on carrying out the destruction of our nation," Yoo writes. Literally speaking, this is true: terrorists have long existed— they were the subject of two novels by Joseph Conrad, *The Secret Agent* and *Under Western Eyes*—but none of them possessed the ability to engage in the level of destruction witnessed on that fateful day. But for Yoo, the unprecedented existence of destructive terrorism is treated figuratively as well as literally; it stands for dangers to the American regime so omnipresent that the government will have to go on an indefinite war footing. Someday the threat posed to America by al-Qaeda will ebb, and at that point, the United States can return to a peacetime form of politics in which "Congress enacts laws, the President enforces them, and the courts interpret them." Yoo does not know when that time will be. For now, we have no choice but to recognize that we are at war, and so long as that is the case, "gravity shifts to the executive branch."

The price of the shift will mean major modifications in the way Americans have understood procedural liberalism: individual rights will have to give way to considerations of national security; the principle of checks and balances, at least as it has been traditionally understood, cannot be invoked to limit the power of the president; the Supreme Court should get out of the business of second-guessing the decisions of the military and the commander in chief; the United States need not be bound by international treaties it has previously signed if the president decides otherwise; and the fact that Congress could, if it wanted to, cut off funding for a war "renders unnecessary any formal process requirement for congressional authorization of a declaration of war before hostilities may begin." Yoo's arguments to the contrary, these are surely radical measures. But what if the assumption underlying them—that the threat from international terrorism constitutes a turning point in modern history—turns out not to be true?

No one can doubt the tragic character and historical significance for Americans of the events of September 11. But nor did the deaths recorded on that day come even close to those recorded during the French Revolution and the subsequent Napoleonic Wars or the horrendous experience of world war and totalitarianism in the twentieth century. Liberal democracy survived the French Revolution; indeed, liberalism went on to experience its greatest period of success in the century that followed. Liberal democracy also managed to emerge from the wreckage of the twentieth century. For all the ingeniousness of his arguments about what the framers intended, John Yoo devotes relatively little attention to justifying his assertion that our times are as tumultuous as he claims, or even, for that matter, as dangerous to liberal democratic values as other momentous historic events. Yet if they are not, much of the reason for reinterpreting the Constitution the way he does is removed.

Not only is the case against suspending liberal proceduralism weak, there is also reason to believe that liberalism's procedural commitments strengthen a society in times of crisis rather than weaken it. The best evidence for this lies not in the way the idea of a unitary executive was justified during the Bush years, but with how the newly emboldened president actually used the discretionary power he claimed. During the eight years of the Bush administration, the United States had a strong president but not a wise one. Alas, both American national security and global stability would have been better enhanced by a wise one than a strong one.

The difference between strength and wisdom was on full display during the war in Iraq. When it came to toppling Saddam Hussein, American military power was strong enough to do the job in record time. But when it came to fighting the insurgency that developed in the wake of Hussein's fall from power, American policy failed, and failed badly. Although the ultimate consequences of the U.S. decision to invade Iraq will not be known for years, the declared objective of the invasion—the creation of a democratic state in the Middle East that will act as a source of stability in a dangerous region—is simply not one of the likely outcomes. This was not the way things were supposed to happen according to the theorists of the unitary executive. Bypassing Congress, ignoring laws, and centralizing authority in the president, they argued, ought to provide the "energy" in the executive branch that was so important to Alexander Hamilton. But if all that energy pushes the machine of the state in the wrong direction, as it clearly did in this case, then centralizing power, rather than becoming a help, becomes a hindrance. The single greatest failure of the theory of the unitary executive is this: if one is forced to make a trade-off between liberal proceduralism and a strong commitment to national security, a case might be made for the latter; but if concentrating power in the presidency undermines historical constitutional values and weakens American security at the same time, it is unquestionably the wrong step to take.

The United States has now failed to achieve its stated objectives in two significant wars, one in Vietnam and the other in Iraq. Both were premised on the idea that the president should have the flexibility to do what is necessary, even if Congress and public opinion have to be ignored. Yet in both, the United States began withdrawing troops before "victory" was achieved. In politics, there rarely exist enough cases to fully test a theory. But two losses in two successive wars suggest that in the world in which we live, Schmittian ideas, offered as a form of hyperrealism, lack relevance to the conditions under which contemporary wars are fought. Toughness of rhetoric, a willingness to fight war even when not attacked in order to take conflict to the enemy, and most relevant of all, a willingness to make decisions without consulting other branches of government—all these actions may make people feel secure. But the security they actually offer is illusory. They substitute wars of the imagination for wars in reality.

One feature of the world in which we live is of special help in understanding why efforts to strengthen the executive weaken the country. For both Schmitt and Yoo, Hamilton is the American founding father to whom we ought to turn. Yet for all his brilliance and grand vision of the American future, Hamilton wrote before the rise of mass democracy and was an opponent of the early forms of democracy he witnessed. In today's world, by contrast, democracy is part and parcel of war-making. Troops have to be found and mobilized. Huge sums of money need to be spent. Long wars—Iraq became the longest war in America's history—require sustained public support if they are to be concluded successfully. Liberal democracies learned during the twenti-eth century that world wars were total wars; they could not be won without shared sacrifice and overwhelming support. In the twenty-first century it has also become clear that even localized wars are something like total wars; without strong and continued public support, victory in neither Vietnam nor Iraq was possible. Any president who wants to win a war rather than just fight one has to be prepared to bring the whole country together behind the effort.

This sharing of the burden is precisely what the theory of the uni-tary executive rejects. The idea behind the theory is that the president can determine how and when to fight when it is perfectly obvious that Congress, which provides the money, will ultimately want to be con-sulted if the fighting does not go well. Lacking the support of Con-gress, the theory of the unitary executive by implication holds that the president does not need to frequently consult the electorate either, since there are congressional elections every two years and presidential ones every four. Any president who therefore tries to win a war without the support of the public will pay the price by losing the crucial backing he needs to follow the war to its conclusion. Indeed, any president who goes even further and calls those who disagree with his decision to go to war traitors or defeatists, by relying so strongly on the friend-enemy distinction at home, undermines the capacity of his administration to muster the necessary unity to achieve his objectives abroad.

And here lies the wisdom of liberal proceduralism. It is true that insisting on the priority of constitutionally agreed-upon rules, even in times of emergency, may delay a democratic society from engaging in military action. But after Vietnam and Iraq, both of which proved dis-astrous for the United States, not going to war may be more important in protecting a country's security than going to war. The more impor-tant point, though, is that if military action does need to be taken in the future, the more widespread the input in that decision, the more seri-ous the commitment to that war will be. If the war is necessary and justified, the chances of actually winning are greater when the dynam-ics of liberal proceduralism are permitted to work. The logic seems inescapable: if there really is a danger to the nation, the whole nation must respond. If the president and the president alone perceives a danger and acts without the need to mobilize the nation, the danger of which the president warns cannot be that serious.

All this, interestingly enough, was anticipated by Benjamin Constant. As if he knew that a thinker such as Carl Schmitt would exist long after him, Constant considered the possibility of a state of exception when he chose "to contrast a regular government with one that is not." Even governments in the normal state, he continued, will sometimes allow themselves to be persuaded that their usual ways of conducting the public business will have to give way in the face of an emergency. Such urges, he believed, ought to be resisted: "When a regular government resorts to arbitrary measures, it sacrifices the very aim of its existence to the means which it adopts. . . . Why do we wish authority to repress those who attack our properties, our liberty and our life? Because we want to be assured of their enjoyment. But if our fortune may be destroyed, our liberty threatened, our life disturbed by arbitrary power, what good shall we derive from the protection of authority?" Perhaps, just perhaps, the costs might be worth paying if going to war protected the liberal procedures society ought to value. But rarely will it do so: "The system of warfare, independent of present wars, carries the seeds of future wars," Constant said. "The sovereign who has entered that path, driven by a fatality that he himself has summoned up, cannot at any time revert to peace." Not everything written by early-nineteenth-century liberals turned out to be prescient, but this prediction did.

As Constant's thoughts on the matter suggest, liberalism's respect for proceduralism is not some obsolete burden from earlier times that must be removed if liberal democracies are to protect themselves against external threats, including those posed by terrorists. On the contrary, proceduralism offers liberal democracies strong advantages that they unilaterally discard if they decide too prematurely and too often to declare states of emergency. Liberals do acknowledge the possibility that procedural rules may have to be temporarily suspended; Lincoln's decision to do so, while criticized by some, is generally regarded as one such example. But that took place during a civil war that constituted the most bloody military engagement of its time. No emergency of such magnitude faces the United States today, not even after September 11. The thing about exceptions is that they really ought to be exceptional. September 11 was tragic, terrible, and devastating, but it did not pose a challenge to the existence of liberal democracy and might have, with a different kind of leadership, strengthened it. The best way to protect liberal values is still to act in a liberal way.

CHAPTER 6

HOW LIBERALS SHOULD THINK
ABOUT RELIGION

WARS OF RELIGION, THEN AND NOW

"The New Wars of Religion"—these were the words that graced the cover of the November 1, 2007, issue of *The Economist*. Across Africa, in the former satellites of the Soviet Union, and even in the quintessentially modern United States, the magazine pointed to a thriving revival of religious fervor—and one with the potential to start a new round of religious conflict not unlike the wars that had plagued Europe in the sixteenth and seventeenth centuries. According to a host of social theorists including both Marx and Freud, this should not have been happening. Modern society was supposed to bring about greater secularism and religious peace. Instead, *The Economist* pointed out, religion continues to offer both succor to its followers and discord between its traditions.

A good bit of exaggeration accompanies such arguments. In actuality, as I argued in a response published in *The Atlantic Monthly,* the world has also been witnessing a rise both of nonbelief and of forms of religious expression that owe a considerable debt to secular ways of conducting public business. The notion that the world is about to experience a new round of religious wars is simply not supported by the dynamics of global religious competition: in both the Third World and in the United States, religion, even in its most conservative forms, has more to do with seeking prosperity and promoting individual mobility than it does with submission to an all-powerful deity. Still, there can be no doubt that religion in one form or another retains its attractions. For those desiring to hear Him, God continues to speak, and people continue to listen.

Given the continued presence of religion in the modern world, liberals need to think more about how they ought to respond to it. Should they, appalled by religion's history of sectarianism and dogmatism, join with the forces of skepticism, even if that means closing oneself off to those moved by the power of faith? Or should liberals, in the name of openness, defend the rights of the faithful to believe as they best see fit, even if some of the more aggressive believers would, if they had the power, extend no such rights to them?

These kinds of questions are strikingly similar to the ones asked by the *philosophes* who helped bring about the Enlightenment in the eighteenth century. Appreciating how those thinkers dealt with questions involving fervor and conflict then ought to help liberals figure out how to think about religion now and in the future.

DARING TO KNOW

Philosophers are not generally known for writing bumper stickers. When Immanuel Kant, among the most abstruse of metaphysicians, nevertheless pondered the meaning of the intellectual revolution taking place around him, he boiled down its significance to a two-word slogan that could easily fit on any of today's economy-size Volkswagens: *Sapere aude,* or "Dare to know." This, Kant held, "is the motto of enlightenment." Kant heard calls for obedience from every quarter— "The officer says: do not argue, just drill! The tax collector says: do not argue, just pay! The clergyman says: do not argue, just believe!" People who blindly follow the orders of their superiors, Kant wrote in his essay "What is Enlightenment?," are immature, and while immaturity has its comforts, rendering it a difficult state from which to escape, escape one must if one is to possess any degree of autonomy.

Kant lived at a time when knowledge of the world, both natural and human, was being accumulated with breathtaking speed. In the face of such developments, he argued, an individual could, for prudential reasons and for a limited period of time, postpone the acceptance of new knowledge. "But to renounce it for his own person, and more still for his descendents, amounts to violating the sacred rights of humanity and to trample them under foot." Enlightened individuals, those who are "not afraid of shadows," have a moral obligation to ensure that future generations not be deprived of the advantages of sunlight they have received.

Kant argued the way he did for a reason: It is difficult to exaggerate just how closed the societies of the *ancien régime* were. This was certainly true of their social and economic structure. In the age of absolutism, the monarchy was of course closed to anyone who was not a member of the royal family, and even among that select group, accession to the throne was shut off to people born in the wrong order or with the wrong gender. The king was surrounded by his court, and the nobles were divided into classes and orders based on birth and privilege. And so it went down the ladder, all the way to workers fortunate enough to be organized into guilds or peasants unfortunate enough to be tied to the land through serfdom. The democratizing spirit of the eighteenth and nineteenth centuries, significantly aided by liberalism, was designed to pry open these restrictive social and economic worlds. Before careers could be open to the talents, positions closed to everyone but the select few had to be abolished.

More than economic positions were being closed by the societies of the old regime, however; minds were as well. The walls built around Europe's major cities were designed to keep out ideas as much as people. Means of communication, including the press, were restricted to a minority, in part because the many lacked literacy and in part because access to information was curtailed through licensing and governmental monopolies. Education was nonexistent for the masses, and for those privileged enough to receive it, up to and including university, it was more bent on inculcating received truths than on exploring new ones. Censorship was a fact of life in the worlds of art, music, and theater. Those fortunate enough to have the right to vote were expected to cast their ballots out of gratitude toward those who ruled them, not to ponder what might be in their own self-interest. And the business of government was carried out in secret, as if it was an obvious fact of political life that people whose lives were influenced by the actions of government should have no knowledge of what their government planned for them.

"What is Enlightenment?" did not amount to a full-throated call for defiance against the powers that were; it contained very kind words for Frederick the Great, for example, just as Diderot and Voltaire had their soft spots for enlightened despots. Yet, along with Locke's *Second*

Treatise and Mill's *On Liberty*, Kant's short essay anticipated a world in which individuals, by developing their own capacities, would become masters of their own fate; daring to know, people would have to grow. The benefits of openness would thus be revealed through time. As Kant put it: "The tendency and the calling to free thinking . . . will gradually extend its effects to the disposition of the people . . . and finally even to the principles of government, which find it to be beneficial to itself to treat the human being, who is indeed more than a machine, in accordance with his dignity."

So much of the old order was closed that the thinkers of the Enlightenment could pick and choose among what needed to be opened. Of all the features of a closed-minded world that attracted their attention, none played a more prominent role than religion. The church certainly appeared to be an antagonist to everything in which liberals believed; ostensibly in the business of saving souls, it had managed to find time for teaching orthodoxy, discouraging tolerance, and promoting obedience. The result was something of a double whammy for a liberal commitment to openness. Sedition—an attack on the monarch—was bad enough. Heresy—criticism of the church—was also subject to punishment. But when church and state combined forces, as they did so frequently in the societies of the old regime, attacks on religion could be persecuted as seditious and heretical simultaneously. This is why for Kant knowing was accompanied by daring. Diderot, after all, had been sent to that prison in Vincennes for mocking the Christian religion.

It was not just because church and state stood together as a bulwark of order and orthodoxy that the problem of religion became so important for liberals to address. There was also the fact that a commitment to open minds could lead to two quite contradictory attitudes toward faith. On the one hand, being enlightened meant supporting reason over revelation, which in turn presumed the emergence of secular ways of thinking and what the Columbia University political philosopher Mark Lilla has called "the Great Separation" between godly authority, not subject to question, and man-made authority, which requires legitimacy and accountability. On the other hand, enlightened thinkers recognized that people possessed inalienable human rights, and so long as one of those rights involved the freedom to believe in and practice something of immeasurable significance to human beings, respect for religion would have to be part of the liberal agenda as well. When it came to religion, liberals knew they wanted to be on the side of openness. They were never quite sure what they should be open toward.

Freedom from religion to promote individual growth or freedom for religion to support diversity and equality? This was the most important question with which they had to deal.

FREEDOM FROM AND FREEDOM FOR

"What could exist without a dominant religion?" wondered Maria Theresa, the eighteenth-century empress of Austria. "Toleration and indifference are exactly the surest ways of destroying the established order. What else is there to harness bad instincts? . . . Nothing is so necessary and beneficial as religion. . . . If there were no state religion and submission to a church, where would we be?" If this is what religion meant, many liberals had few doubts about where they should stand on the matter, and that was in the opposite corner.

One reason the theorists of the Enlightenment could be hostile to religion was the existence of a clergy that made superstition its friend and scientific inquiry its enemy. Although Kant shared much of the Lutheran sensibility that characterized his time and place, and in that sense can be viewed as quasi-religious, he articulated this position with considerable vigor. In calling attention to the immaturity of those who rely on their superiors for guidance in how to think, including their priests and pastors, Kant wrote that immaturity in matters of religion "is the most harmful of all, and hence the most degrading of all." We live in an age of enlightenment, Kant told his readers, but not in an enlightened age, and one of the reasons for the perpetuation of ignorance was that too many of Europe's despots were closer in spirit to Maria Theresa than they were to Frederick the Great.

In addition, as the comments of the empress imply, religion, while distractingly otherworldly, was also disturbingly this-worldly, capable of joining with absolutism to crush dissent, enforce conformity, and suppress liberty. As much as it may evoke images of dark medievalism, the Spanish Inquisition did not go out of existence until 1834, and although it had lost much of its power in its declining years, it was still there during the period of liberalism's birth. "Spain is perhaps the most ignorant nation in Europe," reads one of the entries in Diderot's *Encyclopédie*, written by Nicolas Masson de Morvilliers, a lawyer and geographer. "What else can be expected of a people who wait for a monk to give them freedom to read and to think?" (Authorities in Madrid responded by seizing some 1,700 copies of the offending volume, effectively banning it.) Controversies such as this one reminded European thinkers of the dangers, not only of the suppression of ideas, but of the cooperation between church and state in carrying it out. The Spanish Inquisition, argues Joseph Pérez, emeritus professor of history at the University of Bordeaux, was unique in one respect: "It entrusted the repression of heresy to the civil authorities," introducing "a confusion between the sphere of politics and that of religion." Any political order deserving the label "liberal," to put the legacy of the Inquisition in its rightful place, would have to keep matters of faith distinct from affairs of state, even if that meant, as it ultimately did, saying good-bye to the idea of enlightened despotism.

For both of these reasons, the thinkers associated with the Enlightenment tended to assume that liberty and religion would prove incompatible. Voltaire was typical. A deist, one who believes that God set the world in motion only to retire thereafter to the sidelines, he was the author of many works skeptical of religion, including one, *Le Fanatisme, ou Mahomet le Prophète,* which continues, in this age of substantial Muslim presence in Europe, to attract its share of controversy. Voltaire was by no means alone. Denis Diderot and his friend, the German-born French *philosophe* baron d'Holbach, were even more determined to limit the influence of religion, and they had their English-language counterpart in Tom Paine. Diderot may not have uttered the famous phrase "Man will never be free until the last king is strangled with the entrails of the last priest"—it is unclear exactly who did—but the sentiment was widely shared among his followers; the Revolution, after all, sent to the guillotine France's imperious queen, Marie Antoinette, who happened to be Maria Theresa's daughter. The more people began to think for themselves, these theorists believed, the less they would need a divine power who did their thinking for them.

The story of the Enlightenment's skepticism toward religion is a familiar one. Voltaire in Europe and Tom Paine in the United States have come down to us as men with the courage to challenge the pieties of their time and, in so doing, to set the stage for the emergence of such modern ideas as religious toleration and freedom of thought and expression. There is much truth in such a picture. Still, a number of historians have begun to complicate it, with important implications for how we should think about religion at the present time.

Religion, for one thing, may not have been quite as opposed to reason as we are sometimes led to believe. In *The Victory of Reason,* Baylor University's Rodney Stark has argued that not only was Christianity sympathetic to science, democracy, and modernity, it was solely responsible for all three. Stark's case is too extreme to be taken seriously; he downplays contributions made by other faiths, ignores the Catholic Church's campaign against modernity, and neglects the work of scholars working on the same issues who do not agree with his conclusions. Still, the revisionist sensibility that Stark represents has helped reshape the way we understand the role of religion generally, and Christianity more specifically, in the West. It now seems clear, in ways that were not to Voltaire and Diderot, that such seemingly secular ideals as toleration and democracy have Christian roots. It would be wrong to conclude that Christianity was responsible for liberalism, but it would not be wrong to believe that some of the ideas associated with liberalism had religious origins.

If religion was not that hostile to liberalism, neither was liberalism necessarily hostile to religion. One of the most important liberal thinkers, in fact, was a devout Christian. John Locke's *Letter Concerning Toleration*, first published in 1689, was as much an argument in favor of religion as it was a denunciation of the use of religion for coercive purposes. His strongest condemnatory words were reserved not for the faithful but for "those who persecute, torment, destroy, and kill other men upon pretence of religion." For Locke, being a Christian was impossible "without holiness of life, purity of manners, and benignity and meekness of spirit." Salvation was the purpose of a Christian life, but salvation was meaningful only if brought about through the sincere convictions of individuals themselves. A society determined to respect the beliefs of all—"neither pagan, nor Mahometan, nor Jew, ought to be excluded from the civil rights of the commonwealth because of his religion," Locke wrote—would make a place for faith rather than seek to limit its reach. Locke's arguments have their limitations; finding the resources for tolerance in voluntaristic forms of faith, he was not favorably disposed to religious traditions with strong ideas about clerical authority, especially Catholicism, and he pretty much left Jews to fend for themselves. Still, his *Letter* is one of the classics of liberal political thought, as relevant to today's politics as it was to the memories of the English civil strife that inspired it.

Locke exercised significant influence over the thinkers who came after him in matters of religion as well as in matters of politics. Gertrude Himmelfarb argues that there were at least two Enlightenments, not just one, and that what distinguished the British from the French was primarily their contrasting approaches to religion. At the core of the moral philosophy developed in eighteenth-century Edinburgh and London, she points out, was the notion of sympathy: civil order is made possible, as Adam Smith suggested in *The Theory of Moral Senti-*

ments, by our ability to imagine ourselves through the eyes of others. Religion was no necessary obstacle to such sympathetic ways of thinking and could, if understood as offering compassion or benevolence, be helpful to that end. This explains why thinkers such as Smith "had no quarrel with religion itself—with a benighted or antisocial religion, to be sure, but not religion per se." Indeed, Himmelfarb goes so far as to include within the purview of the British Enlightenment the evangelical John Wesley, both the founder of the Methodist Church and a determined opponent of slavery. One should not make too much of national character in discussing these matters. David Hume, Adam Smith's fellow Scot, was more skeptical than Smith, and John Stuart Mill, who came a generation or two later, was one British thinker whose views on religion were closer to those of French deists than to his countryman John Wesley; he never had to shed religion, Mill wrote in his *Autobiography,* because he never had any to get rid of. Still, the Enlightenment did come in different styles, and one of the most characteristic distinctions among those styles involved the question of whether religion should be treated with skepticism, as was typical among French intellectuals, or with at least some respect, which was more common among the British ones.

The idea that there is an inherent tension between liberalism and faith is further problematic because the country that owed the most to Locke, the United States, did not, especially at its founding, experience any major conflict between the two. To be sure, Thomas Jefferson was not only a deist but so were, in one form or another, four of the five first American presidents, and the odd man out, John Adams, was a Unitarian who denied the existence of the Trinity. The documents written by these politician-activists encompass some of the greatest declarations of religious liberty ever published, including Jefferson's "Bill for Establishing Religious Freedom" and Madison's "Memorial and Remonstrance." Despite claims by contemporary conservative politicians that the founders established a republic grounded in religion, the Constitution they wrote was strongly influenced by the Enlightenment reaction against orthodoxy. Yet neither were the founders, including the deists among them, hostile to people of faith. Like the Constitution in general, the First Amendment was the product of compromise; as the founder and editor in chief of Beliefnet.com, Steven Waldman, points out in *Founding Faith,* evangelicals made as much of a contribution to American church-state separation as Enlightenment philosophers.

It is worth pausing for a moment to consider the career of one of those evangelicals. "I have preached in four hundred and thirty-six meeting houses, thirty-seven court houses, several capitols, many academies and school houses; barns, tobacco-houses and dwelling houses; and many hundreds of times on stages in the open air," John Leland, an itinerant Baptist preacher from Massachusetts, wrote in 1825. A meticulous record keeper, Leland, before he died in 1841 at the age of eighty-seven, estimated that he had delivered roughly 8,000 sermons, baptized 1,524 converts, befriended nearly 1,000 other Baptist clergy, heard more than 300 of them preach, witnessed the deaths of another 300, spoken to congregations as large as 10,000 people, and traveled enough to have traversed the circumference of the globe three times. He did it all out of love of Jesus: "Not the place, but the presence of Christ, and a right temper of mind, makes preaching solemnly easy and profitable," he wrote. But he also knew that despite the Second Great Awakening, the period of evangelical enthusiasm that swept the United States in the 1820s and 1830s, the work of saving souls would never be complete. As he once put it: "My only hope of acceptance with God, is the blood and righteousness of Jesus Christ. And when I come to Christ for pardon, I come as an old grey-headed sinner."

It was, however, neither his remarkable political energy nor his Christian convictions that made Leland the most important American never to have been the subject of a full-length biography. With something like perfect timing, Leland popped up every time a major step in the direction of American religious liberty was taken. After moving to Virginia in 1777, Leland, as did many of his fellow Baptists, objected to the Constitution because it lacked a guarantee of religious freedom. Virginia's leading citizen at the time, James Madison—Jefferson was in Paris—argued that the Constitution's Article VI forbidding religious tests for office was sufficient protection in this regard, but he was unable to persuade Leland. The two men eventually met in the town of Orange, Virginia, and though it is unclear exactly what they discussed, an alliance between them was formed. Leland agreed to support Madison's election to the Virginia Convention called to ratify the Constitution in return for Madison's support for stronger language on religious freedom.

The Orange alliance proved remarkably durable. Leland went on to endorse Madison's election to the first Congress, meeting head-on the opposition of Patrick Henry, who threw his weight behind another future president, James Monroe. (Alas for Henry, Monroe, as one historian puts it, "may have been the most skeptical of the early American presidents.") Madison, in turn, more than delivered on his promise to Leland by working on behalf of the Bill of Rights. Although Leland spent only a portion of his life in Virginia, he played an indispensable political role by offering to the landed gentry the support of plain folk in the more rural regions who developed an attraction to camp meetings and revivalist spiritualism.

Leland also became actively involved in Jefferson's public life. The Constitution does not speak of a "wall" of separation between church and state; we owe that famous metaphor to a letter Jefferson wrote to the Danbury Baptists, a Connecticut-based group strongly committed to church-state separation, in 1802. Leland was with Jefferson on the day he wrote the letter, having delivered to the president a wheel of cheese—weighing, once cured, 1,235 pounds and inscribed with the words "Rebellion to tyrants is obedience to God." (The cheese had been manufactured only from "Republican" cows by good Baptist dissenters from western Massachusetts in thanks to Jefferson for his support of religious liberty.) Knowing that his Danbury letter would expose him to the charge of nonbelief, Jefferson, against his usual inclination, decided to attend one of Leland's sermons—delivered, rather ironically for such strict separationists, in the House of Representatives. If Jefferson and Madison are the fathers of the American church-state separation, Elder John Leland was their enabler; they provided the theory, he supplied much of the practice.

In addition to his political activity, Leland wrote eloquently, if not especially originally, on behalf of religious liberty. "It is more essential to learn *how* to believe than to learn *what* to believe," he wrote in "The Bible Baptist." In the tradition of Locke, Leland opposed all efforts to coerce belief and encouraged the faithful to arrive at their views through the exercise of their mental powers: "A man's mind," he wrote, "should always be open to conviction, and an honest man will receive that doctrine which appears the best demonstrated: and what is more common than for the best of men to change their minds?" A "liberal man"—yes, he used that term—Leland concluded, asks only this: "Let every man speak without fear, maintain the principles that he believes, worship according to his own faith, either one God, three Gods, no God, or twenty Gods; and let the government protect him in so doing, i.e., see that he meets no personal abuse, or loss of property, for his religious opinions." Unlike Madison and Jefferson, Leland constantly invoked the name of Jesus Christ and spoke of the mysteries of the Gospel. Yet like them, he believed that "government has no more to do with the religious opinions of men, than it has with the principles of mathematics." This practicing Christian who never approved of dancing, drinking, or gambling was also opposed to faith statements, missions, public pay for chaplains, official religious holidays, seminaries, and Sunday Schools. One of the key planks in the agenda of modern liberalism—freedom of religion—owes its existence as much to him as it does to the skeptical Thomas Paine.

As the campaign for religious liberty led by Leland illustrates, liberalism cannot tie its fate to the notion that people's destinies are controlled by a power whose authority can never be questioned, especially when that power is reinforced by the punitive capacities of the state. But, as Leland's life and thought just as equally illustrate, liberals can be sympathetic to the religious aspirations of ordinary believers. Liberalism calls for freedom *from* religion; citizens should not be bound by the closed-mindedness associated with dogma and superstition. But it also demands freedom *for* religion; citizens should not only have the right to practice their religion if chosen voluntarily by them, they ought to extend that right to people of other faiths as well. For the one, free-thinking people who opt for strict forms of faith are still enchained. For the other, free societies that do not allow for private religious conviction are not really free. No matter how much liberals may want to ensure that every person thinks for himself, they have to make room for a believer who, in thinking for himself, chooses God.

It may gratify the sensibilities of some contemporary liberals to picture themselves as Kantian heroes, daring to stand for open minds against the forces of religious bigotry lined up against them. And it may be just as comforting for today's conservative critics to insist that behind every liberal is an intolerant secular humanist just waiting for a chance to banish religion from the land. But in truth, liberalism's enemy is not religion but religious oppression and its friend is not skepticism but freedom, including religious freedom. When it comes to matters of religion, it is not always easy for liberals to allow room for the faithful. But that is what they have to do to remain true to their heritage.

A RENEWED ENLIGHTENMENT?

Western Europe is no longer all that religious; even Spain, once the symbol of reaction, has become a primarily secular society, indeed, one of the most liberal countries in Europe on the issue of gay rights. This does not mean that religion, and religious thought, have disappeared from the Continent: Pope Benedict XVI is a theologian of considerable distinction; thinkers such as Jürgen Habermas and Jacques Derrida engaged in a dialogue on the subject of religion in the aftermath of September 11, 2001; and the rise of Islam in Western Europe—it is now the second most adhered to faith in most European countries—has provoked considerable discussion about the mutual compatibility of liberal openness and godly devotion. Yet these debates differ considerably from the ones that provoked Diderot and Kant. Then, religion had the upper hand and liberalism was struggling for recognition. Now, throughout most of Western Europe, liberal values such as toleration and pluralism are widely accepted and religion has to fight for its place in the public arena.

The situation is very different in the United States. It is not just that the United States was founded during the time of the Enlightenment. It is also that with no majority faith and hence no powerful state church it could never have produced a Maria Theresa, let alone a Marie Antoinette. Still, the United States is the one Western liberal democracy that, despite its attractions to modernity in economics and technology, has seen a revival of religion, including a variety of forms of conservative religion, in the last few years of the twentieth century and the first decade of the twenty-first. The extent to which the United States has shifted in matters involving religion from the era of Jefferson and Madison to our own times can be illustrated by returning to the example of John Leland. This time, however, it is not Leland's life but his legacy that is important.

Denominationally, but not ideologically, one can draw a direct line from Leland to the Southern Baptist Convention (SBC), among the most conservative of all of America's contemporary religious denominations. In the 1980s, leaders of the SBC looked out on a land that, in their view, was in the midst of a moral crisis, represented by loose sexual morals, ineffective parental discipline, and the collapse of religious faith. It was time, they believed, to take sides in the culture war that was leading so many political activists on the right end of the political spectrum to campaign against *Roe* v. *Wade*, the 1973 Supreme Court decision legalizing abortion (which the SBC had originally endorsed), as well as to work for the election of conservative Republicans such as Ronald Reagan. Jesus, whose kingdom was not of this world, would now have to be brought down to earth; a church once skeptical of political involvement would have to become deeply political.

The efforts of the SBC have had major consequences for the character of religious liberty in the United States. In the politics of the

1970s and 1980s, liberals had generally lined up in favor of church-state separation while conservatives had argued on behalf of allowing prayer in school, religious symbols in public places, and, eventually, vouchers that parents could use to help pay for private education for their children, if need be in parochial schools. As a staunch defender of church-state separation, America's Baptist leaders were historically reluctant to join forces with those who wanted to see religion play a more direct and visible role in public affairs. At the same time, Baptists were typically conservative in their views about every other issue facing America. The SBC therefore faced a choice: Should it join together with other conservative Protestant churches in their efforts to bring religion back into the public square, thereby turning its back on its own history of Leland-like separationism? Or should it hold fast to a tradition that, in religious terms, had more in common with the Jews—another religion closely identified with church-state separation—than with the conservative Protestants and Catholics with which it was allied politically?

One might think that a church would put its religious understanding before its political commitment, but this is not what the SBC decided to do. SBC leaders like to portray their decision to abandon strict separationism as a continuation of their past beliefs, but what took place in the 1980s was what Barry Hankins, a fair-minded historian writing from within the Baptist tradition, calls "a monumental shift" away from the earlier views of Baptist leaders. Lelandism—a commitment to religious liberty so strong that it opposes any and all effort on the part of the state to endorse one religion over another or even belief over nonbelief—was gone. In its place, the Southern Baptist Convention lined up on behalf of "accommodationism," the idea that church and state could find ways to mesh their common interests, a step toward a more Calvinistic, if not downright Catholic, endorsement of an unofficial religious establishment.

The transformation of the Southern Baptist Convention helped reshape American politics, resulting in the elections of Ronald Reagan and George W. Bush. With these political victories, conservative religion achieved unusual public prominence in American public life. Its issues—abortion, gay marriage—became America's issues. Sectarian, sometimes extremist religious figures bragged of their access to the White House and to Congress. Institutions whose purposes are secular, up to and including the U.S. military, became places filled with evangelical fervor. Politicians in one party bent over backward to appeal to religious voters, while politicians in the other went to great lengths to show that they have religious sensibilities of their own. The United

States is most likely not experiencing another Great Awakening. But after a long period in which politics and religion seemed to go their separate ways, it has been witnessing a much closer connection between them.

For many American liberals, these developments are troubling. If religion proved itself the enemy of reason in the eighteenth century, they are convinced, it continues to play that role in the twenty-first, standing firmly against the teaching of evolution in the schools, arguing for faith-based solutions to problems of overpopulation and global poverty, opposing such potential lifesaving technologies as embryonic stem cell research, and, most troubling of all, basing foreign policy decisions, including the decision to go to war, on calls from divine authority. And, the feeling continues, if religion once joined with the state to enforce orthodoxy and suppress dissent, today's religious conservatives not only seek nothing less than a constitutional revolution that would repudiate the First Amendment in favor of a new religious establishment but now have the justices on the U.S. Supreme Court capable of doing so. The only problem with Tom Paine's *Age of Reason*, for liberals of this sort, is that it was published too early.

The political success of the religious right has led to a reversal of positions between Europe and the United States. Despite Europeans' experiences with absolutism and church-state cooperation, they no longer need fear the blending of religion and politics, while the United States, for all its historical sympathy toward religious liberty and church-state separation, does. The result is that Europe, whose intellectual history includes so many writers attacking faith, is now relatively indifferent to the subject, while the United States, which by and large missed the earlier fireworks of the Enlightenment, has suddenly sprouted authors evoking the spirit of Voltaire and Diderot. Look for those determined to *écraser l'infâme*, and you are more likely to find them in Washington than in Paris or London. Seemingly out of nowhere, the best-seller lists in the United States have been filling up with books dismissing religion as superstitious nonsense that can only stand in the way of political and scientific progress.

Tom Paine was an Englishman who came to America. It therefore seems fitting that one of his most energetic contemporary followers, the essayist Christopher Hitchens, trod exactly the same path. "We are in need of a renewed Enlightenment," Hitchens writes in *God Is Not Great*, "which will base itself on the proposition that the proper study of mankind is man, and woman." (It was actually Alexander Pope, anything but a liberal and skeptic, who pronounced those words, and in a poem meant to demonstrate the existence of a great chain of being with God at the top, man floundering in a fallen state, and woman nowhere to be found.) Name an evil and, according to Hitchens, it has been carried out in the name of God: rape, murder, colonialism, ethnic hatred. Hitchens hardly confines himself to the religious revival in the United States. A world traveler and intrepid reporter, he has only unkind words for Gandhi's spinning wheel, Israeli settlers, South African Calvinists (indeed Calvin himself), Mother Teresa, ashrams, Shiites, Sunnis, and Mormons; even liberation theologians in South America disappoint him. For Hitchens, it is beyond belief that anyone could believe. Patiently, but with touches of bemused contempt, he provides a laundry list of religion's mysteries, denouncing them for their lack of logic, their hypocrisy, their inaccuracies. And, with equal measure on the other side, he praises those men—including Albert Einstein, Mark Twain, and H. L. Mencken—who, he believes, with the courage of their own convictions, dared to stand up to those who would shut them down.

Hitchens is only one of a number of writers in the United States who evoke the side of the Enlightenment that was hostile toward faith. The best-selling writer Susan Jacoby has told the stories of men such as Robert Ingersoll, the late-nineteenth-century orator and author of "Why I Am an Agnostic," who attracted huge crowds to his lectures and, save for his radical views, might well have achieved high political office in the United States. Sam Harris, reacting to the events of September 11, has emphasized the dangers posed to liberal societies from religious extremists, Islamic ones to be sure, but their twins in other religious communities as well. Because conservative Christians continue to argue against modern science, scientists and philosophers influenced by science, including Richard Dawkins and Daniel Dennett, have chipped in to defend reason against superstition and myth. (Dawkins, like Hitchens, is British, and although he has not made the United States his home, his books are very popular there.) Hitchens's call for a renewal of the Enlightenment has been met. The question facing us is just how enlightened this new enlightenment actually is.

From a liberal perspective, this advocacy on behalf of nonbelief is long overdue; liberals must constantly be on guard against those who would shut down free inquiry in the name of religious conviction. The question of whether homosexuals should be free to marry or whether wars ought to be fought in the Middle East should be decided by rules of liberal democratic debate and considerations of the national interest, not by the commands of a supernatural authority. It is healthy for a liberal society to have matters of faith debated—even debated vehemently—rather than treated as so sacred and holy that no one is allowed to question them. One can scarcely imagine modern liberalism in the absence of a Voltaire or a Diderot.

Yet neither can one imagine contemporary liberalism in the absence of a John Locke or a John Leland. If at least some liberal thinkers were able to make a place for religion in earlier times, perhaps liberals ought to be able to make some place for religion now. This is not something that thinkers like Hitchens and company are at all interested in doing. On the contrary, if the mark of a liberal is open-mindedness, there is something decidedly closed-minded about the more zealous of this resurgence of militant nonbelief. It does not sound very liberal to describe Catholic theologians pondering mysteries they take seriously—in this case the conviction that unbaptized babies enter a state of limbo—as, in Harris's words, "a hilarious, terrifying, and unconscionable waste of time" that "begins to exude a truly diabolical aura of misspent human energy"; if anything, as a phrase such as "diabolical aura" suggests, it sounds remarkably like the strictures of disgruntled Old Testament prophets. Nor is it a manifestation of a liberal outlook on the world to argue, as Dawkins does, that political absolutism "nearly always results from strong religious faith . . . and constitutes a major reason for suggesting that religion can be a force for evil in the world," not, at least, after the twentieth century, when the greatest forces for evil in the world—Nazism and communism—were hostile to religion. (Harris's attempt to show that the Nazis were not hostile to religion because their anti-Semitism had Christian origins is equally unpersuasive.) It is perhaps even worse, if you wish to display a liberal temper of mind, to go beyond Dawkins and Harris, who insist only that fascism results from religion, to argue, along the lines of Hitchens, that religion *is* fascism. Damon Linker, a writer on American religion, is right to suggest, as he did in a 2007 essay in *The New Republic,* that nonbelief has historically taken both liberal and illiberal forms, and that much of the resurgence of atheism we have been witnessing in recent years belongs in the latter category.

One knows we are approaching something other than a liberal disposition when Harris argues that moderate believers "are, in large part, responsible for the religious conflict in the world, because their beliefs provide the context in which scriptural literalism and religious violence can never be adequately opposed." This effort to blame moderates for the extremists on their side of the ideological divide is too reminiscent of the ugly political rhetoric of the twentieth century—the kind, for example, in which political reactionaries accused liberals of being Communists at heart, while leftists attacked conservatives as incipient Fascists—to be part of any serious liberal analysis of religion. "While religious people are not generally mad, their core beliefs absolutely are," Harris writes. This is not the language of argument and discussion but of dismissal and contempt. You do not debate mad ideas; you confine them.

It should come as no surprise that a significant number of these critics of religion are evolutionary theorists, since, as I argued earlier, sociobiology constitutes the most popular form that illiberalism takes in the contemporary world. It is nonetheless surprising just how illiberal they are. Let us assume, for the sake of argument, that religion does all the evil things Hitchens and Harris assign to it and, at the same time, maintains things we ought to consider patently absurd. Should citizens of a liberal democracy nonetheless have the right to believe those things? If we cannot be sure that Diderot ever uttered the words attributed to him about hanging kings with the entrails of priests, it has never been definitely established that Voltaire was willing to defend to the death another's right to say something of which he disapproved. Whether or not he said it, however, someone did, and it is now a cornerstone of the liberal sensibility to extend rights to those who hold ideas with which you disagree. By that standard, a moderate enough one, Hitchens qualifies, although just barely, and Harris does not at all.

"To 'choose' dogma and faith over doubt and experiment," Hitchens writes, suggesting "choose" is anything but a choice, "is to throw out the ripening vintage and to reach greedily for the Kool-Aid," the Kool-Aid of course being the one that contained sufficient amounts of cyanide to kill off the flock at Jim Jones's People's Temple in Guyana. Nonetheless, Hitchens is willing to allow believers the right to their own convictions, however grudgingly: "What believers will do, now that their faith is optional and irrelevant, is a matter for them. We should not care, as long as they make no further attempt to inculcate religion by any form of coercion." As intolerant as this may sound, Sam Harris goes further. No person, he argues, can be free "to believe a proposition for which he has no evidence." Anyone therefore claiming freedom for religion "has exercised his freedom to be thought a fool." A more blunt form of the argument that human beings require freedom from religion could hardly be made. If at least one side of the Enlightenment stood for the free exchange of ideas, the renewed enlightenment advocated by Hitchens and Harris contains sufficiently chilling language to suggest that it does not.

One might think that if the theorists of the new enlightenment assert that no one has the right to believe nonsense, believers would respond by insisting on their right to believe in things so meaningful to them. Oddly enough, though, this rarely happens. As they deal with a Hitchens or a Harris, conservative Christians have a problem of their own. If they defend their right to be religious in the face of the hostility they perceive all around them, they find themselves relying on one of the key planks in the liberal platform: the idea of individual rights, after all, is not one we have historically associated with monarchs and priests. Far better to argue that liberalism and religious faith are incompatible—exactly the point that Hitchens and Harris work so assiduously to demonstrate—than to acknowledge that liberalism may be good for religion after all.

Stanley Hauerwas, a theologian at Duke University whose books have a significant following in the conservative Christian world, comes directly to that conclusion. Believers can be considered "resident aliens" in a liberal political order, Hauerwas, along with William H. Willimon, argues; they live there, but, not being full citizens, they are not fully accepted there. Many resident aliens—the real ones, that is—seek to become citizens as soon as they can. But Hauerwas does not believe that genuinely religious people should take steps to overcome their alienated status by joining liberal society. On the contrary: "Liberalism emasculated Christianity in the name of social peace," he has said, "but the kind of societies thus created lack the moral resources to face those who would rather die, and kill, than live religiously unworthy lives." Hauerwas prefers a romantic and heroic tradition of Christian insistence on truth, whatever the price paid, than the mundane compromises and constitutional rules that make liberalism prosper. If the world he wants could be brought back into existence—Hauerwas is fully aware how archaic his views are—teachers would not want students to think for themselves but to think like them; we would all learn to live with the limits God has put upon our lives; and we could come to realize that such reputed liberal virtues as pluralism and tolerance make no sense. Any attempt to reconcile liberalism with Christianity, Hauerwas believes, can take place only on liberalism's terms and therefore no such efforts at reconciliation should be made. For Hauerwas, the choice between freedom from religion and freedom for religion—liberalism's great dilemma—is not a choice at all. Neither idea makes sense to him because both presuppose a world in which individuals make choices in the first place, as opposed to a world in which people ought to live in accord with the received teachings of a church.

Hauerwas writes as a conveyor of uncomfortable truths to a society that does not want to hear them, but he does have allies, not only in the conservative Christian world but also among postmodernists and others suspicious of liberalism and its affinity with reason and moderation. Postmodernists are skeptical of the idea of absolute truth, which Christians are not. They are also generally leftist in their politics, which most conservative Christians certainly are not. And like most other contemporary academics, they are not especially known for their deep religious convictions. But many postmodernists have nonetheless joined forces with theologians such as Hauerwas; the dislike of liberalism is as common in the American academy as belief in a supreme being is rare. The postmodern sensibility has made two major contributions to the American debate over freedom of religion. One is to deny that there is any such thing as religion, at least in any coherent sense of the term. The other is to deny that there is any such thing as freedom.

While serving as dean of students at the University of Chicago Divinity School, Winifred Fallers Sullivan was called by an attorney asking her to serve as an expert witness in a religious discrimination case. Generally willing to testify on behalf of those seeking the right to practice their faith as they best see fit, she agreed, but in the course of her research and testimony it became clear to her that the ways people practice their religion—spontaneously, non-doctrinally, personally—is usually very different from the way that legal systems, with their emphasis on rules and institutional responsibilities, treat religion. Sullivan, a law professor, is anything but a ponderous postmodern theorist. She has powerful narrative abilities and engages her readers in the difficulties of actual cases being debated in real courtrooms. Still, she writes that "we live in a new moment, a time of undifferentiation—in which a postmodern consciousness is reluctant to see sharp divisions such as those historically described as the sacred and the profane." In such a situation of flux and uncertainty, Sullivan concludes that " 'religion' can no longer be coherently defined for purposes of law," and if religion is too fluid and otherworldly to be defined, how can religious liberty exist? Her answer is that, at least for purposes of law, it cannot. To provide for religious freedom, the courts have to define religion, and when they do so, they invariably define it in ways compatible with Protestant ideas about individualism and the right to worship. In this way, the search for religious liberty forces those outside the Protestant tradition to adapt to it. The idea of freedom serves the cause of intolerance.

What Sullivan tries to demonstrate through the practice of religion, others have tried to show at the level of theory. One who has undertaken the task with special vigor is Stanley Fish. As it happens, Fish and Hauerwas were once neighbors and colleagues when both taught at Duke University in North Carolina. Much given to influencing each other's work, it became somewhat inevitable that Fish would write about religion with the same disdain for liberalism that characterizes Hauerwas's theology. Following his usual procedure in discussing liberal ideas, Fish turns to a text: Locke's *Letter Concerning Toleration.* This essay, Fish argues, makes the best ever case for religious freedom. But, like all such efforts to realize liberal principles, it nonetheless fails. The reason is the same as why all forms of liberalism have to fail: liberalism seeks to be neutral between competing ways of life but is itself partisan in arguing only for one way of life, the liberal one. Once we realize this, Fish concludes, it is self-evident that Locke's insistence on tolerance does not protect religion against the state but allows the state to control and tame religion. Because they believe in things that cannot be judged by a liberal insistence on reason, such as the existence of a transcendent creator of the world, Fish argues that religious people should not be tricked into accepting the liberal idea of freedom, not of speech, not of assembly, and certainly not of religion.

Writers such as these are right to point out how dominant liberalism has become in the contemporary world, something of which liberals, who always see threats from other political philosophies, are not persuaded. But they are wrong to hold that liberalism is inevitably unable to accommodate people of faith. True, those kinds of liberals and leftists who denounce religion in unrepentant terms are not likely to make a place at the table for the faithful. But if liberalism responds to the revival of religion, even conservative religion, in the spirit of Locke more than in the spirit of Paine, it may be possible to have liberalism and religion at the same time.

Doing so is not nearly as impossible or foreordained to failure as both liberal skeptics and defenders of the faith argue. It is true that, as Walter Benn Michaels, like Fish a professor of English literature, puts it, "if you believe that Jesus is the way and I don't believe that Jesus is the way, one of us must be wrong." But it does not follow that people with radically opposed conceptions of the truth are bound to be at each other's throats. Despite the failure of the Supreme Court to come up with firm principles on the question of religious liberty, and despite the disagreements among academics about whether they ever can, Americans, inhabiting one of the most religiously diverse societies in the world, have found ways to live together in relative peace. Religion in practice does not show, as Winifred Sullivan holds, that there is no such thing as religious freedom; it shows instead that, however different religions may be in theology and tradition, their lived realities are all shaped by a common culture of individualism and democratic choice. We know that toleration and religious freedom exist because we see them put into practice every day of the year. If we did not, we would be in the midst of a religious war, not debating these matters in books or even resolving them at the ballot box.

LIBERALISM'S TRIPLE DUTY

No one these days is going to be put in prison, as Diderot was, for publishing *Lettre sur les aveugles*, his 1749 work supporting Locke's theory of knowledge and questioning the existence of God. But if it has become less dangerous to argue on behalf of open minds, it has also become more difficult. Diderot had two enemies, the combined forces of church and state, and his overriding objective was to challenge their efforts to enforce religious orthodoxy. Liberalism today has a triple duty. To wage a campaign on behalf of open-mindedness, liberals have to defend their views against conservative denominations that once made religious liberty central to their outlook on the world but no longer do; skeptical intellectuals who, having inherited the scientific bent of the Enlightenment, find religion so hostile to knowledge that no guarantees of religious liberty are necessary; and left-leaning humanities professors persuaded that the Enlightenment, far from liberating people to think and act on their own behalf, influences people to seek false forms of freedom that modern society will never grant them.

If Southern Baptists and other evangelical denominations are no longer willing to keep alive the legacy of John Leland, liberals, including secular liberals, ought to do it for them. Liberals worry that the religious right, by failing to respect the proper boundary between church and state, will move the United States in a more theocratic direction insufficiently appreciative of the benefits of human liberty. That may well be true, but among the first to suffer would be religious conservatives themselves. The religious right would, if it could, create a society in which Christianity's place of privilege would be supported by special access to public funds; public authorities would be charged with enforcing its particular conceptions of morality; restrictions would be imposed on the free speech of atheists and non-Christians; and a foreign policy would be designed to spread its word. Yet by sucking up the air of human liberty, such a society would leave a vacuum in which new religious movements—tomorrow's evangelicalism—would find no place of nourishment. Evangelicalism has always cast its lot as a religion of dissent, not as a force for establishment.

It is therefore not only political liberals who worry about the political seduction of conservative Christianity. Darryl Hart, director of academic programs at the Intercollegiate Studies Institute, is a contemporary conservative Christian inspired by the teachings of fundamentalist theologians who in the early years of the twentieth century led the campaign against modernism. But unlike other conservative Christians, Hart is no aspiring theocrat; he warns that too close a link between religion and politics, even one directed toward such seemingly good ends as promoting compassion and social justice, will cause "religious conservatives, in the name of the love of neighbor, to lose sight of a prior and higher love, namely devotion to God."

Hart's concerns should be taken seriously. Religions that draw too close to politics lose their capacity to engage in matters of the spirit. If they receive government money, they become bureaucracies more interested in balancing their books than saving souls. If their objective is to get out the vote, they will want an obedient flock, not disputatious otherworldly saints. Their clergy will become more comfortable in the country club than on the street corner; worried about their standing, the status of their capital campaign, and their ties to local business, they will lose their ability to speak to the economically marginalized, from whom conservative religion has always drawn the bulk of its new recruits. Their churches may grow, to be sure; indeed, they will develop management objectives, best practices, and consumer surveys to ensure their growth. But the resources of the spirit are limited, and the more that goes into committee work, the less there is for God. Evangelicals were once successful in spreading the word not least because they had little or no political power, something of an advantage if you are seeking support among the dispossessed. Now that they have tasted power, they are less likely to have compelling words to spread. If you are looking for a way to stultify the religious spirit and confine it to the margins of the society, Hart teaches us, your best way would be to establish it in the form of a theocracy. Coerce conviction, drive out dissent, and impose orthodoxy, and the religion you get will not be a religion worth keeping.

Hart's concern is the same one that motivated John Leland two centuries ago. Searching for an appropriate metaphor to register his thoughts on this issue, Leland adopted a marital one. "Let us . . . endeavor to divorce them, to dissolve their unnatural connection," he wrote in 1802, denouncing the intimate relationship that had developed between church and state. What Leland wanted to tear asunder, today's Southern Baptists want to join together. "The go-along, get-along strategy is dead," reflected Richard Land of the Southern Baptist Convention in 1998 as he pondered his new alliance with Christian right activists close to the Republican Party. "No more engagement. We want a wedding ring, we want a ceremony, we want a consummation of the marriage." Lelandism or Landism? The Southern Baptist Convention chose the latter, and the price conservative believers paid is a loss of the prophetic voice of those who once, in the name of Jesus, insisted that the only faith worth preserving is one chosen by freethinking people. Only time will tell how long this marriage will last, but if it does not, this may be one very justifiable divorce.

Liberalism's second duty is to protect tolerance against the shrill voices of its neo-Enlightenment critics. These critics do the cause of reason no favor when they ignore serious arguments advanced on behalf of religion or dismiss them with theologically amateurish rebuttals. For Christopher Hitchens, religion developed at a time when we did not understand much about how the world worked; now that we do, we no longer need it, and any attempt to hold on to it is pathetic. Yet thinkers as impressive as the nineteenth-century Danish philosopher Søren Kierkegaard and the twentieth century's Reinhold Niebuhr met the modern world on its own terms while retaining religious convictions, and surely Hitchens owes his readers more than one brief reference to the former and complete avoidance of the latter. No compelling case for tolerance can be made by railing against religion's weakest defenders. If the arguments for religion are as stupid as Hitchens makes them out to be, foleration is either unnecessary or unnecessarily patronizing. Had he instead engaged religion's strongest defenders, Hitchens would have made a case for toleration that was much more powerful, for the more willing we are to allow to flourish ideas with which we disagree but nonetheless find powerful, the more tolerant we are.

Compared to the weak case Hitchens makes for tolerance, Sam

Harris makes no case at all. Because in his view no one has a right to believe in ideas as idiotic as those associated with religion, steps should be taken to isolate those who do. Harris, of course, does not call for a secular inquisition against the dangers of belief. But he does say that the only sensible response to anyone who takes religion seriously is to grant such a person "an even greater stigma in our discourse." If we want to lessen the amount of violence in the world, we should do a better job at shunning the belief systems that cause so much of it.

Harris should reread John Stuart Mill. Mill was also no friend of revealed religion. But he was especially antagonized by the application of what he called "the social stigma" to ideas we happen not to like. It is true that stigmatization "kills no one" and "roots out no opinions," Mill argued, but "the price paid for this sort of intellectual pacification is the sacrifice of the entire moral courage of the human mind." Mill's principles in *On Liberty* could not be more relevant than to the question of whether people should have the right to hold beliefs others consider foolish: whether those ideas turn out to be true or false, society will be better off if their free expression is allowed. If Harris wants to respond that religious ideas can nonetheless be stigmatized because they violate Mill's harm principle—which holds that the only justification for suppressing ideas is the harm done to others—it is up to Harris to show how the Catholic belief in limbo causes any harm to him or, for that matter, anyone else.

"It is time we recognized that belief is not a private matter," Harris writes. For him, there is no difference between religious beliefs and religious acts; if you think that God condemns homosexuality, you will have to see homosexuality be made illegal, if not worse. On the issue of whether belief cannot be a private matter, conservative Christians could not agree more; for them, religion cannot be private, because if you believe that love of Jesus suffuses all of life, it must suffuse public life as well. Yet one thing that makes liberal society work is that we do not automatically derive our public convictions from our private confessions. If we did, all Christians who treat the Bible as the literal word of God would vote the same way, which, in fact, they do not. It is through the private sphere that we decide for ourselves how to act in the public sphere, and if the richness and diversity of the former is allowed to atrophy, the health of the latter will be damaged. By denying the importance of a private sphere, religion's critics advocate a vision of society that religion's most passionate followers crave. Against both, liberals must insist that belief cannot play a role in public unless it is nourished in private. When it comes to anything involving conscience, liberals ought to be on the side of protecting the right to privacy rather than on the side of claiming that no such thing as privacy exists.

A third and final duty of liberalism is to defend the idea of religious freedom against postmodernists who find it an impossible goal to achieve. Liberals, it must be acknowledged, have not carried out this task well. A number of the most prominent contemporary liberal political theorists, writing under the influence of John Rawls, or at least the early John Rawls who made less room for the faithful in his philosophy than the later one, have argued that liberalism requires a commitment to public reason. As such it has little or no room for people who appeal "to any authority whose conclusions are impervious, in principle as well as in practice, to the standards of logical consistency or to reliable methods of inquiry that themselves should be mutually acceptable," as two political philosophers, Amy Gutmann, president of the University of Pennsylvania, and Dennis Thompson, a political scientist at Harvard, put it. Unlike Locke and Leland, these contemporary liberals do not believe that a society open to all must be open to the faithful. On the contrary, by insisting on a standard of logical consistency as a precondition of debate in a democratic society, they exclude those for whom revelation comes before reason.

When answering the question of how a liberal society should respond to those who do not share a commitment to reason, liberals of this sort offer two proposals, neither of which is liberal in a temperament sense. One is to insist that believers must, as a condition for entry into public debate, put aside their convictions. But this denies to people their right to bring to the public square something of great importance to them and for that reason contradicts liberalism's insistence upon equality: a society that permits secular individuals to bring their convictions into the public square but denies the same right to the faithful treats people unequally. The second is to conclude that, if believers refuse to put their appeals to divine authority aside, they can simply be denied the freedom to choose; just as Sam Harris thinks that no one has the right to hold nonsensical beliefs, the political philosopher Stephen Macedo, in *Diversity and Distrust,* holds that no one has the right to "opt out of reasonable measures designed to educate children toward very basic liberal virtues." To protect liberalism, it would seem, one must deny the option of home schooling, or even faith-based private schooling, to parents who prefer it, an option that fails liberalism's test of allowing individuals the right to put into practice what they believe in theory. It is one thing when conservative Christians and postmodernists, neither of whom make any claim to uphold liberal principles, violate liberal tenets. It is more disturbing when those who insist on their fidelity to liberal principles come up with solutions that show too little respect for liberty and equality.

Such ways of thinking are therefore music to the ears of liberal critics like Stanley Fish. Gutmann and Thompson's conditions for public disagreement strike Fish as an admission of guilt to his charge that liberalism is never neutral, for they all but say flat out that only liberals meet the conditions for public deliberation. Macedo's views, by contrast, Fish finds "positively bracing compared to the pious moralizing of the usual son or daughter of Rawls," for Macedo at least acknowledges that there are real winners and losers in these battles and that liberals want their side to win, a position Fish is happy to accept because it is perfectly compatible with his view that those who are faithful must, as a condition of their faith, fight to win as well.

If we were still living in the age of John Milton, the literary figure about whom Fish has written with great insight, he would be right; in those days, differences over faith were matters of life and death. If we were still living in the period of the French Revolution and its aftermath, Fish would be half right; in that period, forces of clericalism were lined up on one side and forces of anticlericalism on the other, and while some societies found ways for them to live together, not all of them did. But we live in a modern liberal state, and under our political conditions, Fish is wrong. The United States is structured around the idea of what Damon Linker calls "the liberal bargain." In contrast to those who ask believers to check their faith at the door, a liberal society ought to welcome their participation and encourage them to influence public policy in directions they favor, even—indeed, especially—over such contentious issues as abortion, gay marriage, or stem cell research. For this reason, the liberal bargain is not, as postmodern critics insist, hostile to belief; it instead allows belief to flourish, as it in fact does in that most liberal of modern societies, the United States. At the same time, the liberal bargain, because it is liberal, does deny believers one thing: no group belonging to one particular religious tradition can monopolize the violence that the state has at its disposal to impose its views on those belonging to other traditions or to none at all. Since it is close to impossible to create such intimate cooperation between church and state in an age grown used to the benefits of religious liberty and political equality, this is not an especially onerous concession to have to make.

The revival of religion that the United States has been witnessing therefore has little or nothing in common with the European past. The guardians of religious orthodoxy dominant in the Europe of the *ancien régime* would be shocked by its pluralism, its voluntary character, and its democratic engagement. Modernity in the United States, unlike most European societies, has not brought nonbelief in its wake. But nor has it brought about religious orthodoxy. Instead, what we see in the United States is a curious blending of religious faith, technological innovation, and liberal individualism. Secular liberals may find American religiosity dangerous, but genuine religious conservatives are more likely to find it hopelessly compromised. Compared to what Christopher Hitchens would like, it insists on the presence of the divine. Compared to what Voltaire and Tom Paine feared, it is too focused on the needs of the self and too fractured into sects and tendencies to impose, through government, its morality on society as a whole.

Religion's critics nonetheless insist that even a modern and secularized religion is a threat to liberal values. Their argument runs something like this. Liberalism's purpose is not just to create a society of freely choosing people but to help individuals develop their capacities so that the choices they make are wise ones. For them, religion's failure to help people in this process of development is an obvious fact: anyone liberated from religion's preference for superstition, affinity with sectarianism, and inherent biases will be a freer person able to make his or her independent choices outside the coercion of church and clergy. The problem with religion, they insist, is that it does not give an adequate account of the natural world around us, distorts how we think by speaking in parables, and utters conclusions that can never be tested. Those who believe in it have shackled their minds. Uncurious and conformist, they can never be good citizens. A society of the faithful will be a nation of sheep.

If religious believers in contemporary society inherited their faith from their parents and never questioned its assumptions throughout their lifetimes, the position taken by religion's critics would be justified. Liberals such as Kant and Mill insisted on openness precisely on the grounds that exposure to views different from received ones would help individuals grow and develop. In a way not fully appreciated by political theorists such as Amy Gutmann and Stephen Macedo, this searching is precisely what a large number of religious believers actually do. According to the most reliable survey, some 44 percent of Americans switch their faith in the course of their lives; not satisfied with one, they do what modern individuals do in other areas of life and decide for themselves which one makes the most sense to them. When people choose their religion rather than having it chosen for them, they have already taken an important step on the path to self-development upon which liberal theorists have insisted.

Not everyone, of course, treats religion in a self-reflective fashion. I have spent a considerable amount of time over the past decade gathering empirical material by interviewing people about their religious and moral views. I can guarantee today's skeptics that among them are people for whom religion serves as a flight from reality: these are people so set in their convictions, so surrounded by others who think the same way they do, and so hostile to a culture they view as degrading that dialogue with them is impossible. In talking with them, I could not help but feel that their faith, however important to them, was holding them back from experiencing a world different from the one so familiar to them. Had they been exposed to ideas against which they have shut themselves off, they would have broadened their horizons and reduced much of the displaced anger they feel about the world around them. I would not be as quick as Sam Harris to pronounce their views mad and delusional, but I share the concern that if a society contains too many people like this, it will not last long as a liberal political system.

On the other hand, my interviews also yielded up individuals for whom religion had become a powerful tool for making sense out of the world. They were people to whom miracles were not to be dismissed because of their illogic but appreciated because of their wonder. Prayer, for them, was not just a chance to ask God for a favor but an opportunity to reflect on whether the lives they were leading were worthwhile lives. Some were led by their faith to volunteer on behalf of the poor; others were attracted by their beliefs to listen to and love music. For many of them the Bible was not the literal word of God but a work of literature that, like other great works of literature, offered them insights into their own morality and the morality of others. For people of this sort, religion, which is about matters of personal conviction, is also about stimulating the imagination, expressing the power of the symbolic, and interpreting the ambiguities of human existence. As I talked with people like these, I found myself persuaded that their faith had made them far better people, bringing them out of lives of cynicism and loneliness into communion with others. A society without religious people of this sort would be far more illiberal than one with only a few of them.

Liberal society, in short, benefits directly from the presence of citizens whose religious beliefs encourage them to reflect on the question of human purpose; these are exactly the kind of reflective, imaginative, and serious people that a liberal society craves. But it also benefits from the existence of conservative believers who reject, sometimes root-and-branch, the very existence of liberalism. These—the fundamentalist preachers, the legions of the Christian right, the single-minded zealots on behalf of creationism—give liberals the opportunity to prove just how liberal they are, an opportunity that liberals would be foolish to sacrifice. Either way, liberalism is better served by a temperamental openness to people of faith than by a censorious condemnation.

Under conditions such as these, it is a disastrous empirical mistake to argue, as Stanley Fish does, that religion stands in opposition to such liberal ideals as tolerance, pluralism, neutrality, and reason. But it is also myopic for liberals to treat religious believers as if they are the enemy of everything that liberals ought to uphold. Because religion has made its accommodations with liberalism, it is time for liberals to make their accommodation with religion. Reason and revelation need not be in conflict, but even when they are, liberals should have enough confidence in the latter to temper their fear of the former. We no longer live in societies closed to reason, and it demeans liberalism when liberals argue that we do.

RISKS WORTH RISKING

There are risks liberals will face if, in casting their lot on behalf of open minds, they emphasize freedom for religion; watching an administration refuse to allow U.S. Park Rangers to estimate the age of the rocks in the Grand Canyon for fear of offending creationists, as the administration of George W. Bush did, is as difficult as sitting idly by while the same administration insisted, against all evidence, that abstinence was the only appropriate form of birth control. But the proper response to such efforts is to defeat those who support them at the polls, not to deny their right to try to put their convictions into practice. All things considered, liberals should be pleased that conservative religious believers have to make their case by using the same liberal-democratic means—elections, pressure groups, appeals to public opinion—relied on by everyone else; over the long run, such arrangements remain the best way to ensure that reasonable public policies will be chosen. Liberal proceduralism benefits everyone, including those who do not share liberalism's substantive commitments, although, as I pointed out earlier, there are increasing numbers of conservative Protestants who *do* share liberalism's substantive commitments.

In the debate that took place between Rousseau and Kant, Kant's defense of the artifice of culture proved to be far more compatible with a liberal understanding of human purpose than Rousseau's defense of nature. Religion is one of culture's many forms—perhaps its most important, and certainly its most persistent. As such, it serves to remind us of the capacity of human beings, in creating the world they inhabit, to reduce their dependence on natural forces over which they have no control. To be sure, religious believers assert a dependence on a supernatural force instead, and many of them claim that this force controls their lives. But in doing so, they rely on such artifacts as language, myth, traditions, laws, and beliefs, all of which testify to their own powers to shape the world in which they live. All forms of religion in the modern world are cultural rather than natural. Take away their faith and you are not necessarily left with human beings free to think for themselves; you might well be left with human beings who, lacking such a valuable cultural resource, are left without the ability to wonder, to emphasize, to make meaning, to appreciate.

Kant wrote that the generation anticipating an enlightened age was under a moral obligation to pass its knowledge on to the future. We who are the beneficiaries of those who struggled on behalf of open minds in the past are under a similar obligation to refuse to close them now. Religion is not about to disappear any time soon. Liberals are best off respecting it rather than repressing it. It is a truism that freedom of religion, like all forms of freedom, has its limits; respecting the rights of believers does not necessarily mean supporting the continued practice of polygamy, animal sacrifice, or even, to cite the most controversial of recent Supreme Court decisions, the use of peyote among Native Americans. When it comes to religion, as is true of almost any kind of human activity, some limits will always exist.

But for liberals, a disposition to be open to religion showers benefits all around. It supports religion because it gives believers the right to practice something so important to them. It benefits religion's critics because it removes from them the ugly and illiberal temptation to denounce people with whom they disagree as mad or illusory. And it benefits the society both of them share because it gives them something they can hold in common even if they disagree, not only over which gods they hold sacred, but whether any gods should be held sacred at all. There are few such really great bargains in politics. Religious freedom is one of them. Whatever the future of liberalism, a place for religion must be guaranteed.

CHAPTER 7

THE OPEN SOCIETY AND ITS FRIENDS

THE PURPOSE OF OPENNESS

The separation of church and state has become a fact of life in most Western societies today, and the priests among us are more likely to be in the news for running from the law than for upholding it. Monarchs are unable to exercise control over their own children, let alone their subjects, and aristocratic foibles have become the stuff of gossip columns. Towns no longer have walls, not even, in this age of cyberspace, electronic ones. Too few readers constitute a more serious fact of life for newspapers than governmental efforts at censorship. The problem with globalization, say critics from the left as well as the right, is that far from closing the world down too much, it opens it up too far. The goal of an "open society," a term popularized by the Viennese-born, London-based philosopher Karl Popper more than a half century ago at a time when liberalism was threatened by totalitarianism, has by and large been achieved.

The major question now facing liberal societies is not whether they should be open, but how. Three current controversies illustrate the way this question might best be addressed. Liberalism has long been committed to the principle that individuals must be able to hear and say whatever they want, yet whether freedom of speech ought to apply to private corporations who can use their deep pockets to tilt policy-makers in their favor or to those who say hateful or discriminatory things about stigmatized minorities are issues that remain hotly debated. Along similar lines, liberals have long held that societies should welcome strangers from abroad, but not everyone agrees that a commitment to open borders can be maintained when immigration has become as prevalent as it has. From the days of Bentham and Mill, finally, publicity in government has been held to be a key crucial value, yet as the Supreme Court justice Robert Jackson said in 1949, "the Constitution is not a suicide pact," which has led a number of contemporary thinkers to argue that a liberal society, to protect itself against its enemies, may have to keep some of its affairs secret from its citizens.

None of these controversies has easy resolutions, which is one reason liberals can often be found on both sides of them. Yet sometimes lost in the discussion of how much openness there ought to be is the prior question of what purposes openness is expected to serve. Liberals, I will now argue, believe in openness for a reason: it encourages citizens to expand their awareness of the world around them. Without such expansion, openness serves little or no purpose. With it, liberal societies live up to their promise. When it comes to some of the most important debates concerning just how open society ought to be, liberals should remember what they some time ago concluded about open markets: if policies and ideas help people to lead lives of autonomy and dignity, they are a good thing, but if they do not, liberals should be open to additional ways of encouraging people to live up to their full potential as human beings.

OPEN DISCUSSION

Put on trial for questioning religion and corrupting the minds of the young, Socrates, in "The Apology," told his judges that the gods had given to him "my duty to pass my life in the study of philosophy," a post he could no more desert than a soldier could abandon the position to which he has been assigned. I do not fear death, Socrates said, because I do not know what it is. But I do know what injustice is; in the case before us, it would be unjust for me to disobey what I have been commanded to do, and, as a lover of wisdom, I cannot participate in acts so "evil and base." Do what you must, was his advice to his jurors, "either dismiss me or not, since I shall not act otherwise, even though I must die many deaths."

Such eloquent, such implacable words have inspired the imagination of thinkers and artists ever since. One hears echoes of Socrates in Martin Luther's determination to make a stand since he could do no other; Henry David Thoreau's call for civil disobedience against slavery and the Mexican War; and the determination of Henrik Ibsen's Dr. Stockmann, in *An Enemy of the People*, to publicize the unsanitary conditions of his town's baths, despite the hostility of the townspeople and their leaders. These are all people who, in Kant's terms, dared to know, whatever the personal risks to themselves, and it is no wonder that for many a liberal thinker, their examples demonstrate that an open society is one that does not attempt to drive ideas out of existence merely because they are unpopular or challenge conventional ways of doing things.

John Stuart Mill was especially attracted to this understanding of openness. "Mankind can hardly be too often reminded, that there was once a man named Socrates," he wrote in *On Liberty*, "between whom and the legal authorities and public opinion of his time, there took place a memorable collision." The fact that Socrates was put to death as a common criminal, he believed, ought to serve as a reminder both of the timelessness of truth and of the determination of small-minded inquisitors to punish those who utter it. Even when truth is seemingly driven out of existence, Mill wrote, "it may be extinguished once, twice, or many times, but in the course of ages there will generally be found persons to rediscover it, until some one of its reappearances falls on a time when from favourable circumstances it escapes persecution until it has made such head as to withstand all subsequent attempts to suppress it."

Not only did Mill speak in defense of unpopular ideas, he worried that those who advocated them were likely to be persecuted. To be sure, Victorians did not live in ancient Athens, and the men of wisdom among them were not about to be forced to drink hemlock. But lest you think that the days of inquisitions are past, Mill warned, another enemy of freedom of thought, one with which Socrates was quite familiar, lurks dangerously around us: the public. The masses now want a say in how public affairs ought to be run, and Mill believed that their influence would be baleful. No matter the country in which they appear, "they are always a mass, that is to say, collective mediocrity. And what is a still greater novelty, the mass does not now take their opinions from dignitaries in Church and State, from ostensible leaders, or from books. Their thinking is done for them by men much like themselves, addressing them or speaking in their name, on the spur of the moment, through the newspapers."

Under the influence of his friend Alexis de Tocqueville, whose ideas about the tyranny of the majority expressed so cogently in *Democracy in America* appealed to Mill, the great liberal had turned into the great kvetch. When it came to public opinion, mediocrity was to be our lot and the solitary person of genius our Savior. "The initiation of all wise or noble things, comes and must come from individuals; generally, at least, first from some one individual. The honour and glory of the average man is that he is capable of following that initiative; that he can respond internally to wise and noble things, and be led to them with eyes open," Mill wrote. This can be read, I suppose, as a defense of an open mind, but only if, in contrast to Kant, all other minds are prepared to receive instruction from their betters.

On Liberty is a classic work that belongs in the liberal tradition's canon. It is also not always consistent. Those sections of the essay that remind us of how human beings possess the capacity to strive after excellence offer a powerful and optimistic account of what liberal citizens might become, just as those that evoke the tyranny of the majority reinforce the idea that liberal citizens may never amount to much of anything. Mill is right that we should never forget that there was once a man named Socrates, but nor should we forget, as Mill seems to do, that Socrates was neither a liberal nor a citizen of a liberal society. "But why, my dear Crito, should we care so much for the opinion of the many?" Socrates asked one of his followers, who had suggested that the philosopher seek to escape from the death penalty imposed upon him. The multitude might be able to bring about a great evil, just as it might be able to bring about a great good, "but now they can do neither; for they can make a man neither wise nor foolish; but they do whatever chances." It never occurs to Socrates that if the views held by the multitude are wrong, his task is to raise their sights so that in the future they may be right. "The Apology," like *On Liberty*, is a declaration, not a dialogue. Toward the multitude, Socrates is actually rather passive. Indeed, when the verdict comes in and he learns that some Athenians had voted for his acquittal, he is surprised, for he had simply assumed that the judgment against him would be unanimous.

On Liberty, and especially its invocation of Socrates, raises the question of whether there exist alternative ways of fulfilling the liberal commitment to openness without a grumpy dismissal of the public and its all but inevitable closed-mindedness. To try to educate the mass public rather than condemn it is, to a considerable degree, what many of the major thinkers of the Enlightenment had in mind. Exploring the marvels of new printing technologies, Denis Diderot and his colleagues had launched the *Encyclopédie* and, in so doing, they helped shape what Jürgen Habermas calls the public sphere, a place where people would come together more to develop their ideas than to declare them. "Diderot's distinction between written and oral discourse sheds light on the functions of these new gatherings," Habermas has written. "There was scarcely a great writer in the eighteenth century who would not have first submitted his essential ideas for discussion in such discourse, in lectures before the *académies,* and especially in the *salons.*" No longer was it necessary to assume that the public would always and inevitably be ignorant. Instead, the liberal idea of openness was transformed into a quest to bring the individuals together who collectively compose the public so that, through dialogue and discussion, they could enlighten each other.

Kant's "What is Enlightenment?" was certainly part of this search for an informed public. There are times, he believed, when limitations on freedom of expression are necessary; officers in the Army, for example, must obey their superiors. But in the public realm, where reason prevails, using one's intellect is essential; that same officer, Kant continued, in words that have direct relevance to the U.S. war in Iraq, cannot "justifiably be barred from making comments, as a scholar, on the mistakes in the military service and submitting these remarks to judgment by the public." Writing at the time he did, Kant associated the use of reason, as his comment about the military officer suggests, with the minority of the population whose professional conditions of work forced them to justify by the use of logic and argument the decisions they made. Yet, as Habermas insists, Kant's conception of the scholar was not "merely academic." For once a public sphere came into existence, it would expand as more and more people began to read newspapers, participate in public discussion, and eventually vote. "The public sphere," Habermas points out, "was realized not in the republic of scholars alone but in the public use of reason by all those who were adept at it."

Here, then, are two quite different ways of defining what it means for a society to be open. In the one, truth, always fragile, needs protection against complacency; a liberal society will take special steps to ensure that when words of wisdom are uttered, those who speak them will not be prosecuted for their dissent. Even if the unpopular idea is false, moreover, it will require, as Mill insisted, the same amount of protection as if it were true, for society can never know in advance which of the opinions competing for attention will turn out over time to be the correct one. An open society is therefore one committed to the idea of civil liberty: government should simply stay out of the business of policing opinion altogether. Just as the state should not favor one industry over another, it should not favor one opinion over another. Conditions of openness are met when censorship is prohibited and the means of mass communication, such as newspapers and the mass media, are allowed to do their job. In a democracy, the majority may have numbers on its side, but it does not necessarily have right on its side. The more a society is open to minority points of view, whatever they happen to be, the more open it is.

In the competing view, the public is not something already formed, its opinions waiting to be expressed. Like the society of which it is a part, the public is a creature of artifice, not a by-product of nature; technologies such as the printing press may have created the conditions for its emergence, but a public had to fashion itself through its own intentional acts. It is not enough that opinions be expressed; they must also be informed, and the best way to ensure that they are informed is to encourage people to hear ideas other than the ones they are used to hearing. In this process, government cannot and should not be passive; it has means at its disposal to educate citizens, and it should use those means to educate them well. Government is not a referee refusing to take sides in an athletic contest. It is better understood as a tutor, offering its resources to people not to help them win a struggle against others but to improve the kind of people they are.

America's debate over the meaning of the public would come a century later than the one that took place in Europe. When it came, it took the form of one side arguing, under the influence of Tocqueville and Mill, that the mass public was an obstacle to an open society, and the other arguing, much in the spirit of the *philosophes,* that the public was a work in formation requiring cultivation and improvement. Taking the former position, as the media critic Eric Alterman has pointed out, was America's preeminent journalist, Walter Lippmann, whose *Public Opinion* (1922) relied on the newly developing science of psychology to argue that the public is too much attracted to stereotypical thinking and too easily manipulated by propaganda to act rationally. Modern society is a mass society, and because of this, the public official, in order to manufacture consent, "finds himself," as Lippmann put it, "deciding more and more consciously what facts, in what setting, he shall permit the public to know." Democracy can still continue to exist under these conditions, but it will never be based on appeals to reason; enlightenment will come, if it is to come at all, by lowering our sights and doing our best to secure footholds in a world dominated by the power of symbols and stereotypes.

John Dewey, America's best known philosopher at that time, responded to Lippmann, first in an article in *The New Republic* in 1922, and then more thoroughly in *The Public and Its Problems*, published five years later. Like all the great liberal thinkers before him, Dewey took the side of culture over nature: "Everything which is distinctively human is learned, not native," he wrote. "To learn in a human way and to human effect is not just to acquire added skill through refinement of original capacities." We live, Dewey went on to say, in what he called The Great Society, by which he meant the radical expansion of modern forms of social organization that had characterized societies such as the United States in the first decades of the twentieth century. How do we add to our "original capacities" when we no longer work the farm or share the village green with our neighbors? His answer was that we have to rely on forms of mass communication, and that those, in turn, require a healthy and vibrant public: "There can be no public without full publicity in respect to all consequences which concern it. Whatever obstructs and restricts publicity, limits and distorts public opinion and checks and distorts thinking on social affairs."

Dewey is best known today as the father of progressive education. But Dewey's views on education follow directly from his political philosophy. Education, like communication, is a way of forming the public so that it can live up to its responsibilities under modern conditions. Dewey did not deny that psychology had taught us about the potential for human irrationality. But he also believed that the equally emerging science of sociology taught us about how institutions, including the schools and the press, could teach people through experience ways of directing their efforts toward ends collectively determined by themselves.

Any argument between Lippmann and Dewey was bound to attract considerable attention, one reason it continues to reverberate today. Habermas, relying heavily on Dewey as an intellectual predecessor, argues that liberalism requires open and undistorted communication. His ideas, in turn, have inspired those contemporary journalists who believe that the press, rather than just reporting the news, has an obligation to help promote an informed citizenry better prepared to consume it. Lippmann, by contrast, remains too elitist to have a large number of explicit contemporary defenders, but his ideas about the public's irrationality live on in the academic world and his disdain for the rationality of the general public guides those journalists more than willing to offer the public the "soft" news they think the public wants. Every time we discuss what information means—a discussion fueled even more today by new means of communication such as the Internet—we are participating in the debate that Lippmann and Dewey did so much to shape.

Another, equally important debate over the meaning of the public took place at the same time as the one between Lippmann and Dewey. This one focused directly on the First Amendment to the Constitution and its guarantees of freedom of speech, assembly, religion, and the press. Although it had been written in the age of the Enlightenment, the First Amendment, intended to define what openness meant in the most open society in the world, was not subject to judicial interpretation until the outbreak of World War I and the subsequent steps taken by the Wilson administration to regulate speech and conduct. The two thinkers who did the most to frame our understanding of what role freedom of speech should play in American life were both Supreme Court justices, and they were also among the most brilliant writers the liberal tradition ever produced. Because they both wrote in favor of free speech at a time when the Supreme Court was not inclined to countenance it, we tend to forget how different their reasoning was. One, Oliver Wendell Holmes, Jr., a Civil War veteran and cold-eyed realist, argued that the purpose of free speech was to keep government from censoring opinion. The other, Louis D. Brandeis, a leading Progressive, social reformer, and idealistic early Zionist, believed that the purpose of free speech was to improve the quality of what people heard and spoke. Here again one finds echoes in the American context of the earlier European debate over whether the public is a friend or an enemy of an open society.

Jacob Abrams was a left-wing firebrand who, in opposition to American involvement in World War I, got together with his comrades to distribute pamphlets opposing Woodrow Wilson's decision to send troops to Russia in 1918. Convicted under the Espionage Act of 1917 on the grounds that his actions might have harmed the war effort, he appealed to the Supreme Court, where his conviction was upheld by a 7–2 vote. Holmes dissented, somewhat surprisingly since it was Holmes who in an earlier case had upheld the Espionage Act on the grounds that speech which constituted a "clear and present danger" to social order could be regulated. (This was the case in which Holmes made his remark about "falsely shouting fire in a theater.") I can understand why, if you believe something to be true, you would want to ensure that others will accept it as true as well, Holmes now reasoned. "But when men have realized that time has upset many fighting faiths," he continued, "they may come to believe even more than they believe the very foundations of their own conduct that the ultimate good desired is better reached by free trade in ideas—that the best test of truth is the power of the thought itself to get itself accepted in the competition of the market, and the truth is the only ground upon which their wishes can safely be carried out." Like Mill and Lippmann, Holmes worried about the irrationality of the public. But he was too much the liberal to believe that it was government's job to prevent people from hearing wrong ideas. Let the market do the work instead, Holmes reasoned. In a free market of ideas, bad ones—Holmes characterized the speech of Jacob Abrams as, in part, "a silly leaflet by an unknown man"—will be driven out of circulation just as inferior species will not survive the struggle for existence.

Brandeis concurred in Holmes's dissent in *Abrams*. He would have his chance to express his own views about freedom of speech eight years later when Anita Whitney, who had helped establish the Communist Labor Party, was convicted under the Criminal Syndicalism Act of 1919 and appealed to the Supreme Court. For technical reasons, Brandeis joined a unanimous Court in upholding her conviction, but his concurring opinion in the case became his most famous statement about freedom of speech:

Those who won our independence believed that the final end of the state was to make men free to develop their faculties; and that in its government the deliberative forces should prevail over the arbitrary. They valued liberty both as an end and as a means. . . . They believed that freedom to think as you will and to speak as you think are means indispensable to the discovery and spread of political truth; that without free speech and assembly discussion would be futile; that with them, discussion affords ordinarily adequate protection against the dissemination of noxious doctrine; that the greatest menace to freedom is an inert people; that public discussion is a political duty; and that this should be a fundamental principle of the American government.

As this passage makes clear, Brandeis possessed a strong conception of the civic purposes a liberal political system should try to fulfill and was therefore very much a liberal in the Kantian or Deweyan sense of the term. His goal was not just to encourage liberty but to view liberty as an opportunity to develop the capacities of citizens. There will be noxious ideas—no one doubts that. But it is neither the job of the state to censor bad ideas nor the task of the market to weed them out. Elevating the level of public discourse is the best antidote for an ignorant public.

Of these two approaches to free speech, Holmes's would eventually become the more influential. It is not difficult to understand why. Just as the leading theorists of the Enlightenment justified the role of a benevolent despot, Brandeis's approach to these matters seems too patronizing for a society as committed to individual freedom as the United States. Americans are inclined to distrust government intervention in the economy, which means that they are even more likely to distrust government intervention in matters of thought and discussion. From this perspective, if the people are inert, that is their decision, considered or not, and any effort to rouse them interferes with their freedom to choose their own way of life, even if it is a way of life offensive to liberals and their ideas about improving upon human nature. The First Amendment forbids government from interfering with ideas, and if that means that government cannot prevent people from hearing some, it also means it cannot encourage them to hear others.

There is considerable truth in this way of thinking: we have seen too many examples of government doing harm to matters of individual conscience to have much confidence that it could do much good. Yet from the point of view of a Brandeis or a Dewey, first opinions are likely to be unreflective ones, for what best represents what we think will be the views we hold after we have had a chance to think and engage with others. This is why institutions are important; they help take us out of a state of nature, in which our opinions are likely to be emotional, and bring us into a state of society, in which our opinions are more likely to be formed. In this process, government, so long as it is democratic government, is too valuable a resource to be allowed to stand idle. If freedom of speech means that government should encourage citizens to use their full capacities as speakers, something more than laissez-faire is required.

In *Democracy and the Problem of Free Speech,* the Harvard law professor Cass Sunstein makes this point by drawing a comparison between the regulation of business and the regulation of speech. In the days of Adam Smith, liberals believed that government regulation of the economy was something to be avoided. But throughout the nineteenth century, liberals came to understand that the end they sought—the ability of individuals to avoid arbitrary dependence upon others in order to become masters of their own fate—was better obtained by regulating business than by allowing industrial capitalists a free hand. Isn't the same thing true of speech? Sunstein asks. If the purpose of free speech is to help individuals think for themselves so that the ideas they express are genuinely their own, might it not be necessary to establish what Sunstein calls a "New Deal" for speech—a recognition that government has a positive duty to sustain the conditions that make for an open and enlightened citizenry?

Two recent free speech controversies raise the question of whether openness is best pursued by regulating speech or by allowing it to operate without constraints. One involves those forms of speech that minorities find offensive and insulting. The other concerns efforts to make the free speech playing field more equal by regulating the amount of money that can be spent in political campaigning. Both illustrate that the best approach to an open society is not one that relies on abstract principle but one that judges policies by the actual extent to which they contribute to human development.

"Hate speech" refers to the utterance of words or the display of symbols that a group, usually a stigmatized minority group, finds degrading. The most prominent examples are found in Europe. Italy, France, Germany, and Austria, for example, make denying the Holocaust illegal; whatever freedom of speech means there, it does not mean open advocacy of the kind of right-wing extremism that once brought the Nazis to power in Germany. Such laws did not come out of the blue. Europeans have a long history of laws regulating blasphemy, and while nearly all such blasphemy laws only made it illegal to offend Christians, those laws have taken on new life as European Muslims argue that speech insulting to them, such as cartoons caricaturing the Prophet Muhammad published in a Danish newspaper, ought to be regulated as well. Generally without constitutional guarantees of free speech as firm as those contained in the U.S. Constitution, European governments tend to the proposition that treating all groups with equal respect trumps an individual's right to say anything he or she wants.

Laws regulating hate speech in the United States are less common. But they do exist and to some degree are expanding as states, towns, college campuses, and even at times the federal government, responding to attacks on gays or discriminatory language against women and African-Americans, develop policies that would punish offensive comments against them. Typical is Section 422.6 of the California penal code, which says:

> No person, whether or not acting under color of law, shall by force or threat of force, willfully injure, intimidate, interfere with, oppress, or threaten any other person in the free exercise or enjoyment of any right or privilege secured to him or her by the Constitution or laws of this state or by the Constitution or laws of the United States because of the other person's race, color, religion, ancestry, national origin, disability, gender, or sexual orientation, or because he or she perceives that the other person has one or more of those characteristics.

Conservatives, especially religious conservatives, know what they think of such laws; worried that those who oppose feminism or gay rights will be charged with a crime for expressing their opinions, they oppose them. Liberals, by contrast, find in such laws a conflict between the First Amendment's commitment to free speech and the Fourteenth Amendment's assertion of equality. Which should they choose?

If we hold with Brandeis that the purpose of an open society is to encourage people to develop their capacities as citizens, I believe we must avoid regulating hate speech. As offensive as such speech may be, it still represents an attempt to communicate a position on an important public issue. If, like Holocaust denial, the view is false, its falsity will be better revealed through exposure than through censorship. If it is ugly—think of someone wearing a T-shirt calling homosexuals "fags"—it cannot be clear in advance whether the comment represents a sincere religious conviction or an expression of prejudice so awful that it cannot be allowed public expression. Given the ubiquity of such competing attractions as sports, mass entertainment, and celebrity worship, it is difficult enough in modern liberal democracies to involve the public in political discussion at all. From the standpoint of encouraging people to think about the world around them, wrongheaded opinions are better than no opinions. Even though political extremism can be a danger to democracy, at some point liberal democracies must have sufficient confidence in the ability of their own citizens to think for themselves. Here the spirit of the First Amendment should take priority over the spirit of the Fourteenth.

Quite a different conclusion ought to be reached in cases involving campaign finance reform. In June 2007, the Supreme Court ruled that portions of the McCain-Feingold Act of 2002, a campaign finance reform law, were unconstitutional. The law had attempted to ban efforts by interest groups to use their funds in the days immediately before an election to broadcast advertisements aimed at electing or defeating specific candidates. By a 5–4 majority, the Court held that efforts to ban such ads violated the freedom of speech of those concerned enough to spend their funds for such purposes. "The First Amendment requires us to err on the side of protecting political speech rather than suppressing it," wrote Chief Justice John Roberts. From the majority's point of view, its decision was a continuation of the efforts of earlier free speech advocates such as Oliver Wendell Holmes, Jr., to let these matters be decided by the market rather than by government regulation.

For its critics, by contrast, the majority's ruling ignored the obvious fact that if you allow well-financed groups to pour money into elections to help their side win, you give them advantages denied to those whose views are less likely to attract the financial support of rich backers. The case, *Federal Election Commission* v. *Wisconsin Right to Life*, was thus one battle in a larger war over what freedom of speech really means. Money is money, critics of the case believe, while talk is talk; one does not substitute for the other. Not only that, but not all forms of talk are the same: words can be used in propaganda-like fashion to buttress the self-interest of particular groups or they can be used in ways designed to inform and enlighten. It is therefore proper, according to those who support campaign finance reform, not only to limit the amount different sides to an issue can spend in an effort to equalize them but to bring more transparency to the process of helping voters discover who is providing the money and why. Establishing fair rules of campaign finance is not a form of regulation that suppresses free speech but represents an effort to improve the quality of what is spoken. In this area, it makes more sense to side with the Fourteenth Amendment's insistence on equality than on an abstract reading of the First.

The interesting thing about a case such as *Federal Elections Com-*

mission v. *Wisconsin Right to Life* is that neither the majority nor the minority say that they are opposed to freedom of speech; in that sense, one of liberalism's most important commitments to openness is accepted, in theory, across the board. Yet, as the case also illustrates, everything depends on what freedom of speech is taken to mean. If the purpose of freedom of speech is to encourage citizens not only to make decisions but to make wise ones, this case is a giant step backward. For one thing, the speech in question is that of a corporation or interest group, and while corporations can be said to grow in an economic sense, only individuals grow in the developmental sense meant by such thinkers as Kant, Mill, and Dewey. From a Brandeis-like perspective, in addition, campaign finance reform represents an effort to regulate the distortions that inevitably follow when the process of raising political money becomes little more than a legalized form of bribery in which well-endowed contributors gave money to politicians in return for support on matters of public policy important to the givers. Not only does such a system not promote deliberation, it hinders efforts to bring reason and enlightenment to political discussion by encouraging self-interested arguments and calling them information. If we are to value free speech, we need to consider what people are actually saying. And the kind of speech generated by a free market system in the absence of any public regulation is not speech worth much protection.

In an effort to understand the conditions that make an open society possible, the last word should be given to Alexander Meiklejohn, who lived from 1872 to 1964. A philosopher by training, Meiklejohn, who was born in Britain, taught at Brown University, where he eventually became dean of the college. (The peer advising program at Brown to this day bears his name.) A career in university administration followed, first as president of Amherst College and then as the head of experimental colleges at the University of Wisconsin and the School of Social Sciences in San Francisco. Too utopian, too cantankerous, and, truth be told, too imperial in his attitude toward others, Meiklejohn nonetheless remains known as a strong defender of civil liberties in general and academic freedom in particular; the American Association of University Professors names its award in defense of academic freedom after him.

In three lectures published in 1948 as *Free Speech and Its Relation to Self-Government*, Meiklejohn asked and answered the question of what free speech is for. "The First Amendment," he wrote, "is not the guardian of unregulated talkativeness. It does not require that, on every occasion, every citizen shall take part in public debate." Imagine a meeting of twenty people, all of whom have the same view, Meiklejohn said; what purpose, save to make the meeting longer, would it serve to have each of them speak? "What is essential," he continued, "is not that everyone shall speak, but that everything worth saying shall be said." Once we view the people as governing themselves, the key ingredient "is not the words of the speakers, but the minds of the hearers. The final aim of the meeting is the voting of wise decisions. The voters, therefore, must be made as wise as possible."

Like John Stuart Mill or Oliver Wendell Holmes, Jr., Alexander Meiklejohn was an advocate for free speech. But his reasons for supporting it were different from theirs. Mill and Holmes wanted freedom of speech so that the ignorant would not suppress the wise. Meiklejohn wanted free speech so that there would be as few as possible ignorant people. The best guarantee of an open society is not to take heroic measures after freedom of speech has been threatened, but to take preventive action so that it will not be threatened in the first place.

OPEN BORDERS

The societies of the *ancien régime* were not completely closed against foreigners; wars, uncertain boundaries, religious persecution and exile, nascent colonial ventures, linguistic affinities—all produced sufficient cross-border mobility to give at least the cities of the old order a cosmopolitan complexion. But gaining rights of citizenship in a land not originally one's own was another matter entirely. There was always the tendency, as the Dutch-born jurist Hugo Grotius noted in his *Law of War and Peace* (1625), to treat the alien as the enemy. In Great Britain, foreign merchants could not hire fellow aliens; Catholics and Jews were long denied the benefits of full citizenship; and as late as 1793, Parliament passed an Alien Bill requiring shipping companies to report any foreigners on board. In France, foreigners were subject to similar restraints and, in addition, could not draw up wills passing on their property to their children; the *droit d'aubaine* gave the monarch the right to inherit their property in the absence of native heirs. When it took an act of parliament to naturalize a citizen, there were not many citizens to be naturalized: between 1660 and 1790, roughly fifty-two foreign-born people annually were accorded French citizenship.

One might think that the first generation of liberal philosophers, appalled at the restrictions on individual liberty implied by such ways of treating foreign-born people, would have made an argument for societies as open to people as they were to ideas. If governments are formed out of contracts into which individuals voluntarily enter, surely they can contract themselves anywhere they choose. And if individual liberty is tied to the idea of free markets, then the buyers and sellers of human labor, like the buyers and sellers of any other commodity, should be allowed to move around in search of the best bargains.

None of the most prominent British liberal thinkers, however, engaged in a sustained discussion of immigration. John Locke did envision a situation where men could engage in "withdrawing themselves, and their obedience, from the jurisdiction they were born under . . . and setting up new governments in other places," but he then went on to argue that because of the idea of tacit consent—once you have benefited from a contract, your retroactive consent to it is implied—a person's right to leave one contract in order to enter into another is severely limited. Adam Smith, who attacked nearly all the restrictions on economic activity imposed by mercantilism, never wrote a defense of what today we would call a free market immigration policy. Aside from some remarks on the better bargaining power of labor in the American colonies, *The Wealth of Nations* simply does not contain a sustained discussion of the advantages of workers moving from one country to another in search of better opportunities, let alone of employers seeking workers from abroad in search of higher profits. Even though John Stuart Mill later tried to justify state intervention into the economy in ways contrary to Adam Smith, Mill shared Smith's lack of interest in immigration; *Principles of Political Economy* refers to emigration in twenty-eight different paragraphs and to immigration in only three.

It may be that this lack of discussion about immigration was due to the fact that Great Britain was too busy sending large numbers of its residents abroad to worry about the relatively few who were arriving on its shores. Since so many of them were leaving for the American colonies, the situation on the other side of the Atlantic, in matters of immigration as in matters of religion, was something of a thought experiment designed to see if things could be done differently than they had been done in Europe. For all of Adam Smith's silence on immigration, the Declaration of Independence contains a stirring defense of the right of the colonies to receive new members. The Declaration was by no means alone; its rhetoric, in fact, paled in comparison to Tom Paine's *Common Sense:* "O ye that love mankind! Ye that dare oppose, not only the tyranny, but the tyrant, stand forth! Every spot of the old world is overrun with oppression. Freedom hath been hunted round the globe. Asia, and Africa, have long expelled her.— Europe regards her like a stranger, and England hath given her warning to depart. O! receive the fugitive, and prepare in time an asylum for mankind."

Despite the need to populate the nation, however, the American colonies, and then the United States, were not unabashedly in favor of opening themselves to all who wanted to come. Ben Franklin, a liberal man on most things, was a xenophobe when it came to German immigrants. The Declaration's author, Thomas Jefferson, worried that too many foreigners would undermine republican conceptions of virtue. Of all the founders, the most enthusiastic on behalf of immigration was Alexander Hamilton, himself an immigrant, and Hamilton was much closer to European conservatism than he was to North American liberalism. No wonder, then, that American history is filled with examples of restrictive sentiment designed to regulate, or even stop, the flow of immigrants; every campaign on behalf of restricting the borders could appeal to the ambivalence of the framers, reiterating Franklin's concern that "those who come hither are generally of the most ignorant Stupid Sort of their own nation," or Jefferson's that "they will bring with them the principles of the governments they leave, imbibed in their early youth; or, if able to throw them off, it will be in exchange for an unbounded licentiousness, passing, as is usual, from one extreme to another."

Immigration is now an issue facing all liberal societies, not just the United States, and Europeans are just as uncertain as Americans about how to react to it. They have welcomed guest workers to take low-paying jobs, but they have also been generally unwilling to grant the benefits of citizenship to them—or even to their children and grandchildren. As much as the leaders of these societies protest against those who carry out acts of genocide, they are not especially generous in granting asylum within their countries to genocide's victims. As they have opened themselves up to each other through the European Union, they have grown increasingly closed within, rediscovering their Christian identity in the face of Muslim immigration or reasserting the uniqueness of their individual national cultures. When it comes to time-tested policy considerations such as how and whether to regulate the economy, European societies have a history of liberal theory upon which they can rely. But the same is not true when it comes to dealing with immigrants; in this especially contentious arena of public debate, there is not all that much in the liberal tradition to which they can turn.

As a result of this liberal vacuum, a substantial part of the public debate over immigration has been dominated by illiberal voices. The most insistent of such voices in both Europe and the United States belong to those politicians who promise to protect the presumed cultural integrity of the homeland against the alleged degeneracy of the alien. There can be little doubt that the bulk of the messages conveyed by the more extreme anti-immigrant politicians in both the United States and Europe are illiberal through and through. One finds in them no generosity of spirit toward people whose conditions of life have been difficult in the extreme; no heartwarming accounts of their courage in leaving one land to try and achieve success in another; no sense that all cultures have something to value; no appreciation of the underlying universality of all people whatever their national differences; no recognition of the fact that peace among cultures is a worthier objective than war between them; and no acknowledgment that the society being protected, far from being flawless, could use an injection of new ideas and entrepreneurial energy. Nowhere do conservatives of this particular inclination—there are other conservatives, such as those associated with *The Wall Street Journal,* who are supporters of immigration—seem more deserving of the epithet "reactionary" than when it comes to immigration; mobility of people around the globe is a fact of life, and they react to it out of anger and fear.

Because they reach out and welcome people from distant shores, multiculturalists find themselves on the opposite side of the political spectrum from xenophobes. Yet this does not mean that multiculturalism is by definition liberal. It is axiomatic among many multiculturalists that newcomers, living in an environment hostile to their way of life, need to preserve many of the cultural practices they bring with them. In such a way do the imperatives of multiculturalism and the demands of liberalism come into conflict: if we extend autonomy to groups, we allow them to engage in practices—arranged marriages, gender segregation, religious indoctrination, to name three—that can stand in conflict with the rights of the individuals within those groups. At least one important theorist in this tradition, the Canadian political philosopher Will Kymlicka, has tried to make the case that considerations of group solidarity are not inherently illiberal, yet his arguments are not especially persuasive. If Mill's emphasis on the importance of determining one's own life plan means anything, it is that we not only get to choose for ourselves the best way to live but that such choices, by frequently bringing us into conflict with the ways of life into which we were born, demand that we be able to break with the power that groups in general, and inherited groups in particular, have over us. It is for this reason that multiculturalism has been criticized not only from the right but from political philosophers who strongly identify with the liberal political tradition.

How, then, should liberals treat the vexing question of what to do about national borders? The answer is to recall that liberals believe not only in openness but in the growth of individual capacity that openness encourages. From such a perspective, liberals should insist that openness is a two-way street. Kant is a helpful guide here. He teaches us that the circumstances in which we find ourselves always have to be judged against the circumstances in which, but for an arbitrary roll of the dice, we might have found ourselves. From this perspective, it is inherently unfair that someone who happens to be born in the United States is likely to live longer and to have a greater capacity to choose the kind of life he or she wants to lead than someone born in Kenya. This does not mean that the United States has to open its borders to everyone from Kenya who wishes to come. But it does mean that a New Yorker should recognize that any advantages he may have over the Nairobian are as much due to an accident of birth as they are to any notion that he may be a more deserving person. No system of perfect justice is ever possible, but from the perspective of a Kantian commitment to openness, the least an American can do is to welcome a certain amount of immigration from Africa. Given liberalism's history, no society can close its borders to the deserving and call itself liberal; however capacious liberalism's definition, xenophobia never meets it.

If openness is something we value in one direction, however, it is also something we must value in the other; once a society admits new members, those members are also under an obligation to open themselves to their new society. Liberalism distinguishes itself from xenophobia by welcoming newcomers. But it also is different from multiculturalism because it makes demands on them. There is a liberal bargain with respect to immigration as there is with respect to religion. Its basic premise is this: we will be open to you if you are open to us.

An illustration of the liberal approach to borders can be found in a well-meaning effort to control incidents of racism against Muslim immigrants in Great Britain led by the Runnymede Trust, an organization committed to a multicultural Britain. The Trust constructed an eight-part test designed to see whether the views that native Britons had of Muslims were open or closed: an open-minded person would be more likely to view Islam as diverse rather than monolithic, different rather than inferior, a partner rather than an enemy, and a sincere religion rather than a manipulative ideology. The questions are thoughtful and likely to uncover what people really do think of the strangers in their midst, but no similar account of how Muslim immigrants view their hosts was included in the Runnymede Trust report, *Islamophobia*. Yet surely it matters whether immigrants view the inhabitants of their new country as hostile or welcoming, sincere or racist, a friend or an enemy. If the native-born refuse to reach out to newcomers, racism and xenophobia follow. But if the newcomers do not reach out to the native-born, exclusion and isolation follow.

These issues moved from the academic to the practical realm in 2006 when Great Britain's former foreign minister, Jack Straw, raised concerns about the burqa, the full-body covering worn by some Muslim women. (As home secretary in 1997, Straw had launched the Runnymede Trust's report on Islamophobia.) Straw made clear in his remarks that he defended the right of any woman to wear less intrusive head scarves and that he was conscious of the fact that men ought not to tell women what to wear. Yet he also felt that something is seriously wrong when, in conversation with another person, he cannot engage in face-to-face interaction. Without explicitly using the term "openness," Straw was saying that a decision to wear the burqa is a decision to close yourself off from everyone around you. He was not, like a xenophobe, saying that Muslims do not belong in Great Britain. He was not saying, as many multiculturalists do, that Muslims should be allowed to wear whatever traditional garb they believe best expresses their cultural and religious sensibilities. Nor was he asking for the full assimilation of immigrants to British customs. Straw was instead, through a carefully chosen example, illustrating what it means to open up to others while expecting a certain openness in return.

When immigration is viewed as a two-way street, the liberal promise of individual development works in both directions. Multiculturalists are right about one important thing: the benefits immigrants bring to their new country are cultural as well as economic. Because they represent so many different faiths, immigrants expand the religious pluralism that serves as the best protection of religious liberty. Because they bring with them a different perspective on such matters as family, friendship, and community, immigrants frequently rejuvenate the literary, musical, and artistic sensibilities of the countries to which they move; one way of knowing when immigration has been successful is when novels written by immigrants or their children win literary prizes or dominate best-seller lists. When immigration works, the horizons of the native-born expand. They become better people because they live in a more cosmopolitan society. No longer do they need to travel abroad, as the children of the aristocracy did centuries ago, to learn about ways of life different from their own. All they need to do is to go out and buy groceries.

At the same time, immigration offers similar benefits to the new-comers. One can understand why, living in a foreign country they may perceive as hostile, immigrants would close themselves off from others. And it's true that some host countries, especially France, may be too hasty in demanding from immigrants an acceptance of new ways of life, for example by banning head scarves in schools. But it is also the case that attempting to live a closed life in an open society is bound to be as self-limiting as it is self-defeating. Liberalism's promise is not just that it will make room for newcomers, although, given the fact that so many immigrants arrive from highly illiberal countries, making room for them is no small thing. People come in order to become; they learn that new ways of life unavailable, or even unimaginable, to them in the societies they left are now within view. Fearful of changes of this magnitude, immigrants, and especially their children, are sometimes led to rededicate themselves to traditional practices in their new society, including, on rare but nonetheless dramatic occasions, practices that can lead to or excuse away acts of terrorism. But over time, liberal society exercises such a strong and seductive hold on people that subsequent generations find its appeals almost impossible to resist. That, for multiculturalists, is precisely the problem. They tend to view liberalism's seductiveness as the imposition of an alien way of life upon a more genuine one. But liberals ought to be proud of the fact that the opportunity to shape a life of one's own choosing, once experienced, is not easily given up. When immigrants arrive in liberal societies, the number of liberal citizens in the world ultimately expands.

Immigration does not follow the usual left-right lines that divide liberal societies: opponents and proponents can be found on both sides of the ideological divide. Big business generally likes it while labor does not; some racial minorities fear it even as others welcome it. It also frustrates those looking for clear and unambiguous rules that can resolve the tensions immigration brings. No society can completely close its borders, for even if it tried to do so, immigrants would still arrive, and no society can completely open its borders, for if it did so, no conception of citizenship worth possessing would remain. If one is looking for an abstract principle to follow on questions of immigration, liberalism cannot provide it.

But liberalism can offer other things. One is a guideline: a liberal society will allow people in and make exceptions for conditions under which they must be kept out rather than keeping people out and making an occasional exception for when they ought to be allowed in. Another is a willingness to view the world as teeming with potential that, however threatening to ways of life taken for granted, forces people to adapt to new challenges rather than try to protect themselves against the foreign and unknown. And the third is a focus not only on what we can offer immigrants but on what they can offer us. The goal immigration seeks—openness—is a goal worth seeking, especially if openness encourages those on both sides of once firm national borders to become better people in the process.

OPEN GOVERNMENT

"Political secrecy," writes the historian Robin J. Ives in an article in the journal *French History*, "was in many ways the defining feature of *ancien régime* political culture." Two individuals deserve special credit for shaping that culture. The theory behind the *politique du secret* was formulated with impressive verve by the sixteenth-century Frenchman Jean Bodin, who revived the Roman notion of *arcana imperii*, or mysteries of state, to argue that without the ability to keep his affairs secret, the monarch's sovereignty would exist in name only. In Europe, Bodin's ideas were put into practice primarily by France's Cardinal Richelieu. "It was under his stewardship," Ives writes, "that there emerged a sophisticated framework of censorship (underpinned by guild controls), centralized administration (vested in the office of the *secrétaire d'état*), and financial secrecy (underpinned by *ordonnances de comptant*)." Lasting right up until the day after the French Revolution, the idea that the people had no right to inquire into the business of the monarch was as central to the politics of the old order as the notion that they did have such a right was fundamental to the Enlightenment.

Of all the realms of darkness upon which the *philosophes* hoped to shed light, the secrets protected by government were among the most important. "Liberals," the sociologist Paul Starr writes in *Freedom's Power*, his attempt to identify what is valuable in the liberal tradition, "held that government, rather than being the private domain of a ruler or venal office-holders, exists for the public's benefits and ought to serve its interests. And to ensure that government does, liberals sought to make it more transparent—to publish laws, to open up trials and legislative proceedings, to require government officials to disclose their actions, and to allow the press to circulate political news and critical discussion that would enable citizens to form their own judgments." Just as they supported efforts to open minds through free speech, liberals supported attempts to open government through publicity.

Great Britain offers an interesting example of such efforts. In Britain, nineteenth-century reformers took up the cause of openness as part of the case for government reform in general. Jeremy Bentham called publicity, or exposure, "the grand security of securities," and defined it as a commitment to the principle of "whatever is done by anybody, being done before the eyes of the universal public. By these means," he continued, "appropriate moral aptitude may be maximized, appropriate intellectual aptitude may be maximized, appropriate active attitude may be maximized." John Stuart Mill may not have been the greatest fan of the multitude, or for that matter of Bentham, but this did not mean that, in his view, the public should not be permitted access to the affairs of its government. Reflecting on the collapse of the French military under Napoleon III, Mill expressed his view that "when a government is continually requiring its functionaries to commit rascalities for its sake, they will go on committing rascalities for their own: and as there can be no publicity and no effectual system for the detection of abuse when the government has an interest in concealment, the funds intended for the service of the State find their way into private pockets."

Efforts by liberals such as Bentham and Mill to open government to public scrutiny would not prove very successful. Great Britain has an Official Secrets Act, first passed in 1911 and amended in 1920 and 1989. Unlike the Freedom of Information Act in the United States, the British approach attempts to protect government against public scrutiny rather than to provide public access to governmental deliberations; the 1989 changes, for example, were aimed at stopping leaks by public officials of confidential material. Such powers do not lie unused. Britain's Official Secrets Act was invoked in May 2007 against officials who revealed the details of a 2004 conversation between Prime Minister Tony Blair and President George W. Bush. Because acts of terrorism have occurred in Britain in recent years, especially the July 7, 2006, bombings, it seems highly unlikely that the act will be significantly liberalized in the near future.

The U.S. Constitution, as it happens, was drafted in secret (even if James Madison's notes have since become essential to understanding the process by which it was), and it contains a clause, Article I, Section 5, justifying the way it was drafted: "Each House shall keep a Journal of its Proceedings . . . excepting such Parts as may in their Judgment require Secrecy." Still, the American experience in these matters, lacking anything like an absolute monarchy, was as different from Europe in the realm of governmental publicity as it was on questions of religion or immigration. The idea that leaders can protect themselves from public scrutiny by invoking *raisons d'état* is so foreign to the American experience that the major exceptions to the principle—the Alien and Sedition Acts of 1798, which among other things allowed the deportation of aliens deemed to be dangerous to the United States, and the Espionage Act of 1917, which criminalized efforts to interfere with the American war effort—stand out for their singularity.

Nowhere else in the world did liberalism's commitment to openness combine with democracy's belief in equality to create a political system as transparent as in the United States. The fact that the same country also possessed an energetic entrepreneurial culture that produced lively and popular means of mass communication made that commitment even stronger. Dewey and Brandeis, both strongly committed to openness in government, argued for publicity along the lines of Bentham and Mill, but unlike their English cousins, the Americans at least for a time, had a considerable impact on the way their countrymen thought about the issue.

In line with America's historical traditions on these matters, substantial portions of the Espionage Act of 1917 were repealed after World War I. But the frequency with which the United States went to war in the twentieth century slowly brought to an end the American commitment to public transparency. This was especially true of the Cold War, for this one was not only being fought against an enemy, the Soviet Union, that itself was secretive in nature, but (or so it was assumed) the war would continue indefinitely. Breaking with its tradition of open government, the United States, as the Cold War began, created a national security apparatus expected to operate in the dark, and put into place a series of understandings between government and the media that would restrain the latter from informing the public of everything it knew about the former.

Secrecy was surely required to fight the Cold War, for, as we now know, the Soviet Union was busily engaged in recruiting agents within the United States and managed to snare some remarkably large fish. Yet, as Senator Daniel Patrick Moynihan came to understand when he wrote a book on the subject, secrecy harmed as well as helped the efforts of the United States in the Cold War. Moynihan points out, with considerable astonishment, that America's secret intelligence agencies did not pass on the information they had collected about spies in high places to President Harry Truman, all the while sending him unfounded rumors and thirdhand innuendo about others. Bureaucracies love secrecy because it turns information into a valuable commodity; agencies in possession of such a resource, experience time and again proves, are more likely to hold on to it rather than to share it, whatever the consequences for national security. Secrecy may protect a society against its enemies but it also protects itself all too often from the truth.

No wonder, then, that the organization created in the early years of the Cold War to gather intelligence turned out to be such a failure. Protected by secrecy, the Central Intelligence Agency, as Tim Weiner's *Legacy of Ashes* makes abundantly clear, was unable to insulate itself against the irresponsibility of its own leaders, the demands of presidents to tailor intelligence in politically acceptable ways, and the temptation, once secrecy was used in places where it belonged, to expand it to places it did not. Secrecy, Weiner writes, reached its "peak" in 1971: "The CIA, the NSA, and the FBI were spying on American citizens. Defense Secretary Melvin Laird and the Joint Chiefs of Staff were using electronic eavesdropping and espionage to keep tabs on Kissinger. Nixon, improving on the work of Kennedy and Johnson, had bugged the White House and Camp David with state-of-the-art voice-activated microphones. Nixon and Kissinger wiretapped their own close aides and Washington reporters, trying to stop leaks to the press." If any of this protected national security, Weiner is unable to find evidence for it.

The Cold War, to the surprise of many, did have an end, but the quest for governmental secrecy did not. Richard Nixon did not merely exhibit a penchant for secrecy; his other major contribution to the question of governmental transparency was to invoke the doctrine of executive privilege, or, as he defined it, the idea that if the president does something, it is for that reason legal. Executive privilege in theory meant that the president was superior to the other branches of government, but Nixon used it not only to shield himself against scrutiny from Congress and the courts, and not only to protect the United States against its enemies, but to defend himself against his critics. With Watergate, Americans received their first real glimpse of what eighteenth-century European liberals most feared: claims that the executive was accountable to no one but himself, made on behalf of information to which no one but himself was privy.

Appalled at the implications of Nixon's view of executive power, Congress put in place numerous reforms in the wake of Watergate, from campaign finance procedures to the creation of special prosecutors, in an effort to restore a balance between open government and the need for executive flexibility. But some key officials were convinced that the Nixon-era reforms designed to open government to greater public inspection constituted a serious mistake. Among them were two men, Donald Rumsfeld and Dick Cheney, both of whom had served as chief of staff to Nixon's replacement, Gerald Ford. In a tribute to their persistence, Rumsfeld and Cheney would wait patiently for another chance to put into place their enthusiasm for shutting down government's business from public scrutiny. George W. Bush gave them that chance.

From the moment terrorists attacked the United States on September 11, 2001, officials in the Bush administration began urging the need for secrecy in government to combat this insidious enemy. But a penchant for secrecy had characterized the administration even before the attacks on the World Trade Center and the Pentagon. Almost immediately upon assuming office, Vice President Cheney made it clear that he would resist any efforts to provide a list of those who attended a task force created by the administration to make recommendations on energy policy. In Cheney's view, the executive's right to decide trumped the public's right to know. Power would have to shift back toward the president, which meant that information would have to shift away from the people. Secret trials, secret interrogation techniques, secret wiretaps, off-budget expenditures, resistance to congressional oversight, classifying records when inconvenient, declassifying them when convenient—all would follow as Cheney proved himself a master of bureaucratic intrigue during the Bush years, even going so far as to claim, before the idea was withdrawn due to the excessive ridicule it provoked, that because the office of the vice president was neither fully in the executive nor legislative branches, its affairs could not be overseen by anyone. Cardinal Richelieu, but for the incompetence, would have approved.

There is a need, often an overwhelming need, for secrecy in war. The benefits of good intelligence have been proven time and again, and just as a society must keep its own intelligence-gathering operations secret, it also needs to keep secret the result of its monitoring of the enemy's similar efforts. True of wars in general, the need for secrecy is an obvious truth of a war on terror; penetrating terrorist cells before they carry out a strike is the single best way to prevent such a strike. After September 11, Democrats and Republicans, liberals and conservatives, agreed that it was intelligence failures that made the attack possible and that intelligence successes would be necessary if a response was to be effective. You do not protect yourself against terrorism by allowing potential terrorists to know what you are doing.

Yet, as important as good intelligence may be, an obsession with secrecy is not always the best means of obtaining it. Terrorist cells need to be infiltrated, but terrorists also need to come out into the open to produce successful actions; they require financial transactions, networks of sympathizers, governments willing to look the other way, diversionary tactics, passports, access to weapons, and numerous other unanticipated encounters with the world outside their cell. The very means of communication that secrecy advocates distrust—newspapers, public records, data sharing—are the very means by which potential terrorists communicate with each other. To be effective against terrorists, one needs as many eyes and ears as possible. Call it, if you will, open source intelligence. Just as software developers believe in sharing codes so as to improve their software, sharing information, in an age of terror, may well gain in intelligence gathering what it loses in publicity. Because such ways of thinking about security are anathema to those bent on protecting governmental secrecy, the Bush administration sacrificed one of the most powerful forms of counterterrorism available to it: the kind of public support and trust on the part of ordinary people around the world that would encourage them to call a police station or notify an authority when they encounter suspicious activity. If you repeatedly tell people you are not interested in sharing information with them, they are less likely to want to share it with you.

Secrecy can contribute to failure not only in the field, where the gathering of intelligence is performed, but also at home, where intelligence must be analyzed and put to good use. Before the U.S. Senate

Committee on the Judiciary, Jack Goldsmith, the Bush administration figure who resigned in disagreement with the extreme positions of John Yoo and other key officials, testified in October 2007 that "too much secrecy can be counterproductive." He cited as an example the very problem earlier identified by Senator Moynihan: the reluctance of agencies within the executive branch to share important information with each other. "This extreme internal secrecy," Goldsmith continued, "was exacerbated by the fact that people inside the small circle of lawyers working on these issues shared remarkably like-minded and sometimes unusual views about the law. Closed-looped decision-making by like-minded lawyers resulted in legal and political errors that would be very costly down the road for the administration." Strict defenders of governmental secrecy typically argue that open government is inefficient government. It is more likely the case that closed government is error-filled government. We do not need secrecy because the decisions facing officials are too tough. We do need openness to prevent them from making decisions that are too easy.

Openness in government is not the obstacle to national security that those intent on closing it insist it is. Closed government, by comparison, is and must be an obstacle to the development of the kinds of informed citizenry in which liberals believe. Closing off public scrutiny means shutting down public curiosity. Those who advocate secrecy in government are essentially claiming that liberal democratic citizens are, and ought to be, ignorant, all the while taking steps based on the assumption that they are not; a society of incurious people, after all, would have no need for secrecy because there would be no public to keep secrets from. Protecting people from themselves is the ultimate form of contempt for democracy. Insisting that they know what the public should not know, extreme advocates of secrecy in government claim for themselves privileges that no rulers in a liberal democratic age ought to be allowed to possess. They view openness as one of liberalism's greatest vulnerabilities when in fact it is one of liberalism's greatest strengths, for the more public affairs are open to public scrutiny, the greater the extent to which the public can rise to the challenges placed before it. The Constitution should indeed never be a suicide pact. It is more likely to become one, not when it is followed but when it is ignored.

OPEN SOCIETIES AND HUMAN PURPOSE

Liberalism does not stop with minds open to new ideas, countries receptive to new citizens, and governments exposed to public scrutiny. The world of the liberal is filled with additional wonders: new cures for old diseases, stabs at public policies never before tried, efforts to create equality upsetting once-taken-for-granted hierarchies, experiments in living questioning the conventional, technologies that change how human beings communicate with each other. Liberals believe that fear of the unknown ought to give way to excitement about the unexpected. There is always something new in the world, and one should always be prepared to be open to it.

Those skeptical of liberalism find in this proclivity toward openness a significant chink in the liberal armor. To be open to experience, they insist, is to be closed to judgment; when new and unexamined ideas are given the same status as old and tried-and-true ones, no idea can ever be viewed as better than others. Liberalism's curiosity is thus a thin disguise covering its irresponsibility: it refuses to set standards, insist on distinctions, impose penalties, convey hard-earned rewards. Liberals fail to acknowledge the fundamental urge to belong; open to all, they deny the fierce attachments people have to national borders, neighborhoods, ethnic groups, traditions, and religious communities. We should trust most what we know best, critics assert. Liberal generosity toward people we do not know or to generations not yet born, however appealing in the abstract, comes at the cost of solidarity with those nearest to them. Far better to rely on the comfortable than to flirt with the unproven.

If one believes that human beings are inherently flawed creatures rarely capable of looking beyond their own self-interest, it makes sense to warn them against the excesses of openness. Driven by our fears and protective of our immediate environment, we would have no need to be curious about worlds far removed from us, and any such curiosity, should we nonetheless manifest it, would only lead to the disasters of misplaced idealism, unexpected consequences, and meddling in the affairs of others. No wonder, then, that for people who think this way, liberalism's commitment to free speech is transformed into filthy speech, its willingness to open its borders leads to lawlessness, and its calls for transparency in government contribute to its own death wish. Laws must conform to human nature; if they do not, nature, one way or another, will take its revenge.

To argue in favor of openness, by contrast, means taking a more positive position on the kinds of creatures we human beings are. This is what such twentieth-century liberals as Louis D. Brandeis, John Dewey, Alexander Meiklejohn, and Jürgen Habermas have done. For them, and for liberals who follow in their wake, free speech, open borders, and transparency in government are worthwhile in themselves. But they serve another purpose as well. Our political and legal arrangements ought to reflect not only who we are but what we are capable of becoming. Speech is worth having because it can introduce us to ideas unfamiliar, and often challenging, to the ones we hold. Open borders are important because the more diverse our society, the more we are brought into contact with ways of life so different from our own that they cause us to reflect on who we are. Open government is necessary because we are not only protected by government but participants in shaping the kind of government we have. Our debates about the meaning of an open society do not oppose freedom against unfreedom; they instead ask us what kind of freedom best accords with human beings as creatures capable of building upon nature to direct their affairs toward self-chosen ends.

This conception of freedom is the one Isaiah Berlin warned us against. Positing a direction toward which we should aim, and then relying on the state to guide us in our journey, he insisted, inevitably leads to cumbersome social planning at best and totalitarian excess at worst. But if there are dangers involved in an active state telling us what to think and whom to welcome among us, there are also dangers in a state that, either by treating all forms of speech as equal in worth, or by closing itself off to newcomers, or by keeping its affairs safely out of the hands of its citizens, forces us to deny our long-established eagerness to grow and explore. There are no easy answers to the dilemmas posed by free speech, immigration, and secrecy in government. The least we can do, as we continue to ponder them, is to treat people's curiosity about the world and capacity to grow as advantages to be cultivated rather than obstacles to be overcome.

CHAPTER 8

WHY CONSERVATIVES CAN'T GOVERN

OUR LISBON EARTHQUAKE

Thirty-four years before the French Revolution launched the modern debate about equality, another great historical event shook Europe. "Shook" in this context is meant to be taken literally. The earthquake began at 9:40 in the morning on November 1, 1755.

> *That was the year that Lisbon-town*
> *saw the earth open and gulp her down*

wrote the poet and physician Oliver Wendell Holmes, Sr., father of the U.S. Supreme Court justice, a little more than a century later.

> *It was on the terrible earthquake day*
> *That the Deacon Finished the One-Hoss Shay.*

Most likely measuring near 9 on the Richter scale, the earthquake and subsequent fires and tsunamis destroyed nearly all of Lisbon and caused havoc as far away as Morocco, resulting in as many as 90,000 deaths. Scientists would eventually address why such enormous devastation happened, but its meaning became a major eighteenth-century preoccupation, prompting an outpouring of moral, political, and theological reflection.

The Lisbon earthquake, for one thing, raised important questions about the nature of God. To the more strictly confessional, the earthquake was clearly a sign, not unlike those found in the Bible, of His displeasure with our sinful conduct. But, responded other theologians, if God is all-powerful and good, how could He have allowed such a terrible thing to take place? Because eighteenth-century Europeans did not live in biblical times but in increasingly enlightened ones, the latter question attracted more interest than the former assertion. As there was no obvious answer to it, merely posing it dealt a severe blow to conservative forms of Christianity.

Although the age was enlightened, Enlightenment thinkers had no easy explanations for the Lisbon earthquake either. Jean-Jacques Rousseau, who blamed human beings for the earthquake rather than assigning the responsibility to God, saw the devastation as proof of just how bad it was for us to live together in those artificial entities called cities, yet live in cities we nonetheless continue to do. Voltaire concluded from it that perhaps everything was not for the best in the best of all possible worlds after all. Kant, fascinated with the earthquake, was led to ask not why God would do such a thing but why a seemingly ordered physical world could suddenly appear without order. Mostly, as the contemporary philosopher Susan Neiman points out, the Lisbon earthquake changed the way Europeans thought about good and evil. No human being brought the earthquake about: in the absence of any motive for it, was the whole experience, from a philosophical or religious perspective, meaningless? Nothing less than modern philosophy was born out of the Lisbon earthquake, Neiman argues. From this time forward, she writes, we would no longer use the term "moral" to describe a phenomenon that, however horrifying, was strictly natural in origin; events could now be described as immoral only when some human beings engaged in deliberate cruelty toward others. Yet if the Lisbon earthquake made people far more discriminating in their understanding of morality, it in no way answered the question of why they nonetheless lived with tragedy.

Our Lisbon earthquake took place in the last days of August 2005. Much as eighteenth-century Europeans had, twenty-first-century Americans watched nature's fury launched against a major city and immediately began to wonder why it had caused such total devastation. Hurricane Katrina did not raise that many I-told-you-so invocations of God's displeasure, although one could hear, off on the distant right, cries to the effect that the easy sex available in New Orleans angered Him to the point of taking revenge. Nor were ours primarily questions of theodicy, or how a good God could be responsible for bad things; in spite of its religious revival, even the United States is too secular in modern times to have such a discussion. We did not adopt the Rousseauian posture of denouncing cities; we were too urban for that. Hurricane Katrina did not even put a significant dent into America's spirit of optimism, the kind of belief in inevitable progress that Voltaire had mocked in *Candide*—or, for that matter, that leads Americans to build vacation homes in the path of storms. Instead, as Americans watched the devastation on television, talk turned immediately to politics. The federal government's response was slow and out of sync with the depth of the tragedy, and Americans wanted to know why.

Just as the Lisbon earthquake resulted in deep discussions of the nature of morality, Hurricane Katrina provoked serious reflection about the dynamics of governance. Starting in the late nineteenth century and continuing to the present time, modern people made the effort to govern nature rather than to be governed by it; in so doing they turned to the state as the most effective instrument for managing the task. As that happened, liberals and conservatives began to develop different views about the role and scope of the public sector. Understanding that only through public action could individuals avoid becoming dependent on forces outside their control, liberals left behind their once-strong commitments to laissez-faire in favor of reliance on government. With that shift, they simultaneously helped modern people to shape their destiny and opened themselves up to charges of promoting bloated bureaucracies and requiring higher taxes to sustain them.

Conservatives in the United States and to a lesser degree Great Britain did the opposite: they abandoned their conviction that government could play an important role in strengthening the social order in favor of the libertarian ideal that government should be kept as far removed from people's lives as possible. This change left conservatives on terrain as uncertain as that occupied by liberals. Conservatives, to be sure, could now claim to be the party in favor of lower taxes, but, not fully convinced that government had a role to play even in such man-made phenomena as poverty and economic insecurity, they found themselves unprepared to take action when nature launched its fury against the people of the Gulf Coast. The response to Hurricane Katrina became a test case for the conservative understanding of the role of government, and it was a test that conservatism failed. From that failure, we have learned that liberal approaches to governance, however flawed, nonetheless remain preferable to conservative ones that deny the legitimacy of the best management tool available for dealing with the uncertainties of modern life.

PLANNED INCOMPETENCE

George W. Bush, the most conservative president of modern times, had been elected, at least in 2000, on the issue of competence. Bush was America's first MBA leader, a man who had attended business school at Harvard and there had developed a well-thought-out management philosophy. Compared to the helter-skelter approach of the Clinton administration that preceded him, he would, he claimed, bring to government the experience and wisdom of private-sector executives who knew something about budgets and bottom lines. His argument was that it was time for the adults to take over the business of running the country. Taxes would be cut, not necessarily because government itself would be cut back—in fact, Bush developed a version of compassionate conservatism that suggested new tasks for government—but because government would be run more efficiently.

Yet when the hurricane struck, the federal government he oversaw was nowhere to be found. The main responsibility for disaster relief belonged to the Federal Emergency Management Agency (FEMA), created by President Jimmy Carter in 1979 as a response to pleas made on behalf of the nation's governors for federal coordination in this area. In subsequent years, many presidents had come to view FEMA as a place for rewarding political supporters. It was not completely surprising therefore that as Katrina hit land, the man in charge of the agency, Michael Brown, who had padded his résumé and was in any case a failed lobbyist, knew little or nothing about the tasks for which his agency was responsible. Brown's inexperience quickly showed. Not only did he fail to appreciate the magnitude of the storm, even as its destructive power was already known to anyone watching television, he delayed the provision of aid to the area and then, to the utter astonishment of people on the ground, refused to allow emergency responders from outside New Orleans to move in: "It is critical," Brown reasoned, "that fire and emergency departments across the country remain in their jurisdictions until such time as the affected states require their assistance." As a series of released e-mails would reveal, Brown seemed more concerned with his looks and clothes than with helping people in severe distress.

When President Bush responded to these events by praising

Brown for the job he was doing, critics of the administration began to focus on its almost surreal level of incompetence. This was not without reason; the administration had shown a similar incompetence in foreign policy, failing to act promptly and professionally in the wake of its invasion of Iraq and relying on campaign volunteers to staff positions in Baghdad. In politics, bragging is a double-edged sword, and by claiming expertise in the first place, the administration made itself vulnerable for its failures in the second.

Unmodified, however, "incompetence" is not quite the right word to describe the Bush administration's response to Katrina. The conservatives who worked for Bush had a well-developed philosophy of how to treat issues such as disaster relief and responded to Katrina by putting their philosophy immediately—one is even compelled, save for the poor execution, to say competently—to work. That philosophy had been articulated by Brown's predecessor as head of FEMA, Joseph Allbaugh. Allbaugh, who had been Bush's campaign manager in 2000, also knew little or nothing about disaster relief. But this did not prevent him from outlining strong views on the subject when he testified before a Senate subcommittee in May 2001. "It is not the role of the federal government to tell a community what it needs to do to protect its citizens and infrastructure," he said on that occasion. "Many are concerned that federal disaster assistance may have evolved into both an oversized entitlement program and a disincentive to effective state and local risk management. Expectations of when the federal government should be involved and the degree of involvement may have ballooned beyond what is an appropriate level. We must restore the predominant role of state and local response to most disasters. Federal assistance needs to supplement, not supplant, state and local efforts."

As the use of the words "oversized entitlement program" suggests, officials of the Bush administration came to power convinced that the federal government existed not to meet the needs of citizens but to convince those citizens that they were not entitled to things they had come to expect. When Katrina hit New Orleans, the administration's first instinct was to delegate the responsibility for dealing with the disaster to state and local officials, and then to keep tight control on the federal purse strings to prevent use of federal money for purposes they deemed frivolous. To the degree the administration was incompetent, then, it was not because of errors of omission; on the contrary, the inability of the Bush administration to respond to the disaster was a form of planned incompetence, a direct result of its view of government's proper role in society.

Because so many administration officials shared this conservative vision of government, Michael Brown's unwillingness to act in the face of Katrina's destructive power was matched by that of his colleagues. Despite warnings of potential disaster, Brown's supervisor, Secretary of Homeland Security Michael Chertoff, never went to his office in the two days before Katrina struck the Louisiana and Mississippi coastlines and, like Brown, was extremely slow to acknowledge the seriousness of what was taking place. Although presented with numerous opportunities to declare Katrina a catastrophic event, thereby assigning it the government's highest priority, Chertoff opted instead to call it an "incident of national significance," making clear that the federal government would not assume full control of the relief effort. ("Chertoff's actions," Douglas Brinkley noted in *The Great Deluge,* "cost lives.") Nor did President Bush feel any particular need to respond. When the distraught governor of Louisiana, Kathleen Blanco, appealed for funds, Bush, according to Brinkley, "didn't pursue the matter actively enough. Louisiana was a notorious black hole for pork-barrel funds. He wasn't going to write a blank check. He also wouldn't be inclined to make up for Blanco's inexperience; if she was floundering, he didn't leap to save her reputation."

Any doubts about how determined conservatives were to fit Hurricane Katrina into the way they thought about government were resolved when right-wing activists and intellectuals began to ponder the longer-term implications of the disaster. On September 12, 2005, two weeks after the hurricane hit, the Heritage Foundation, a conservative think tank, published a paper repeating the essence of Allbaugh's earlier testimony to the effect that disaster relief should not be a federal responsibility, urging instead the creation of "opportunity zones" based on free market principles. Jack Kemp, once a Republican candidate for president, similarly viewed Katrina as a "great opportunity" for conservatives to get their ideas across. "Bush has what Social Security and tax reform lacked," the conservative policy analyst Tod Lindberg said in the same vein, "a real sense of crisis that places his opponents in an awkward position. He can make demands in the name of New Orleans, including demands for substantive policy changes, that he could never obtain in the absence of a crisis." Mike Pence, a Republican congressman from Indiana, told *The Wall Street Journal* at the time that "the desire to bring conservative, free-market ideas to the Gulf Coast is white hot. We want to turn the Gulf Coast into a magnet for free enterprise. The last thing we want is a federal city where New Orleans was." And when President Bush endorsed some of these ideas, such as

relying on school vouchers or personal accounts for the poor, Rich
Lowry, editor of the conservative *National Review,* noted liberal opposition to them and expressed the view that "the objection to these Bush
proposals isn't fiscal, but philosophical. They serve to undermine the
principle of government dependency that underpins the contemporary
welfare state, and to which liberals are utterly devoted. In a reversal of
the old parable, liberals don't want to teach people how to fish if they
just give them federally funded seafood dinners instead."

Why do we have government in the first place? From where does
its power derive? When are its actions legitimate and when are they
not? Is it our friend, ready to help us in times of danger, or a seducer,
holding out false allures that we must be determined to resist? Are we
too dependent upon it? Would we be better off if we weaned ourselves
from it in favor of reliance on the market or private charity? Must it
corrupt, and corrupt absolutely? If bad things happen, can government
make them better? If we are to have it, should its authority stand as a
symbol of the nation and the community it defines, or are its powers so
awesome that, to control its abuses, its authority should be divided and
kept as close to home as possible? These are, one hastens to add, not
theological questions: they can be answered without reference to a
supreme being. But they are philosophical and moral questions, and
they deserve serious attention. It is in that sense a credit to conservatives that they raised them before and after Hurricane Katrina. But in
doing so, they also managed to demonstrate, as sin-obsessed religious
thinkers did in eighteenth-century Lisbon, that their descriptions of
how the modern world does work were as irrelevant as their prescriptions for how it should.

THE STATE'S CURSE

One of the most fascinating figures produced by the Lisbon earthquake
was neither a theologian, a poet, nor a philosopher; he was, in fact, an
administrator—Sebastião José de Carvalho e Melo, the marquis de
Pombal. Portugal at that time was governed by a monarch, Dom José I,
and Pombal, the man who served as his prime minister, was hardly a
liberal; he is remembered, certainly by the Jesuits, as a man determined
to persecute his enemies, and he held on to power with all the zeal of a
dictator. But while not a liberal, Pombal was a reformer, and an
enlightened one at that. Taking charge of the country in the wake of
the earthquake, he not only rebuilt Lisbon (along the way contributing

the term "pombaline" to refer to its new architectural style), he reorganized Portugal's industries, modernized its educational system, equalized its tax system, abolished its reliance on Indian slavery, and ended the form of discrimination against Jews known as the distinction between old and new Christians. Long before Baron Haussmann re-created Paris and Robert Moses redeveloped New York, the marquis de Pombal proved how someone could transform the world in which he and his fellow citizens—and, indeed, all those who came after him—lived.

The Lisbon earthquake was a natural disaster that, in the hands of the marquis de Pombal, was transformed into a political agenda. But it was not Pombal's vision that made his life's work possible; it was his ability to use the authority of government, or, as Europeans of the time liked to call it, the state. Government possessed the power to tax, which provided not only a power to destroy, as the American jurist John Marshall would put it, but also a power to create. It could confiscate property and commandeer resources. It was capable of ordering people to do things they did not wish to do and then of punishing them if they refused. It could decide who would be a citizen and who would not. Matters of war and peace were left in its hands. Government could tell you what time it was, what language you had to speak, and what you should do with your children. In theory, God's power was more awesome. In practice, the state's power was more worrisome.

The marquis de Pombal deserves to be remembered as a founder of what we now call public administration; one of his ideas was to enact the *Lei da Boa Razão*, or Law of Good Reason, which demanded that any policy adopted by the Portuguese state justify itself by reference to natural law. (Needless to say, the law was usually ignored by influence peddlers and court acolytes.) Public administration, as Pombal's work shows, was a by-product of the Enlightenment; eighteenth-century thinkers from all over Europe and North America, with their passion for constitution writing and their concern with procedural justice, not only devoted considerable attention to how government ought to be organized, they also spent considerable time thinking about how it ought to be run. If the Catholic Church, rife with corruption and favoritism, offered a model of bad governance, science and reason would show the way toward good governance. Citizens must be ruled by their leaders, but their leaders ought to be ruled by disinterest and dispassion. Administration was to be public, not just private, and the word "public" itself was filled with Enlightenment connotations, suggesting a sphere in which the common good would be given pride of place. As a form of knowledge, public administration's contribution to the way modern people live should not be underestimated. To say we are shaped by culture rather than enslaved by nature is to say that we can influence our own fate, and no other institution gives us the capacity to do so more than government. If we are to use it, thinkers of the Enlightenment believed, we should use it wisely.

Because government and its activities are at the heart of politics, one would expect any political philosophy to offer a coherent theory about how the powers of government ought to be used. Yet as government came to play a greater role in the life of Western liberal democracies throughout the nineteenth and twentieth centuries, its scope and proper activities created difficulties for all the major political philosophies of the period. This was a time in which five approaches to politics came to fruition: liberalism, conservatism, socialism, nationalism, and Romanticism. Each of them was subject to what can be called the curse of the state; once government became a significant force, none of them would survive unscathed.

Romanticism's curse, as we have already seen, was militarism. It was one thing to look to the battlefield for heroes who could rise above the pettiness of everyday life and inspire their fellow citizens to yearn after great things. But no sooner did the Romantic poets find inspiration in arms than the state began to systematize their purchasing and deployment. The Romantic hero was an amateur, and proud of it; instinct ruled his decisions and courage motivated his actions. Actual soldiers, as well as the men who led them, proved in the age of modern government to be professionals, cautious in the extreme, especially when life was at stake, and more likely to have majored in engineering than in English. The fact that Romantic militarism continues to flourish among contemporary neoconservatives by no means proves that it has escaped its curse; if anything, Romantic militarism's illusions in the face of modern war suggest that its curse hangs over every war it advocates and fights.

Ironically enough, nationalism's curse proved to be the nation-state. In the early nineteenth century, especially in Germany, philosophers were filled with praise for the *Volk,* from whose legends, language, customs, and music would be discovered the ties that bind the community together. The nation-state, however, unlike the nation, came into existence not through some world historical spirit but by the actions of bureaucrats and technicians. The tension between these two imperatives—one, the nation, natural and organic, the other, the state, artificial and constructed—would eventually be resolved in favor of those Max Weber called "specialists without spirit, sensualists without heart." Lacking bankers, urban centers, and businessmen—lacking, in short, all those dreadfully mundane calculators of the bourgeois mentality—Germany would have remained the collection of duchies and municipalities it had been under the Holy Roman Empire. Nationalism lived on in Germany and would even experience a late flourishing that produced that ugly mixture of nationalism and the nation-state called Nazism. But the defeat of Nazism also represented the nation-state's triumph over nationalism; in its wake, there would be nation-states aplenty, but relatively few that were willing to court their own destruction to keep a mythology of national and racial superiority alive.

Socialism promised, in the words of Friedrich Engels, the withering away of the state. It would be difficult to find anywhere in the modern world a promise more resolutely broken. Some forms of socialism moderated their revolutionary character in the nineteenth century and found ways to make themselves compatible with liberal democracy in the twentieth. But where socialism took power by force, which happened in all of those societies that came to be called Communist, it not only failed to deliver on its promises of equality but brought into being a state marked as much by its inefficiency in economic matters as its efficiency in violating the most basic of civil liberties. And, as the experience of post-Soviet Russia under Vladimir Putin suggests, the state survived even when socialism did not. Socialism's legacy proved to be a mechanism for paving the way for an especially rapacious form of capitalism.

For conservatives, the state's curse turned out to be opposition to the state, or what is usually called laissez-faire. Conservatives of the old-fashioned sort had no problem with government; as Alexander Pope reminded his eighteenth-century contemporaries:

> For forms of government let fools contest
> Whate'er is best administered is best.

To be sure, the spirit of public administration was enlightened and in that sense liberal, or at least pre-liberal. But smart conservatives have always been able to use liberal innovations for conservative purposes, and from the eighteenth until the twentieth century, this proved to be true of the state. For those intending to keep the lower classes obedient, government possessed powers too important to be ignored; ministers of justice, with the secret police at their disposal, were the natural allies of conservative politicians. The conservative affinity with government, however, involved not just its repressive capacities. The enlightened nineteenth-century Toryism of Benjamin Disraeli, the novelist and statesman who served as prime minister in 1868 and from 1874 to 1880, reminds us how a class certain of its inherent right to govern had little or no problem with the idea of governing. That legacy would extend well into twentieth-century Britain among Tory "wets," the term used to describe conservatives such as Harold Macmillan of the publishing family, who served as prime minister from 1957 until 1963; the "wets" were intent on having an active role for government in regulating the economy and improving the lot of the poor.

Laissez-faire changed all that. Because they distrusted the very state that conservatives of the *ancien régime* had been willing to use, earlier advocates of laissez-faire such as Herbert Spencer had called themselves liberals, and even as late as the mid-twentieth century, one of the most determined of them, F. A. Hayek, continued to insist that he was not a conservative. But all that would change by the time Barry Goldwater wrote his *Conscience of a Conservative* in 1960 and Margaret Thatcher led her later campaign against the Harold Macmillans of her party. In becoming such firm advocates for laissez-faire, contemporary conservatives placed upon themselves a curse that previous conservatives had been able to avoid. It is impossible to imagine the conservatives of the Bush administration responding to a disaster the way an earlier Republican like Herbert Hoover did; Hoover, an engineer by training, before the misfortune of the presidency fell upon him, had accepted an offer from Woodrow Wilson to be the U.S. Food Administrator, leading the efforts to reduce starvation in post–World War I Europe with Pombal-like energy. Today's conservatives, by contrast, fed a steady diet of laissez-faire gospel, are more likely to denounce government than to use it to reestablish order.

Liberals, too, have had problems developing a coherent theory of the state. Liberalism's schizophrenia on the subject is on full display in the writings of John Stuart Mill, who (in *On Liberty*) could sound like Herbert Spencer while (in the revised versions of *Principles of Political Economy*) anticipating John Maynard Keynes. Let the question be one of free speech or freedom of religion, and liberals can be as libertarian as any conservative denouncing occupational health and safety measures; but should the question be one of funding elementary schools or offering food stamps, liberals can be as pro-government as conservatives are when talking about fighting crime or supporting the troops.

Given the ubiquitous role government plays in modern life, not being able to make up your mind how you feel about it can be a distinct liability.

The curse the state visits upon liberalism is Progressivism. When liberals opted to rely upon the state to become more directly involved in the economy, they also opened the door for the state to become more invasive of people's civil liberties. The Wilson administration in the United States, for example, was responsible for both the Federal Reserve Bank, which helped government regulate the economy, and the Palmer raids, which used the powers of the state to crush dissent and arrest and deport dissenters. Progressivism is a crucial feature of contemporary liberalism—without a role for government managed by disinterested experts, there would be no liberalism—but progressivism will always be a discordant element within it; progressivism's firm insistence that it knows what is right conflicts with temperamental liberalism's lack of certainty, and its preference for ends undermines procedural liberalism's respect for means. This is not meant to suggest, as some historians and pundits have, that historically Progressivism shares something in common with twentieth-century fascism; for all its flaws, Progressivism in the United States operated within the parameters of liberal democracy and supported reforms that brought about greater popular control over business and government. But the progressive urge does constitute a warning for liberals that too much reliance on government to achieve its objectives can stand in tension with other long-established liberal values such as a commitment to openness.

It may seem odd, given the modern state's ubiquity, that none of our dominant political philosophies contains a theory of how it should work, but it also makes a certain amount of sense; the state, after all, can do bad and the state can do good. Its badness is not some product of the past but is very much alive today. The fact that torture was practiced by leaders of a liberal democratic society in the aftermath of September 11 should remind everyone why they might feel justified in fearing the state; government, when all is said and done, still has the power to kill and maim. No wonder, then, that when the state takes on activities not quite as harmful as those involving torture, it is still a force to be feared. In the abstract, states ought to be able to use powers such as eminent domain to advance the public good; but if your home or business is the one confiscated, you are likely to view its authority as invasive and arbitrary. The state's task of raising armies will always be controversial when troops are selected not through voluntary methods but through the coercive authority of a draft. Liberals have every right to worry that, in their determination to protect people against terror-ism, state officials will listen in on too many phone conversations and arrest too many innocent people. One reason why we lack an adequate theory of the state is because the state itself is so unattractive. Few argue that it is good. Its defenders are far more likely to point out that it is less bad than something else.

At the same time, states have grown over the past two centuries or so because it is impossible to realize the good life without them. States build roads and provide the infrastructure that makes society function. They insure people against the vagaries of sudden job loss. They have improved the living conditions of the elderly. They provide for the common defense. They make the streets safe. Without them, it would be difficult to have museums, schools, libraries, and concert halls. Gov-ernment, in a nutshell, is a synonym for civilization. One can, if one chooses, imagine a society without it—this is the favorite pastime of anarchism, the least important political philosophy of our time—but the moment one begins to picture a society in which human needs are met, there one will find government. And while it generally does not receive that much attention in more normal times, the fact that natural disasters happen can and should remind people why states are blessings in disguise. Past a certain point, nature can wreak so much havoc that not only does a role for government become inevitable but the bigger, better financed, and more comprehensive the government, the better for the people facing nature's wrath.

Not very many people today believe that there exists a God so vengeful that He would launch earthquakes and hurricanes upon inno-cent people, causing horrendous death and destruction along the way. It may someday be equally beyond human comprehension that in August 2005, public officials found reasons not to use the powers the state had at its command. The arguments made by policymakers to jus-tify their inaction, moreover, may someday have the same credibility as arguments to the effect that there must be divine reasons for earth-quakes even if we ordinary mortals can never understand exactly what God had in mind. Do you really mean to tell me, some future skeptic will likely ask, that serious people really believed back then that it made a difference whether the local, the state, or the federal government should be first on the ground at a time when so many were dying? Human beings want to avoid suffering. In the aftermath of Katrina, they saw people dying of thirst and hunger through no fault of their own, and they could not settle for reassurances that, however tragic that seemed, nothing much could be done about it because—for reasons no one seemed to be able to make clear—the powers possessed by the federal government to limit the damage had to be held in abeyance. Arguing about which level of government should be the first to respond under conditions like these is the twenty-first century's version of arguing over how many angels can fit on the head of a pin.

Hurricane Katrina should therefore be viewed as a decisive event in the history of political philosophy, at least as far as the United States is concerned. Before it happened, American conservatism possessed a certain credibility; its pervasive distrust of government was a bit odd, to be sure, so distinct was it from conservatism historically and from conservatism in countries other than Great Britain. But it nonetheless seemed at least plausible that governments closer to where people actually lived might best be relied on in comparison to the government in Washington, D.C., or that private efforts at relief would be superior to public ones. After Katrina, no one except the most ideological can still take these as axioms of political life.

There are times when we must rely on the federal government, including exceptionally dramatic times, and it is at those times that contemporary conservatism fails us. The idea that disasters of this magnitude should be viewed as an opportunity—and no less, as an opportunity to put into place an ideology that, by weakening government further, will make it even more difficult for people in the future to respond to natural disasters—testifies to a blindness about human suffering that defies imagination. What took place in August 2005 should never again be permitted to happen in a society that calls itself civilized.

MAN-MADE DISASTERS

The failure of government helped destroy New Orleans, but the success of government had originally helped build it. As everyone now knows, New Orleans exists below sea level, surrounded on nearly all sides by water that constantly threatens the city with flooding. It may seem frivolous to have located a metropolitan area there but, as one geographer has put it, New Orleans was as inevitable as it was impossible: a major port city, and one of the world's most culturally diverse, was bound to be established at the foot of the Mississippi River. Nature had to be held at bay to make New Orleans possible. A way would therefore be found to hold nature at bay.

Even before New Orleans became part of the United States,

French and Spanish settlers tried to build levees to protect the area, yet, as Craig Colten writes in *An Unnatural Metropolis,* "privately built structures were notoriously inconsistent in design and effectiveness, and floods continued to break these ever-lengthening urban embankments." The Louisiana Purchase did not alter this pattern of failed flood control efforts; private initiatives could displace water from one area, but only by sending it somewhere else. Efforts by the several states to control flooding turned out to be not much of an improvement on private ones. Not only was the flooding problem larger than New Orleans; it was, given the length and breadth of the Mississippi, larger than Louisiana. Flooding was responsible for the outbreak of infectious diseases that lay beyond the ability of any private firm or state and local government to control. If it was inevitable that a city such as New Orleans would be built, it was just as inevitable that the federal government would become its protector. Although the last half of the nineteenth century witnessed the triumph of private industry in the United States, Congress in 1879 created the Mississippi River Commission, symbolizing the transfer of responsibility for protecting New Orleans against flooding to the federal government. From that point on, the U.S. Army Corps of Engineers became the primary builder of the levee system surrounding the city.

The term we usually use to describe what the Army Corps of Engineers does is "public works." The concept is an old one in American history, and has its origins in the writings of Alexander Hamilton and the campaign for internal improvements led by the nineteenth-century perennial presidential candidate Henry Clay. But no period in American history was marked by as strong a commitment to public works as the Great Depression of the 1930s. When we debate the legacy of the New Deal in the contemporary world, we usually focus on policies such as Social Security that gave rise to the welfare state. Yet the Social Security Act, which was passed in 1937, came five years after Franklin Delano Roosevelt's initial electoral victory. The earliest years of the New Deal were devoted to the establishment of the Works Progress (later Projects) Administration, the Civilian Conservation Corps, the Tennessee Valley Authority, and other agencies charged with building or rebuilding the American infrastructure. These activities are frequently viewed as a form of "pump-priming" aimed at getting people back to work as fast as possible in the hopes of stimulating the economy. A new school of historical interpretation sees in them something more, "a revolution," as the historian Jason Scott Smith writes in *Building New Deal Liberalism,* that was "awesome in both scale and scope."

The New Deal's public works activities transformed the American nation. "These programs," Smith argues, "secured the foundations for forging a national market after 1945, spurred dramatic advances in economic productivity, built networks of roads and airports, drew up blueprints for national highways, improved military bases, foreshadowed the rise of the Sunbelt, and gave New Dealers a policy tool that could be used to shape overseas development, from the onset of the Cold War continuing through the Vietnam War."

Now that the infrastructure put in place during the New Deal is so visibly crumbling, it is important to remind ourselves why government took such dramatic steps in the first place. New Deal public works were part and parcel of a political philosophy, and the philosophy behind them was liberalism. It has been a staple of liberal political thought since Locke and Kant that human beings, not content to live by the dictates of nature, are capable of transforming it according to purposes established by themselves. Public works apply the same basic idea to the collective, as well as the individualistic, activities of a people; through them, we reach beyond the limits imposed by the size of mountains, the flow of rivers, and the dictates of the seasons to build places in which human beings can live and work. It does no good to possess mastery without the means necessary to master. Government was there, and government would be used.

Presidential speeches are rarely devoted to matters of political philosophy, but so severe were the conditions under which FDR assumed the presidency that he used his inaugural address to remind his listeners about these liberal propositions. That speech has become so famous for its insistence that "the only thing we have to fear is fear itself" that we tend to forget what it was we were fearing in the first place. It was not nature. "We are stricken by no plague of locusts," FDR declared. "Compared with the perils which our forefathers conquered because they believed and were not afraid, we have still much to be thankful for. Nature still offers her bounty and human efforts have multiplied it." Our problem, rather, was that we were neglecting our ability to build upon what nature offers us. "Plenty is at our doorstep, but a generous use of it languishes in the very sight of the supply. Primarily this is because the rulers of the exchange of mankind's goods have failed, through their own stubbornness and their own incompetence, have admitted their failure, and abdicated."

It was obvious to Roosevelt, and he tried his best to make it obvious to his fellow Americans, that if they were "not to be ministered unto but to minister to ourselves and to our fellow men," they would have to find ways "to stimulate and reorganize the use of our natural resources" in order to recapture "the old and permanently important manifestation of the American spirit of the pioneer." Roosevelt was as much a progressive as a liberal, and his way of moving forward—"as a trained and loyal army willing to sacrifice for the good of a common discipline"—sounds disturbingly militaristic to contemporary ears. Yet his choice of a military metaphor also underscores that war, as well as depression, would require that society mobilize its resources through conscious and deliberate action if human beings were to lead purposeful lives.

Before a role could be carved out for the state to play in meeting the conditions of modern life, the notion that economies operated by natural laws impervious to human intervention, which we associate with such thinkers as Herbert Spencer, would first have to be discredited. No one played a more important role in doing this than the British economist John Maynard Keynes. Keynes was flatly averse to biological explanations of human behavior; not only did he reject Spencer's version of them, he also reacted against Spencer's leading critic, Thomas Hill Green, for being too sympathetic to organic ways of thinking. (Green, after all, was an Oxford man, while Keynes was a Cambridge don.) Keynes, like the marquis de Pombal, was no democrat. A proud member of a then very elitist British elite, Keynes distrusted democracy because he trusted intelligence; better that experts run complicated things such as an economy, he believed, than that we subject our fate to the whims of public opinion.

Although not much of a democrat, Keynes was very much a liberal. Other than a few occasional pieces, he did not write extensively on political philosophy. But he did address the questions raised by Rousseau and Kant and came down directly in favor of the notion that we are better off living in society than conforming our needs to the presumed dictates of nature. Expressing himself in no uncertain terms, Keynes, in a pamphlet written for the British general election of 1929, wrote that "the Conservative belief that there is some law of nature which prevents men from being employed, that it is 'rash' to employ men, and that it is financially 'sound' to maintain a tenth of the population in idleness for an indefinite period, is crazily improbable—the sort of thing which no man could believe who had not had his head fuddled with nonsense for years and years." Better, Keynes wrote, to put people to work "with the confidence, the bold optimism, the push and the drive which tackled more formidable problems in the war, and delivered the goods up to the scheduled date." If one were looking for a twentieth-century heir to the insistence on the importance of society characteristic of eighteenth-century liberals such as Kant, Keynes would be the obvious choice.

Keynes's magnum opus, *The General Theory of Employment, Interest and Money,* published in 1936, is not, like Mill's *On Liberty,* an easily absorbed entry into the pantheon of readable liberal classics. Although written for specialists, it is not difficult for lay readers to grasp its central insight, which, as Keynes put it, is that "we must not conclude that the mean position . . . determined by 'natural' tendencies . . . is, therefore, established by the laws of necessity." Once Keynes demonstrated theoretically that there was no one natural point of equilibrium in an economy but many possible ones that could be established by governmental action, the way was open for societies to control their economic life rather than be controlled by it. A society suffering from insufficient levels of demand had the choice of stimulating greater demand through macroeconomic measures such as deficit spending. Herbert Spencer had thought that by demonstrating the extent to which the laws of economics were written by nature, we would realize our powerlessness to alter them. The joke, it seems, was on him. Once rivers were dammed, rural areas electrified, cities transformed, and even natural areas protected against private encroachment, it was a short step to the position that society need not suffer the ills of massive unemployment and desperate poverty.

The General Theory was published too late to be viewed as the inspiration for the public works programs undertaken by the early New Deal. But Keynes was no stranger either to the New Deal or to the idea of public works. Not all the early New Dealers supported a radical expansion of the public sector, but one who did was the future Supreme Court justice Felix Frankfurter. Frankfurter had met Keynes during the 1919 Paris Peace Conference and had sponsored the publication of portions of Keynes's brilliant book on that event, *The Economic Consequences of the Peace,* in *The New Republic.* In 1933, Frankfurter assumed the Eastman Professorship at Oxford University and, while in England, persuaded Keynes to publish "An Open Letter to President Roosevelt" in *The New York Times.* Keynes used the platform to urge the new American president to pursue a vigorous program of public works. When Keynes later arrived in New York to be honored by Columbia University, Frankfurter arranged for a meeting between him and the president; alas for history, they seemed to talk past each other.

Still, Keynes had his popularizers and advocates in the United States, and they brought to Washington the conviction that government could, by stimulating the economy, help counter the brutalizing effects the Great Depression had brought to the country.

Unlike such advocates for equality as T. H. Green and R. H. Tawney, Keynes was no Christian expressing religious sentiments to an increasingly secular public. But he was a secular moralist writing prose with decidedly religious overtones. For an economist, Keynes was disdainful of economic questions, believing them technical at root, capable of being solved, and therefore of not much interest to future generations. Once we move beyond them, he insisted, we will be able to rid ourselves of "pseudo-moral principles which have hag-ridden us for two hundred years, by which we have exalted some of the most distasteful of human qualities into the position of the highest virtues" and "return to some of the mostly sure and certain principles of religion and traditional virtue—that avarice is a vice, that the extraction of usury is a misdemeanour, and the love of money detestable." It would take at least a century, Keynes warned, before "we shall once more value ends above means and prefer the good to the useful," but he still looked forward "in days not so very remote, to the greatest change which has ever occurred in the material environment of life for human beings in the aggregate."

It was a long way from public works to the post-economic paradise of which Keynes spoke, but the first step would be an expansion of the activities of government from measures of economic recovery to those providing greater economic security. When people do not work, they do not contribute to the overall prosperity of the society in which they live. If they are too poor, they suffer, and so do all those dependent upon them and upon whom they depend. Let disease wreck their lives, and not only may their lives be cut short but everyone else, in one way or another, will assume the cost. We might like to think that everyone is responsible for his or her own fate, but what about those too young to make decisions or those too old to avoid dependence on others? The Lisbon earthquake taught us that the category of evil makes no sense when applied to events caused by nature; in its aftermath, people wrestled mightily with the meaning of morality. Much the same happened in the aftermath of the Great Depression. The evils of want and despair were caused neither by nature nor by God; they were the result of a set of political and economic arrangements that made it impossible to correct the negative consequences of the business cycle. The New Deal—and, in its own way, Keynesianism—taught us that social evils could be corrected in our time the way natural evils could be in previous eras. Under modern political conditions, it had become immoral to allow suffering to persist when we possessed the knowledge of how to prevent it. Of all of liberalism's contributions to the way we live now, this is without doubt the most important.

Lyndon Baines Johnson, a young Texas congressman and a master at the politics of public works provision, was one of the most fervent of the New Dealers. When he later became president of the United States, Johnson put a bust of FDR in his office, brought a number of old New Dealers back to the White House, and modeled his Great Society on the New Deal experience. The unifying element behind so many of the reforms passed during the period of the Great Society was the same liberal impetus that had characterized the New Deal: individuals, through government, could gain some degree of mastery over their lives. In the face of arguments from white supremacists that black citizens were naturally inferior to whites, the Civil Rights Act of 1964, and then the Voting Rights Act of 1965, finally realized the idea that every citizen, regardless of race, has an equal right to participate in the life of the nation. Against the idea that poverty was a permanent fixture of human nature, the War on Poverty was designed to give people the tools that would help them improve their condition. Johnson was unable to provide a system of national health insurance, but the adoption of Medicare enabled the elderly to avoid the dependencies long associated with old age. Before Johnson, in disgrace because of the catastrophe in Vietnam, decided not to run for reelection in 1968, he brought American liberalism to the highest point it had ever reached.

In the years since Johnson left office, more Republicans have been elected to the presidency than Democrats, and one of the reasons for their political success has been their attack on the excesses of the 1960s. It is therefore worth reminding ourselves how permanent the accomplishments of the Great Society, like those of the New Deal, have proven to be. No one with any credibility opposes the Civil Rights Act of 1964, which helped transform the United States from a nation that tolerated segregation to one that elected an African-American for the presidency. Unlike their support for Civil Rights Act, conservatives have mobilized to oppose extensions of the Voting Rights Act, but their efforts have met substantial resistance and have been unsuccessful.

Medicare is as widely accepted as Social Security; in fact, George W. Bush, so conservative in so many things, sponsored a significant extension of its benefits in his first years in office. The environmental programs endorsed by Johnson's wife, Lady Bird, are politically untouchable. Federal spending on education was once considered a radical idea; in the first years of the twenty-first century, No Child Left Behind, which provided additional federal funding for schools in return for wider use of assessment testing, made it a principle of school governance. The Office of Economic Opportunity, to be sure, was dismantled in 1973, at least in part because of its controversial Community Action Program, but many of its other programs, such as Head Start and Vista (now called AmeriCorps), survive in other federal departments. Just as Dwight D. Eisenhower when president legitimated the New Deal by not dismantling it, Republican presidents since Richard Nixon have solidified the Great Society by not curtailing some of its features while dramatically enhancing others.

With the Great Society, the United States had finally come to accept what Europeans had long understood: government, for better or worse, is an unavoidable fact of modern existence. We—that is to say, just about everyone in the modern world—believe, whatever our substantive political views, that some of the things we value most, from protecting our nation against foreign threats to protecting the savings we have spent our lives building up to lifting the burden of our aging from our children to the amelioration of the effects of poverty to eliminating the stigmas associated with race and gender, cannot be accomplished by our individual efforts alone. Not only are such ambitious projects collective in nature, they require some degree of disinterested management to be successfully carried out. We would no more do without them than we would without roofs over our heads or food in our bellies. The more we realize that arbitrary unfairness and mere caprice need not seal our doom, the more we call upon government to add stability and security to our lives. Government grows because, all things considered, we would rather lead better lives than miserable lives. Reject government, and the lives we lead would be impoverished in more ways than just economically.

It makes a certain amount of sense, then, that the last liberal to hold the presidency before Hurricane Katrina struck the Louisiana coast, Bill Clinton, had elevated the Federal Emergency Management Agency to cabinet status, appointed a highly regarded professional, James Lee Witt, to head it, and allowed him to end the practice of using the agency for purposes of political patronage and to build up its preparedness functions. For Clinton, as well as for Witt, government at its best was not an entitlement program run amok but a continuation of the efforts of FDR and LBJ to use government as an instrument of public purpose. Nothing like Hurricane Katrina struck the United

States while Witt was head of FEMA, but a major earthquake in Los Angeles did take place in 1994, and Witt was as prepared as any government official has ever been for a natural disaster. Witt's performance in the aftermath of that event—his quick visit to the scene, his willingness to work with state and local officials, his ability to get money directed to where money needed to be spent—seemed to settle the case about government once and for all. No one could prevent another natural disaster from hitting the United States. But Americans had witnessed an example of the extent to which the state they so often feared could rush to their protection when one did.

In a less ideologically driven political universe than the one that had come to characterize the United States, the Clinton years should have put an end to controversies over the role of government in modern life. In the last few decades of the twentieth century, a consensus around the proper role of government had begun to come into existence. Right-wing politicians, although promising tax cuts and attacking government waste, did not really try to dismantle popular programs, while a Democrat such as Bill Clinton, sensitive to the way the political winds were blowing, expediently proclaimed that the era of big government was over even while appointing competent people such as Witt to run it. So long as public programs served some well-understood purpose and taxes were not viewed as burdensome, most Americans, pragmatic to their core, were happy to accord government its proper role in managing the conditions of modern life. It may have taken most of a century to establish the point, but the lessons taught by Roosevelt in his first inaugural appeared to have been absorbed. Alexander Pope had gotten it right; that which is best administered really is best.

BARRY GOLDWATER'S DREAM

Alas for the cause of effective government, the United States *had* become a highly ideological political system. Especially for those on the political right, the long period that began with the New Deal and ended in the Clinton administration was not viewed as an opportunity to celebrate the emergence of a pragmatic consensus over government but instead represented the triumph of a set of ideas they considered alien to the American way of life. These determined conservatives held that the New Deal had been a mistake, state and local governments were always preferable to federal action, and the private sector would be better at carrying out activities that other societies routinely assigned to the state. The last conservative to run for president before the Great Society came into existence, Barry Goldwater, made such themes central to his 1964 campaign; he would, he said, sell the Tennessee Valley Authority and make Social Security voluntary. Phyllis Schlafly, a key conservative activist, wrote a book during the campaign called *A Choice, Not an Echo*. It was a good title. Americans were given a choice. They chose to reject laissez-faire about as thoroughly as a political idea could be rejected.

Goldwater's defeat created a severe political dilemma for conservative American politicians. As their performance in office suggests, conservative leaders never actually tried to make Goldwater's dream a reality. The reasons were obvious enough. It is not just that the programs associated with the welfare state had become too popular for even politicians such as Margaret Thatcher in Great Britain or Ronald Reagan in the United States to roll back. It was also the case that the wealthy and powerful voted for conservative parties for the same reason that the poor and vulnerable voted for liberal ones: in both cases, winning politicians could offer what government had at its disposal. Big business as well as small farmers, Southern real estate developers as well as Western cattle ranchers, military contractors as well as Wall Street brokers, pharmaceutical companies as well as doctors, even, in the form of faith-based initiatives, the religious right—none of them supported conservative parties to *reduce* the number of governmental contracts thrown their way. Modern politics is all about dividing up and relying upon what the state has to offer, not about cutting back what it provides. Preach Goldwaterism, and you can get your party's nomination. Practice it, and you will spend your time in office encountering fervent opposition from every interest group that supported you in the first place.

Conservative politicians continued to preach Goldwaterism nonetheless. Like the senator from Arizona, none of them was willing, at least at the level of rhetoric, to make a positive case for government. Typical in this regard was American conservatism's favorite conservative, Ronald Reagan. As if he were engaged in a direct dialogue with Roosevelt, Reagan, in *his* first inaugural address, said that "government is not the solution to our problem; government is the problem." As was also the case with Roosevelt, Reagan's line became so famous that we ignore the reasons he gave for it. Liberalism, in FDR's view, was based upon the idea that because we can govern ourselves, we ought to be able to govern society. Reagan argued the exact opposite: "If no one among us is capable of governing himself," he asked, "then who among us has the capacity to govern someone else?" Because he came out so strongly against the idea of government, Reagan distanced himself from eighteenth-century conservatives such as Alexander Hamilton who not only believed in the state but wanted to see its power concentrated in the federal government. Reagan instead sided with Hamilton's opponents when he said that "the Federal Government did not create the States; the States created the Federal Government." Reagan somewhat softened his remarks by saying that he did not intend to "do away with government." His first inaugural, moreover, like so many of his speeches, was filled with the language of hope. But he also denigrated, in unsparing language, the one institution that Americans had been relying upon since the New Deal to realize their hopes in practice.

For conservative politicians, attacks on government have their political uses, none more so than their appeal to diverse groups in the Republican coalition that might otherwise have little in common. For businesspeople, they offer an escape from regulations and taxes that cut into profits. Younger voters, for whom the New Deal is a distant historic event, hear in such rhetoric both a call for economic opportunity and a socially libertarian message that appeals to lifestyles filled with personal choice. Westerners like the language of states' rights because, far from Washington, they tend to believe, incorrectly, that they are less dependent on the federal government than folks back east. It is the language that rallies those Southerners who hear in attacks on government a defense of the notion of states' rights that had once been employed to try to preserve and protect racial segregation. So appealing is antigovernmental talk in conservative political circles that supply-side economics, which calls for radical tax cutting as a mechanism for reducing the size of government, has become the same kind of litmus test for Republicans that support for abortion rights once was for Democrats, even if the budget deficits produced by supply-side economics stand in direct contrast to principles of fiscal responsibility that conservatism once articulated. The more that modern people of all political persuasions came to rely on government, the more ideologically driven became the conservative case against it.

The looming clash within contemporary American conservatism did not come to fruition until the administration of George W. Bush. For the first time in modern American political history, a conservative party now controlled the presidency, both houses of Congress, and, depending on the issues involved, a majority of the Supreme Court. Not only that, the party in question, once composed of both hard-line and moderate conservatives, had gradually been losing the moderates and filling its ranks with the hard-liners. Finally, the man who led them, President Bush, was as strongly committed to tax cuts, the key plank in the laissez-faire program, as any president had ever been; never once, either during his campaigns or in the years he held power, no matter what the conditions of the economy or the world, did Bush ever backtrack from his tax-cutting zeal. The political forces had aligned themselves in a way conservatives of previous years could scarcely believe. Goldwater's dream of cutting government down to size—captured by the conservative activist Grover Norquist's metaphor of washing the state down the bathroom drain—could finally become reality.

It never did. Unlike Goldwater, but like all modern Republican presidents before him, Bush lacked the courage of his free market convictions. Although happy to call for tax cuts, he was unwilling to risk political unpopularity by cutting widely supported government programs in order to balance the budget (although, late in his second term, he did veto nearly all the domestic legislation passed by a Democratic Congress, including a bill that would have provided increased health insurance for children). Not only did he therefore quickly run through the budgetary surplus built up by his Democratic predecessor, he opted to fight a hugely expensive war without including its costs in the regular federal budget, and proposed expensive new programs in education and health care for the elderly without any visible means to pay for them. And when a financial crisis hit Wall Street in the fall of 2008, President Bush led the efforts to provide governmental assistance designed to help the credit markets recover—over the determined opposition of hard-right libertarians within his own party for whom Goldwater's dream had never died. A favorite Washington sport in the first eight years of the twenty-first century involved watching one after another libertarian come to the dawning realization that George W. Bush was fiscally and politically irresponsible. Yet however irresponsible President Bush may have been, the Republicans who opposed Barack Obama's 2009 economic recovery program without a plan of their own, took political irresponsibility to even new heights.

The libertarian critique of the Bush presidency will no doubt continue to resonate. It was one thing for liberals to criticize the Bush administration, but when thinkers long identified with right-wing think tanks such as the Cato Institute joined the fray, cracks in the conservative movement could be heard all over Washington. There was, as well, something refreshingly honest about the libertarian dismay with Mr. Bush. In comparison with neoconservatives who strongly supported the war in Iraq, libertarians were as critical of an all-powerful state in matters of foreign policy as they were in matters domestic; not only did some of them oppose the war itself, nearly all of them protested the concentration of power in the presidency and the curtailment of civil liberties that came with it. In addition, libertarians, once they realized the degree to which Bush's kind of conservatism was leading the Republican Party in a directly opposite direction from the one charted by Goldwater, were not hesitant about making their unease known—a rare quality in a city in which people tend to moderate their dissent, if they engage in dissent at all, just in case some future administration might invite them into power. Libertarians did not have much influence, but they did make a considerable amount of noise.

Although they agree from time to time on some issues, such as civil liberties or concerns about a militaristic state, liberals and libertarians do not agree on everything, and they especially disagree on the role the state should play in modern life. Libertarians, skeptical of government, are also skeptical of governance; good government, by making the state's coercive powers appear less oppressive and dangerous, is, from a strictly libertarian point of view, even worse than bad governance. Only this can explain why, when searching for a term that could best characterize an administration of which they were so critical, libertarians tended to dismiss Bush as a "liberal." Outside of libertarian circles, such a charge made little sense. But the world of libertarianism contains only two poles: big government, which is both liberal and bad; and small government, which is both conservative and good. Since Bush presided over an expansion of government, he must, from a libertarian perspective, have been a liberal.

Liberals thought otherwise. To be sure, it did not particularly bother liberals that Bush expanded the role of government; that, done well, is something in which liberals believe. But Bush did it very poorly. It was not just the failure to win in Iraq and the unwillingness to respond to Katrina. In nearly every area of public policy it touched, the Bush administration's simultaneous use of and contempt for government all but guaranteed administrative failure. Its reform of Medicare was made needlessly expensive and complicated in order to pay back the drug companies that so strongly supported it; to cite only the most egregious example, state governments were forbidden to negotiate downward the price of the drugs whose costs they would be covering. Its approach to economic regulation stimulated lobbyists to demand even more from government every time government offered them something in the first place. Wherever government has proven its effectiveness in the past, the Bush administration appointed individuals whose mission was to prevent it from being effective in the future.

Documenting this history of one conservative failure after another, one liberal, Greg Anrig, vice president for policy at the Century Foundation, turned back to Reagan's first inaugural: "Today, in the United States," he wrote in *The Conservatives Have No Clothes*, "conservatism is not the solution to our problem; conservatism is the problem." From a liberal perspective, conservatives cannot govern for the same reason that vegetarians cannot prepare a world-class *boeuf bourguignon;* if you believe that what you are called upon to do is wrong, you are not likely to do it very well. Unable ever to remove themselves fully from the spell that Goldwaterism cast over them, those who inherited Goldwater's dream paid a severe political price when they made the mistake of believing in their own ideas.

It took staggering levels of mismanagement to bring liberals and libertarians into a contest over which could be more critical of the administration of George W. Bush. For all their agreement, however, libertarianism and liberalism point in different directions when it comes to repairing the damage to public life caused by conservatism's failure at governance. For libertarians, Goldwater's dream, though turned into the nightmare of George W. Bush, can still be realized; the example of bad governance becomes an argument for little or no governance. For liberals, the fact of bad governance makes the case for good governance; the sooner Goldwater's dream is revealed for the illusion it is, the sooner we can return to the lessons taught by the New Deal and the Great Society. For all their consistency—perhaps because of their consistency—libertarians have no major political party to call their own; the party that uses the name is likely to be a third or fourth party of American politics for the foreseeable future. Because the legacy of the New Deal and the Great Society has lasted so long, liberals do: it is called the Democratic Party. The most important question liberals face is what they will do with government if and when they again find themselves in charge of it.

OLD NEW IDEAS

There exists a widespread feeling in contemporary society that political ideologies easily become stale and require the constant infusion of new ideas. In the United States, those who argue along these lines frequently point out that the political right was quicker to understand the wisdom of this way of thinking than the political left. "Some of the ideas emanating from the *rive droite* may be far-fetched," John Micklethrait and Adrian Wooldridge, two British journalists associated with *The Economist,* note in *The Right Nation* (2004). "Still others may be shop-soiled. Yet the Right clearly has more intellectual vitality than the Left—at least when it comes to suggesting practical policies." In their telling of the tale of contemporary U.S. politics, "the sound that we have been hearing in the background of American political life for the past thirty years is the melancholy, withdrawing roar of liberalism." A new, forward-looking, and politically aggressive conservatism is there to fill the vacuum. This conservative momentum could be lost, Micklethrait and Wooldridge believe, especially if Republicans turn their backs on racial minorities or tie their fortunes so closely to business that they sever them with everyone else. But the two journalists see little reason for that to happen. America, they argue, is as conservative in practice as earlier writers held it to be liberal in theory. Conservatives, they conclude, are not only on the right, they believe they are in the right, and their self-confidence gives them a huge political advantage.

If there exists a well-told tale of conservative success, there also exists an equally well told narrative of liberal failure. Democrats might win back political power because of Republican incompetence, the journalist Matt Bai maintains in *The Argument* (2007), but they lack the kinds of bold ideas that once inspired the New Deal and the Great Society. They too could have created Washington think tanks replete with policy papers and staff ready to assume positions of power should the Democrats again win the presidency. But this they did not do. Instead, the energy flowed to the "netroots," bloggers and activists who, though long on new technologies and anger, were short on actual policy prescriptions. Refusing to adopt new ideas, liberals, for better or worse, were stuck with the old ones. More intent on being right than building majorities, Bai notes, they will never again inspire Americans until they aspire to new ways of thinking.

There are a number of reasons why these stories, though frequently told, fail to correspond with reality. Two are worth emphasizing. One is that conservatives in reality developed relatively few new ideas. The other, more important point is that one of liberalism's oldest ideas— that government exists to help people attain control of the conditions under which they live—remains as viable as ever.

The conservative intellectual and policy wonks who flocked to Washington think tanks in recent years, rather than developing new ideas, took the one idea that has possessed the right since F. A. Hayek and Milton Friedman—the idea that the market is always preferable to the state—and gave it new names. Fully aware that modern people rely on the state to protect themselves against economic and natural catastrophes, conservatives, rather than simply reiterating the by now stale bromides of laissez-faire, became advocates for what, at first glance, seemed cutting-edge economic thinking: rational choice theory, game theory, public choice theory, and, most famously of all, supply-side economics. But all of it was a reformulation in one way or another of the never-to-be-challenged proposition around which contemporary conservatives had rallied fifty years ago. It was all about repackaging, not about rethinking. However discredited Goldwater's dream may have been in politics, in the think tanks and in Congress it was still alive.

For this reason, the presumably new ideas that came to the attention of Republican politicians in recent years were actually less original than those associated with Herbert Spencer in Victorian England. Spencer, after all, had the quite interesting new idea of relying upon Darwinian evolutionary theory to strengthen his case for capitalism; right or wrong—most of it turned out to be wrong—it was ingenious in its own way. No one in the early-twenty-first-century Washington scene, moreover, rivals Spencer in the breadth of his interests; he was not a thinker who confined himself to economics but theorized about every aspect of the world around him. Spencer, finally, was arguing against the state before the modern state assumed its present size and shape. His goal was to prevent something from happening that he feared.

Today's antigovernment conservatives, by contrast, are calling for a shrinking of government at a time when government is all around us— not only a more difficult task, but one so ambitious that it would require the assistance of the very state to which conservatives are so opposed to carry it out. The kind of conservatism on public display during the eight years of the Bush administration not only failed to measure up to a Victorian libertarian such as Spencer; it could not hold a candle to a Victorian conservative such as Benjamin Disraeli, who anticipated with chilling brilliance what would happen to conservatism in another country and at another time. In his novel *Coningsby*, published in 1844, the future prime minister wrote about a form of conservatism that "discards Prescription, shrinks from Principle, disavows Progress; having rejected all respect for antiquity, it offers no redress for the present, and makes no preparation for the future."

Even if contemporary conservatism were flush with new and sweeping ideas, it does not follow that they should be adopted. It is more important that an idea be correct than that it be new, and the liberal idea of using the state to help improve the quality of people's lives is a correct one. FDR's words, though delivered some time ago and under radically different economic conditions, still ring true: we have the capacity to control our fate, so long as we are willing to use the institution that represents us as a people.

But if this means that liberals should not apologize for relying upon government, it also means that they should not become apologists for it. Liberals ought to be well aware that, in using the state, they are not adopting a panacea. The state, as I have already suggested, tends to curse all contemporary political philosophies. Bureaucracies can become inefficient and the solutions they propose counterproductive to the problems they set out to correct. Governmental officials will develop interests of their own and they will use the state to further them. The fiscal costs of relying on government can be high, and while public spending can stimulate the economy, it can also have inflationary effects. Micromanagement of the choices of private individuals and institutions can lead them to innovate and experiment less. Regulation of unsafe industrial practices ought to be as welcome as regulation of individual rights ought to be shunned, but it is not always easy to draw a sharp line between the two. And yes, there is such a thing as too high a tax burden.

Fortunately, there is a way for liberals to defend the state while warning against its dangers. Liberalism has never been in favor of the state as an end itself; *étatisme,* as the French call it, was long associated with right-wing movements in Western history, not, except for Leninism and some of its offshoots, with leftist ones. The key liberal idea has instead been self-mastery: a good society, from a liberal perspective, is one in which people get to decide the kinds of lives they want to lead. Liberals may once have believed that self-mastery would be best furthered by laissez-faire, but the growth of large corporations and the experiences of debilitating business cycles convinced them that most people, in the absence of the protection that government offered, would be as powerless against economic forces beyond their control as they had once been powerless in the face of nature's onslaughts. One of the most prolific of twentieth-century American liberals, the economist John Kenneth Galbraith, wrote some thirty-five books, too many to have gotten everything right, but he was correct in his concept of "countervailing power." Modern citizens experience forces more powerful than themselves all the time. Their only hope lies in an institution capable of counteracting private power, and that institution would have to be the state.

Programs that enable people to bring the conditions of their lives under their own control ought to be passionately supported by liberals. When conservatives say that they want to add private accounts to help relieve the fiscal pressures on Social Security, liberals are right to be skeptical, for behind many such efforts are attempts to cut back on the idea that old age creates conditions of dependency that can best be met by ensuring benefits to people without conditions attached. For similar reasons, liberals need to support the expansion of medical insurance. Liberalism's goals are best fulfilled when people are not forced for lack of coverage to forgo care that would help improve their lives. The work of the New Deal and the Great Society is not yet finished. So long as dependency on forces larger than themselves exists, people will need government, and liberals, who believe in government, are the ones best able to provide it.

If the state is viewed as a means to help individuals lead autonomous lives, however, the state becomes a problem when it interferes with their capacity to do so.

Liberals should question reliance on the state on the same grounds that undergird their support for it: if governmental programs create rather than overcome dependencies, significantly undermining the ability of people to choose the kinds of lives they want to lead, the time has come to rethink them. There are at least two major issues in contemporary American politics where liberals ought to be open to reforms that would lower the amount of governmental involvement in American life.

One was Bill Clinton's contentious effort to "end welfare as we know it." For some liberals, including some who worked for him and resigned in protest, Clinton was viewed as attacking a government program, Aid to Families with Dependent Children, that was a direct outgrowth of the Social Security Act of 1937. By criticizing a piece of New Deal legislation, Clinton was implicitly criticizing the New Deal itself. His "neoliberalism," as critics took to describing efforts by both Clinton and Tony Blair to roll back well-established governmental benefits, deserved the prefix, in their view, because it was not really liberalism at all. Welfare reform was viewed as the best example of "triangulation," Clinton's effort to position himself midway between liberalism and conservatism in the hopes of solidifying his political popularity.

It makes more sense, I believe, to view Clinton's welfare reforms as compatible with rather than hostile to liberal objectives. People should be helped out in difficult times, but what had actually happened in the case of Aid to Families with Dependent Children was the creation of a permanent welfare class, a group of people whose dependency on government was passed down from generation to generation. If we are to advance the liberal goal of helping people to achieve control over their lives, it is appropriate to put conditions upon the provision of welfare to encourage such people to leave the rolls. Whether or not forcing mothers of young children into the workforce was the appropriate way to do this can and should be questioned, but the notion of overcoming dependency should not be. It is not liberalism's task to reproduce premodern conditions of subservience in the modern world.

School choice is another area in which liberalism's commitment to government has been sorely tested, yet also one from which liberalism can emerge stronger. There are good liberal reasons to support the principle of public schooling, including the importance of teaching common values of citizenship, as well as offering a benefit of equal worth to every child whatever the income of his or her parents. From John Dewey to Senator Edward M. Kennedy, public education has been an important plank in the liberal program. As the political scientists Ira Katznelson and Margaret Weir have pointed out in *Schooling for All*, public education is to Americans as the welfare state is to Europeans. Americans have been very slow to adopt universal health care, but they were one of the world's first societies to adopt universal public schooling.

The equality that public schooling offers can only be realized when everyone relies on public schools. That, for better or worse, does not happen in the United States. Wealthy people have always found ways to exercise school choice, either by paying the costs of private schooling themselves or by moving to suburban communities where high taxes guarantee good schools. If some people can exercise choice, it violates conditions of equality to forbid others from so doing. Vouchers, charters, and other efforts to allow school choice tend to be extremely popular among inner-city parents desperate to find better opportunities for their children. The liberal goal of helping people control the conditions of their lives is best served not by neglecting their needs but by supporting their desires. This becomes even more true when considerations of race enter the picture, as they inevitably do when black children are more likely not to have school choice than white children. School choice is an idea developed by libertarians that liberals should endorse.

Because of the curse of the state, there are unlikely ever to exist firm principles that tell us when to rely on government and when not to. But the world is filled with enough examples of misfortune—from hurricanes to the crippling dependencies of old age to the failures of inner-city schools—to reach one conclusion about the modern state: it makes far more sense to accept it as legitimate and attempt to correct its flaws than to view it as evil, decentralize its powers in ways that prevent them from being effectively used, and rush haphazardly to rely upon it when it cannot be avoided. If the state's curse can never be removed, its effects can be modified. The best way to prevent the abuses that attend reliance on the state is to welcome the need for the state. You do not improve the state's performance by commanding it to disappear.

Faced with the inevitable fact of the state's existence in modern society, conservatives could reject a libertarian commitment to laissez-faire that, for all its admirable consistency, cannot deal with the realities of modern life. Were it to do so, conservatives might consider returning to the ideas of Alexander Hamilton and John Marshall in the United States or Benjamin Disraeli and the "wets" of twentieth-century Great Britain. This would not be a conservatism that used government to pay off friends and punish enemies, but one that sought to use government to stabilize society, create conditions of order, and avoid periodic crises. Any such "big government conservatism" would not be liberal; although there would be a significant role for the state, government would not, under such a program, be in charge of helping as many people as possible to lead autonomous lives. But at the very least, a conservatism of this sort would not, by rejecting government, also reject governance. Had we had such conservatives in power when Hurricane Katrina struck, not nearly as many lives, it seems safe to suggest, would have been lost.

There is little prospect of such an old-fashioned form of conservatism reemerging, especially in the United States. Ideologies need political parties to spread and apply their ideas, and a right-wing base that wants to hear little more than attacks on government and calls for lower taxes still exercises significant influence within the Republican Party. Good governance was once an Enlightenment ideal that far-sighted conservatives were willing to adopt. For reasons known only to themselves, contemporary conservatives abandoned the terrain of good governance—not the smartest tactic when government is so essential to the way we live now. In so doing, they left the whole question of how best to manage the complications of modernity to liberals (just as liberals, alas, left so many questions of morality to conservatives). That, in retrospect, was a gift—one that will keep on giving and for which liberals ought always to be grateful.

CHAPTER 9

LIBERALISM'S PROMISE

IDEAS HAVE (SOME) CONSEQUENCES

"The enemy within is modern liberalism, a corrosive agent carrying a very different mood and agenda than that of classical or traditional liberalism," begins Robert Bork's *Slouching Toward Gomorrah*, one of the more ill-tempered of the attacks on liberalism that have recently appeared in the United States. Bork, a former law professor and judge who was denied a seat on the Supreme Court in 1987 because of the extremism of his views, compares the threat modern liberalism poses to Western civilization to earlier ones represented by the Nazis, Communists, and even the Germanic tribes that once descended on Rome— and finds it worse. We really are on an inevitable path to perdition, he believes, tempted by a political worldview that is leading us astray. Modern liberalism may be "intellectually bankrupt," but this "diminishes neither its vitality nor the danger it poses. A bankrupt philosophy can reign for centuries and, when its bankruptcy becomes apparent, may well be succeeded by an even less coherent outlook."

Bork's book raises a number of important questions, including this one: Can a political philosophy, any political philosophy, really have the power to cause so much havoc to civilization as we know it? Bork believes that it can: "The mistake the Enlightenment founders of liberalism made about human nature," he writes, "has brought us to this—an increasing number of alienated, restless individuals without strong ties to others, except in the pursuit of ever more degraded distractions and sensations." Richard Weaver, an English professor at the University of Chicago and an admirer of the Southern way of life, published *Ideas Have Consequences,* a major statement of conservative philosophy, in 1948. Bork agrees with the title: liberalism very definitely has had consequences and nearly all of them have been dreadful.

No one in my line of business can doubt that both Weaver and Bork are on to something—I would not be writing a book about liberalism if I thought ideas did not matter—but it is questionable whether ideas have the importance we sometimes assign to them. It is better to say that ideas have some consequences, even important ones, but by themselves their influence is limited. Philosophers can help explain the world. They are unable to direct its course.

The evidence advanced by Bork to demonstrate liberalism's pernicious qualities illustrates the limited role that political ideas actually play. From time to time, Bork singles out a liberal or leftist writer to criticize, although far more of them are leftists than liberals. But such important modern thinkers as John Rawls and Richard Rorty never appear in his pages, let alone earlier liberals such as Benjamin Constant or Immanuel Kant. Developments on the ground rather than ideas in the air fuel Bork's scorn. Unbridled hedonism has brought us forms of popular culture barely distinguishable from pornography. Relentless quests for equality produce little more than envious rage. A feminist insistence on individual rights has destroyed the family and obscured inherent biological differences between men and women. A general refusal to impose standards and apply discipline results in massive and uncontrollable crime. The unwillingness of modern people to accept the authority of a supernatural force paves the way for the mistaken belief that everything is of equal value. These are all, if one is as conservative as Bork, perfectly appropriate criticisms to make. To the extent that they involve ideas, however, they are, at best, at second remove from those who formulate them.

Ideas about politics do not take root and influence large numbers by themselves; they must in addition speak to the social forces shaping the world in which they are formulated and propagated. All those pressures from women to become equal to men did not flow directly from people reading John Stuart Mill's *The Subjection of Women* but had more to do with such economic and technological factors as the rise of industrialization, the impact of wars, the improvement of birth control, the spread of two-income families, and the weakening authority of religion. Indeed, Mill recognized as much when he made the case for equality based on the decreasing importance of force in the world. Nor did religion lose its authority because of the attacks launched upon it by Diderot and Voltaire; more important were the spread of mass education and the extraordinary breakthroughs of modern science. Classical music did not eventually give way to rock and roll because of anything written by Kant on the philosophy of aesthetics, but because new technologies brought music out of the concert halls, into people's homes, and finally into the iPods of teenagers.

If all the innovations that created the world we know remained in place, and none of the great liberal thinkers had ever been born, the world that would have resulted would very much resemble the world that exists. Robert Bork, like so many contemporary conservatives, attacks liberalism, but his real enemy is modernity. No wonder his anger seems so misplaced. He is firing his rhetorical ammunition at the wrong target.

Liberalism faces a number of challenges both now and in the future, and in this final chapter I will describe and analyze some of the most important of them. But before doing so it is important to recognize that it was not liberalism that created the modern world; the modern world made possible the achievement of liberalism. The challenge of politics in our times is not to find the most logically consistent political philosophy, the one with the most tragic vision of life, or the one that is best expressed in sound bites; it is instead to find the political philosophy best capable of understanding our situation and anticipating our future. By now, it ought to be clear which one that is. Of all the political philosophies that arose in the wake of the modern revolution, liberalism is the one left standing with the least wobble in its legs.

MANAGING MODERNITY

When exactly the modern world came into being, what its major features are, and whether or not it has come to an end are questions that are debated endlessly, not only by political philosophers but by anyone interested in the fate of the world in which we find ourselves. For debates as vigorous and far-reaching as these, however, there is an unusual consensus that something called the modern world does exist; that it began as a reaction against the societies of the *ancien régime* and therefore was set in motion by the American, French, and industrial revolutions; and that the most significant of those forces involved the triumph of industry over agriculture, the growth of urban areas, the spreading of the scientific revolution, increasing democratization, and the development of a bureaucratic state with the capacity both to raise armies and to shape a national consciousness. Nor is there all that much doubt that these forces continue to shape Western societies down to the present time, bringing into being such realities as increased personal freedom, greater equality, religious diversity, social mobility, sustained economic growth, technological dynamism, global expansion, and an unshakable conviction on the part of ordinary people that even if they choose not to become involved in politics, their voice ought nonetheless to be the final say on what is permissible and what is not. Even those who claim that modernity has been replaced by postmodernity understand the latter as a more extreme version of the former.

To appreciate the demands that modernity imposes upon politics, consider what it means to manage a world like the one we inhabit. If you were put in charge of running any contemporary society, you would immediately realize that you were not selected because you had inherited a throne; on the contrary, you had to persuade the public to vote for you and you must be constantly prepared for the possibility that, should you fail, they may be inclined to vote for someone else. You can claim, as rulers of old did, that your authority derives from God and that therefore your decisions should be accepted without question. But people in the society you govern, belonging as they do to many different religious traditions, will challenge you by asking precisely which God you have in mind—or even whether it is legitimate for you to invoke God at all. As the leader of your society, you have significant political power at your disposal, but your power is not unlimited; you cannot, for example, simply assassinate someone who threatens you and hope to hold on to whatever power you have. Power matters to you, but it also matters to everyone else, which means you will have to share a large portion of it, either with the legislative branch of government or with courts charged with discovering whether your actions can be considered constitutional.

The complexities of modernity do not stop there. Whatever you do, when it is not subject to other branches of government, will be scrutinized by the media, and the more you antagonize them, the more likely they are to pay careful attention to you. The people you govern do not belong to the same gender, race, income group, or region; indeed, these days significant numbers of them are likely to have been born in another country. And even if you should be successful enough to win the love and respect of your people, your country will face both economic and military competition from other countries and you must do whatever you can to improve its position relative to them. You can, with appropriate political skills, try to govern such a world, but its pluralism, its democratic instincts, and its openness will also govern you.

Modernity is a brute fact of contemporary social life; as the popular World War I song put it, "How ya gonna keep 'em down on the farm (after they've seen Paree)?" Modernity cannot be wished away. Its spread to ever-newer parts of the globe can be slowed but is unlikely ever to be stopped. Human beings can no more reverse its course than spiritualists can bring the dead back to life. But they can answer the question of the best way to manage it. And it is with respect to managing modernity that liberalism best demonstrates its strengths: the dispositions that give liberalism its meaning are most in accord with how the modern world functions.

The modern world unleashes forces as dramatic as they are unpredictable, which suggests that it is best managed by learning from experience and manifesting a willingness to grow and develop as the world changes. The fact that modern societies allow people with different conceptions of the common good to express themselves means that it requires agreement on procedures so as to permit disagreement on substance. The pressures toward equality associated with modernity undermine arguments in favor of inherited status and inherent difference. If modernity puts unprecedented powers in the hands of leaders, society will have to find ways to rely on that power to accomplish purposive goals, but also to check its concentration to protect individual rights. Modern societies are open to the world, which suggests that attempts to shut them down will always be unsuccessful. Most important of all, modern citizens believe that the world they inhabit is one they made, and that any attempts to go back to a state of nature, or to convince themselves that they are mere pawns in the hands of supernatural forces beyond their control, or that all efforts to improve the conditions of their lives are doomed to fail, however much asserted, rarely become the basis for their actual decisions and actions. Liberalism may not have created modernity, but liberalism is the answer for which modernity is the question. Flexibility is built into the way we live now. It ought to be built into the way we govern now.

Liberalism's elective affinity with modernity makes all the more strange the vehemence of the attacks against it. For all the hostility conservatives manifest toward liberalism, they are the first to invoke John Stuart Mill's ringing defense of unorthodox ideas when they find themselves on campuses dominated by leftists. They speak of reverence for God and the priority of revelation over reason, yet they make their case by citing statistics and engaging in debate, methods of persuasion a capricious and all-powerful God would likely disdain but a liberal trained in the logic of modern social science would welcome. One hears from them frequent complaints about stigmatized minorities seeking what they call "special rights," yet they tend to view themselves as persecuted victims oppressed by the secular liberals they believe to be in control of all the major institutions of power. When in power they like to skirt proceduralist ideals about fairness and neutrality, but when they are out of power, they are among the first to demand commitments to them.

Even Robert Bork, whose attack on liberalism is as strong as they come, is a liberal manqué; he claims to be a friend of equality compared to the elitism he finds on the left, and he criticizes feminism, not because it insists on a woman's right to choose but because he believes that it denies women the choice of leading traditional lives. Not everything conservatives say borrows from liberalism—their inclination to tar the people with whom they disagree with the ugly epithet "enemies within" does not—but the very passion they bring to their convictions testifies to the fact that, no longer having the power to impose their ideas by fiat, they live for better or worse in a world of pluralism and disagreement. We are definitely *not* all liberals now. But we do all live in a liberal world, which is why conservative attacks on liberalism so frequently amount to hating the society that sustains you. If modern liberalism really is as dangerous and bankrupt as Bork says, there would be no such thing as modern conservatism.

It is not, in short, liberalism's failure that has caused it to be a curse word in modern politics but its success. Liberals no longer write pathbreaking books because the most important paths have already been broken. Modern people do not need to know why liberty, or society, or rights, or peace, or even equality are good things; the cases for them have already been made, and even if they had not been, citizens of liberal democracy have grown quite used to living with them. The conditions that led Kant to dare to know or Mill to defend liberty so passionately no longer exist, which is good for liberal societies even if it is not so good for the vibrancy of liberal political philosophy. To be sure, liberals, politically speaking, are often on the defensive, but while their opponents may control the play, liberals own the field. They need be neither frightened about the inevitable power of nonliberal ideas nor complacent about their own inherent wisdom. Instead, they should take a deep breath and remind themselves that their record has been a good one and their relevance never more apparent. Their task is less to know new things than to apply things long known to new conditions.

This does not mean that we are at the end of history. Modernity does not reach a stage where it suddenly stops, which means that liberalism, modernity's accompaniment, will continue to be tested in the years ahead. John Dewey delivered his 1934 lecture "The Future of Liberalism" at a time when the Great Depression was still in its early stages. The need for government action to combat economic hard times was obvious to him and he concluded, as nearly all liberals of his time did, that under such conditions, liberty had to mean more than the freedom of businessmen to do anything they wanted. But Dewey also looked beyond the Great Depression. Liberalism, he argued, possessed a cultural as well as an economic dimension. "The full freedom of the human spirit and of individuality," he said, "can be achieved only as there is effective opportunity to share in the cultural resources of civilization." Three questions about how the cultural resources of civilization will be distributed—one dealing with liberalism at home, the other two abroad—seem especially significant.

At home, liberalism, while the political philosophy most compatible with modernity, is neither always compatible with it nor the only political philosophy to have survived modernity's rigors. Conservatism has shown its relevance as well, in large part by adapting itself to modern political conditions, and although certain forms of contemporary conservatism amount to little more than demagoguery, others raise important questions about liberalism's not always comfortable relationship with modern democracy. On some of the most serious issues facing American politics, including abortion and racial and sexual equality, what liberals think most appropriate is not always what the majority of citizens find acceptable. Liberalism's most serious domestic challenge is what it should do when liberal commitments lack public support, especially in an era when conservative positions on those issues appear to have widespread backing. Liberals are frequently accused of elitism and it is a charge to which they must respond.

The challenges confronting liberalism from abroad come in two forms. One, post-liberal in nature, argues that globalization undermines the liberal belief in progress: far from making the world more cosmopolitan, critics of globalization argue, contemporary capitalism is plunging the world into forms of chaos that are likely to result, if it is possible to manage this emerging anarchy at all, in new forms of authoritarianism. The other, pre-liberal by disposition, focuses on the faith-inspired terrorist. Religious fundamentalism, a throwback to the past rather than an anticipation of the future, will either win its war against weak-willed liberal societies or force them, at the cost of their own survival, to question their commitments to liberal principles. But in either case, liberalism is as threatened by tribalism as it is by globalism. In the worst of all possible scenarios, the two link up—the one, by breaking down the nation-state and bringing all the haters in the world in touch with one another, preparing the ground for the other.

Only time will tell whether the threats to liberalism in the remainder of the twenty-first century will be as severe as those that gave rise to liberalism in the late eighteenth. But the idea that liberalism is on its way to obsolescence is, as Jeremy Bentham described the idea of rights rooted in nature without law to enforce them, "nonsense upon stilts." Liberalism is not some new kid on the block. It has been with us as long as any other modern political philosophy, and it is likely to continue to be with us for some time coming. Of all the political worldviews at our disposal, the most appropriate political philosophy for our times has the best chance of being the most appropriate for our children and grandchildren as well.

THE DANGERS OF CONSERVATIVE POPULISM

Out of those earth-shattering events that sped the creation of the modern world in the late eighteenth century, only conservatism remains a significant challenge to liberalism. It is not difficult to understand why. We all know what it means to conserve. There is something we value, the nuclear family, for example, or our faith, or our national Constitution. It has been in existence for a long period of time, and over that time, it has either proven its worth or won our respect simply because of its longevity. Why experiment with something new when we already have something old? To be sure, as Don Fabrizio's nephew Tancredi put it in Giuseppe Tomasi di Lampedusa's novel *The Leopard,* "If we want things to stay as they are, things will have to change." But the urge to prefer our way of life to that of strangers, to resist radical experiments in public policy, or to be skeptical about promised utopias appeals to emotions as fundamental as they can be seductive. Whatever their other differences—and they can be many—conservatives are united by a widely shared conviction that time-tested arrangements should always be given the benefit of the doubt.

In a conservative world, conservatism would be the natural governing philosophy. But we live in a modern world, and because modernity happened, conservatives find themselves in an awkward position. Inclined by temperament to fight against so much of what modernity stands for, conservatives can insist that the whole modern experience was one vast mistake, and when they do, nostalgic conservatism rings with a certain conviction. Conservatism of this sort is one vast thought experiment: it asks us to judge how we live against a standard by which we no longer can live. Like the jeremiad, the classic Puritan sermon that viewed the world outside the church as one long march downward into hell, its implacability gives conservatism a distinct prophetic quality. The price it pays, however, is the likelihood of becoming "superfluous"—the term Albert Jay Nock, the early-twentieth-century conservative author of *Our Enemy, the State,* used to describe himself.

No one who hopes to influence the world in which he or she lives can be expected to deliberately choose irrelevance, however, and as a result, conservatives, as we see among so many of the critics of contemporary liberalism, are more inclined to accept selected features of modernity while condemning others. They can hardly be blamed for that. It is enormously difficult to defend class privileges in societies that pride themselves on their lack of class differences. Making the case for hierarchy is not the easiest thing to do in democratic times when the people themselves decide which case is best. It is one thing to insist on the need for order but another to preserve order at a time when people expect to do pretty much what they want most of the time. The essence of conservatism is that it wants to limit the reach of liberty and equality while the essence of modernity is to expand them. Instead of denouncing liberty and equality as unworkable, conservatives are therefore better off claiming them as their own. And this, in the United States, a liberal society if there ever was one, is what conservatives, a few odd remnants excepted, have always done.

Examples of conservatives willing to compromise with conservative principles throughout American history are legion. The Whigs set themselves up in opposition to Jacksonian democracy, but to have any chance of defeating Jacksonianism, they found themselves appealing to the masses in ways that were uncomfortable for their sense of themselves as a governing class. Conservative clerics played down strict Calvinist ideas about predestination to emphasize the egalitarian potential of everyone being born again in Christ. Southern defenders of slavery sounded like left-wing Marxists when they informed Northern businessmen that their employees were in reality wage slaves. Twentieth-century isolationists abandoned the internationalism of Alexander Hamilton, America's greatest conservative, for nativist sentiments more likely to win them votes. Such decisions kept conservatism alive, but in compromised form. Conservatives used the language of liberty to restrict freedom and the appeal of democracy to protect privilege. Because they did, a conservative in America became someone who advocated ends that could not be realized through means that could not be justified, at least not on conservative terms. In such fashion could conservatism retain its relevance, but at the cost of considerable intellectual inconsistency. No wonder that by the mid-twentieth century Lionel Trilling famously dismissed conservatism as "irritable mental gestures which seek to resemble ideas."

In our own times, this tendency of conservatives to adapt to the conditions of modernity can best be described as "conservative populism." On the one hand, such a political worldview, despite its willingness to borrow liberal language, is, if Robert Bork's views are any indication, truly conservative; it is unmoved by actual economic inequality and, even in its heart of hearts, thinks that inequality is actually good for disadvantaged people because it forces them to take responsibility for their failures in life. We should never forget what a constricted vision of life this is. Lacking in sympathy and compassion, it sees no affront to carefully constructed ideas of fairness and social justice that have become part of what Western societies stand for. In the minds of those who think this way, it is only proper that the most well rewarded get even more of society's rewards.

Conservatives of this sort express their concern for the moral values of ordinary people, but in fact theirs is a politics of indifference toward the frequently mind-boggling moral dilemmas less wealthy people in modern societies face. Conservatives have proven themselves so ill at ease in relying on government because they know that government is all too often the most appropriate mechanism for making the conditions of life fairer for those treated most unfairly, and this is not a purpose with which they identify. Conservatives can attach the adjective "compassionate" to their self-description, but when they get the chance to put their ideas into practice, compassion rarely follows.

At the same time, conservative populism is, in key respects, really populist. When it attacks liberal elites, it does so for their elitism as much as their liberalism. It has little truck with the idea of scientific expertise and its ideals of dispassion and disinterest. Its foreign policy, whether in interventionist or isolationist form, is above all else nationalist. Conservatives these days love to go after the modern university, finding it to be a den of political correctness and left-leaning activism, evoking a long tradition of anti-intellectual contempt associated with populists of the past. Populism's appeal has always been not to those at the very bottom of the economic scale but to those just above them, and this is exactly where contemporary American conservatism finds its political base. Appealing to religion, playing off one section of the country against another, rallying around the flag—all such political strategies were as prominent in the late nineteenth century as they have become ubiquitous in the twenty-first.

By definition, contemporary liberals cannot be conservatives; they are committed in substantive terms to liberty and equality in ways that conservatives are not. At the same time, liberals, by disposition, should be wary of populism. To be sure, older forms of populism, such as those associated with the three-time presidential candidate William Jennings Bryan, the advocate of a policy of "free silver" that would have helped poor farmers pay off their debts, resonate with ideas of social justice and in that sense remain appealing to the left to this day. But even though populism shares something substantive with liberalism, it is deeply illiberal temperamentally. Populism attempts to rouse people out of fear rather than to appeal to them through hope. It is strongly tempted to divide the world into friends and enemies. It has never been sympathetic toward those who live outside its rather restricted moral universe. It looks back with nostalgia toward a simpler past rather than anticipating a more complex future. Although Bryan himself evinced few signs of religious bigotry, populism in general did. Its response to the openness of the modern world was to try to close it against forces it considered alien and dangerous.

Put populism and conservatism together in one package and you have one very dangerous brew. If one believes, as Edmund Burke did, in the viability of the "little platoon" somewhere between the individual and the state that sustains lives of tradition, conservative populism abolishes it in the name of uniformity. It is not to individuals that conservative populists appeal but to masses: ethnic groups, public opinion, collective frenzy. Rather than limit the powers of government, as conservatives have not very successfully sought to do, conservative populism expands them, offering a public response to every kind of imagined private complaint. Gone is the idea that a leadership class can play a restraining role, elevating ordinary people to reach for something higher in life; instead, class resentments are mobilized to reinforce class inequalities. Standing alone, Edmund Burke and William Jennings Bryan represent admirable traditions. Blended, they are a danger to moderation, reason, and stability.

If liberals should be wary of populism, does it follow that they should be sympathetic toward elitism? Under certain, hopefully limited conditions, the honest answer has to be yes. Democracy and liberalism have worked well together at most times because both share a commitment to equality. But they have not worked well together at all times. Immanuel Kant's soft spot for enlightened despotism, John Stuart Mill's contempt for the masses, and, in our own day, Ronald Dworkin's defense of highly unpopular judicial decisions on issues ranging from euthanasia to affirmative action all represent instances when liberals opted for freedom or equality as they understood them rather than democracy as it has usually been practiced. Because of the close association between modernity and democracy, this is dangerous ground for liberals to explore. If they stand too much against what most people want, they will soon find themselves on the same path toward political irrelevance trod by conservatives of the nonpopulist variety.

Still, there are and always will be issues in which liberalism's commitments to openness, proper procedure, or fairness will come into conflict with democracy's insistence not only on fulfilling the will of the majority but on doing so as rapidly as possible. Under such circumstances, conservative populists, who have no trouble identifying themselves with the concerns of ordinary people against the designing schemes of the elites, will be quick to charge liberalism with hypocrisy—or worse. This is a charge that liberals ought to face squarely. For all their commitment to equality, liberals do believe that the political views people sometimes hold are not, if they had more knowledge and were open to more deliberation, the political views they should hold. It is fair enough to call such a position elitist. But that should not end the discussion. Instead, it should provoke conversation about when, and under what conditions, democracy requires leadership. Some recent examples of where liberal forms of leadership have been offered suggest ways of thinking about the issue.

The United States was not ready for a giant step to be taken in the direction of racial equality when the U.S. Supreme Court handed down its 1954 decision in *Brown* v. *Board of Education,* theoretically ending segregation in public schools. Still, the liberals responsible for that decision—in those days, the term "liberal" could include a Republican chief justice, Earl Warren, appointed by a Republican president, Dwight D. Eisenhower—did not consider public opinion a trump card, especially in the Southern states in which its holding would be most directly applied. The result was an opinion that not only announced what the law would be but did so in a way designed to win over likely opponents. "Chief Justice Warren's decision in *Brown*," writes the Yale Law School professor Jack Balkin, "is a model of eloquence and understatement, brief and statesmanlike, fully aware of political context and deliberately designed to avoid confrontation and to conserve the Court's legitimacy."

Another way of making the same point is to suggest that the *Brown* decision constituted an exercise in liberal leadership. Understanding that large numbers of people held ideas that were incompatible with the basic liberal principles for which their own country stood, it opted to give those people, and the political institutions that represented their views, sufficient time to grow into the position they ought to have rather than the one they did have. Ten years later, Congress passed the Civil Rights Act of 1964, giving the decision in *Brown* ex post facto democratic legitimacy. The lesson was clear: liberals could and should break with public sentiment in order to ensure that what was popular and what was right could become the same thing.

The methods by which liberals brought into being a historic consensus on racial equality—one that had been conspicuously missing from most of American history before the 1960s—were so successful that even conservatives who once opposed civil rights legislation came to support it. Their new support of racial equality, in fact, became a key plank in the conservative populist critique of liberalism. The Civil Rights Act of 1964 committed the nation to the principle of color blindness, they maintain. After all, Senator Hubert Humphrey, a civil rights firebrand, said so himself in the debates over the legislation when he assured the nation that passage of the act would not "require hiring, firing, or promotion of employees in order to meet a racial 'quota' or to achieve a certain racial balance. . . . In fact, the very opposite is true." By committing themselves in the aftermath of the 1964 act to affirmative action, liberals, this line of argument continues, committed a double sin. On the one hand, they supported the idea that group membership counts for more than individual achievement, a violation of a key liberal principle. On the other, they relied upon undemocratic institutions such as courts and administrative agencies to bring affirmative action into being, recognizing full well, and hence determined to bypass, the depth of the opposition toward quotas on the part of ordinary people. If the Civil Rights Act constitutes a model of how the public can and should be moved, affirmative action would seem to offer the exact opposite: liberal elitism run rampant in ways that can be corrected only by popular movements against it.

The conservative populist critique of affirmative action is not without merit: affirmative action is unpopular, and whenever measures restricting it are put on the ballot in the form of initiatives or referenda, they invariably pass. Yet the populist critique of affirmative action does not really hold up. For one thing, affirmative action was not imposed by liberals on society without public input. There was in fact little such input, but conservatives were as responsible for that as liberals. Affirmative action has had many parents. The most important one was Richard Nixon, who had cleverly hoped to win over white working-class votes by having his Labor Department side with blacks in the Philadelphia construction trades. (My father, my grandfather, and my father's three brothers were all members of the Philadelphia union in question, which means that, under the rules as they existed before Nixon intervened, I could have joined, but the African-American laborers with whom I worked during summer vacations could not.) Nor was Nixon alone. The only justice appointed to the Supreme Court because of his race was appointed by a Republican. The large business corporations that routinely support the Republican Party also practice affirmative action in order to capture new markets or to find undiscovered talent. However unpopular quotas may be, especially when they take rigid form, softer forms of affirmative action are routine features of political and social life in the United States. It was not liberal elitism that brought affirmative action into being so much as everyday common sense.

In addition, affirmative action does not necessarily stand in opposition to liberal principles. Just as government intervention into the economy is needed to help people gain the economic security that will help them direct the conditions of their lives, affirmative action can and does enable people who were prevented from reaching their full potential because of the racism of others to do so with assistance from the state. The issue is a difficult one, and affirmative action can result in clear cases of injustice; Barbara Grutter, a white woman who was denied admission to the University of Michigan School of Law, *was* unfairly passed over because of her race. Yet it is also reasonable to conclude, based on liberal commitments to individual growth, that institutions such as law schools benefit intellectually from the presence of a diverse student body, as the Supreme Court ruled in Grutter's case. Affirmative action does not offer as clear and defensible an example of liberal leadership as civil rights, but it nonetheless represents a situation in which a seemingly obvious truth—quotas are always bad and should be illegal in all forms—loses what is obvious about it when human beings are viewed as capable of self-development.

The one decision by the U.S. Supreme Court that did more to further the cause of conservative populism than any other was *Roe* v. *Wade*, the 1973 case legalizing abortion. For those who believe that abortion is tantamount to murder, *Roe*, and its companion *Doe* v. *Bolton*, are, in Robert Bork's words, "equal in their audacity and abuse of office to *Dred Scott* v. *Sanford*. Just as *Dred Scott* forced a Southern pro-slavery position on the nation, *Roe* is nothing more than the Supreme Court's imposition on us of the morality of our cultural elites." Conservative populists believe that *Roe* was decided in such an undemocratic manner and its decision was so shocking to our conventional teachings on morality that the Court's actions were, in effect, illegitimate. Americans were right to resist it, they insist, and it is a source of some pride among conservative populists that Republican presidents were elected bent on appointing justices who would, by eventually overturning the decision, restore public opinion to its rightful place in a democratic society. (Ironically, had Bork's nomination to the Supreme Court been approved, Justice Anthony Kennedy would not be on the Court and a foolproof anti-*Roe* majority would now be in place.)

Of all the criticisms made by conservative populists against liberal elitism, the one made against *Roe* has the greatest credibility. It is not that, from a liberal perspective, the Court reached the wrong conclusion: if liberalism means control over the conditions of one's life, women must be allowed to control their own bodies. But the Court reached its decision not only badly but contemptuously. *Roe* is invariably compared to *Brown*, and the comparison does not work in its favor. "Blackmun's opinions in *Roe* and *Doe*," Jack Balkin observes, "by contrast [to Warren's in *Brown*], although filled with scholarship and medical history, are long-winded and devote a significant amount of space to technical legal issues." Justice Harry Blackmun made no attempt to use the Court's decision as a bully pulpit from which to encourage opponents of a woman's right to choose to reconsider their opinion. He did nothing to recognize the fact that different states were struggling with the question of abortion in different ways and that it might make sense, given the opposition around the country, to allow the political process more room to find its way to the right position. If *Brown* offered a model of how to lead the public to a liberal position it had not yet endorsed, the problem with *Roe* is that here liberal leadership failed to lead.

Supporters of *Roe* respond by saying that since those opposed to abortion are acting out of religious conviction, no political compromise would have been possible; abortion is an issue in which liberal principles of autonomy inevitably clash with conservative views about the sanctity of life, and one or the other has to be chosen. Yet public opinion in the United States has consistently supported a woman's right to choose, even if it also supports restrictions that stop well short of abortion as an absolute or fundamental right. The fact is that the political materials for a compromise on abortion have been in place for some time. Because they have, *Roe* did indeed shut off public debate in a way that left supporters of abortion triumphant, opponents furious, and everyone in the middle frustrated. As committed as liberals are and must be to a woman's right to choose, they also must commit themselves to a process in which those who do not share liberalism's commitments are allowed to make their views count. Hopefully, liberals ought to believe, they will change their minds. If they do not, then liberals must accept the fact of compromise, even when they are otherwise persuaded that what is being compromised is a fundamental right.

Conservative populism very much represents a scattershot approach to politics. There is something disingenuous, if not downright dishonest, when conservative populists argue for tax cuts for the rich on the grounds that they will benefit the poor or claim that it is necessary to privatize Social Security in order to preserve it. But not all forms of conservative populism are quite so insincere. Liberalism fits modernity so well that one of its temptations will be triumphalism: the sense that its views, and its views alone, represent all that is principled and wise. Often they do; on racial equality, affirmative action, and abortion, liberalism's positions do allow for greater personal autonomy and growth than conservative ones. But as long as liberal societies contain people with very different views of how the world should be organized, it is not enough to be right. Liberals must be prepared to argue on behalf of unpopular points of view, even if doing so makes them elitist. They can even go further and rely on the undemocratic branches of government such as courts to proclaim such rights, bringing their elitism to an ever-higher level. But they also have to know when the education necessary to bring people to a view of the world they do not share turns into a coercive instrument for making them share it. When that moment happens, liberals ought to be challenged by conservative populism—and they ought to back off.

Conservative populism did not achieve much success with the McCain-Palin Republican ticket in 2008, which suggests that its heyday may be over. It is impossible to know what the future will bring. But if it is true that the only way conservatism can remain viable in a liberal society is by appealing to the fears and concerns of ordinary people, liberalism's future will inevitably bring forth uncomfortable moments when what helps people grow will not necessarily be what people want. When those moments occur, whether they involve defending people's right to know in the face of calls for greater national security or protecting the dignity of a stigmatized group at the height of periods of hysteria, liberalism will have no future if it abdicates a liberal understanding of human purpose. Liberalism is both a philosophy of governance and an exercise in leadership. If it is to manage modernity's next stage, it must continue to shape the views of the public and not just reflect them.

GLOBALISM'S CHALLENGE

In the years after the French Revolution, two of liberalism's rivals besides conservatism, Romanticism and nationalism, linked forces, developing along the way a significant following in the German lands that had not yet become unified into a nation-state. One of the most interesting thinkers among them, Friedrich List, was not some delver into the past trying to discover an authentic German *Volk* but an economist concerned primarily with issues of international trade. Born in the same year that the French Revolution erupted, List became a professor of administration at the University of Tübingen and a deputy in the Württemberg legislature. An avid reformer, List lost both positions due to his political activity, and after being sentenced to hard labor in prison he escaped and eventually entered into an agreement with the authorities to exile himself to the United States. His seven-year stay in America brought him personal wealth and exposure to the ideas and policies of Alexander Hamilton and Henry Clay, both of whom had argued that government should play a major role in financing national economic development. In 1832, List moved back to Germany to become the American consul in Leipzig. Physical and financial problems led him to turn down a position with a newspaper in Cologne—the job was then offered to and accepted by Karl Marx—and, despondent over his declining prospects, List committed suicide in 1846.

His most famous book, *The National System of Political Economy*, was published in 1841. In it, List reviewed the history of economic development in nearly all parts of Europe, from the Iberian peninsula to Russia. His aim was to criticize Adam Smith's *Wealth of Nations* for failing to understand the limits of free trade. England did not become wealthy because of laissez-faire, List maintained; its growth was facilitated not by a search for the cheapest goods wherever they might be found in the world but by a willingness to strengthen its own domestic industries. In truth, England only turned to free trade once it possessed significant advantages over other countries, and only then for the purpose of maintaining its own superiority. The lesson for List was clear. Any country wishing to grow—none more so than his native Germany—needed to protect itself against global competition:

> Modern Germany, lacking a system of vigorous and united commercial policy, exposed in her home markets to competition with a foreign manufacturing power in every way superior to her own, while excluded at the same time from foreign markets by arbitrary and often capricious restrictions, and very far indeed from making that progress in industry to which her degree of culture entitles her, cannot even maintain her previously acquired position, and is made a convenience of (like a colony) by that very nation which centuries ago was worked upon in like manner by the merchants of Germany, until at last the German states have resolved to secure their home markets for their own industry, by the adoption of a united vigorous system of commercial policy.

Like the other German Romantics of his era, List disdained both individualism and cosmopolitanism in favor of strong feelings of national identity; only a system of national political economy could work in a world of nations, and nations could only flourish if people's wills could be guided toward collective ends. "The unity of the nation," List wrote, "forms the fundamental condition of lasting national prosperity. . . . Only where the interest of individuals has been subordinated to those of the nation, and where successive generations have striven for one and the same object," he elaborated, "have [nations] been brought to harmonious development of their productive powers." After his death, List's nationalism would be expropriated by German anti-Semites such as Eugen Dürhing, a philosopher and economist who would be forgotten were it not for the fact that Friedrich Engels, Karl Marx's collaborator, wrote a book attacking him. Nationalism can have its ugly side, as so much of European and especially German history suggests, and when it did, List's talk about the unity of the nation was bound to sound appalling.

Nationalism, however, can also have its positive side, especially when it comes to defending the capacity of the nation-state to provide greater equality among its citizens or greater protection of its workers. List himself, for all his criticisms of eighteenth-century liberalism, was anything but a reactionary, and his economic nationalism has taken left-wing as well as right-wing forms. The nineteenth-century American economists who admired List, such as Henry Carey, a critic of laissez-faire who believed that the interests of capital and labor could be harmonized through government-sponsored industrial policies, were the progressives of their day. America's own path to economic supremacy was Listian in its reliance on protective tariffs and governmental subsidies to business.

Other nations in the world, such as Japan and Korea, show a propensity to invoke List to spur their own economic development. It is not surprising, therefore, that American liberals worried about rapidly increasing inequality within the United States produced by such free trade institutions as the World Trade Organization (WTO) or the North American Free Trade Agreement (NAFTA) adopt a language that resonates with List's ideas. "I am a citizen of the United States, not a citizen of the WTO or NAFTA," writes the liberal economist Robert Kuttner in *The Squandering of America.* "Regulation of labor, health, the environment, taxation, and provision of social goods are all necessarily done by national governments. The embryonic European Union is making an effort to accomplish some of this on a continental scale, so that it can carry on the project of balancing commercial goals with social ones. NAFTA, which has no civic component, is a pure triumph of commerce over democratic citizenship."

Although the United States has by far the most productive economy in the world, many contemporary Americans feel that international developments are undermining long-established ways of life. The rise of China and India as centers of manufacturing, the downsizing of American corporations and the reassignment of jobs to countries where the costs of labor are considerably cheaper, increased immigration, and free trade agreements such as NAFTA have begun to prompt heated arguments to the effect that globalization works to the detriment of Americans of all social classes and regions. To some degree these arguments are heard on the right end of the political spectrum: those who oppose immigration, such as the conservative commentator Patrick Buchanan, are also likely to oppose free trade. As the economist Edward Gresser, a centrist Democrat associated with the Progressive Policy Institute, points out, this is as it should be: since the days of the McKinley Tariff, the legislation of 1890 that set a 48 percent duty on imported goods, Republicans, especially conservative Republicans, have tried to protect American businesses against foreign competition.

More surprising has been the popularity of protectionist sentiments among liberals, many of whom no longer share the free trade inclinations of Franklin Delano Roosevelt and Harry Truman. Although Bill Clinton had been a strong advocate of free trade, most prominent Democrats who have followed in his wake have had reservations about it. Such reservations have not put a serious dent in free trade policies; even if they campaign against free trade in primaries, Democratic presidents typically wind up supporting it in office. Given the balancing act they carry out, it is likely that their future support will be more conditional. It is axiomatic among contemporary Democrats that conditions have to be attached to any agreements dealing with international trade. The heyday of American liberalism's commitment to an open global economy, which produced such breakthroughs in the 1940s as the Bretton Woods system to coordinate monetary policy and the General Agreement on Tariffs and Trade (GATT), the predecessor to the World Trade Organization, is clearly over.

At least American liberals critical of free trade have not turned their backs on the modern world. The same cannot be said for Britain's John Gray, who teaches European thought at the London School of Economics and has emerged as one of the most scathing critics of globalization anywhere in the Western world. Gray holds that the Enlightenment's insistence on progress is responsible for much that is wrong with the world around us. Enlightenment thinkers believed that they were developing an alternative to millennial religion, but they were just as likely to become utopian and chiliastic. They thought that constitutions and agreed-upon procedures could bring peace to the world, but "a conflict-free existence is impossible for humans, and wherever it is attempted the result is intolerant to them." One might be tempted to think that the ideas of the Enlightenment stand in opposition to such illiberal movements as Nazism and radical Islam, but for Gray both are, at least in part, products of the Enlightenment itself. Promising us light, the Enlightenment, he claims, has only produced a dark mass symbolized by a rapacious free market that, not content with destroying the cohesion of one domestic society after another, now is about to destroy the prospects for any stability in the globe as a whole.

False Dawn, John Gray's antiglobalization manifesto, never mentions Friedrich List, although it is indebted to another continental romantic, Joseph Schumpeter, one of the few twentieth-century economists who had praised List's insights. But List's spirit, with one significant exception, dominates Gray's book. Both List and Gray treat Adam Smith with disdain. Both view Continental Europe as engaged in an effort to resist a laissez-faire ideology associated with Britain and the United States. Both worry about what List, even in the mid-nineteenth century, had the foresight to call "the supremacy of America." Still—and this is the difference that matters—List believed that nations could protect themselves against global laissez-faire through protectionist policies. Gray's vision is much darker than that. Compared to what transpired in the nineteenth century, he writes, sovereign states are losing their authority to control *any* kind of economic activity beyond their borders: "The reality of the late-twentieth-century world market is that it is ungovernable by either sovereign states or multinational corporations." Not only can we no longer call upon the nation-state to manage our affairs, we cannot call upon anything. Liberalism is bankrupt, Gray says, because in a fundamental sense all political philosophies, if they are understood to make sense of and give direction to the world, are bankrupt. If modernity means that we are guided by rules, globalization means that all rules have been suspended.

A condition of no rule is called anarchy. Nineteenth-century anarchists hoped to bring such a condition into being. Twenty-first-century anarchists assume it already exists. Anarchistic sentiments exercise significant influence over the global activists who gather in the streets when officials of the World Bank, the International Monetary Fund, or the General Agreement on Tariffs and Trade meet to set the conditions for global commerce. Engaged in dramatic street theater, willing to confront the police forces massed against it, claiming support from activists in every country, the antiglobalization movement has become the most visible form of left-wing political activity in the contemporary world. Its targets are sweatshops and free trade zones. Its enemies are multinational corporations. Its allies are meant to be workers in the Third World who make a fraction of what their counterparts in the industrialized world earn. Its goals are . . . well, there is the problem. Unable to imagine any kind of alternative to the world in which we find ourselves, the antiglobalization movement has little to offer but endorsements of efforts by local governments to buy fair-traded goods. Leftists in the past believed that they could, through protest, move the world in a direction they favored. It is hard to do that when you are convinced that the world lacks both a sense of direction and a statement of purpose.

Having given up on the nation-state, antiglobalization activists share little in common with List's protectionism; his autarky is their anarchy. But unlike the more moderate critics of free trade to be found among politicians and policy intellectuals in the Democratic Party, they very much share List's romanticism. The antiglobalization movement is too diffuse to have widely accepted theorists, but those who have tried to explain the movement and its rationale are romantic through and through. *Empire,* by Michael Hardt and Antonio Negri, which had such favorable things to say about the Nazi thinker Carl Schmitt, offers the most ambitious theoretical justification for the antiglobalization movement. It argues that today's forms of global capitalism, unlike the industrial capitalism upon which Karl Marx focused, lack coordination and are therefore best explained by postmodernist appreciations of fluidity and formlessness. But the real heroes of the book are not contemporary postmodern theorists in France but the Romantics of early-nineteenth-century Germany. *Empire* cites such German Romantics as Johann Gottlieb Fichte and Johann Gottfried Herder, and even goes so far as to claim that "the Romantic counterrevolution was in fact more realistic than the Enlightenment revolution." No wonder, then, that when its authors look for rebels against empire, they find them not in any organized segment of society such as the working class but among romantic protestors filled with anarchist fervor.

Another writer close to the antiglobalization movement, the Canadian journalist Naomi Klein, displays the same romantic sensibility. Like John Gray, Klein does not believe that the free market is really free; people are inclined to resist the imposition of global capitalism on their ways of life, she argues in *The Shock Doctrine,* and the only way it can be imposed is through force. But rather than argue her point empirically, she demonstrates it dramatically. In one chapter, she tells the story of the mad scientist who, with the help of the CIA, induced people to undergo dangerous electric shock therapy. In another she discusses debt repayment plans developed by the International Monetary Fund. The former, in her view, leads directly to the latter. This is analy-

sis by way of street theater: if free markets work through shock treatment, critics of globalization have to use shock illustrations to drive
their point home. Klein tells great stories. Whether they have much to
do with the actual realities of globalization is another matter.

Whether they take the form of romantic protest or simple queasi-
ness about free trade, antiglobalization sentiments, like those associated with conservative populism, will continue to present one of the
main challenges facing liberals in the years to come. How should they
respond? The question is widely debated, and perhaps nowhere so
prominently as in the Economics Department of Columbia University.
In one corner stands Joseph Stiglitz, former chairman of the Council of
Economic Advisers in the Clinton administration and a winner of the
Nobel Prize, while in the other can be found Jagdish Bhagwati, university professor at Columbia, senior fellow of the Council on Foreign Relations, and one of the world's most distinguished free trade
theorists.

Like most economists, Stiglitz believes in free trade in theory. But
he also thinks that critics of globalization, including the more radical
ones, have a point. Stiglitz uses the term "Washington consensus" to
characterize the commitment to free trade fashioned by laissez-faire
advocates in the 1980s, and he argues in *Globalization and Its Discontents* that its results "have not been encouraging: for most countries
embracing its tenets development has been slow, and where growth has
occurred, the benefits have not been shared equally." It is simply not
true, Stiglitz believes, that countries long under authoritarian leadership, such as Russia, can receive a quick injection of market-based economics and flourish. Nor does it make sense to impose strict conditions
upon debt repayment in poor countries when the problem to begin
with is their poverty. Markets can work, but, in contrast to those who
insist on "market fundamentalism," or the idea that laissez-faire is to be
relied upon at all times and in all places, markets can also fail. Wise
policy will find ways to distinguish between them.

Jagdish Bhagwati is anything but a market fundamentalist, but he
does think that critics of globalization have their facts wrong. Globalized forms of capitalism have not brought about what Marx called
"immiseration" but have increased the quality of life in countries such
as China and India. Nor have American workers lost out because
of global competition; jobs have been sent overseas, but at the same
time overseas companies have created jobs within the United States.
The idea that globalization creates a "race to the bottom" in which

economies compete with each other to degrade their living standards or environmental commitments in the hopes of attracting business is not, Bhagwati argues throughout *In Defense of Globalization*, supported by any evidence. Taking on his departmental colleague directly, Bhagwati points out that institutions such as the World Bank are not committed to market fundamentalism; the Bank's objective is to spend, and if its approach to developing countries is too punitive, it will, if it chooses to restrict funds, contradict its own mission. Questions remain about globalization, in particular the question of how fast it should take place. Bhagwati is open to the idea that it was forced upon Russia too fast and backfired. But globalization is, overall, a positive development that people interested in social justice ought to welcome.

When economists at this level of distinction disagree, what is a noneconomist to do? The proper answer is to suggest that globalization is not just about economics but raises fundamental questions about what Dewey called "the cultural resources of civilization." Once the terrain shifts to that issue, antiglobalization activists believe they are on strong ground. Those who theorize on their behalf are not liberals; if anything, they believe that globalization signifies the end of liberalism and its naïve beliefs in social reform. But like conservatives on the opposite end of the political spectrum from them, they borrow from liberalism to establish the criteria against which globalization should be judged. If liberalism's major substantive commitment is to a world in which as many people as possible are free to lead lives of their own choosing, the conditions under which globalized manufacturing take place, they argue, deny that possibility at every turn.

Take, for example, the export processing zones established in the Philippines or China to manufacture goods for the world's markets. These are not places that allow people to organize into unions so that they can reduce the oppression associated with low wages and long hours; instead, as Naomi Klein puts it in *No Logo*, they have "been carefully planned to squeeze the maximum amount of production out of this swath of land." The trouble with globalization, John Gray argues in *False Dawn*, is that bad forms of capitalism, because they are more exploitative, will always drive out any good forms that remain. It follows that if one takes any of the problems that once accompanied the development of domestic capitalism—exploitation, corruption, environmental degradation, authoritarian control over the lives of ordinary people—global free trade makes them worse. Follow down that path, and you will end up with a world as unfree as it is inegalitarian. The situation could not be bleaker. "We cannot expect feasible alternatives to global *laissez-faire* to emerge," Gray concludes, "until there has been an economic crisis more far-reaching than we have experienced thus far." The same disasters that help capitalists solidify their rule are the only hope we have to bring their rule to an end.

Before entertaining such apocalyptic scenarios, liberals might consider a point made by Bhagwati. Discussing the efforts made to defend the traditional ways of life of indigenous people against the arrival of international capitalism, he writes that "the pull of modernity in many ways has been the source of the outmigration of rural young people to urban areas in search of a different, morally alluring lifestyle. There is no reason to think that it does not work in the case of indigenous groups as well." Globalization, from this perspective, is best appreciated as a contemporary version of a long historical process, as wrenching as it can be liberating, of bringing people into contact with a wider world; if it follows the path established by the rise of industrial capitalism, people will wind up freer to lead lives chosen by themselves than if they had remained behind in the rural areas of their countries. True of men, this will prove even truer of women, who, once outside the authority of traditional religious practices and stifling local customs and superstitions, will be in a position to exercise greater personal autonomy. One need not take the frequently rosy-eyed view of a globalization booster such as the *New York Times* columnist Thomas L. Friedman to realize that such possibilities exist and even, in some countries, have already been achieved. To judge its moral effects, we should compare the world created by free trade not against an ideal but to the world that existed when forces of tradition chained people to land, stunted their individual growth, and kept them ignorant of the larger world. By that comparison, globalization, because it is the engine of modernization, is also a force for liberalization.

Globalization's benefits involve more than liberation from rural ways of life. The fact that companies hire workers irrespective of national boundaries and sell their goods all over the world, from a Kantian point of view, is an expression of cosmopolitanism; in a globalized world, we are more likely to learn about languages and cultures other than our own and to take the point of view of people different from ourselves. The Victorian manufacturer and liberal politician and writer Richard Cobden viewed international trade as establishing the conditions for world peace by reducing the influence of militarism, and in recent years, he has been proven correct. Whatever else might be said about the period of the last few decades in which capitalism has spread its wings so widely, it cannot be said that it has led to the kinds of world wars that characterized more protectionist periods. Globalization has been accompanied by new technologies—from the Internet to the iPhone—that open up the world more dramatically than newspapers did in the early nineteenth century. If one side of globalization involves the World Bank and the International Monetary Fund, another includes the Universal Declaration of Human Rights and the International Court of Justice. From a globalized perspective, the problem with the United States is not that its commitments to free trade reduce the amount of social justice in the world but that its failure to commit itself to international norms increases it. Liberalism is, from this point of view, threatened not by too much globalization but by too little.

None of this means that globalized free markets should rule without any attempts to control them. As committed as liberalism has been to the goal of increasing people's ability to control their lives, it has also long recognized that such a goal is best achieved by directing the efforts people make toward common purposes established by themselves. What was true of the domestic economy ought to be just as true of the international one; as Bhagwati writes, globalization must "be managed so that its fundamentally benign effects are ensured and reinforced. Without this wise management, it is imperiled." For all the fervor that the debate between them sometimes reaches, Stiglitz and Bhagwati differ over means rather than ends, and even their differences over means are not that significant. "Globalization with a human face," as Stiglitz calls it, is the only kind of globalization compatible with liberalism as it has historically evolved. Trying to achieve it makes greater moral sense than either welcoming it unmanaged or denouncing it as the Enlightenment's dark shadow.

Perhaps the most important thing liberals need to maintain as they approach the question of globalization is a positive outlook on the world. Even when they identify problems they believe ought to be corrected by modifying the effects of free trade, they should avoid not only the doom-and-gloom rhetoric of the antiglobalization activists but the cries of those who say that Americans are being treated unfairly or, even worse, that they are victims of some kind of international conspiracy. This is not something they always do; just as right-wing politicians turn their backs on the world when they attack immigrants flowing in, left-wing politicians do the same when they criticize capital flowing out. The issue facing liberals is not whether they should seek to attach conditions to free trade agreements designed to protect domestic jobs or the environment; under some conditions they should and under others they should not. The issue instead is whether they ought to be as open to the world today as they have been in the past.

Once begun, globalization is unlikely to stop. Yet if globalization is something new, it is also something with which liberals have been long familiar, for it takes us back to the late eighteenth and early nineteenth centuries when the goals of liberty and equality, proclaimed in one country, quickly spread to so many others. Liberalism's birth was decidedly worldwide. As Jay Winik describes it:

> Thomas Paine left England to rouse a fledging America in 1776, then he traveled to France, joined the revolutionary Assembly, and was almost beheaded, released only due in part to pleas by James Monroe. Thomas Jefferson advised the budding French revolutionaries while Gouverneur Morris counseled the king. Voltaire hugged Franklin while listening to his friend Empress Catherine; Rousseau found a home in Jefferson's Republican Party, and Franklin and Jefferson were studied by the Russian reformers. . . . Militarily, John Paul Jones, America's great naval hero, circumnavigated the globe and joined Catherine the Great's imperial navy to fight the Muslims, and then died a pitiful death in Paris. Another dramatic hero of the American Revolution, Polish-born Thaddeus Kosciuszko, would return home to lead a revolution that was ruthlessly crushed by Catherine's Russia. And Lafayette, after heroically serving under Washington's wing in America, fled the very French Revolution he helped start, landing in an Austrian prison, while Talleyrand, the notorious French foreign minister, would spend the bloody days of the Terror in exile in the United States, befriend Hamilton, and return home to serve the Directory (and then Napoleon), only to turn on his former American hosts.

With a past like that, liberalism has little to fear from a globalized future. A world in which people and capital move about is one in which ideas catch fire.

TERRORISM'S THREAT

It is not that difficult to draw a portrait of the global capitalist whose insatiable quest for profit is believed to undermine such long-standing liberal ideals as income equality and economic security. For all the havoc he wreaks upon the world, he aspires to a civilized life of the first order: expensive art collections, multilingual fluency, Davos hobnobbing, Gulfstream jet-setting, philanthropic foresight. Belonging to no nation in particular—the country of his birth is the least interesting thing about him—he is a true citizen of the world, a member in good standing of the "superclass," as David Rothkopf, who worked on trade policy during the Clinton administration, has called it. Roughly six thousand people in all, these globalists live in exclusive special neighborhoods or buildings—Kensington Park Gardens in London, 740 Park Avenue in Manhattan—and can be seen or, more frequently, not seen "working together, doing deals together, even attending gala events together—all those things that help forge the networks that empower and define the superclass," as Rothkopf puts it. Our future is now in the hands of an elite as cosmopolitan in its tastes as it is ruthless in its tactics.

Western societies have another enemy besides this one, and his picture is not difficult to paint either. Even if born in conditions of wealth, he lives in a cave in one of the remotest regions of the world. His aim is not only to practice his faith but to restore his religion to a state of doctrinal purity and position of dominance it has not enjoyed for a thousand years. In his world, women obey the word of their husbands, everyone who is not a friend is an enemy, and the use of violence to reward and punish has holy sanction. Only when all traces of hedonism, from drinking to dancing, have been eliminated will the world be ordered once again. His law is the law of the jungle, and, as Lee Harris puts it in *The Suicide of Reason,* "whenever the law of the jungle becomes the final arbiter of any conflict, those who are the most stubborn inevitably have the advantage over those who are the most reasonable." If the campaign of terror he unleashes is successful, the world will not be transformed into a gigantic shopping mall but reduced to a Hobbesian state of war of all against all.

Globalism and terrorism seem, at first glance, to be polar opposites, the one the embodiment of a cosmopolitan sensibility so refined that it loses all touch with down-to-earth realities, the other worshipping the particular and the primitive and so fierce in its communalism that it

cannot appreciate any cause but its own. Yet we should not be fooled by
the apparent differences between them, a number of contemporary cultural commentators insist, for both can best be understood as a reaction
to the fact that the forces unleashed by modernity can no longer be
controlled. The Jihadi sensibility, the political scientist Benjamin Barber writes in *Jihad vs. McWorld,* "may seem . . . to be a throwback to premodern times: an attempt to recapture a world that existed prior to
cosmopolitan capitalism and was defined by religious mysteries, hierar-
chical communities, spellbinding traditions, and historical torpor." But
this is not quite correct, for "Jihad . . . is itself a dialectical response
to modernity whose features both reflect and reinforce the modern
world's vices and virtues." John Gray makes a very similar argument.
Al-Qaeda, he notes, "is a by-product of globalization"; its existence is
indicative not of an effort to reject modernity, but of the very kind of
anomie and rootlessness characteristic of modern capitalism in its most
rational form. The corporate executive in his Lear jet and the terrorist
in his cave turn out to be first cousins, both taking advantage of modernity's unhappy consciousness to impose themselves on the world by
force.

According to those who think this way, not only are the globalists
and the terrorists presumably united in their rejection of the modern
world, both are held to pose significant threats to liberalism, the political philosophy that has long accompanied modernity's success. Critics
from the left worry that the globalist threatens government's ability to
manage the domestic economy, thereby undermining liberal commitments to the welfare state. Those coming from the right, by contrast,
believe that the terrorist represents a far more insidious danger to our
way of life. For these writers, no question is more important to the survival of liberal societies than whether they can defend themselves
against Islamic terrorism, and a surprising number of them believe that
they cannot. In the wake of 9/11, their writings contribute to an aura of
defeatism within the liberal world, a palpable sense that the political
philosophy that emerged in the late eighteenth century committed to
the proposition that people can be free to grow to their full capacity
represents an ideal whose time has come and may, alas, be gone.

Norman Podhoretz, the neoconservative thinker, considers everyone who disagrees with him a defeatist, making it a bit odd to attach
the term to himself. Yet in the long struggle between liberal societies
and what he calls "Islamofascism," Podhoretz is uncertain of the former's prospects. True, he says in *World War IV,* the United States has
had two great assets: the courage of its troops and the determined lead-

ership of George W. Bush, a man he views as a resolute defender of freedom. But in the war against Islamic terrorism, Americans will need to live up to the sense of duty and sacrifice they manifested during World Wars II and III. (For Podhoretz, the Cold War was a world war won by the United States and we are fighting World War IV now.) Podhoretz sees little evidence that they will. If the Democrats are in power, will they be willing to overcome their proclivity toward political correctness, preference for a law enforcement approach to terrorism instead of a military one, and tendency to ask for support from European allies or the United Nations? Can they be trusted to put aside their scruples against using torture or their commitments to civil liberties? "From the way the Democrats have been acting and speaking, especially since Bush's reelection in 2004, all the answers would seem to be no." Roughly half of the American population votes Democratic; for Podhoretz, then, the United States is already halfway to defeat. No one can properly call the author of *World War IV* an optimist.

Podhoretz is widely regarded as one of the most prominent conservative writers in the United States today, which makes it worth pointing out that his defeatism, compared to that of others addressing the same topic, is actually rather moderate. Podhoretz is not, he insists, naïve enough to believe that Islam is capable of undergoing a reformation that would make it resemble Christianity and Judaism. Islam was once a religion that imposed its will on the world by force, and "there is no chance today of an inverse instant transformation of Islam by force of American arms." Still, all is not lost: "There is . . . at least a fighting chance that a clearing of the ground and a sowing of the seeds out of which new political, economic, and social conditions can grow will gradually give rise to correlative religious pressures from within." If the United States puts enough pressure on the Muslim world, it just might be able to encourage Islamic theologians "to find warrants in the Qur'an and the *shari'a* under which it would be possible to remain a good Muslim while enjoying the blessings of decent government, and even of political and economic liberty."

Not so, claims Lee Harris. For Harris, the struggle between Islam and the West is the latest in a long line of battles between reason and fanaticism. We like to believe that with the achievement of modernity, reason has won, but, Harris warns, modernity is "a self-protective myth." In actuality, fanaticism cannot die out because it speaks to a fundamental fact of the human condition. Islam represents for him a warrior culture premised above all else on a rejection of the West's confidence in Enlightenment principles. Borrowing, as so many writers critical of liberalism do, from the literature of sociobiology, Harris characterizes Islamic hostility toward the West this way: "popular Muslim fanaticism acted as a societal defense mechanism against alien influences, operating as automatically as the body's immune system operates when it comes into contact with foreign microbes. Or to use the language of Richard Dawkins, popular Muslim fanaticism functioned as a method for expelling or eliminating those dangerous foreign memes that, if permitted to invade Dar el-Islam [the Islamic world], might sooner or later bring about a disruption of their collective tradition."

Many of those worried about the terrorist threat to the West rely on Samuel P. Huntington's argument that we face a "clash of civilizations" between increasingly antagonistic religious worldviews. Harris finds Huntington's gloomy scenario far too optimistic. We do not live in a world in which Islam and the West are fighting over ideas and territory, he believes; we instead confront a process of decivilization in which every value we once held dear is threatened. The West's natural response is to stand fast to the commitment to reason that has guided it for two hundred years; but this would be a disastrous, indeed, a fatal mistake "that may well destroy us." Reason is not some universalistic value to which all people aspire; it "represents a specific cultural tradition." They, the Muslim enemy, have their way of life. We, the modern liberal democrats, have ours. The only way we can defeat them is by mobilizing our tribe against their tribe. But since our tribe believes that fanaticism unleashes dangerous passions, our side can never win.

Harris's views overlap with segments of conservative opinion in Europe, where levels of immigration from Muslim countries are much higher than can be found in the United States. Bat Ye'or, the pseudonym of Gisèle Littman, an Egyptian-born British writer of decidedly alarmist views, looks at Europe's demography, considers the leverage Arab countries possess because of their oil, examines Western Europe's history of anti-Semitism, and concludes in *Eurabia* that "European countries have engaged consistently in policies of appeasement and are often opposed to confronting the Jihadi threat—including threats against modernist European Muslims living in their midst." Bruce Bawer, an American living in Norway, found himself, as a gay man, especially shaken by the assassination of the gay Dutch politician Pym Fortyn. That event, along with the murder of the Dutch filmmaker Theo van Gogh, the violent protests by Muslims of Danish cartoons they considered blasphemous, and the general atmosphere of political correctness he believes to be enveloping intellectuals and politicians in Western liberal countries, led him to the conclusion that, like England many years ago, Europe finds itself in a stupor.

"Europe is even now entering another chapter in its long history of violent struggle," Bawer writes in *While Europe Slept*. "The enemy can't be wished or talked away. And what's at stake isn't just the sovereignty of one or two nations but modern democratic civilization." Although the stakes are as high as one can imagine, Bawer cannot muster much confidence that Europeans will meet them. "In the end," he concludes, "Europe's enemy is not Islam, or even radical Islam. Europe's enemy is itself—its self-destructive passivity, its softness toward tyranny, its reflexive inclination to appease, and its uncomprehending distaste for America's pride, courage, and resolve in the face of a deadly foe."

It ought not to be surprising that conservatives of this sort have mixed feelings at best about the survival of liberal values. While some of them, such as Bawer, defend liberalism's commitment to free speech, the others are too extreme in their views to find much of anything of value in the liberal tradition at all. A more serious case for the dangers facing liberalism in a time of terrorist violence comes from writers within the liberal tradition itself. The September 11 attacks, the repressive nature of so many Islamic societies, and periodic *fatwas* and protests violating principles of freedom of expression have forced liberals to think more seriously about their tradition and how it can best defend itself against such threats.

This way of thinking builds on a movement toward a more robust foreign policy that had preceded September 11. In reaction to the Vietnam War, many liberals, both in the United States and abroad, had become extremely wary of any efforts on the part of Western countries to intervene in the affairs of other states, especially those in the Third World. Although reflecting the quite sensible conclusion that the disasters of Vietnam should not be replicated elsewhere, such a left-wing retreat from global involvement also left Western countries helpless in the face of genocide. This affected not only Cambodia, which was itself a legacy of the Vietnam War, but the subsequent genocides in Rwanda and the former Yugoslavia. Against such ostrichlike behavior, two liberals in particular, Michael Ignatieff, the writer and deputy leader of Canada's Liberal Party, and Samantha Power, the Harvard expert on human rights, have argued separately that commitments to human rights can neither stop at national borders nor be stymied by dictators invoking Westphalian principles of national sovereignty to brutalize their own people. It would be difficult to cite any books in recent years written with the same combination of liberal sensibility and moral urgency as *The Lesser Evil* and *"A Problem from Hell."* If liberals did not take a stand against genocide, and also call for appropriate military actions to end it, it is difficult to know what they would ever be for.

Iraq under Saddam Hussein was one of the countries identified by Samantha Power as genocidal. Describing Saddam's use of chemical weapons against both the Iranians and the Kurds, Power can barely contain her fury at American inaction: "Nothing in U.S. behavior signaled Hussein that he should think twice about now attempting to wipe out rural Kurds using whatever means he chose." Of all the criticisms liberals have made of U.S. foreign policy since they rediscovered the need for a more interventionist approach, this one would appear to have been rendered irrelevant by the decision of George W. Bush to do what his father never did: push Saddam out of power by military force. When he made the decision to do so, Bush all but issued a challenge to all those liberals who had come to accept the necessity of military force to protect basic human rights: would they remain true to their antigenocidal convictions and support him?

A few were willing. Though harboring doubts about the way Bush chose to fight the war in Iraq, the war itself was supported by a number of prominent liberal thinkers: the writer and translator Paul Berman in the United States; the journalists Oliver Kamm and Nick Cohen in Great Britain; and Christopher Hitchens in both. (Michael Ignatieff at first supported the Iraqi war but later had second thoughts. Samantha Power raised questions about the war from the start and eventually became a strong critic not only of American intervention in Iraq but of the "war on terror" of which it was presumed to be a part.) Sharing the conviction that liberals must oppose genocide, these writers also insisted that liberalism must stand against totalitarianism. Influenced by the Iraqi dissident Kanan Makiya, who had written eloquently of Saddam's crimes against his own people, they concluded that distinct similarities existed between the threats posed to liberal society by earlier totalitarian movements such as communism and Nazism and the threat represented by Saddam. Liberal societies responded to the earlier dangers with considerable conviction and they should do the same for these more recent developments.

Antitotalitarian liberals were correct to point out that much leftist opinion in Europe and the United States had been unable to recognize evil not only in Iraq but in a number of other regimes that might from time to time have called themselves progressive, but which were in fact deeply reactionary. Along with the signers of the "Euston Manifesto"—a statement of principles meant to evoke an earlier era in which liberals such as George Orwell had stood up to totalitarianism—these writers properly condemned a worldwide reflexive anti-Americanism that led people to become apologists for Saddam. One such was the notorious George Galloway, described by Nick Cohen as "a Scottish MP who combined blood-curdling rhetoric with a whining sentimentality, like many a political thug before him." The spirit in which these critiques of the left were offered was bracing. It had been a giant step forward for contemporary liberals to make questions of genocide central to their outlook on the world; any retreat from that position would constitute an equivalent step back. Liberals ought to oppose genocide for the same reason they should support globalization. If they do not, they give in to a narcissistic self-protectionism, content to enjoy liberal benefits for themselves while unwilling to support access to them for others who might just need them more.

Liberals, however, must learn from experience, and the experience of liberal antitotalitarianism, however brief, proved to be filled with unexpected complications. It is now fairly obvious, except to die-hard neoconservatives, that deposing Saddam by military force did not increase American national security. But it is equally true that America's difficulties in Iraq raise serious questions about liberal antitotalitarianism's programs and methods. It is not just that a more successful war than the one launched by George W. Bush still might well have unleashed sectarian furor and revealed unsolvable problems of self-governance in Iraq. There is also the problem that not all forms of humanitarian intervention are the same. For all the efforts made by liberal writers to view Saddam's Iraq as a form of totalitarianism comparable to communism and Nazism, those who lived under the latter evils were, for the most part, grateful to be liberated by American power, while those who live with undemocratic regimes in the Muslim world—including Iraq and Iran—are unlikely to be so thankful. Yesterday's liberator is today's occupier. Relying on military power to stop genocide can work; the situation in the former Yugoslavia proved that. But there is no guarantee that it will always work; the situation in Iraq proved that as well. Because the Iraq war teaches us that it is more complicated to stand up to evil than was apparent at the time that Ignatieff and Power wrote their books, it is imperative for liberals to reexamine what at first seemed a clear-cut imperative to oppose genocidal totalitarianism.

The writer who can help us here is the most passionate of all the antitotalitarian liberals, Paul Berman. Berman's acute historical sensibility and compelling moral voice make his analysis of how liberals should respond to the war on terror persuasive. At the same time, especially in his important book *Terror and Liberalism,* he reveals antitotalitarian liberalism's fatal flaw. One of Berman's criticisms of the way Bush chose to fight the war on terror is the president's "failure to take up the war on ideas." By this, Berman presumably means that defeating Islamic terrorism requires a profound commitment to the proposition that liberalism has more to offer to the world than totalitarianism. Yet Berman himself does not take up the war of ideas either. There is, his analysis suggests, one problem we face if we rely on liberalism to vanquish Islamic fascism: it might not be able to do so. Although Berman avoids the trap of those on the right who condemn liberal societies as too hopelessly decadent to fight the war against Islamic extremism effectively, he also expresses a surprising lack of confidence in basic liberal ideas. The same aura of defeatism hanging over so many neoconservatives hangs over him.

One form that liberal defeatism takes is a willingness to give the opponent more credit than he deserves. Like Lee Harris, Berman expresses a certain admiration for Islamic fundamentalism. Berman holds Sayyid Qutb to be the founder of radical Islam. Yet he describes Qutb's *In the Shade of the Qur'an* as "sometimes demented," "bristling with hate," and "cruel," but "a vast and elegantly constructed architecture of thought and imagination, a work of true profundity, vividly written, wise, broad, indignant," "tolerant," "grave," and "poetic." It is as if Berman, the liberal, cannot let go of the romantic appeal of those determined to confront the modern world and resist it with all the determination they can muster. His discussion of Qutb's writings suggests the uncomfortable proposition that for Berman, liberalism, lacking in romantic heroism, simply cannot compete with the appeals of radically illiberal political ideologies. As he puts it toward the end of *Terror and Liberalism,* totalitarian movements "arise because of failures in liberal civilization, but they flourish because of still other failures in liberal civilization, and if they go on flourishing, it is because of still more failures—one liberal failure after another." At no point does Berman express the confidence that such failures of liberal civilization, which he never concretely identifies, will correct themselves.

Berman accentuates this mood of liberal defeatism by inflating the power of the enemy liberal societies face. "Totalitarianism in decline?" he writes of Saddam Hussein's Iraq. "It was a spectacular error to have imagined any such thing in 1989—a curious error, an almost laughable example of the self-absorbed delusions of the Eurocentric imagination. As if the Muslim world didn't exist!" Berman's identification of the entire Muslim world, not just radical Islam, with totalitarianism is more than just a careless slip. Berman, like Norman Podhoretz, simply does not believe that the West should put much faith in the capacity of Islam to reform itself from within. Depending upon how he is read, the theologian Tariq Ramadan, the grandson of one of the founders of the Muslim Brotherhood in Egypt and now a professor at Oxford University, is trying to do just that. Don't be fooled by this man, Berman warns Western intellectuals.

In a long essay on Ramadan published in *The New Republic,* Berman is careful to note that he is not attacking Islam itself, as if regretting some of the language he used in *Terror and Liberalism.* But he also leaves no doubt that anyone like Ramadan, who tries to negotiate his way between his Islamic roots and modern liberal democracy, will fail. By dismissing so thoroughly the possibility that Islam is capable of liberalizing itself, Berman perhaps inadvertently undercuts liberalism's appeal, as if ideas about human rights, respect for others, and the capacity to grow simply cannot compete with religious fatalism. This is an odd conclusion to reach for someone committed to a war of ideas between liberalism and militant Islam, for it denies the possibility that his side can ever win.

If Berman is any indication, liberal antitotalitarianism suffers from a crisis of conviction. It ought to recognize that liberalism's greatest asset in a time of terror is liberalism itself. There is evil in the world. Dictators do practice genocide on their own people. Terrorists, many of whom are inspired by militant forms of Islam, do kill innocent people. Corrupt regimes offer sanctuary to them. No one—and certainly no liberal—ought to be naïve about any of these things. But just as you do not fight ruthlessly antiliberal enemies by copying their methods of secrecy, torture, and unchecked executive power, nor do you take on terrorism and genocide by tying one hand of your own political philosophy behind your back. If liberals do not believe that their way of life is the best way of life, they will indeed find themselves at a disadvantage in a world characterized by evil. They must resist forces to their left claiming that any declaration to the effect that all people long for freedom and democracy is an imperialistic effort to impose our way of life on the Other. But they must just as strongly resist the notion that liberalism's enemies somehow feed off liberalism's weaknesses.

The situation is the exact reverse. Concede the war of ideas to liberalism's opponents—an all too common failing of both the neoconservative right and the antitotalitarian left—and before you know it, there will be no war of ideas to fight. It would be lovely if the last examples of terrorism and genocide have already been experienced, but it is highly unlikely. The future will no doubt contain more than its share of bad ideas and evil people, all the more reason it should also contain a vibrant liberalism to compete with the one and contain and at times defeat the other.

HONESTY TOWARD THE WORLD

Because liberalism is at one and the same time procedural, temperamental, and substantive, it will always be open to challenge: its commitment to proceduralism presupposes a clash of ideas; its temperamental openness welcomes dissents to its own ways of thinking; and its substantive ideals are intended to be partisan and therefore subject to debate. As much as liberals ought to want to see their ideas win over their opponents, they should not seek unconditional surrender. A world in which the only ideas were liberal ideas would not be a liberal world.

Liberalism nonetheless has one significant advantage over its competitors: because it is the political philosophy most capable of managing the complexities of modernity, it can, since we live in a very modern world, be honest about what it stands for. None of the philosophical outlooks that emerged in the late eighteenth and early nineteenth centuries can make the same claim. Nationalists in an age of globalization rail against capital flowing out and immigrants coming in, but their rhetoric expands in demagoguery as they prove themselves incapable of achieving autarky. Romantics call upon liberal societies to sacrifice for some noble and higher good but, worried about losing political support, they refrain from imposing the obligations that would make those sacrifices real. Socialists went out of business some time ago. Conservatives appeal to the time-tested truths of the past, but since the past includes such unpleasant realities as the existence of slavery and segregation, limited suffrage, rampant economic inequality, and deference to clerical authority, they generally ignore it in favor of appeals to democratic sentiment they would not ordinarily share. Modernity cannot be managed by pretending that modernity never happened.

- the condition of self-sufficiency - esp. economic of a state

Liberalism, by contrast, does not have to pretend to stand on the side of democracy because, with the exception of its occasional flirtations with elitism, it has backed movements to extend the suffrage and to increase racial and gender equality. It does not have to become enthusiastic for war because it views war as a failure in the quest for peace. It can stand up for freedom of speech and association because it really believes in them. It defends the concept of an open society because it truly detests those that are closed. It need not venerate an ugly past because it has a decided confidence about the future. It distrusts otherworldliness because it is grounded in this world. Liberalism does not proclaim that government is evil because it knows that it has been a force for good. It takes modernity as a fact of life, recognizing its gains, accepting its terms, and seeking to improve upon it.

That is what liberalism does. What liberals do is another matter. All too often, liberal politicians lack the courage of liberalism. Especially in the United States, but elsewhere as well, liberals act as if conservatives are the natural governing party of the contemporary world and that they, the liberals, only get to take over when the right goes on a temporary leave of absence. Liberals read the books written by Ann Coulter, Robert Bork, and other conservative populists and conclude that they are more right than wrong. Yes, we really are too elitist, they say to themselves. To win people to our side we ought to pander to how people feel rather than appeal to what they think. Our greatest enemy really is ourselves; our ideas are too nuanced, our policies too demanding, our approach to politics too intellectual to win the majorities we need. Far better to appear more conservative, more nationalistic, and even more romantic than we really are than to stand for what we have long been. Liberalism is honest about itself. Liberals, all too often, are not.

The challenge facing liberalism in the future, then, is not to beat out its rivals; because of modernity, it has already done that. Its biggest challenge is to get liberals to once again *believe* in liberalism. Once upon a time they did, and it was in those days that they made such great gains in overcoming economic catastrophe, building up society's infrastructure, advancing equality of incomes, gender, and race, and confronting with confidence the enemies they faced. No contemporary liberal can look back on the eloquence of a Louis D. Brandeis, the more sensible reforms of the Progressive Era, the massive public works projects of the New Deal, the willingness to stand up first to Nazism and then to communism, and the accomplishments of the Great Society without feeling that it has all been downhill since. Put that record against high protective tariffs, Social Darwinism, rigid adherence to the gold standard, isolationism, McCarthyite witch hunts, and today's Christian right, and liberalism's record ought to speak for itself. That a political outlook which has accomplished so much can lose elections so frequently to one that has accomplished so little is bound to be a source of constant frustration.

Convinced that what people want are lower taxes, firmer borders, support for the troops, and genuflection to religious convictions, liberal politicians are too intent on winning office to pay much attention to liberalism's achievements. They may be right in their calculations. I strongly believe that a deeper appreciation of what liberalism stands for combined with a greater determination to be proud of its accomplishments can help liberal politicians in the rough-and-tumble of contemporary campaigns, but I am not a campaign consultant and I could be wrong. Still, this is too good a political philosophy to dare not speak its name. No other contemporary political worldview comes close to liberalism in its appreciation of how much individuals can grow and how much society can achieve. It is a proud record—and one that ought never be lost.

Politics can be easy and politics can be hard. When it is at its easiest, politicians respond in good populistic fashion by seeming to give people what they want. When it is hard, it asks people to see through demagoguery and confront the world as it actually is. It is axiomatic to believe that faced with a choice between the easy and the hard, people will always choose the easy. But this has not always been the case and, with luck, it will not always be the case in the future. There cannot be a challenge unless there is a challenger. Liberal politicians in the modern world have not challenged enough: not themselves, not those who vote for them, and not even, for that matter, those who vote against them. Liberalism is always about growth. It will grow again when liberals face the future by growing to meet the challenge of their own tradition.

ACKNOWLEDGMENTS

I owe a special debt to Leon Wieseltier, who not only read part of the manuscript but has inspired and challenged me over the years; I continue to find it amazing that Leon realized that I was a liberal before I did. Damon Linker offered extremely valuable feedback that helped me organize my chapters. Jerome Copulsky, Susan Shell, Sanford Levinson, and Bernard Yack read portions of the manuscript and offered constructive advice. Chris Beneke helped with bibliographic leads. Erik Owens engaged me in almost daily conversation. Thanks to all of them.

The staff of the Boisi Center at Boston College provided major assistance. A special thanks to Susan Richard, John Crowley-Buck, Suzanne Hevelone, and Hillary Thompson.

Andrew Stuart has been a terrific agent. Jon Segal's editing made my arguments sharper and, I hope, my examples more compelling. I also benefited from the assistance of Kyle McCarthy and Joey McGarvey.

I have learned so much from so many friends and colleagues, but I am not going to mention them all by name for fear that once I start, I will not be able to stop. I say this not to claim that I have a huge number of friends and colleagues; I mention it only because the meaning and purpose of liberalism is a topic that has engaged so many people. I hope I have added something to the discussion.

From time to time I borrowed a sentence or two—in some cases a page or two—from my previously published writings. Portions of my article "Why Conservatives Can't Govern" are reprinted here with permission from *The Washington Monthly,* Copyright by Washington Monthly Publishing LLC. Other material upon which I have relied includes "A Fascist Philosopher Helps Us Understand Contemporary Politics," *Chronicle of Higher Education,* April 2, 2004, pp. B16–17; "What God Owes Jefferson," *The New Republic,* May 23, 2005, p. 541; and "Mobilizing the Religious Left," *The New York Times Book Review,* October 21, 2007, p. 23.

My three children are now all adults. This book is dedicated to them with all the gratitude I can muster.

NOTES

CHAPTER 1   THE MOST APPROPRIATE POLITICAL PHILOSOPHY FOR OUR TIMES

3 "In the beginning": John Locke, "The Second Treatise: An Essay Concerning the True, Original, Extent, and End of Civil Government," in *Two Treatises on Government and A Letter Concerning Toleration*, ed. Ian Shapiro (New Haven: Yale University Press, 2003), 121.

4 "Locke's little book": Thomas Jefferson to Thomas Mann Randolph, May 30, 1790, in Joyce Appleby and Terence Ball, eds., *Jefferson: Political Writings* (Cambridge, U.K.: Cambridge University Press, 1999), 261.

4 generated fierce controversy: Rogers Smith, "Beyond Tocqueville, Myrdal, and Hartz: The Multiple Traditions in America," *American Political Science Review*, 87 (September 1993), 549–66. See also James T. Kloppenberg, "In Retrospect: Louis Hartz's *The Liberal Tradition in America*," *Reviews in American History*, 29 (September 2001), 460–76.

5 Lockean truths: Louis Hartz, *The Liberal Tradition in America: An Interpretation of American Political Thought Since the Revolution* (New York: Harcourt Brace & World, 1955), 58.

5 twice as many Americans say: Ipsos Public Affairs, March 5–7, 2007, at http://www.ipsos-na.com/news/client/act_dsp_pdf.cfm?name=mr070309-2topline.pdf&id=3399.

6 John Rawls: *A Theory of Justice* (Cambridge, Mass.: Belknap Press of Harvard University Press, 1971).

6 some French intellectuals ... stopped instead: Two important French works that can be said to be broadly within the liberal tradition are Tzvetan Todorov, *On Human Diversity: Nationalism, Racism, and Exoticism in French Thought*, trans. Caroline Porter (Cambridge, Mass.: Harvard University Press, 1993), and Pierre Rosanvallon, *The New Social Question: Rethinking the Welfare State*, trans. Barbara Harshav (Princeton: Princeton University Press, 2000).

6 many of Germany's most important thinkers: See Jürgen Habermas, *The Inclusion of the Other*, ed. Ciaran Cronin and Pablo de Grief (Cambridge, Mass.: MIT Press, 1998), and Hans Joas, *Pragmatism and Social Theory* (Chicago: University of Chicago Press, 1993).

6 endless books pour out: One of the more impressive of these, but where the authors explicitly claim not to be writing for the general public, is Amy Gutmann and Dennis Thompson's *Democracy and Disagreement* (Cambridge, Mass.: Belknap Press of Harvard University Press, 1996).

6 some prominent journalists have written: See, e.g., E. J. Dionne, *Stand Up, Fight Back: Republican Toughs, Democratic Wimps, and the Politics of Revenge* (New York: Simon & Schuster, 2004); Michael Tomasky, *Left for Dead: The Life, Death, and Possible Resurrection of Progressive Politics in America* (New York: Free Press, 1996); and Peter Beinart, *The Good Fight: Why Liberals—and Only Liberals—Can Win the War on Terror and Make America Great Again* (New York: HarperCollins, 2006).

6 joined by academics who write for: Paul Starr, *Freedom's Power: The True Force of Liberalism* (New York: Basic Books, 2007); Robert B. Reich, *Reason: Why Liberals Will Win the Battle for America* (New York: Knopf, 2004); Eric Alterman, *Why We're Liberals: A Political Handbook for Post-Bush America* (New York: Viking, 2008); and Paul Krugman, *The Conscience of a Liberal* (New York: W. W. Norton, 2007).

7 to remind themselves of the great leaders and policies: Beinart's *The Good Fight* is the best example.

7 to "frame" their beliefs: George Lakoff, *Whose Freedom?: The Battle over America's Most Important Idea* (New York: Picador, 2007).

7 to the power of emotions: Drew Westen, *The Political Brain: The Role of Emotion in Deciding the Fate of the Nation* (New York: Public Affairs Press, 2007).

7 Feminists defending a woman's right: This is the thesis of Will Saletan, *Bearing Right: How Conservatives Won the Abortion War* (Berkeley: University of California Press, 2003).

7 to urge the creation of a religious left: Jim Wallis, *God's Politics: Why the Left Gets It Wrong and the Right Does Not Get It* (San Francisco: HarperCollins, 2005).

7 "The 'L word' implies": Neil Jumonville and Kevin Mattson, "Introduction," in Jumonville and Mattson, *Liberalism for a New Century* (Berkeley and Los Angeles: University of California Press, 2007), 3 (emphasis in the original).

8 "saw the savagery of the 9/11 attacks": Patrick D. Healy, "Rove Criticizes Liberals on 9/11," *New York Times,* June 23, 2005, p. A13.

8 "have rendered our society": Sean Hannity, *Deliver Us from Evil: Defeating Terrorism, Despotism, and Liberalism* (New York: Harper, 2004), 9, 10, 12.

8 "when the nation is under attack": Ann Coulter, *Treason: Liberal Treachery from the Cold War to the War on Terrorism* (New York: Crown Forum, 2003), 1.

8 they actually caused it: Dinesh D'Souza, *The Enemy at Home: The Cultural Left and Its Responsibility for 9/11* (New York: Doubleday, 2007).

9 the Fascist variety as well: Jonah Goldberg, *Liberal Fascism: The Secret History of the American Left, from Mussolini to the Politics of Meaning* (New York: Doubleday, 2008).

9 denounced for their egoism and taste for luxury: The French theorists of the Counter-Enlightenment. See Darrin M. McMahon, *Enemies of Enlightenment: The French Counter-Enlightenment and the Making of Modernity* (Oxford: Oxford University Press, 2001).

9 their absurd belief in progress: The Vatican's 1864 "Syllabus of Errors." See http://www.papalencyclicals.net/Pius09/p9syll.htm.

9 their overweening rationalism: George Fitzhugh, the American defender of slavery. See Arnaud B. Leavelle and Thomas I. Cook, "George Fitzhugh and the Theory of American Conservatism," *Journal of Politics* 7 (May 1945), 145–68.

9 their rootless cosmopolitanism: German Romantic nationalists such as Julius Langbehn and Arthur Moeller van den Bruck. See Fritz Stern, *The Politics of Cultural Despair: A Study in the Rise of the Germanic Ideology* (Berkeley and Los Angeles: University of California Press, 1961).

9 their affinity with madness: Juan Donoso Cortés, "Letters to the Editor of *El He-raldo*," in *Selected Works of Juan Donoso Cortés*, ed. Jeffrey P. Johnson (Westport, Conn.: Greenwood Press, 2000), 95.

9 their naïve failure to recognize: Carl Schmitt, *The Crisis of Parliamentary Democracy*, trans. Ellen Kennedy (Cambridge, Mass.: MIT Press, 1988), 35.

9 "this monster of our times": Fr. Félix Sardá y Salvany, *Liberalism Is a Sin*, trans. Condé B. Pallen (Rockford, Ill.: Tan Books, 1993), 1, 7, 22.

10 although I confess to having done so: Especially concerning Dinesh D'Souza. See Alan Wolfe, "None (But Me) Dare Call It Treason," *New York Times Book Review*, January 21, 2007, p. 6.

11 "Men are not born free": Guido De Ruggiero, *The History of European Liberalism*, trans. R. G. Collingwood (Boston: Beacon Press, 1959 [1927]), 32.

12 "*Society* was the great": James Oakes, "Radical Liberals, Liberal Radicals: The Dissenting Tradition in American Political Culture," *Reviews in American History*, vol. 27, no. 3 (September 1999), 507.

14 "Everything is what it is": Isaiah Berlin, "Two Concepts of Liberty," in Berlin, *The Proper Study of Mankind: An Anthology of Essays* (New York: Farrar, Straus & Giroux, 1998), 197.

14 Liberalism's substantive commitments: I am indebted on this point, indeed on many points, to Stephen Holmes, *Passions and Constraints: On the Theory of Liberal Democracy* (Chicago: University of Chicago Press, 1995), 13–41.

16 "solitary, poor, nasty": Thomas Hobbes, *Leviathan* (New York: Oxford University Press, 1998 [1651]), 84.

16 certainly not the anti-ideological conservatism: see Michael Oakeshott, *Rationalism in Politics, and Other Essays* (New York: Basic Books, 1962).

16 importance of the American founding: For an example, see Herbert J. Storing, *Toward a More Perfect Union* (Washington, D.C.: AEI Press, 1995).

17 a "procedural republic": Michael Sandel, *Democracy's Discontent: America in Search of a Public Philosophy* (Cambridge, Mass.: Belknap Press of Harvard University Press, 1996), 3–119.

17 Stanley Fish: See Stanley Fish, *The Trouble with Principle* (Cambridge, Mass.: Harvard University Press, 1999).

18 There *is* something amiss: This frequently appears to be the case with Ronald Dworkin; see, e.g., *Freedom's Law: The Moral Reading of the American Constitution* (Cambridge, Mass.: Harvard University Press, 1996).

18 those who call themselves communitarians: For a recent articulation, see Amitai Etzioni, *The Common Good* (Cambridge, U.K.: Polity Press, 2004).

19 the word "liberal" existed: See Philip Hamburger, "Liberality," *Texas Law Review*, 78 (May 2000), 1215–85.

19 A conservative who opposes: For evidence that this happens, see Arthur C. Brooks, *Who Really Cares: The Surprising Truth About Compassionate Conservatism: America's Charity Divide Who Gives, Who Doesn't, and Why It Matters* (New York: Basic Books, 2006).

20 lacking a skeptical sensibility: See Andrew Sullivan, *The Conservative Soul: How We Lost It, How to Get It Back* (New York: HarperCollins, 2006).

22 It is one thing for conservatives: George A. Panichas, ed., *The Essential Russell Kirk* (Wilmington, Del.: ISI Books, 2006).

22 even to add fox-hunting: Roger Scruton, *On Hunting: A Short Polemic* (South Bend, Ind.: St. Augustine's Press, 2001).

23 J. G. Merquior: See Merquior's *Liberalism: Old and New* (Boston: Twayne Publishers, 1991), 149.

23 The last years of the eighteenth century: Jay Winik, *The Great Upheaval: America and the Birth of the Modern World, 1788–1800* (New York: Harper, 2007).

24 how the Enlightenment project failed: See Alasdair MacIntyre, *After Virtue: A Study in Moral Theory,* 2nd edn. (Notre Dame, Ind.: University of Notre Dame Press, 1984).

25 artificial attempts to create equality: See J. L. Talmon, *The Origins of Totalitarian Democracy* (London: Secker & Warburg, 1952).

29 The ever-engaging but often over-the-top British philosopher: John Gray, *Straw Dogs: Thoughts on Humans and Other Animals* (London: Granta, 2002); John Gray, *Black Mass: Apocalyptic Religion and the Death of Utopia* (New York: Farrar, Straus & Giroux, 2007).

29 but merely the last days of Europe: Walter Laqueur, *The Last Days of Europe: Epitaph for an Old Continent* (New York: St. Martin's Press, 2007).

29 The future of the United States: Samuel P. Huntington, *Who Are We?: The Challenges to America's National Identity* (New York: Simon & Schuster, 2004).

29 it actually has launched World War IV: Norman Podhoretz, *World War IV: The Long Struggle Against Islamofascism* (New York: Doubleday, 2007).

CHAPTER 2   IN PRAISE OF ARTIFICE

31 "the stupid Moslem": Jean-Jacques Rousseau, "The First Discourse: Discourse on the Sciences and Arts," in *The Social Contract and The First and Second Discourses,* ed. Susan Dunn (New Haven: Yale University Press, 2002), 48.

32 "The needs of the body"and the quotes that follow: Ibid., 48, 50.

32 "the herd known as society": Ibid., 50.

32 "we have nothing but a deceitful": Jean-Jacques Rousseau, "The Second Discourse: Discourse on the Origin and Foundations of Inequality Among Mankind," in ibid., 138.

32 "it ends in": Ibid., 140.

32 "If you reflect": Ibid., 140–41.

33 a refugee from totalitarian-torn Europe: See Judith N. Shklar, "A Life of Learning," in Bernard Yack, ed., *Liberalism Without Illusions: Essays on Liberal Theory and the Political Vision of Judith N. Shklar* (Chicago: University of Chicago Press, 1996), 275.

33 "the insane Socrates": Edmund Burke, "Letter to a Member of the National Assembly," in Issac Kramnick, ed., *The Portable Edmund Burke* (New York: Penguin Books, 1999), 512.

33 those who wanted to restore the authority: Darrin M. McMahon, *Enemies of the Enlightenment: The French Counter-Enlightenment and the Making of Modernity* (New York: Oxford University Press, 2001), 35.

34 "The hypochondriac": Immanuel Kant, "Anthropology from a Pragmatic Point of View, Part 2, Section E," in *Toward Perpetual Peace and Other Writings on Politics, Peace, and History,* ed. Pauline Kleingeld (New Haven: Yale University Press, 2006), 169, 167.

34 "The human being": Ibid., 167–68.

35 as Kant famously put it: Immanuel Kant, "Toward Perpetual Peace: A Philosophical Sketch," in ibid., 90.

35 "which embodies the highest degree": Ibid., 170.

35 "brutishness to culture": Immanuel Kant, "Idea for a Universal History from a Cosmopolitan Perspective," in ibid., 7.

35 "far from being the solution": Leo Damrosch, *Jean-Jacques Rousseau: Restless Genius* (Boston: Houghton Mifflin, 2005), 237.

35 "be realized only in society": "Idea for a Universal History," in Kleingeld, ed., *Toward Perpetual Peace*, 8.

36 placed into one of two camps: See Thomas Sowell, *A Conflict of Visions: Ideological Origins of Political Struggles* (New York: William Morrow, 1987).

37 Calvinist Geneva . . . rigorously monitored: William G. Naphy, "Calvin and Geneva," in Andrew Pettegree, ed., *The Reformation World* (London and New York: Routledge, 2000), 309–22, and Robert M. Kingdon, *Adultery and Divorce in Calvin's Geneva* (Cambridge, Mass.: Harvard University Press, 1995).

37 "Rousseau's view of human nature": Robert N. Bellah, "Rousseau on Society and the Individual," in Bellah and Steven M. Tipton, eds., *The Robert Bellah Reader* (Durham, N.C.: Duke University Press, 2006), 182.

38 "Sin is a transgression": Jerry Falwell, *Listen America!* (Garden City, N.Y.: Doubleday, 1980), 64.

38 "I here propose": Ibid., 63.

39 "Sin brings reproach": Ibid., 64.

39 "we have become ": Ibid., 248.

40 "We are living in a society": Ibid., 62.

40 "The hope of reversing": Ibid., 21, 63, 47.

42 "to make propaganda among gullible laypeople": Richard Dawkins, *The God Delusion* (Boston: Houghton Mifflin, 2006), 133.

42 "Any creative intelligence": Ibid., 31.

42 "The central insight of Darwinian theory": Paul Bloom, *Descartes' Baby: How the Science of Child Development Explains What Makes Us Human* (New York: Basic Books, 2004), 61.

42 scientists and philosophers trained in: Daniel Dennett, *Breaking the Spell: Religion as a Natural Phenomenon* (New York: Viking, 2006), and Sam Harris, *The End of Faith: Religion, Terror, and the Future of Reason* (New York: W. W. Norton, 2004).

42 "It's not that people": Steven Pinker, *How the Mind Works* (New York: W. W. Norton, 1997), 518.

42 He would later take pains to argue: Dawkins, *The God Delusion*, 215.

43 "Believing, with Max Weber": Clifford Geertz, *The Interpretation of Cultures* (New York: Basic Books, 1973), 5.

43 "It is civilization": Emile Durkheim, "The Dualism of Human Nature and Its Social Conditions," in *Emile Durkheim on Morality and Society: Selected Writings,* Robert N. Bellah, ed. (Chicago: University of Chicago Press, 1973), 149.

43 "sensory appetites": Ibid., 151.

43 a "dyed-in-the-wool monist": Dawkins, *The God Delusion*, 180.

44 "to supply a comprehensive theory": Ibid., 196.

44 romantic love: For examples, see Helen E. Fisher, *Why We Love: The Nature and Chemistry of Romantic Love* (New York: Henry Holt, 2004); Matt Ridley, *The Origins of Virtue: Human Instincts and the Evolution of Cooperation* (New York: Viking, 1997); and Daniel Dennett, *Breaking the Spell*.

44 "an innate part": Steven Pinker, "The Moral Instinct," *New York Times Magazine*, January 13, 2006, p. 36.

45 the leading defenders of inequality: See William Graham Sumner, *What Social Classes Owe Each Other* (New York: Harper, 1883) and Herbert Spencer, *The Principles of Sociology* (New York: D. Appleton, 1895–97).

45 "conservatives need Charles Darwin": Larry Arnhart quoted by Patricia Cohen, "A Split Emerges as Conservatives Discuss Darwin," *New York Times,* May 5, 2007, p. A1. See also Larry Arnhart, *Darwinian Conservatism* (New York: Imprint Academic, 2005).

45 theories of international relations: Stephen Peter Rosen, *War and Human Nature* (Princeton: Princeton University Press, 2004).

46 It is wrong . . . to confuse a scientific theory: Pinker, *How the Mind Works,* 47–58.

46 "From the content of": David Brooks, "Human Nature Redux," *New York Times,* February 18, 2007, sec. 4, p. 12.

47 swimming pools, the data show: Steven D. Levitt and Stephen J. Dubner, *Freakonomics: A Rogue Economist Explores the Hidden Side of Everything,* rev. and exp. edn. (New York: William Morrow, 2006), 135.

47 citing the psychologist: Judith Rich Harris, *The Nurture Assumption: Why Children Turn Out the Way They Do* (New York: Free Press, 1998).

47 "Most of the things that matter": Levitt and Dubner, *Freakonomics,* 161.

48 "each of us is trapped": Daniel Gilbert, *Stumbling on Happiness* (New York: Knopf, 2006), 125, 171.

48 "super-replicators" . . . "The production of wealth": Ibid., 216, 219.

48 "We are . . . nodes": Ibid., 222.

48 "Incessantly we obey rituals": Rousseau, "The First Discourse," ed. Dunn, 50.

49 "What makes us think": Gilbert, *Stumbling on Happiness,* 230.

49 that human beings "have faculties": John Stuart Mill, "Utilitarianism," in *On Liberty and Other Essays,* ed. John Gray (Oxford and New York: Oxford University Press, 1998), 138.

49 "Human nature is not a machine" . . . "it is better": Mill, "On Liberty," in ibid., 66, 140.

50 "For two thousand years" . . . "the sentence is": Gilbert, *Stumbling on Happiness,* 36–37.

51 "God gave the world to men": John Locke, "The Second Treatise: An Essay Concerning the True, Original, Extent, and End of Civil Government," in *Two Treatises on Government and A Letter Concerning Toleration,* ed. Ian Shapiro (New Haven: Yale University Press, 2003), 114.

51 "the source of all man's misfortunes": Rousseau, "The Second Discourse," ed. Dunn, 96.

52 today we consider the bourgeois virtues: Deirdre McCloskey, *The Bourgeois Virtues: Ethics for an Age of Commerce* (Chicago: University of Chicago Press, 2006).

52 "possessive individualism": See C. B. Macpherson, *The Political Theory of Possessive Individualism: Hobbes to Locke* (New York: Oxford University Press, 1962).

52 "the earth is given as a common": Thomas Jefferson to Rev. James Madison, October 28, 1795, in Joyce Appleby and Terence Ball, eds., *Jefferson: Political Writings* (Cambridge, U.K.: Cambridge University Press, 1999), 107.

52 "man was created": Jefferson to Francis W. Gilmer, June 7, 1816, in ibid., 143.

52 Rousseau's unceasing self-absorption: Rousseau's relationship with Hume is described in loving detail in David Edmonds and John Eidinow, *Rousseau's Dog: Two Great Thinkers at War in the Age of Enlightenment* (New York: Ecco, 2006).

52 "conceived of commerical self-interest": Stephen Holmes, *Passions and Constraints: On the Theory of Liberal Democracy* (Chicago: University of Chicago Press, 1995), 60.

53 This is not how behavioral economists: See, for example, Dan Ariely, *Predictably Irrational: The Hidden Forces that Shape Our Decisions* (New York: HarperCollins, 2008). I explore the issues raised by this and similar books in Alan Wolfe, "Hedonic Man: The New Economics and the Pursuit of Happiness," *The New Republic,* July 9, 2008, 47–55.

53 "He who lets the world": Mill, "On Liberty," in *On Liberty and Other Essays,* 65–66.

54 its "narrow theory of life": Ibid., 69.

54 "It is not by wearing down": Ibid., 70.

54 "It really is": Ibid., 66.

54 "In proportion to the development": Ibid., 70.

54 Even religion is improved: John Locke, "A Letter Concerning Toleration," in *Two Treatises on Government and A Letter Concerning Toleration,* ed. Shapiro.

55 "Even if there were such a thing": Ronald Bailey, *Liberation Biology: The Scientific and Moral Case for the Biotech Revolution* (Amherst, N.Y.: Prometheus Books, 2005), 236.

56 "a shortsighted and improverished vision": See http://www.firstthings.com/onthe square/?p=418.

56 the ethicist . . . and the political philospher: Leon Kass, *Life, Liberty, and the Defense of Dignity: The Challenge for Bioethics* (San Francisco: Encounter Books, 2002), and Francis Fukuyama, *Our Posthuman Future: Consequences of the Biotechnology Revolution* (New York: Picador, 2002).

56 one of the more powerful ideas: Pierre Manent, *The City of Man*, trans. Marc A. LePain (Princeton: Princeton University Press, 1998).

56 "crunchy cons": Rod Dreher, *Crunchy Cons: How Birkenstocked Burkeans, Gun-Loving Organic Gardeners, Evangelical Free-Range Farmers, Hip Homeschooling Mamas, Right-Wing Nature Lovers, and Their Diverse Tribe of Countercultural Conservatives Plan to Save America (or at Least the Republican Party)* (New York: Crown Forum, 2006).

57 "the Earth would do fine": Alan Weisman, *The World Without Us* (New York: Thomas Dunne Books, 2007), 274.

57 "The human race ought": Kant, "Anthropology," in *Toward Perpetual Peace*, ed. Kleingeld, 167.

57 "It is an intensely disturbing idea": Bill McKibben, *The End of Nature*, 10th anniv. edn. (New York: Anchor Books, 1999), 182.

58 *The Bell Curve:* Richard Herrnstein and Charles Murray, *The Bell Curve: Intelligence and Class Structure in American Life* (New York: Free Press, 1994); for critiques, see Steven Fraser, ed., *The Bell Curve Wars: Race, Intelligence, and the Future of America* (New York: Basic Books, 1995).

58 the DNA co-discoverer: For something of a defense of Watson's position, see Will Saletan, "Created Equal," at http://www.slate.com/id/2178122/entry/2178123/.

58 Feminists such as the psychologist: Carol Gilligan, *In a Different Voice: Psychological Theory and Women's Development* (Cambridge, Mass.: Harvard University Press, 1993).

58 "black children are": Andrew Hacker, *Two Nations: Black and White, Separate, Hostile, Unequal*, exp. and updated edn. (New York: Ballantine Books, 1995), 177.

59 "Cosmopolitanism . . . starts": Kwame Anthony Appiah, *Cosmopolitanism: Ethics in a World of Strangers* (New York: W. W. Norton, 2006), 134–5.

59 "There is something appealing": Michael Sandel, *The Case Against Perfection: Ethics in the Age of Genetic Engineering* (Cambridge, Mass.: Belknap Press of Harvard University Press, 2007), 99–100, 97.

60 the man who has been called the inventor: Joshua Foa Dienstag, *Pessimism: Philosophy, Ethic, Spirit* (Princeton: Princeton University Press, 2006), 49.

CHAPTER 3   EQUALITY'S INEVITABILITY

62 the West's most important political philosophers: See Sanford A. Lakoff, *Equality in Political Philosophy* (Cambridge, Mass.: Harvard University Press, 1964), 88–125.

63 "is at once the most natural": *Philosophical Dictionary*, cited in ibid., 91.

63 that "monstrous fiction": Edmund Burke, *Reflections on the Revolution in France*, ed. Frank M. Turner (New Haven: Yale University Press, 2003 [1790]), 32.

63 One twentieth-century writer: See J. L. Talmon, *The Origins of Totalitarian Democracy* (New York: W. W. Norton, 1970).

63 "the people subsist": Russell Kirk, "The Prescience of Tocqueville," in George A. Panichas, ed., *The Essential Russell Kirk* (Wilmington, Del.: ISI Books, 2007), 165.

64 "the rights of man": Lynn Hunt, *Inventing Human Rights: A History* (New York: W. W. Norton, 2007), 130.

64 "Does Mr. Burke": Tom Paine, *The Rights of Man,* cited in ibid., 134.

65 "Either no individual": Condorcet, "On the Admission of Women to the Rights of Citizenship," cited in ibid., 170.

67 "However brutal a tyrant": John Stuart Mill, "The Subjection of Women," in *On Liberty and Other Essays,* ed. John Gray (Oxford and New York: Oxford University Press, 1998), 504.

67 anticipated by Wollstonecraft: Mary Wollstonecraft, *A Vindication of the Rights of Woman; and, The Wrongs of Woman, or, Maria,* ed. Anne Mellor and Noelle Chao (New York: Pearson Longman, 2007).

67 "was a founding document": Richard Reeves, *John Stuart Mill: Victorian Firebrand* (London: Atlantic Books, 2007), 414.

67 "convert what was a mere": Mill, "The Subjection of Women," in *On Liberty and Other Essays,* 475.

67 "The truth is": Ibid., 477.

68 "Human beings are no longer": Ibid., 488.

68 "We are entering": Ibid., 518.

68 "All praise of civilization": John Stuart Mill, "Nature," in *Nature and Utility of Religion,* ed. George Nakhnikian (Indianapolis: Bobbs Merrill, 1958), 15.

68 "conduct, and conduct alone": Mill, "The Subjection of Women," in *On Liberty and Other Essays,* 560.

68 "the liberty of each" . . . "Any society": Ibid., 576, 574.

69 "Government . . . ought to fit": James Fitzjames Stephen, *Liberty, Equality, Fraternity,* ed. Stuart D. Warner (Indianapolis: Liberty Fund, 1993 [1873]), 136.

69 Stephen shared with Carlyle: See Thomas Carlyle, *Sartor Resartus: The Life and Opinions of Herr Tuefelsdröckh in Three Books,* ed. Rodger L. Tarr (Berkeley and Los Angeles: University of California Press, 2000 [1840]).

69 "To establish by law": Stephen, *Liberty, Equality, Fraternity,* 136.

70 "the physical differences": Ibid., 138.

70 "Political power": Ibid., 154–55.

71 A recent biography argues: See Mark Francis, *Herbert Spencer and the Invention of Modern Life* (Ithaca, N.Y.: Cornell University Press, 2007).

71 argued in dissent that: *Lochner* v. *New York,* 195 U.S. 45 (1905), at http://www.law .cornell.edu/supct/html/historics/USSC_CR_0198_0045_ZS.html.

71 "Every man has freedom": Herbert Spencer, *Social Statics* (London: Routledge, 1996 [1851]), 103.

71 "to drop connection with": Ibid., 206.

71 "can give us no direct": Ibid., 250.

72 the "idlers": Herbert Spencer, *The Man Versus the State* (Caldwell, Idaho: Caxton Printers, 1940 [1892]), 22.

72 "The defective natures": Ibid., 53.

72 "There is a notion": Ibid., 23.

72 "a Who's Who for letters": Richard Hofstadter, *Social Darwinism in American Thought, 1860–1915* (Philadelphia: University of Pennsylvania Press, 1945), 34.

72 Spencer did not like: See Francis, *Herbert Spencer,* 103–5 .

72 "It is a great delusion": William Graham Sumner, *What Social Classes Owe to Each Other* (New York: Harper & Bros., 1920 [1883]), 69.

73 "radically erroneous" . . . "The yearning after": Ibid., 166, 168.

73 "In an age of helter-skelter": Hofstadter, *Social Darwinism,* 51.

74 "As soon as the state": F. A. Hayek, *The Road to Serfdom* (Chicago: University of Chicago Press, 1994 [1944]), 119.

74 "it cannot refuse" . . . "inequality is": Ibid., 118, 117.

75 "primitive equality": See Michael Walzer, *Spheres of Justice: A Defense of Pluralism and Equality* (New York: Basic Books, 1983).

77 The welfare state has many parents: See Gøsta Esping-Andersen, *The Three Worlds of Welfare Capitalism* (Princeton: Princeton University Press, 1990).

77 a spirited debate over evolution: T. H. Green, "Mr. Spencer on the Relation of Subject and Object," in Thomas Hill Green, *Works,* ed R. L. Nettleship (New York: Longmans, Green, 1885–90), Vol. I, pp. 373–409; Herbert Spencer, "Professor Green's Explanations," in *Essays: Scientific, Political, and Speculative* (London: Williams & Norgate, 1891), Vol. II, pp. 321–32.

77 Readers interested: See the discussion in Judith Wilt, *Behind Her Times: Transition England in the Novels of Mary Arnold Ward* (Charlottesville: University of Virginia Press, 2005), 46–81.

77 For Green: Green's ideas are best expressed in his *Lectures on the Principles of Political Obligation, and Other Writings,* ed. Paul Harris and John Morrow (New York: Cambridge University Press, 1986). For a good overview, see *Melvin Richter, The Politics of Conscience: T. H. Green and His Age* (London: Weidenfeld & Nicolson, 1964).

77 his brother was an alcoholic: See Richard A. Chapman, "Thomas Hill Green (1836–1882)," *Review of Politics,* 27 (October 1965), 527.

77 "the men whose heart": cited in ibid., p. 530.

78 "the state was ultimately": Andrew Vincent and Raymond Plant, *Philosophy, Politics and Citizenship: The Life and Thought of the British Idealists* (Oxford: Basil Blackwell, 1984), 34.

78 a "new Toryism": Spencer, *The Man Versus the State,* 3.

78 "Gambling is the vice": Walter Rauschenbusch, *Christianity and the Social Crisis in the Twenty-First Century: The Classic That Woke Up the Church,* ed. Paul Raushenbush, (San Francisco: HarperSanFrancisco, 2007 [1907]), 216.

78 "a new temperance crusade": Ibid., 305.

78 "exalts selfishness": Ibid., 215.

78 "nations do not die": Ibid., 228–29.

78 "Equality . . . is the only basis": Ibid., 203.

78 "personal gifts" . . . "are concerned": R. H. Tawney, *Equality* (New York: Capricorn Books, 1961 [1931]), 38.

79 "violent contrasts": Ibid., 79.

79 "is to liberate": Ibid., 84.

79 "Culture . . . is not an assortment": Ibid., 88–89.

80 Marshall . . . while clearly a moralist: A. H. Halsey, "T. H. Marshall and Ethical Socialism," in Martin Bulmer and Anthony M. Rees, eds., *Citizenship Today: The Contemporary Relevance of T. H. Marshall* (London: Routledge, 1996), 81–100.

81 "What matters": T. H. Marshall, *Class, Citizenship, and Social Development: Essays by T. H. Marshall,* ed. Seymour Martin Lipset (Garden City, N.Y.: Doubleday, 1964), 102.

81 "It was increasingly recognized": Ibid., 82.

81 "the extension of social": Ibid., 102, 106.

82 a series of dams: See Walzer, *Spheres of Justice.*

83 the welfare state transforms: See Brian M. Barry, *Why Social Justice Matters* (Cambridge, U.K.: Polity Press, 2005).

84 because individuals make decisions: F. A. Hayek, "The Use of Knowledge in Society," *American Economic Review,* XXXV (September 1945), 519–30.

84 "We have never designed": F. A. Hayek, *Law, Legislation, and Liberty*. Vol. III: *The Political Economy of a Free People* (Chicago: University of Chicago Press, 1979), 164.

84 "directive intelligence": John Maynard Keynes, "The End of Laissez-Faire," in *The Collected Writings of John Maynard Keynes*. Vol. IX: *Essays in Persuasion* (London: Macmillan, 1973 [1926]), 292.

85 "is a mutual benefit arrangement": T. H. Marshall, *The Right to Welfare, and Other Essays* (New York: Free Press, 1981), 88.

85 "the welfare state is": Robert E. Goodin, *Reasons for Welfare: The Political Theory of the Welfare State* (Princeton: Princeton University Press, 1988), 3.

86 "Equality, properly understood": Margaret Thatcher, "Reason and Religion: The Moral Foundations of Freedom." James Bryce Lecture, September 24, 1996, at http://www.margaretthatcher.org/speeches/displaydocument.asp?docid=108364.

86 no such thing as society: Margaret Thatcher, Interview with *Woman's Own*, at http://www.margaretthatcher.org/speeches/displaydocument.asp?docid=106689.

86 "the speech": Ronald Reagan, "Rendezvous with Destiny," Address on Behalf of Senator Barry Goldwater, October 27, 1964, at http://www.reaganfoundation.org/reagan/speeches/rendezvous.asp.

86 there was a significant retrenchment: See Paul Pierson, *Dismantling the Welfare State?: Reagan, Thatcher, and the Politics of Retrenchment* (New York: Cambridge University Press, 1994).

87 Mrs. Thatcher's political demise: See Geoffrey Wheatcroft, *The Strange Death of Tory England* (London: Penguin, 2005).

87 One study of public attitudes: See Clem Brooks and Jeff Manza, *Why Welfare States Persist: The Importance of Public Opinion in Democracies* (Chicago: University of Chicago Press, 2007), 80.

87 "Whatever the level of support": Ibid., 123.

88 called "more equality" harder to come by: Herbert J. Gans, *More Equality* (New York: Pantheon, 1973).

89 Liberals frequently react: See, e.g., Michael B. Katz, *The Undeserving Poor: From the War on Poverty to the War on Welfare* (New York: Pantheon, 1989).

CHAPTER 4　　WHY GOOD POETRY MAKES BAD POLITICS

93 Trained to be a prodigy: The best account remains Mill's own: John Stuart Mill, *Autobiography*, ed. Jack Stillinger (Boston: Houghton Mifflin, 1969 [1873]).

94 was "the great questioner": John Stuart Mill, *On Bentham and Coleridge* (New York: Harper Bros., 1950), 41, 55, 66, 68.

94 "Prejudice apart": Jeremy Bentham, *The Rationality of Reward*, Bk. III, chap. 1, at http://www.la.utexas.edu/labyrinth/rr/rr.b03.c01.html#c01p08. Mill, p. 95, misquotes Bentham.

95 "the one demanding the extinction": Mill, *On Bentham and Coleridge*, 140.

95 "the stupidest party": John Stuart Mill, "Considerations on Representative Government," in *On Liberty and Other Essays*, ed. John Gray (Oxford: Oxford University Press, 1881), 307.

95 "I never meant to say": Cited in Richard Reeves, *John Stuart Mill: Victorian Firebrand* (London: Atlantic Books, 2007), 4.

95 "the natural means ": Mill, *On Bentham and Coleridge*, 167.

95 although some, especially in France, tried: The most famous example is Joseph de Maistre, *Considerations on France*, trans. and ed. Richard A. Lebrun (New York: Cambridge University Press, 1994 [1797]).

95 an underappreciated political force: The exception is Nancy Rosenblum's *Another Lib-*

eralism: Romanticism and the Reconstruction of Liberal Thought (Cambridge, Mass.: Harvard University Press, 1987). See also Jonathan Mendilow, *The Romantic Tradition in British Political Thought* (Totowa, N.J.: Barnes & Noble, 1986).

96 the images they fashioned of war: I am indebted to Simon Bainbridge, *British Poetry and the Revolutionary and Napoleonic Wars* (New York: Oxford University Press, 2003), for this insight.

96 "the thought of Goethe": Marshall Berman, *All That Is Solid Melts into Air: The Experience of Modernity* (New York: Simon & Schuster, 1982), 96.

97 "Whoever could master": Mill, *On Bentham and Coleridge,* 102.

97 The most impressive eighteenth-century arguments: See Albert O. Hirschman, *The Passions and the Interests: Political Arguments for Capitalism Before Its Triumph* (Princeton: Princeton University Press, 1977).

98 "Riddance": Cited in Rosenblum, *Another Liberalism,* 12.

98 "And ever since": Canto I, XXVI, in *Byron's Poetry,* ed. Frank D. McConnell (New York: W. W. Norton, 1978), 33.

99 "is not vehement expressions": Carl von Clausewitz, *On War,* ed. Anatol Rapoport (London: Penguin Books, 1982 [1832]), 147.

99 "one cannot demand": Immanuel Kant, "Toward Perpetual Peace," in *Toward Perpetual Peace and Other Writings on Politics, Peace, and History,* ed. Pauline Kleingeld (New Haven: Yale University Press, 2006), 96–97.

100 that "poet in action": Rosenblum, *Another Liberalism,* 20.

100 "Hayne cast himself": William R. Taylor, *Cavalier and Yankee: The Old South and American National Character* (New York: George Braziller, 1961), 110.

100 the region's peculiar bellicosity: See Rollin G. Osterweis, *Romanticism and Nationalism in the Old South* (New Haven: Yale University Press, 1949), and John Hope Franklin, *The Militant South* (Cambridge, Mass.: Belknap Press of Harvard University Press, 1956).

101 others downplay the South's distinctiveness: See, e.g., Marcus Cunliffe, *Soldiers and Civilians: The Martial Spirit in America, 1775–1865* (Boston: Little, Brown, 1968); Michael C. C. Adams, *Our Masters, the Rebels: A Speculation on Union Military Failure in the East, 1861–1865* (Cambridge, Mass.: Harvard University Press, 1978); and R. Don Higginbotham, "The Martial Spirit in the Antebellum South: Speculations in a National Context," *Journal of Southern History,* LVIII (February 1992), 3–26.

101 "sectional self-interest": Samuel P. Huntington, *The Soldier and the State: The Theory and Politics of Civil-Military Relations* (New York: Vintage Books, 1964), 212.

101 "The military man": Ibid., 69.

101 A good deal of what passes for conservatism: For an analysis of some of the similarities between the New Left and the New Right, see Mark Lilla, "A Tale of Two Reactions," *New York Review of Books,* May 14, 1998, pp. 4–8.

102 an embodiment of: John Patrick Diggins, *Ronald Reagan: Fate, Freedom, and the Making of History* (New York: W. W. Norton, 2007), 21–54.

102 "Battles bring out the coward": Victor Davis Hanson, *Carnage and Culture: Landmark Battles in the Rise of Western Culture* (New York: Doubleday, 2001), 8.

102 "the power and mystery of culture": Ibid., 16, 22.

103 "The suburban soccer fields": Victor Davis Hanson, *Between Peace and War: Lessons from Afghanistan to Iraq* (New York: Random House, 2004), 18–19.

104 The first-generation neoconservatives: See Francis Fukuyama, *America at the Crossroads: Democracy, Power, and the Neoconservative Legacy* (New Haven: Yale University Press, 2006), 19.

105 "realistic Wilsonianism": Ibid., 9–10.

106 is not between Mars and Venus: Robert Kagan, *Of Paradise and Power: America and Europe in the New World Order* (New York: Knopf, 2003).

106 "The idea, sometimes invested": Isaiah Berlin, "Nationalism," in Isaiah Berlin, *The Proper Study of Mankind: An Anthology of Essays* (New York: Farrar, Straus & Giroux, 1998), 601.

107 "men belong to a particular human": Ibid., 590.

107 "Those who speak the same language": Johann Gottlieb Fichte, *Addresses to the German Nation,* trans. R. F. Jones and G. H. Turnbull (Westport, Conn.: Greenwood Press, 1979 [1806]), 223.

108 "This is tantamount to saying": Berlin, "Nationalism," 591.

108 "If my group": Ibid., 592.

109 "was legal rather than social": Louis Hartz, *The Liberal Tradition in America: An Interpretation of American Political Thought Since the Revolution* (New York: Harcourt Brace & World, 1955), 109.

109 is achieved rather than ascribed: Michael Ignatieff, *Blood and Belonging: Journeys into the New Nationalism* (New York: Farrar, Straus & Giroux, 1993), 6. See also David Hollinger, *Postethnic America* (New York: Basic Books, 1995).

109 Holding the integrity: Ignatieff, *Blood and Belonging,* 7.

110 "Too many people were killed": Anatol Lieven, *America Right or Wrong: An Anatomy of American Nationalism* (New York: Oxford University Press, 2004), 31.

110 the concept of "constitutional patriotism": Jürgen Habermas, "Historical Consciousness and Post-Traditional Identity: The Federal Republic's Orientation to the West," in Habermas, *The New Conservatism: Cultural Criticism and the Historians' Debate,* trans. Sherry Weber Nicholson (Cambridge, Mass.: MIT Press, 1989), 249–67. See also Patchen Markell, "Making Affect Safe for Democracy: On 'Constitutional Patriotism,' " *Political Theory,* 28 (February 2000), 38–63.

110 "that political attachment": Jan-Werner Müller, *Constitutional Patriotism* (Princeton: Princeton University Press, 2007), 1.

110 Lieven acknowledges: Lieven, *America Right or Wrong,* 117.

110 "as in the European countries": Ibid., 221.

111 Huntington asks who Americans are: Samuel P. Huntington, *Who Are We?: The Challenges to American National Identity* (New York: Simon & Schuster, 2004).

111 creedal rather than cultural: I elaborate this point in Alan Wolfe, "Native Son: Samuel Huntington Defends the Homeland," *Foreign Affairs,* 83 (May–June 2004), 120–25.

112 "Becoming a citizen of the world": Martha Nussbaum, "Patriotism and Cosmopolitanism," *Boston Review,* 19 (Fall 1994), at http://www.soci.niu.edu/~phildept/Kapitan/nussbaum1.html.

112 "What holds a society together": Ignatieff, *Blood and Belonging,* 7.

113 Constitutional patriotism is: See Ciaran Cronin, "Democracy and Collective Identity: In Defense of Constitutional Patriotism," *European Journal of Philosophy,* 11 (2003), 1–28.

113 such notions as "free thought": Emmet Kennedy, " 'Ideology' from DeStutt de Tracy to Karl Marx," *Journal of the History of Ideas,* XL (July–September 1979), 358.

114 "Please explain to me"; Jefferson . . . responded: John Adams to Thomas Jefferson, December 16, 1816; Thomas Jefferson to John Adams, January 11, 1817, both in ibid., 361–62.

114 "lessening differences": Anthony Trollope, *The Prime Minister* (London: Penguin Classics, 1994 [1876]), 584.

115 Great Britain experienced a flowering: Helpful treatments include Michael Freeden, *The New Liberalism: An Ideology of Social Reform* (Oxford: Clarendon Press, 1978), and Peter Weiler, *The New Liberalism: Liberal Social Theory in Great Britain, 1889–1914* (New York and London: Garland, 1982).

115 Green's respect for social institutions: Thomas Hill Green, *Lectures on the Principles of*

Political Obligation, and Other Writings, ed. Paul Harris and John Morrow (Cambridge and New York: Cambridge University Press, 1986). I found especially useful Avital Simhony, "T. H. Green's Complex Common Good: Between Liberalism and Communitarianism," in Shimony and D. Weinstein, eds., *The New Liberalism: Reconciling Liberty and Community* (Cambridge: Cambridge University Press, 2001), 69–91.

116 "moments of madness": Aristide Zolberg, "Moments of Madness," *Politics and Society,* 2 (1972), 183–207.

116 "cold rules": Rosenblum, *Another Liberalism,* 53.

116 "out of the crooked timber": Isaiah Berlin, *The Crooked Timber of Humanity: Chapters in the History of Ideas* (London: John Murray, 1990).

117 "the conscious and the unconscious": Lionel Trilling, Preface to *The Liberal Imagination,* in *The Moral Obligation to Be Intelligent: Selected Essays,* ed. Leon Wieseltier (New York: Farrar, Straus & Giroux, 2000), 546.

117 "an awareness of complexity": Ibid., 548.

117 the historical figures liberals love: Richard Hofstadter, *The American Political Tradition and the Men Who Made It* (New York: Knopf, 1948), and *The Age of Reform: From Bryan to FDR* (New York: Vintage, 1955).

117 that while we intend by our acts : Robert K. Merton, "The Unanticipated Consequences of Purposive Social Action," *American Sociological Review,* 1 (December 1936), 894–904.

118 were among the first to perceive: Daniel Bell, ed., *The New American Right* (New York: Criterion Books, 1955); Richard Hofstadter, *The Paranoid Style in American Politics, and Other Essays* (New York: Knopf, 1965).

118 "the vital center": Arthur Schlesinger, Jr., *The Vital Center* (Boston: Houghton Mifflin, 1948), 41.

118 "because so many of our dreams": Reinhold Niebuhr, *The Irony of American History* (New York: Scribner's, 1952), 2, 42.

119 "few 'classic' liberals insist": Daniel Bell, *The End of Ideology: On the Exhaustion of Political Ideas in the Fifties* (Glencoe, Ill.: Free Press, 1960), 373, 371, 375.

119 "an ethic of responsibility" and the quotes that follow: Max Weber, "Politics as a Vocation," in Hans Gerth and C. Wright Mills, eds., *From Max Weber: Essays in Sociology* (New York: Oxford University Press, 1946), 115.

119 "that he shall not crumble": Ibid., 128.

120 foreign to a romantic sensibility: Bell, *The End of Ideology,* 289.

120 a bit soft on the student movements: Norman Podhoretz, *Breaking Ranks: An Intellectual Memoir* (New York: Harper & Row, 1979), 276–82.

121 "An ideal liberal society": Richard Rorty, *Contingency, Irony, and Solidarity* (Cambridge and New York: Cambridge University Press, 1989), 60, 65.

121 "The social glue": Ibid., 84, 87, 94.

122 "never reasoning about wholes": Mill, *On Bentham and Coleridge,* 53, 48.

122 "The attack on everything": Isaiah Berlin, "Nationalism," 572.

123 "It must be exciting for you": Cited in Tabassum Zakaria, "Bush Says if Younger, He Would Work in Afghanistan," *Reuters,* March 13, 2008, http://www.reuters.com/article/politicsNews/idUSN13331111120080313.

123 "Armies are microcosms": Dan Reiter and Allan C. Stam, *Democracies at War* (Princeton: Princeton University Press, 2002), 65.

124 a much needed corrective: Diggins, *Ronald Reagan, passim.*

124 "What is at stake": http://www.jfklibrary.org/Historical+Resources/Archives/Reference+Desk/Speeches/JFK/003POF03Yale06111962.htm.

125 "Politics . . . is a strong and slow": Weber, "Politics as a Vocation," 128.

CHAPTER 5   MR. SCHMITT GOES TO WASHINGTON

126 a "sublime genius": Benjamin Constant, "The Liberty of Ancients Compared with
     That of Moderns," in Constant, *Political Writings,* trans. and ed. Biancameria Fontana
     (New York: Cambridge University Press, 1988), 318.
127 it "demands that the citizen": Ibid.
127 "All private actions": Ibid., 311–12.
127 "For each of them": Ibid., 310–11.
128 "a disastrous anachronism": "The Spirit of Conquest and Usurpation and Their Rela-
     tion to European Civilization," in Ibid., 55, 65.
129 "would talk of national independence": Ibid., 64.
129 "Within the political realm": Stephen Holmes, *Benjamin Constant and the Making of
     Modern Liberalism* (New Haven: Yale University Press, 1984), 130.
129 "If all men were angels": James Madison, *Federalist Papers* No.51, in David Woot-
     ton, ed., *The Essential Federalist and Anti-Federalist Papers* (Indianapolis: Hackett,
     2003), 246.
130 free rein to fulfill his ambition: Ibid.
131 "ironically avoids the constraints": Carl Schmitt, *Political Romanticism,* trans. Guy
     Oakes (Cambridge, Mass.: MIT Press, 1986 [1919]), 72, 24.
131 could nonetheless be classified: See ibid., 149.
132 "Where it exists": Carl Schmitt, *The Crisis of Parliamentary Democracy,* trans. Ellen
     Kennedy (Cambridge, Mass.: MIT Press, 1988 [1923]), 14.
132 "The situation of parliamentarism": Ibid., 6.
132 "Legislation is *deliberare*": Ibid., 45.
132 for "energy" in the executive: Hamilton, *Federalist Papers* No. 70, in Wootton, ed., *The
     Essential Federalist,* 275.
132 "In case public safety": http://www.zum.de/psm/weimar/weimar_vve.php#Third%
     20Chapter.
133 that it should be interpreted: Ellen Kennedy, *Constitutional Failure: Carl Schmitt in
     Weimar* (Durham, N.C.: Duke University Press, 2004), 160.
133 "The exception . . . is always more interesting": Carl Schmitt, *Political Theology: Four
     Chapters on the Concept of Sovereignty,* trans. George Schwab (Chicago: University of
     Chicago Press, 2005 [1922]), 15.
133 "has the monopoly over": Ibid., 13, 55–56.
134 "the Führer protected": Cited in Jan-Werner Müller, *A Dangerous Mind: Carl Schmitt
     in the Post-War European Tradition* (New Haven: Yale University Press, 2003), 37.
134 Schmitt opened and closed the conference: See Raphael Gross, *Carl Schmitt and the
     Jews,* trans. Joel Golb (Madison: University of Wisconsin Press, 2007), 69–75.
134 including Leo Strauss: Heinrich Meier, *Carl Schmitt and Leo Strauss: The Hidden Dia-
     logue,* trans. J. Harvey Lomax (Chicago: University of Chicago Press, 2006).
134 his party number: Müller, *A Dangerous Mind,* 37.
135 "The political is the most intense": Carl Schmitt, *The Concept of the Political,* trans.
     George Schwab (Chicago: University of Chicago Press, 1996 [1932]), 29.
135 "All genuine political theories": Ibid., 61.
135 "maintains that we are in an age": Ibid., 75.
135 "it joins their side": Ibid., 51.
135 "When a state fights": Ibid., 54, 61.
136 although undergoing an important revival: See, e.g., Tzvetan Todorov, *A Passion for
     Democracy: Benjamin Constant,* trans. Alice Sebbury (New York: Algora, 1999).
137 One group of intellectuals clearly not happy: An overview can be found in Michael

O'Meara, *New Culture, New Right: Anti-Liberalism in Post-Modern Europe* (Bloomington: 1st Books, 2004). See also Alain de Benoist, *On Being a Pagan*, trans. John Greaham (Atlanta: Ultra, 2004).

137 "The liberal state": Alain de Benoist and Charles Champetier, "The French New Right in the Year 2000," at http://home.alphalink.com.au/~radnat/debenoist/alain9.html.

138 "grim truths that democratic idealists": Paul Edward Gottfried, *Carl Schmitt: Politics and Theory* (New York: Greenwood Press, 1990), 38.

138 Strauss wrote a review: His review can be found in *The Concept of the Political*, 83–107.

139 "In extreme situations": Leo Strauss, *Natural Right and History* (Chicago: University of Chicago Press, 1953), 160.

139 the "prerogative": John Locke, "The Second Treatise: An Essay Concerning the True, Original, Extent, and End of Civil Government," in *Two Treatises on Government and A Letter Concerning Toleration*, ed. Ian Shapiro (New Haven: Yale University Press, 2003), 172.

139 "natural right must be mutable": Strauss, *Natural Right*, 161.

140 the most influential and representative works: See Jacques Derrida, "Force of Law: The Mystical Foundation of Authority," in Drucilla Cornell, Michel Rosenfeld, and David Gray Carlson, eds., *Deconstruction and the Possibility of Justice* (New York: Routledge, 1992), 3–67.

140 a best-selling neo-Marxist manifesto: Michael Hardt and Antonio Negri, *Empire* (Cambridge, Mass.: Harvard University Press, 2002), 16.

140 the dazzling wordsmith: See Slavoj Žižek, *The Sublime Object of Ideology* (London: Verso, 1989); *The Ticklish Subject: The Absent Centre of Political Ontology* (London: Verso, 1999); and *The Universal Exception: Selected Writings, Vol. 2* (London: Continuum, 2006).

140 "has today reached its maximum worldwide": Giorgio Agamben, *State of Exception*, trans. Kevin Attell (Chicago: University of Chicago Press, 2005), 87.

140 "brilliant," "pertinent": All four terms appear in the course of two sentences in Chantal Mouffe, *The Return of the Political* (London: Verso, 2005), 118.

140 "Many people . . . will find it perverse": Ibid., 4–5.

140 "more relevant than ever": Ibid., 12.

140 "a dangerous liberal illusion": Ibid., 127.

141 "However, . . . if a form of speech": Stanley Fish, *The Trouble with Principle* (Cambridge, Mass.: Harvard University Press, 1999), 39, 41.

141 "many bad things": Ibid., 2.

142 "the presence of Marxists" . . . "My argument against hewing": Ibid., 89, 75.

143 Jan Werner-Müller is therefore correct: See Müller, *A Dangerous Mind*, 241.

144 There are many reasons for the marked increase in ideological politics: I discuss these reasons in *Does American Democracy Still Work?* (New Haven: Yale University Press, 2006).

145 You do not call publicly: See Ann Coulter, "The Democrats' Laboratory: The Host Organism Dies" at http://www.uexpress.com/anncoulter/index.html?uc_full_date=20030813.

146 "the costs of inaction": John Yoo, *The Powers of War and Peace: The Constitution and Foreign Affairs After 9/11* (Chicago: University of Chicago Press, 2005), x.

146 "To pretend that rules written": John Yoo, *War by Other Means: An Insider's Account of the War on Terror* (New York: Atlantic Monthly Press, 2006), 22.

147 "a unitary, energetic executive": Yoo, *The Powers of War and Peace*, 108.

147 Out of such concerns developed the notion: For the application of this theory to

recent history, see Christopher S. Yoo, Stephen Calabresi, and Angelo Colangelo, "The Unitary Executive in the Modern Era," *Iowa Law Review*, 90 (2005), 601–731.

148 To be fair here: Schlesinger's arguments on behalf of a strong presidency are best illustrated by the biographies he wrote: Arthur Schlesinger, Jr., *The Age of Jackson* (Boston: Little, Brown, 1945); *The Age of Roosevelt* (Boston: Houghton Mifflin, 1957); and *A Thousand Days: John F. Kennedy in the White House* (Boston: Houghton Mifflin, 1965). His later critique of the strong executive can be found in Arthur Schlesinger, Jr., *The Imperial Presidency* (Boston: Houghton Mifflin, 1973).

148 "It is inconceivable": Yoo, *War by Other Means*, 114, 121.

149 "want to overturn American historical": Ibid., 124.

149 In his most infamous memo: See http://news.findlaw.com/hdocs/docs/doj/bybee 80102ltr.html.

149 was "unwise": Yoo, *War by Other Means*, 200.

149 twice as many times: Charlie Savage, *Takeover: The Return of the Imperial Presidency and the Subversion of American Democracy* (New York: Little, Brown, 2007), 230.

150 *Hamdan* v. *Rumsfeld*: 126 S. Ct. 2749 (2006).

150 "displayed a lack of judicial": Yoo, *War by Other Means*, 237.

150 "our grandchildren will not believe": Constant, "The Spirit of Conquest," 642.

150 "Law is critically important": Yoo, *War by Other Means*, xii.

150 a number of legal scholars: See, e.g., Peter Lindseth, "Unchecked Power: The Echo of an Ugly History," at http://www.morningsentinel.com/News/2004/0622/ Commentary_Cent/090.html; Sanford Levinson, "Learning from the Past?" at http://www.tnr.com/blog/openuniversity?pid=37248; and Scott Horton, "Carl Schmitt and the Military Commissons Act of 2006," at http://balkin.blogspot.com/2006/10/ carl-schmitt-and-military-commissions_16.htm.

150 "an extravagant interpretation": Richard Posner, *Not a Suicide Pact: The Constitution in a Time of National Emergency* (New York: Oxford University Press, 2006), 68.

150 "doesn't care about": Cited in Jane Mayer, "The Hidden Power," *The New Yorker*, July 3, 2006, p. 44.

150 Jack Goldsmith, a conservative lawyer: Jack L. Goldsmith, *The Terror Presidency: Law and Judgment Inside the Bush Administration* (New York: W. W. Norton, 2007).

151 the two defects of the rule of law: Harvey Mansfield, Jr., "The Case for the Strong Executive," *Claremont Review of Books*, vol. VII, no. 2 (Spring 2007); http://www .claremont.org/publications/crb/id.1335/article_detail.asp.

151 "An extreme situation": Strauss, *Natural Right*, 160.

151 "In quiet times": Mansfield, "The Case for the Strong Executive."

151 "The rule of law": William E. Scheuerman, *Carl Schmitt: The End of Law* (London: Rowman & Littlefield, 1999), 4.

151 to undermining the assumptions: See, in particular, Carl Schmitt, *Legality and Legitimacy*, trans. Jeffrey Seitzer (Durham, N.C.: Duke University Press, 2004).

152 "We (along with Israel)": Yoo, *War by Other Means*, xii.

152 "Congress enacts laws": Ibid., 234.

153 "renders unnecessary any formal": Yoo, *The Powers of War and Peace*, 294.

156 "to contrast a regular government": Constant, "The Spirit of Conquest," 85, 134–35.

156 "The system of warfare": Ibid., 63.

CHAPTER 6   HOW LIBERALS SHOULD THINK ABOUT RELIGION

157 "The New Wars of Religion": *The Economist*, November 3, 2007, available at http:// www.economist.com/opinion/displaystory.cfm?story_id=10063829. For a scholarly

treatment along these lines, see Philip Jenkins, *The Next Christendom: The Coming of Global Christianity* (New York: Oxford University Press, 2002).

157 the world has also been witnessing: Alan Wolfe, "And the Winner Is . . .", *The Atlantic*, 30 (March 2008), 56–63.

158 "is the motto of enlightenment": Immanuel Kant, "An Answer to the Question: What is Enlightenment?" in *Toward Perpetual Peace and Other Writings on Politics, Peace, and History*, ed. Pauline Kleingeld (New Haven: Yale University Press, 2006), 17–19.

158 "But to renounce it": Ibid., 21, 23.

160 "The tendency and the calling": Ibid., 23.

160 "the Great Separation": See Mark Lilla, *The Stillborn God: Religion, Politics, and the Modern West* (New York: Knopf, 2007).

161 "What could exist without a dominant": Cited in William Doyle, *The Old European Order, 1660–1800*, 2nd edn. (Oxford: Oxford University Press, 1992), 156.

161 "is the most harmful of all": Kant, "An Answer," in *Toward Perpetual Peace*, 22.

161 "Spain is perhaps the most ignorant": Cited in David Goodman, "Intellectual Life Under the Spanish Inquisition: A Continuing Historical Controversy," *History*, 90 (July 2005), 375.

161 Authorities in Madrid responded: Ibid., 376.

162 "It entrusted the repression": Joseph Pérez, *The Spanish Inquisition: A History*, trans. Janet Lloyd (New Haven: Yale University Press, 2005), 204.

162 the emergence of such modern ideas as religious toleration: See Susan Jacoby, *Freethinkers: A History of American Secularism* (New York: Metropolitan Books, 2004).

162 not only was Christianity sympathetic: Rodney Stark, *The Victory of Reason: How Christianity Led to Freedom, Capitalism, and Western Success* (New York: Random House, 2005).

163 scholars working on the same issues: See Charles Freeman, *The Closing of the Western Mind: The Rise of Faith and the Fall of Reason* (New York: Knopf, 2003).

163 such seemingly secular ideals as: See Perez Zagorin, *How the Idea of Religious Toleration Came to the West* (Princeton: Princeton University Press, 2003), and Hugh Heclo, *Christianity and American Democracy* (Cambridge, Mass.: Harvard University Press, 2007).

163 was a devout Christian: See John Dunn, *The Political Thought of John Locke: An Historical Account of the Argument of the "Two Treatises on Government"* (Cambridge: Cambridge University Press, 1969).

163 "those who persecute, torment": John Locke, "A Letter Concerning Toleration," in *Two Treatises on Government and A Letter Concerning Toleration*, ed. Ian Shapiro (New Haven: Yale University Press, 2003), 216, 215.

163 "neither pagan, nor Mahometan": Ibid., 249.

164 "had no quarrel with religion": Gertrude Himmelfarb, *The Roads to Modernity: The British, French, and American Enlightenments* (New York: Knopf, 2004), 51.

164 the evangelical John Wesley: Ibid., 116–30.

164 he never had to shed religion: John Stuart Mill, *Autobiography*, ed. Jack Stillinger (Boston: Houghton Mifflin, 1969 [1873]), 28.

164 To be sure, Thomas Jefferson was not only a deist: On the Enlightenment convictions of the founders, see Darren Staloff, *Hamilton, Adams, Jefferson: The Politics of Enlightenment and the American Founding* (New York: Hill & Wang, 2005).

164 four of the five first American presidents: See David L. Holmes, *The Faiths of the Founding Fathers* (New York: Oxford University Press, 2005); also Brooke Allen, *Moral Minority: Our Skeptical Founding Fathers* (Chicago: Ivan R. Dee, 2006).

164 evangelicals made as much of a contribution: Steven Waldman, *Founding Faith: Politics, Providence, and the Birth of Religious Freedom in America* (New York: Random

House, 2008). See also Mark DeWolfe Howe, *The Garden and the Wilderness: Religion and Government in American Constitutional History* (Chicago: University of Chicago Press, 1967); William Lee Miller, *The First Liberty: America's Foundation in Religious Freedom*, exp. and updated edn. (Washington, D.C.: Georgetown University Press, 2003); and Philip Hamburger, *Separation of Church and State* (Cambridge, Mass.: Harvard University Press, 2002).

165 "I have preached": "Events in the Life of John Leland," in L. F. Greene, ed., *The Writings of John Leland* (New York: Arno Press, 1969), 35.

165 estimated that he had delivered: Ibid., 35, 39.

165 "Not the place": Ibid., 35.

165 After moving to Virginia in 1777: Biographical information on Leland comes from L. H. Butterfield, "Elder John Leland, Jeffersonian Itinerant," *Proceedings of the American Antiquarian Society*, 62 (April 16, 1952–October 15, 1952), 155–242.

165 "may have been the most skeptical": Holmes, *The Faiths of the Founding Fathers*, 107.

166 we owe that famous metaphor: Thomas Jefferson, "To Messr. Nehemiah Dodge, Emphram Robbins, and Stephen S. Nelson, a Committee of the Danbury Baptist Association in the State of Connecticut," January 1, 1802, in Joyce Appleby and Terence Ball, eds., *Jefferson: Political Writings* (Cambridge: Cambridge University Press, 1999), 397.

166 Leland was with Jefferson: Daniel L. Dreisbach, *Thomas Jefferson and the Wall of Separation Between Church and State* (New York: New York University Press, 2002), 17, 21.

166 "It is more essential": John Leland, "The Bible Baptist," in Greene, ed., *The Writings of John Leland*, 78.

166 "A man's mind": John Leland, "The Rights of Conscience Inalienable," in Ibid., p. 181.

166 A "liberal man": Ibid., 184.

167 This practicing Christian: William G. McLoughlin, *New England Dissent, 1680–1883: The Baptists and the Separation of Church and State* (Cambridge, Mass.: Harvard University Press, 1971), Vol. II, pp. 931–32.

168 Pope Benedict XVI is a theologian: See James V. Schall, *The Regensburg Lecture* (South Bend, Ind.: St. Augustine's Press, 2007).

168 thinkers such as Jürgen Habermas: See Giovanna Borradori, *Philosophy in a Time of Terror: Dialogues with Jürgen Habermas and Jacques Derrida* (Chicago: University of Chicago Press, 2003).

168 and the rise of Islam in Western Europe: See, e.g., Jytte Klausen, *The Islamic Challenge: Politics and Religion in Western Europe* (New York: Oxford University Press, 2005), and Tariq Ramadan, *Western Muslims and the Future of Islam* (New York: Oxford University Press, 2004).

169 "a monumental shift": Barry Hankins, *Uneasy in Babylon: Southern Baptist Conservatives and American Culture* (Tuscaloosa: University of Alabama Press, 2002), 148.

170 it continues to play that role in the twenty-first: For examples, see Chris Mooney, *The Republican War on Science* (New York: Basic Books, 2005), and Esther Kaplan, *With God on Their Side: How Christian Fundamentalists Trampled Science, Policy, and Democracy in George W. Bush's White House* (New York: New Press, 2004).

170 today's religious conservatives: Barry W. Lynn, *Piety and Politics: The Right-Wing Assault on Religious Freedom* (New York: Harmony Books, 2006).

170 "We are in need of a renewed Enlightenment": Christopher Hitchens, *God Is Not Great: How Religion Poisons Everything* (New York: Hachette, 2007), 283.

171 has emphasized the dangers posed to liberal societies: Sam Harris, *The End of Faith: Religion, Terror, and the Future of Reason* (New York: W. W. Norton, 2004). See also Michele Goldberg, *Kingdom Coming: The Rise of Christian Nationalism* (New York:

W. W. Norton, 2006); Kevin Phillips, *American Theocracy: The Peril and Politics of Radical Religion, Oil, and Borrowed Money in the Twenty-First Century* (New York: Viking, 2006); and James Rudin, *The Baptizing of America: The Religious Right's Plans for the Rest of Us* (New York: Thunder's Mouth Press, 2006).

172 "a hilarious, terrifying, and unconscionable": Sam Harris, *Letter to a Christian Nation* (New York: Knopf, 2006), 66.

172 "nearly always results from strong religious faith": Richard Dawkins, *The God Delusion* (Boston: Houghton Mifflin, 2006), 286.

172 Harris's attempt to show: Harris, *The End of Faith*, 101.

172 that religion *is* fascism: Hitchens, *God Is Not Great*, 229–52.

172 that nonbelief has historically taken: Damon Linker, "Atheism's Wrong Turn," *The New Republic*, December 10, 2007, pp. 16–18.

172 "are, in large part, responsible". Harris, *The End of Faith*, 45.

173 "While religious people": Ibid., 72.

173 "To 'choose' dogma and faith": Hitchens, *God Is Not Great*, 278.

173 "What believers will do": Ibid., 96.

173 "to believe a proposition": Harris, *The End of Faith*, 71, 77.

174 considered "resident aliens": Stanley Hauerwas and William H. Willimon, *Resident Aliens: A Provocative Assessment of Culture and Ministry for People Who Know That Something Is Wrong* (Nashville, Tenn.: Abingdon Press, 1989).

174 "Liberalism emasculated Christianity": Stanley Hauerwas, *Dispatches from the Front: Theological Engagements with the Secular* (Durham, N.C.: Duke University Press, 1994), 17.

175 "we live in a new moment": Winifred Fallers Sullivan, *The Impossibility of Religious Freedom* (Princeton: Princeton University Press, 2005), 151.

176 One who has undertaken the task: See Stanley Fish, *The Trouble with Principle* (Cambridge, Mass.: Harvard University Press, 1999), 162–86.

176 foreordained to failure: Steven D. Smith, *Foreordained Failure: The Quest for a Constitutional Principle of Religious Freedom* (New York: Oxford University Press, 1995).

176 "if you believe that Jesus": Walter Benn Michaels, *The Trouble with Diversity: How We Learned to Love Identity and Ignore Inequality* (New York: Metropolitan Books, 2006), 175.

178 will cause "religious conservatives": Darryl Hart, *A Secular Faith: Why Christianity Favors the Separation of Church and State* (Chicago: Ivan R. Dee, 2006), 239.

179 "Let us . . . endeavor to divorce them": "Virginia Chronicle," in Greene, ed., *The Writings of John Leland*, 119. Also cited in Philip Hamburger, *Separation of Church and State* (Cambridge, Mass.: Harvard University Press, 2002), 167.

179 "The go-along, get-along strategy": Cited in Hankins, *Uneasy in Babylon*, 109.

179 one brief reference to the former: Hitchens, *God Is Not Great*, 71.

180 "an even greater stigma": Harris, *The End of Faith*, 77.

180 "the social stigma": John Stuart Mill, "On Liberty," in *On Liberty and Other Essays*, ed. John Gray (Oxford and New York: Oxford University Press, 1998), 37–38.

180 "It is time we recognized": Harris, *The End of Faith*, 45.

181 "to any authority whose conclusions": Amy Gutmann and Dennis Thompson, *Democracy and Disagreement: Why Moral Conflict Cannot Be Avoided in Politics and What Should Be Done About It* (Cambridge, Mass.: Belknap Press of Harvard University Press, 1996), 56.

181 contradicts liberalism's insistence upon equality: On this point, see Martha Nussbaum, *Liberty of Conscience: In Defense of America's Tradition of Religious Equality* (New York: Basic Books, 2008).

181 to "opt out of reasonable measures": Stephen Macedo, *Diversity and Distrust: Civic Education in a Multicultural Democracy* (Cambridge, Mass.: Harvard University Press, 2000), 201.

182 "positively bracing compared to": Fish, *The Trouble with Principle*, 210.

182 "the liberal bargain": Damon Linker, *The Theocons: Secular America Under Siege* (New York: Doubleday, 2006), 220–23.

183 According to the most reliable survey: See the Pew Forum on Religion and Public Life, "The U.S. Religious Landscape Study," http://religions.pewforum.org/reports.

184 I have spent a considerable amount of time: See Alan Wolfe, *One Nation, After All: What Middle-Class Americans Really Think About God, Country, Family, Racism, Welfare, Immigration, Homosexuality, Work, the Right, the Left, and Each Other* (New York: Viking, 1998).

185 the age of the rocks in the Grand Canyon: "How Old Is the Grand Canyon?: Park Service Won't Say," Public Employees for Environmental Responsibility," December 28, 2006, at http://www.peer.org/news/news_id.php?row_id=801.

CHAPTER 7   THE OPEN SOCIETY AND ITS FRIENDS

187 a term popularized by: Karl R. Popper, *The Open Society and Its Enemies* (London: Routledge, 1945).

188 "the Constitution is not a suicide pact": *Terminiello* v. *City of Chicago*, 337 U.S. 1 (1949) at http://supreme.justia.com/us/337/1/case.html.

188 may have to keep some of its affairs: See, e.g., Richard Posner, *Not a Suicide Pact: The Constitution in a Time of National Emergency* (New York: Oxford University Press, 2006).

188 "my duty to pass my life": Plato, "The Apology of Socrates," in *The Works of Plato*, trans. Henry Cary (London: George Bell & Sons, 1881), 16–17.

189 "Mankind can hardly be too often reminded": John Stuart Mill, "On Liberty," in *On Liberty and Other Essays*, ed. John Gray (Oxford and New York: Oxford University Press, 1998), 29, 34.

189 "they are always a mass": Ibid., 73.

190 "The initiation of all wise": Ibid., 74.

190 "But why, my dear Crito": Plato, "The Crito," in *The Works of Plato*, 32–33.

191 "Diderot's distinction between written and oral": Jürgen Habermas, *The Structural Transformation of the Private Sphere: An Inquiry into a Category of Bourgeois Society*, trans. Thomas Burger (Cambridge, Mass.: MIT Press, 1991), 34.

191 "justifiably be barred": Immanuel Kant, "An Answer to the Question: What is Enlightenment?," in *Toward Perpetual Peace and Other Writings on Politics, Peace, and History*, ed. Pauline Kleingeld (New Haven: Yale University Press, 2006), 19.

191 not "merely academic": Habermas, *The Structural Transformation*, 105.

192 Taking the former position: Eric Alterman, *When Presidents Lie: A History of Official Deception and Its Consequences* (New York: Viking, 2004), 13.

193 "finds himself": Walter Lippmann, *Public Opinion* (New York: Harcourt Brace, 1922), 247–48.

193 "Everything which is distinctively human": John Dewey, *The Public and Its Problems* (Athens: Ohio University Press, 1991), 154.

193 "There can be no public": Ibid., 167.

193 Habermas, relying heavily on Dewey: See Jürgen Habermas, *The Theory of Communicative Action*, trans. Thomas McCarthy, 2 vols. (Boston: Beacon Press, 1984–87).

194 explicit contemporary defenders: Jay Rosen, *Getting the Connections Right: Public Journalism and the Troubles in the Press* (New York: Twentieth Century Fund, 1996).

194 but his ideas . . . live on: For a recent example, see Bryan Caplan, *The Myth of the Rational Voter: Why Democracies Choose Bad Policies* (Princeton: Princeton University Press, 2007).

194 were both Supreme Court justices: For an excellent discussion of their differences, see Cass Sunstein, *Democracy and the Problem of Free Speech* (New York: Free Press, 1993), 23–28.

195 constituted a "clear and present danger": *Schenck* v. *U.S.*, 249 U.S. 47 (1919), at http://www.law.cornell.edu/supct/html/historics/USSC_CR_0249_0047_ZS.html.

195 "But when men have realized": *Abrams* v. *U.S.*, 250 U.S. 616 (1919), at http://www.law.cornell.edu/supct/html/historics/USSC_CR_0250_0616_ZD.html.

195 "a silly leaflet": Ibid.

195 "Those who won our independence": *Whitney* v. *California*, 274 U.S. 357 (1927), at http://supct.law.cornell.edu/supct/html/historics/USSC_CR_0274_0357_ZS.html.

197 Cass Sunstein makes this point by drawing: Sunstein, *Democracy and the Problem of Free Speech*, 17–51.

198 "No person, whether or not acting": http://caselaw.lp.findlaw.com/cacodes/pen/422.6-422.95.html.

199 In June 2007, the Supreme Court ruled: *Federal Election Commission* v. *Wisconsin Right to Life, Inc.*, at http://www.supremecourtus.gov/opinions/06pdf/06-969.pdf.

200 "The First Amendment . . . is not the guardian": Alexander Meiklejohn, *Political Freedom: The Constitutional Powers of the People* (New York: Harper & Bros., 1960), 26.

201 Hugo Grotius noted: Cited in Peter Sahlins, *Unnaturally French: Foreign Citizens in the Old Regime and After* (Ithaca, N.Y.: Cornell University Press, 2004), 43.

201 foreign merchants could not hire fellow aliens: Aristide Zolberg, *A Nation by Design: Immigration Policy in the Fashioning of America* (Cambridge, Mass.: Harvard University Press, 2006), xx, 90.

201 In France, foreigners were subject: Sahlins, *Unnaturally French*, 31–56, 317.

202 "withdrawing themselves": John Locke, "The Second Treatise: An Essay Concerning the True, Original, Extent, and End of Civil Government," in *Two Treatises on Government and A Letter Concerning Toleration*, ed. Ian Shapiro (New Haven: Yale University Press, 2003), 150–51.

202 a person's right to leave one contract: Ibid., 153.

202 remarks on the better bargaining power: Adam Smith, *The Wealth of Nations* (New York: Modern Library, 2000 [1776]), 609.

202 refers to emigration in twenty-eight different paragraphs: John Stuart Mill, *Principles of Political Economy* (London: Longmans, Green, 1907), with considerable help from the search engine at http://www.econlib.org/index.html.

203 "O ye that love mankind!": Thomas Paine, "Common Sense," in *Common Sense and Other Writings*, ed. Joyce Appleby (New York: Barnes & Noble Classics, 2005 [1776]), 46.

203 American history is filled with examples: See, e.g., Desmond King, *Making Americans: Immigration, Race, and the Origins of the Diverse Democracy* (Cambridge, Mass.: Harvard University Press, 2000); Rogers Smith, *Civic Ideals: Conflicting Visions of Citizenship in U.S. History* (New Haven: Yale University Press, 1997); and Mae M. Ngai, *Impossible Subjects: Illegal Aliens and the Making of Modern America* (Princeton: Princeton University Press, 2004).

203 "those who come hither": Cited in Zolberg, *A Nation by Design*, 54, 80.

204 It is axiomatic among many multiculturalists: See, e.g., Bhikhu Parekh, *Rethinking*

Multiculturalism: Cultural Diversity and Political Theory (Cambridge, Mass.: Harvard University Press, 2000).

204 At least one important theorist: See Will Kymlicka, *Politics in the Vernacular: Nationalism, Multiculturalism, and Citizenship* (New York: Oxford University Press, 2001).

205 from political philosophers who strongly identify: For an example, see Brian Barry, *Culture and Equality: An Egalitarian Critique of Multiculturalism* (Cambridge, Mass.: Harvard University Press, 2001).

205 a well-meaning effort to control incidents: Runnymede Trust, *Islamophobia: A Challenge to Us All* (London: Runnymede Trust, 1997).

206 raised concerns about the burqa: Straw's comments can be found at http://www.guardian.co.uk/commentisfree/story/0,,1889081,00.html.

208 "Political secrecy . . . was in many ways": Robin J. Ives, "Political Publicity and Political Economy in Eighteenth Century France," *French History*, 17 (March 2003), 1, 3.

209 "Liberals . . . held that government": Paul Starr, *Freedom's Power: The True Force of Liberalism* (New York: Basic Books, 2007), 55.

209 "the grand security of securities": Jeremy Bentham, "Principles of Judicial Procedure, with an Outline of a Procedural Code," in *The Collected Works of Jeremy Bentham*, ed. John Bowring (New York: Russell & Russell, 1962 [1838–43]), Vol. II, p. 8.

209 "when a government is continually": John Stuart Mill to Charles Loring Brace, January 19, 1871, "The Later Letters of John Stuart Mill, 1849–1873, Part IV," in *The Collected Works of John Stuart Mill*, ed. Francis E. Mineka and Dwight N. Lindley (Toronto: University of Toronto Press, 1972), 1,799.

209 Efforts by liberals such as Bentham and Mill: See David Vincent, *The Culture of Secrecy: Britain, 1832–1998* (Oxford: Oxford University Press, 1998).

210 created a national security apparatus: For an overview, see Stephen Graubard, *Command of Office: How War, Secrecy, and Deception Transformed the Presidency from Theodore Roosevelt to George W. Bush* (New York: Perseus, 2004).

211 secrecy harmed as well as helped: Daniel Patrick Moynihan, *Secrecy: The American Experience* (New Haven: Yale University Press, 1998).

211 "The CIA, the NSA": Tim Weiner, *Legacy of Ashes: The History of the CIA* (New York: Doubleday, 2007), 318.

212 Nixon used it not only to shield himself: See Mark J. Rozell, *Executive Privilege: The Dilemma of Secrecy and Democratic Accountability* (Baltimore: Johns Hopkins University Press, 1994), 82.

212 Secret trials, secret interrogation techniques: A catalogue of the Bush administration's penchant for secrecy can be found in U.S. House of Representatives, Committee on Governmental Reform, Minority Staff, *Secrecy in the Bush Administration*, September 14, 2004. An even more comprehensive review is Charlie Savage's *Takeover: The Return of the Imperial Presidency and the Subversion of American Democracy* (New York: Little, Brown, 2007).

214 "too much secrecy can be": Testimony of Jack Landman Goldsmith, October 2, 2007, at http://judiciary.senate.gov/testimony.cfm?id=2958&wit_id=6693.

CHAPTER 8   WHY CONSERVATIVES CAN'T GOVERN

217 "That was the year": Oliver Wendell Holmes, Sr., "The Deacon's Masterpiece, or the Wonderful One-Hoss Shay," in Oliver Wendell Holmes, *The One-Hoss Shay, with its Companion Poems* (Boston: Houghton Mifflin, 1891), 13.

218 the Lisbon earthquake changed the way: See Susan Neiman, *Evil in Modern Thought: An Alternative History of Philosophy* (Princeton: Princeton University Press, 2002).

220 "It is critical . . . that fire": Douglas Brinkley, *The Great Deluge: Hurricane Katrina, New Orleans, and the Mississippi Gulf Coast* (New York: William Morrow, 2006), 254.

221 "It is not the role": Testimony of FEMA director Joe M. Allbaugh before the Veterans Affairs, Housing and Urban Development and Independent Agencies Subcommittee of the Senate Appropriations Committee, at http://www.fema.gov/about/director/ allbaugh/testimony/051601.shtm. (I have changed the capitalization to match the usage throughout this book.)

222 never went to his office: Brinkley, *The Great Deluge*, 270.

222 an "incident of national significance": Ibid., 410, 412.

222 "Chertoff's actions": Ibid., 270.

222 "didn't pursue the matter": Ibid., 266.

222 published a paper repeating: See Edwin Meese III, Stuart M. Butler, and Kim R. Holmes, "From Tragedy to Triumph: Principled Solutions for Rebuilding Lives and Communities," at http://www.heritage.org/Research/GovernmentReform/sr05 .cfm.

222 a "great opportunity" for conservatives: Jack Kemp, "Imagining the Unimaginable," *Human Events*, September 6, 2005, at http://www.humanevents.com/article.php? id=8908.

222 "a real sense of crisis": Tod Lindberg, *Washington Times*, August 20, 2005, p. A17.

222 "the desire to bring conservative": John R. Wilke and Brody Mullins, "After Katrina, Republicans Back a Sea of Conservative Ideas," *Wall Street Journal*, September 15, 2005, p. B1.

223 "the objection to these Bush proposals": Rich Lowry, "Bold, Persistent, Experimentation," *National Review*, September 20, 2005, at http://www.nationalreview.com/ lowry/lowry200509200816.asp. I am grateful to two bloggers, Digby and Rick Perlstein, for these quotes; see http://commonsense.ourfuture.org/katrina_slow_molasses and http://commonsense.ourfuture.org/katrina_golden_opportunity.

223 he was, in fact, an administrator: Kenneth Maxwell, *Pombal, Paradox of the Enlightenment* (New York: Cambridge University Press, 1995).

224 which provided not only a power to destroy: *McCulloch* v. *Maryland*, 17 U.S. 316 (1819), at http://www.law.cornell.edu/supct/search/display.html?terms=McCulloch&url=/ supct/html/historics/USSC_CR_0017_0316_ZO.html.

224 one of his ideas was to enact: Maxwell, *Pombal*, 180.

224 not only devoted considerable attention to how government: David K. Hart, "The Virtuous Citizen, the Honorable Bureaucrat, and 'Public' Administration," *Public Administration Review*, 44 (March 1984), 110–20.

226 "specialists without spirit": Max Weber, *The Protestant Ethic and the Spirit of Capitalism*, trans. Talcott Parsons (New York: Routledge, 2001 [1930]), 124.

226 the withering away: Friedrich Engels, *Anti-Dühring: Herr Eugen Düring's Revolution in Science* (New York: International Publishers, 1966 [1885]), 307.

226 For those intending to keep the lower classes obedient: See Don Herzog, *Poisoning the Minds of the Lower Orders* (Princeton: Princeton University Press, 1998).

227 continued to insist that he was not a conservative: F. A. Hayek, *The Constitution of Liberty* (Chicago: University of Chicago Press, 1960), 397–415.

227 But all that would change: Barry Goldwater, *The Conscience of a Conservative* (New York: Hillman, 1960).

228 as some historians and pundits have: See, e.g., John P. Diggins, *Mussolini and Fascism: The View from America* (Princeton: Princeton University Press, 1972), and Jonah Goldberg, *Liberal Fascism: The Secret History of the American Left, from Mussolini to the Politics of Meaning* (New York: Doubleday, 2008).

230 as one geographer has put it: Peirce Lewis, cited in Craig E. Colten, *An Unnatural*

Metropolis: Wrestling New Orleans from Nature (Baton Rouge: Louisiana State University Press, 2005), 2.

231   "privately built structures": Ibid., 20.

231   A new school of historical interpretation: For examples, see Jordan A. Schwarz, *The New Dealers: Power Politics in the Age of Roosevelt* (New York: Knopf, 1993), and Jason Scott Smith, *Building New Deal Liberalism: The Political Economy of Public Works, 1933–1956* (Cambridge: Cambridge University Press, 2006).

232   "These programs": Smith, *Building New Deal Liberalism,* 259.

232   "We are stricken by no plague": http://www.yale.edu/lawweb/avalon/presiden/inaug/froos1.htm.

233   was an Oxford man: Robert Skidelsky, *John Maynard Keynes.* Vol. II: *The Economist as Savior, 1920–1937* (London and New York: Penguin Books, 1992), 224.

233   "the Conservative belief that there is some law": John Maynard Keynes, "Can Lloyd George Do It?" in *The Collected Writings of John Maynard Keynes.* Vol. IX: *Essays in Persuasion* (London: Macmillan, 1973), 90–91.

234   "we must not conclude": John Maynard Keynes, "The General Theory of Employment, Interest, and Money" in *The Collected Writings.* Vol. XII, 254.

234   the future Supreme Court justice: Schwarz, *The New Dealers,* 133–34.

235   "pseudo-moral principles": John Maynard Keynes, "Economic Possibilities for Our Grandchildren," in *Essays in Persuasion,* 229, 330–31.

236   Johnson put a bust of FDR: William E. Leuchtenberg, "Lyndon Johnson in the Shadow of Franklin Roosevelt," in Sidney M. Milkis and Jerome M. Mileur, eds., *The Great Society and the High Tide of Liberalism* (Amherst: University of Massachusetts Press, 2005), 198.

239   "government is not the solution": http://www.reaganfoundation.org/reagan/speeches/first.asp.

240   supply-side economics . . . has become the same kind of litmus test: Jonathan Chait, *The Big Con: The True Story of How Washington Got Hoodwinked and Hijacked by Crackpot Economics* (Boston: Houghton Mifflin, 2007), 80–114.

241   one after another libertarian: Bruce R. Bartlett, *Imposter: How George W. Bush Bankrupted America and Betrayed the Reagan Legacy* (New York: Doubleday, 2006); Bruce Fein, *Constitutional Peril: The Life and Death Struggle of Our Constitution and Democracy* (New York: Palgrave Macmillan, 2008); and Andrew Sullivan, *The Conservative Soul: How We Lost It, How to Get It Back* (New York: HarperCollins, 2006).

243   "Today, in the United States": Greg Anrig, *The Conservatives Have No Clothes: Why Right-Wing Ideas Keep Failing* (Hoboken, N.J.: John Wiley, 2007), 230.

244   "Some of the ideas": John Micklethwait and Adrian Wooldridge, *The Right Nation: Conservative Power in America* (New York: Penguin, 2004), 234–35, 254.

244   Democrats might win back political power: Matt Bai, *The Argument: Billionaires, Bloggers, and the Battle to Remake the Democratic Politics* (New York: Penguin, 2007).

245   "discards Prescription": Cited in Geoffrey Wheatcroft, *The Strange Death of Tory England* (London: Penguin, 2005), 150.

246   wrote some thirty-five books: For a bibliography, see http://www.jfklibrary.org/Historical+Resources/Archives/Archives+and+Manuscripts/bib_galbraith.htm.

246   his concept of "countervailing power": John Kenneth Galbraith, *American Capitalism: The Concept of Countervailing Power* (Boston: Houghton Mifflin, 1952).

247   to "end welfare as we know it": The best analysis of this issue is R. Kent Weaver, *Ending Welfare as We Know It* (Washington, D.C.: Brookings Institution, 2000).

248   There are good liberal reasons to support: See, e.g., Stephen Macedo, *Diversity and Distrust: Civic Education in a Multicultural Democracy* (Cambridge, Mass.: Harvard University Press, 2000).

248 public education is to Americans: Ira Katznelson and Margaret Weir, *Schooling for All: Class, Race, and the Decline of the Democratic Ideal* (New York: Basic Books, 1985).

248 If some people can exercise choice: These issues are explored in Alan Wolfe, ed., *School Choice: The Moral Debate* (Princeton: Princeton University Press, 2003).

CHAPTER 9   LIBERALISM'S PROMISE

250 "The enemy within": Robert Bork, *Slouching Toward Gomorrah: Modern Liberalism and American Decline* (New York: ReganBooks, 1997), 4.

250 "The mistake the Enlightenment founders": Ibid., 63.

255 he claims to be a friend of equality: Ibid., 108.

255 it denies women the choice of leading: Ibid., 204.

256 "The full freedom": John Dewey, "The Future of Liberalism," address at the twenty-fourth annual meeting of the American Philosophical Society, Eastern Division, New York University, December 28, 1934, at http://fce.ufm.edu/catedraticos/mpolanco/dewey1934.htm.

257 "nonsense upon stilts": Jeremy Bentham, "Nonsense Upon Stilts, or Pandora's Box Reopened," in *Rights, Representation and Reform: Nonsense Upon Stilts and Other Writings on the French Revolution*, ed. Philip Schofield, Catherine Pease-Watkin, and Cyprien Blamires (New York: Oxford University Press, 2002), 317–401.

257 We all know what it means to conserve: See, e.g., Andrew Sullivan in *The Conservative Soul: How We Lost It, How to Get It Back* (New York: HarperCollins, 2006).

257 "If we want things": Giuseppe Tomasi di Lampedusa, *The Leopard*, trans. Archibald Colquhoun (New York: Avon Books, 1975), 35.

258 Conservatism of this sort: See, e.g., José Ortega y Gasset, *The Revolt of the Masses*, trans. Anthony Kerrigan (Notre Dame: University of Notre Dame Press, 1985 [1932]); Irving Babbitt, *Representative Writings*, ed. George A. Panichas (Lincoln: University of Nebraska Press, 1981); and Roger Scruton, *A Political Philosophy* (London: Continuum, 2006).

258 of becoming "superfluous": Albert Jay Nock, *Memoirs of a Superfluous Man* (New York: Harper, 1943).

259 "irritable mental gestures": Lionel Trilling, *The Liberal Imagination: Essays on Literature and Society* (Garden City, N.Y.: Anchor Books, 1953), vii.

259 Lacking in sympathy: See Michael Kazin, *A Godly Hero: The Life of William Jennings Bryan* (New York: Knopf, 2006).

260 the "little platoon": Edmund Burke, *Reflections on the Revolution in France*, ed. Frank M. Turner (New Haven: Yale University Press, 2003 [1790]), 40.

261 defense of highly unpopular judicial decisions: See Ronald Dworkin, *A Matter of Principle* (Cambridge, Mass.: Harvard University Press, 1985).

262 "Chief Justice Warren's decision": Jack Balkin, ed., *What Roe v. Wade Should Have Said: The Nation's Legal Experts Rewrite America's Most Controversial Decision* (New York: New York University Press, 2005), 23.

262 "require hiring, firing, or promotion": Cited in John David Skrentny, *The Ironies of Affirmative Action: Politics, Culture, and Justice in America* (Chicago: University of Chicago Press, 1996), 5.

263 Barbara Grutter, a white woman: *Grutter* v. *Bollinger*, 539 U.S. 306 (2003). See also Barbara A. Perry, *The Michigan Affirmative Action Cases* (Lawrence: University Press of Kansas, 2007).

264 "equal in their audacity": Bork, *Slouching Toward Gomorrah*, 173–74.

264 "Blackmun's opinions in *Roe* and *Doe*": Balkin, ed., *What Roe v. Wade Should Have Said*, 23.

265 Yet public opinion in the United States has consistently supported: Morris P. Fiorina, with Samuel J. Abrams and Jeremy C. Pope, *Culture War?: The Myth of a Polarized America* (New York: Pearson Longman, 2005), 34–54.

266 Born in the same year: For the details, see Roman Szporluk, *Communism and Nationalism: Karl Marx Versus Friedrich List* (New York: Oxford University Press, 1988), 96–114.

267 "Modern Germany, lacking a system": Friedrich List, *The National System of Political Economy*, trans. Sampson S. Lloyd (London and New York: Longmans, Green, 1928 [1841]), 91–92.

267 "The unity of the nation": Ibid., 132.

268 wrote a book attacking him: Friedrich Engels, *Anti-Dühring: Herr Eugen Dühring's Revolution in Science* (New York: International Publishers, 1966 [1885]).

268 "I am a citizen": Robert Kuttner, *The Squandering of America: How the Failure of Our Politics Undermines Our Prosperity* (New York: Knopf, 2007), 70.

269 the conservative commentator: See Patrick Buchanan, *State of Emergency: The Third World Invasion and Conquest of America* (New York: St. Martin's Press, 2007).

269 As the economist Edward Gresser: See his *Freedom from Want: American Liberalism and the Global Economy* (Brooklyn, N.Y.: Soft Skull Press, 2007), 55–57.

269 "a conflict-free existence": John Gray, *Black Mass: Apocalyptic Religion and the Death of Utopia* (London: Allen Lane, 2007), 17.

269 for Gray both are . . . products: Ibid., 37, 69.

270 had praised List's insights: Joseph Schumpeter, *History of Economic Analysis* (New York: Oxford University Press, 1954), 504.

270 "the supremacy of America": List, *The National System of Political Economy*, 340.

270 "The reality of the late-twentieth-century": John Gray, *False Dawn: The Illusions of Global Capitalism* (London: Granta Books, 2002), 70.

271 the antiglobalization movement has little to offer: See, e.g., Naomi Klein, *No Logo* (New York: Picador, 2002), 410–19.

271 "the Romantic counterrevolution": Michael Hardt and Antonio Negri, *Empire* (Cambridge, Mass.: Harvard University Press, 2000), 165.

271 But rather than argue: See Naomi Klein, *The Shock Doctrine: The Rise of Disaster Capitalism* (New York: Metropolitan Books, 2007).

272 "Washington consensus" . . . "have not been encouraging": Joseph Stiglitz, *Globalization and Its Discontents* (New York: W. W. Norton, 2003), 16, 86.

272 "market fundamentalism": Ibid., 221.

272 "immiseration" . . . "race to the bottom": Jagdish Bhagwati, *In Defense of Globalization* (New York: Oxford University Press, 2004),55–56, 162–65.

273 "been carefully planned to squeeze": Klein, *No Logo*, 203.

274 "We cannot expect": Gray, *False Dawn*, 235.

274 "the pull of modernity": Bhagwati, *In Defense of Globalization*, 116.

274 the frequently rosy-eyed view: See Thomas L. Friedman, *The World Is Flat: A Brief History of the Twenty-First Century* (New York: Farrar, Straus & Giroux, 2005).

274 The Victorian manufacturer: Richard Cobden, *The Political Writings of Richard Cobden* (London: Frank Cass, 1886).

275 globalization must "be managed": Bhagwati, *In Defense of Globalization*, 35.

275 "Globalization with a human face": Stiglitz, *Globalization and Its Discontents*, 247–52.

276 "Thomas Paine left England": Jay Winik, *The Great Upheaval: America and the Birth of the Modern World, 1788–1800* (New York: HarperCollins, 2007), 576–77.

277 "working together": David Rothkopf, *Superclass: The Global Power Elite and the World They Are Making* (New York: Farrar, Straus & Giroux, 2008), 124.

277 "whenever the law of the jungle": Lee Harris, *The Suicide of Reason: Radical Islam's Threat to the West* (New York: Basic Books, 2007), 8.

278 "may seem . . . to be a throwback": Benjamin R. Barber, *Jihad vs. McWorld* (New York: Times Books, 1995), 157.

278 "is a by-product of": Gray, *Black Mass*, 177.

279 "From the way the Democrats": Norman Podhoretz, *World War IV: The Long Struggle Against Islamofascism* (New York: Doubleday, 2007), 209.

279 "there is no chance": Ibid., 215.

279 "a self-protective myth": Harris, *The Suicide of Reason*, 8.

280 "popular Muslim fanaticism acted": Ibid., 207.

280 "that may well destroy us": Ibid., 59, 83.

280 "European countries have engaged": Bat Ye'or, *Eurabia: The Euro-Arab Axis* (Madison, N.J.: Fairleigh Dickinson University Press, 2005), 38.

281 "Europe is even now": Bruce Bawer, *While Europe Slept: How Radical Islam Is Destroying the West from Within* (New York: Broadway Books, 2006), 157.

281 "In the end": Ibid., 233.

281 Michael Ignatieff: See *The Lesser Evil: Political Ethics in an Age of Terror* (Princeton: Princeton University Press, 2004).

282 "Nothing in U.S. behavior": Samantha Power, *"A Problem from Hell": America and the Age of Genocide* (New York: Basic Books, 2000), 187.

282 the war itself was supported by: See Paul Berman, *Terror and Liberalism* (New York: W. W. Norton, 2003); Christopher Hitchens, *A Long Short War: The Postponed Liberation of Iraq* (New York: Plume Books, 2003); Oliver Kamm, *Anti-Totalitarianism: The Left-Wing Case for a Neo-Conservative Foreign Policy* (London: Social Affairs Unit, 2005); and Nick Cohen, *What's Left: How Liberals Lost Their Way* (London: Fourth Estate, 2007).

282 but later had second thoughts: Michael Ignatieff, "Getting Iraq Wrong," *New York Times Magazine*, August 5, 2007, at http://www.nytimes.com/2007/08/05/magazine/05iraq-t.html?pagewanted=3&_r=1&sq=michael%20ignatieff%20iraq%20wrong&st=nyt&scp=1.

282 raised questions about the war from the start: See Samantha Power, "Bush's Illiberal Power," *The New Republic*, March 3, 2003; Samantha Power, "Our War on Terror," *New York Times Magazine*, July 29, 2007.

282 who had written eloquently: Kanan Makiya, *The Republic of Fear: The Politics of Modern Iraq* (Berkeley and Los Angeles: University of California Press, 1989).

283 "Euston Manifesto": http://eustonmanifesto.org/?page_id=132.

283 "a Scottish MP who": Cohen, *What's Left*, 290.

284 "failure to take up the war": Berman, *Terror and Liberalism*, 195.

284 those on the right who condemn liberal societies: Dinesh D'Souza, *The Enemy at Home: The Cultural Left and Its Responsibility for 9/11* (New York: Doubleday, 2007)

284 "sometimes demented": Berman, *Terror and Liberalism*, 101.

284 "arise because of failures": Ibid., 206.

284 "Totalitarianism in decline?": Ibid., 156.

285 the theologian Tariq Ramadan: See Ramadan's *Western Muslims and the Future of Islam* (New York: Oxford University Press, 2004).

285 In a long essay on Ramadan: Paul Berman, "The Islamist, the Journalist, and the Defense of Liberalism," *The New Republic*, June 4, 2007.

INDEX

THE END OF REFORM
New Deal Liberalism in Recession and War
by Alan Brinkley

The End of Reform shows how the liberalism of the early New Deal—which set out to repair and, if necessary, restructure America's economy—gave way to its contemporary counterpart, which was less hostile to corporate capitalism and more solicitous of individual rights. Clearly and dramatically, Brinkley identifies the personalities and events responsible for this transformation while pointing to the broader trends in American society that made the politics of reform increasingly unpopular. It is both a major reinterpretation of the New Deal and a crucial map of the road to today's political landscape.

Politics/History/978-0-679-75314-8

THE AMERICAN POLITICAL TRADITION
And the Men Who Made It
by Richard Hofstadter

First published in 1948, *The American Political Tradition* has become one of the most influential and widely read historical volumes of our time. The author himself called it "a young man's book," but its elegance, passion, and iconoclastic erudition laid the groundwork for a totally new understanding of the American past. By writing a "kind of intellectual history of the assumptions behind American politics," Richard Hofstadter changed the way Americans understand the relationship between power and ideas in their national experience. Like only a handful of American historians before him—Frederick Jackson Turner and Charles A. Beard among them—Hofstadter was able to articulate, in a single work, a historical vision that inspired and shaped an entire generation.

History/978-0-679-72315-8

SOCIAL AND POLITICAL PHILOSOPHY
Readings from Plato to Ghandi
Edited by John Somerville and Ronald E. Santoni

An anthology of basic statements by the most influential social and political philosophers of Western civilization. The book contains selections from the following: Plato, *The Republic*; Aristotle, *Politics*; Thomas Hobbes, *Leviathan*; John Locke, *The Second Treatise on Civil Government*; Jean Jacques Rousseau, *The Social Contract*.

Philosophy/978-0-385-01238-6

THE PARANOID STYLE IN AMERICAN POLITICS
by Richard Hofstadter

In *The Paranoid Style in American Politics*, Hofstadter examines the competing forces in American political discourse and how fringe groups can influence—and derail—the larger agendas of a political party. He investigates the politics of the irrational, shedding light on how the behavior of individuals can seem out of proportion with actual political issues, and how such behavior impacts larger groups. With such other classic essays as "Free Silver and the Mind of 'Coin' Harvey" and "What Happened to the Antitrust Movement?," *The Paranoid Style in American Politics* remains both a seminal text of political history and a vital analysis of the ways in which political groups function in the United States.

History/978-0-307-38844-5

THE AGE OF AMERICAN UNREASON
by Susan Jacoby

A cultural history of the last forty years, *The Age of American Unreason* focuses on the convergence of social forces—usually treated as separate entities—that has created a perfect storm of anti-rationalism. These include the upsurge of religious fundamentalism, with more political power today than ever before; the failure of public education to create an informed citizenry; and the triumph of video over print culture. Sparing neither the right nor the left, Jacoby asserts that Americans today have embraced a universe of "junk thought" that makes almost no effort to separate fact from opinion.

History/Current Affairs/978-1-4000-9638-1

EUGENE McCARTHY
And the Rise and Fall of Postwar American Liberalism
by Dominic Sandbrook

Dominic Sandbrook traces one of the most remarkable and significant lives in postwar politics, a career marked by both courage and arrogance. Sandbrook draws on extensive new research—including interviews with McCarthy himself—to show convincingly how Eugene McCarthy's political experience embodies the larger decline of American liberalism after World War II. These were tumultuous times in American politics, and Sandbrook vividly captures the drama and historical significance through his intimate portrait of a singularly interesting man at the heart of it all.

History/Biography/978-1-4000-7790-8